Frances Hodgson Burnett
BEYOND
THE SECRET GARDEN

About the Author

Ann Thwaite is a Fellow of the Royal Society of Literature and has an Oxford doctorate. She wrote children's books before publishing her first biography in 1974, the life of Frances Hodgson Burnett. Her other biographies are *A.A. Milne: His Life*, reissued in 2006 by Tempus, *Edmund Gosse: A Literary Landscape, Emily Tennyson: The Poet's Wife* and *Glimpses of the Wonderful,* the life of Philip Henry Gosse. She has recently completed a history of her own family (1845-1945), tentatively entitled *Passageways* as it is a story of emigration across the world. She lives in Norfolk with her husband, the poet Anthony Thwaite.

Frances Hodgson Burnett
BEYOND
THE SECRET GARDEN

ANN THWAITE

TEMPUS

FOR ANTHONY

of course

"One does it all one's life ... Everybody dances, everybody hears the music, everybody sometimes wears a sash and a necklace and watches other White Frocks whirling by—but was there ever anyone who really went to the Party?"

Cover Illustration: Frances Hodgson Burnett, *c.*1908. Courtesy of the Collections of the Library of Congress.

First published in 1974 as *Waiting for the Party*
by Martin Secker & Warburg Limited.
This edition first published 2007.

Tempus Publishing Limited
The Mill, Brimscombe Port,
Stroud, Gloucestershire, GL5 2QG
www.tempus-publishing.com

British Library Cataloguing in Publication Data.
A catalogue record for this book is available from the British Library.

ISBN 978 0 7524 4138 2

Typesetting and origination by Tempus Publishing Limited
Printed and bound in Great Britain

Contents

List of Illustrations

between pages 192 and 205

Foreword and Acknowledgements

Many people have asked me how I came to write this book. I can trace my first consideration of the possibility to a passage in John Rowe Townsend's useful study of children's literature *Written for Children* (1965).

> Frances Hodgson Burnett was a more powerful and I believe a more important writer than Miss Yonge or Mrs Ewing or Mrs Molesworth. On the strength of only three books ... I believe she must be acknowledged as standing far above every other woman writer for children except E. Nesbit; and there are depths in Mrs Hodgson Burnett that Nesbit never tried to plumb. It is hard to account for her neglect (neglect by critics that is; she has not been neglected by readers). I do not know of any modern study of her work beyond an eighteen-page chapter in a book by Marghanita Laski ... True, Mrs Hodgson Burnett's personal character was flamboyant and unappealing; in the years of her success she suffered a gross inflation of the ego; and Miss Laski justly says she emerges from the pages of her son's book *The Romantick Lady* as "aggressively domineering, offensively whimsical and abominably self-centred and conceited". But if we were to judge writers by their personal qualities rather than their work—a mistake which Miss Laski does not make—the map of English literature would be

a very odd one. I think myself that a large part of the explanation lies in the notoriety of *Little Lord Fauntleroy*. Instead of adding to its author's reputation, as it should, this book hangs albatross-wise round her neck.

Until I read this, I had no idea that Mrs Burnett was considered to have been flamboyant and unappealing. Could the author of *The Secret Garden* really have been so self-centred and unattractive a character? I could not believe it, and I wanted to find the evidence. *The Secret Garden* was one of the three or four most important books of my own childhood, in that it was read and re-read, and the atmosphere of it became part of my own life. I knew Mary Lennox better than most of the children in my own form at school and Misselthwaite Manor better than many places I had lived in. Marghanita Laski, in the study referred to by John Rowe Townsend, says of *The Secret Garden*: "It is the most satisfying children's book I know." I have found countless people share this view.

I would like to express my thanks to both Mr Townsend and Miss Laski—to the latter in particular for her bibliography, which first put me on the track of many books I had never heard of and which is the basis of my own fuller one. It was Miss Laski who first drew my attention to the fact that Mrs Burnett was not only the author of three outstanding children's books but of numerous adult novels and plays. She did not begin as a writer for children—her first novel was compared favourably with those of George Eliot—and even after the phenomenal success of *Little Lord Fauntleroy* she continued to devote much more of her time to the adult market.

I must also acknowledge my debt to Vivian Burnett's book about his mother: it was published by Scribner's in New York in 1927 but never appeared in England. If Mrs Burnett emerges from this book as domineering, conceited and the rest, it was certainly not because Vivian saw her that way. His book is an act of filial piety. It is written in a style which, forty-five years later, we find unbearably fey but it *is* strong on facts and surprisingly frank at times. I have whenever possible gone back to original sources and I have read hundreds of letters, newspaper interviews and news items, some of them quoted in that book. It is interesting to find that the only consistent cuts in Vivian's quotations from letters are in references to smoking. Israel Zangwill is not allowed to wish Frances "cigarettes and peppermints ad lib", nor is she permitted to call one of the rooms at Maytham a smoking-room. There are other letters, of course, particularly during the short years of his mother's marriage to Stephen Townesend, which Vivian did not use at all. My most important source outside the family and the hundreds of unpublished letters to and from Frances in the Scribner archives at Princeton University, was an unpublished memoir, including a number of her letters, by Henry Hadfield which I found in Manchester Public Library. This added considerably to my knowledge of her early years which is otherwise based largely on her own memories recorded in 1892 in *The One I Knew the Best of All*.

Throughout I have remembered R.L. Stevenson's dictum, "It must always be foul to tell what is false and it can never be safe to suppress what is true", and I am very grateful to the Burnett family for their cooperation. I know they did not welcome the idea of a new biography. They knew how much Vivian had suffered all his life from his identification with Little Lord Fauntleroy. They were worried that a biographer would turn psychiatrist and analyse with cruelty that mother–son relationship. They felt that Vivian had written Mrs Burnett's life and that that should be enough. But once they accepted I really was writing the book, Vivian's daughter, Dorinda, and her husband Robert Le Clair could not have been kinder and more helpful—sending me fat parcels of old letters and encouraging me with their sympathetic interest in the task I had set myself.

I have used the name Frances throughout for convenience, although she was rarely called that. As a child, she was Fannie; later it was Fluffy or Dearest or Mrs Burnett or Mrs Townesend.

With a man it is simple to use his surname throughout; with a woman it is more complicated. If "Frances" suggests a degree of intimacy she would never have allowed me, I am sorry.

Some people may find the plot-paraphrases and reviews of books and plays irritating and prefer to get on with the life; but it seemed to me essential, when so many of her books and plays are totally forgotten, to give considerable space to them. I have not been consistent in my treatment. Mrs Burnett wrote too much for me to cover fully the contents and reception of everything she produced. I have preferred to be influenced more by the interest of the material available than by the importance I place on the book or play. *The Lady of Quality*, for instance, has no permanent value. I would not recommend it to anyone. But contemporary reactions to it are interesting enough for me to give it a good deal of space. Conversely, *Miss Defarge or A Woman's Will* is a book I admire but I have come across no related material, so the space given to it is slight. If *Fauntleroy* dominates my book, it is inevitable, for it dominated Frances' life and changed it and her.

When I was in Boston talking to Vivian's daughter and her husband, I was also fortunate enough to meet Vivian's widow, Constance Burnett. She received me at her home on Beacon Hill and spoke of the past. She had herself written a brief children's biography of Frances called *Happily Ever After*. I queried the title. On the surface, of course, Frances' life was an extremely successful one. The young girl, who had picked wild grapes on the hillside in Tennessee to pay for the postage on her first stories, had gone on to write one of the best sellers of the century, admired by Gladstone, the Prime Minister of England. She had been a friend of an American president, an extremely rich and famous woman whose opinions were sought on every subject. Henry James had addressed her as "noblest of neighbours and most heavenly of women". But "Happily Ever After"?

She wanted life to be a fairy story. She wanted to make dreams come true—her own and, other people's. She wanted all her life to be at the Party. But again and again throughout her life reality was a disappointment. It was only in her books that she could make things go the way she wanted them to. It was only in my own favourite of all her adult novels, *Through One Administration*, that she admitted an ending close to life as she knew it. In that book, more completely perhaps than in any other, she deals in what George Eliot called "the half-tints of real life". Her own life was too often in technicolor, an uncomfortable blaze. I said to her daughter-in-law that I thought in many ways it had been a tragic life, and the younger Mrs Burnett, now herself an old lady, nodded in agreement.

I would also like to thank the staff of the Lincoln Center Library of the Performing Arts, New York, whose excellent filing system made my work much easier; the staff of the Division of Rare Books and Special Collections, Princeton University Library, where I was given every help when I worked on the Scribner archives; Miss Pollyanna Creekmore and Mr William J. MacArthur of the McClung Historical Collection, Knoxville, Tennessee, who dug out a great deal of material relating to Frances' early days; the staff of the Local History Library, Manchester Public Library; Mr Fred Johnson of the Town Clerk's Department, Manchester, who helped me to find the houses Frances lived in, and the Librarian of the Medical College Library, St Bartholomew's Hospital, London.

I am grateful to Mr Tom Rosenthal for his continuous enthusiasm for my project; Miss Valerie Bradshaw, who put at my disposal the results of her own considerable researches; Mrs Marion de Kay Rous, Mr Ormonde de Kay and Lady Hodgkin; Miss Gillian Avery, Mr Terry Coleman, Miss Janet Dunbar, Professor Leon Edel, the Hon. Mrs Fraser (Pamela Maude), Mr Kenneth Fahnestock, Mrs Gill Frayn, Mrs Anne Harvey, Mrs Penelope Lively, Miss Sophia Macindoe, Mr Raymond Mander and Mr Joe Mitchenson, Miss Philippa Pearce, Professor and Mrs Christopher Ricks, Lord Scarborough, Dr Ann Zito, Air Commodore E.J.D. Townesend, Lt. Col. G.A.F. Townesend, Mr and Mrs G.D.P. Townesend and Mrs G.M. Townesend, Miss

Winnie Comber, Mrs Alice Freeborn, Mr Harry Millum and others at Rolvenden, Kent. And, most of all, to my family, whose help and toleration made the whole thing possible.

I also acknowledge assistance from the Arts Council of Great Britain which allowed me to spend much more time on the book than would otherwise have been reasonable.

My publishers and I would like to thank the following for their kind permission to reproduce illustrations: Institute of Cost and Management Accountants (63 Portland Place); Collections of the Library of Congress (Washington, D.C., in 1880); McClung Collection, Lawson McGhee Library (Knoxville, Tennessee, in 1865); Manchester Public Libraries (Manchester City Trade Directory of 1852); Mansell Collection (Henry James); National Portrait Gallery (Israel Zangwill); New York Public Library (play-bill of the 1903 American production of *The Little Princess*); Radio Times Hulton Picture Library (Mary Pickford in the film of *Little Lord Fauntleroy*).

A.T.

1974

In 2003 I was pleased to be invited by Angelica Carpenter to speak at the first ever conference entirely devoted to Frances Hodgson Burnett. This was at California State University in Fresno. There I was happy to have the chance to meet Burnett's great-grand-daughter, Penny, her husband, Tom Deupree, now guardians of the flame, and also Gretchen Gerzina, a more recent biographer, who was able, thanks to the Deuprees, to use some family papers I had not seen. I am glad to say nothing has turned up to alter in any substantial way the story I first told, over thirty years ago, under the title *Waiting for the Party*. I must record my gratitude to Sophie Bradshaw of Tempus, who suggested reprinting this book when Faber had let their 1994 edition go out of print.

A.T.

2007

1

Preparing for the Party
1849–1865

There is in front of me *A Plan of Manchester and Salford* ("with their Vicinities, Embracing every Improvement, from Actual Survey"), dated 1848. At the northern edge of the map, York Street, Cheetham Hill, where Frances Hodgson Burnett was born the following year, looks a pleasant place, backing on to open country, with trees and grass and lakes. A few miles away in Salford, in the bend of the River Irwell, there is a jungle of streets and courts, dark on the map, marked Islington. Close at hand is the New Bailey Prison, the railway and the coal wharves of the Bury Canal. It was to this area that small Frances Hodgson moved in 1855, following the death of her father. The contrast between light and dark, comfort and poverty, was the dominant theme of her books.

Friedrich Engels was living in Manchester at this time and saw both worlds: "Right and left, a multitude of covered passages led from the main streets into numerous courts and he, who turns in thither, gets into a filth and disgusting grime the equal of which is not to be found." Engels wrote of the "coal-black foul-smelling streams full of debris and refuse", of the tanneries, bone-mills and gas-works.

Cheetham Hill, on the other hand, like Chorlton on Medlock, Ardwick and Pendleton on the outskirts of Manchester, had "free, wholesome country air" and "fine comfortable homes". Engels noted that "the members of the money aristocracy can take the shortest road through the middle of all the labouring districts to their places of business, without ever seeing that they are in the midst of the grimy misery that lurks to the right and to the left".

Edwin Hodgson, Frances' father, had his business at 62 King Street, Deansgate and it was certainly a short and easy journey down York Street, over Ducie Bridge, down Long Mill Gate, past the Cathedral and into Deansgate. Mr Hodgson was not one of the money aristocracy but he lived comfortably enough on their trade. He was a General Furnishing Ironmonger and Silversmith and provided them with chandeliers and plated goods and all sorts of articles to adorn their splendid homes—demand for the kind of goods he supplied was stimulated by the magnificent hardware section in the Great Exhibition of 1851.

Edwin Hodgson and Eliza Boond had been married in the Church of St John, Manchester on 28th November 1844. Both Edwin and his father, John Hodgson, gave their occupations as "Manufacturer". William Boond, Eliza's father, is described as a "Collector", presumably of rents. The story went that John Hodgson had been one of the first to introduce the spinning jenny into his factory and had met with the usual fierce opposition of the operatives. William Boond had apparently come down in the world, for Frederick Boond, Frances' cousin, once described their mutual grandfather as "a well-known dyer, connected with one of the older dyeing establishments in Manchester". Moreover the family believed that the Boonds were descended from "Elizabeth Wyddeville and Sir John Grey of Groby in Cheshire" and further back from an extraordinary Anglesey chieftain called Cadraad Haard, who was often invoked when particular toughness in the face of difficulties was called for.

There was the strong feeling that both families had seen better days and that better days might come again with hard work, good reading and a careful attention to manners and standards a little more demanding than those of most of their neighbours. A candlestick-maker might consider himself a cut above a butcher and a baker.

The Hodgsons began their married life after a long court-ship. Edwin was now twenty-eight and his wife a year older. He wrote to his mother-in-law on the first day of his married life, in the only letter of his which is preserved. He was telling her of their safe arrival at Lockwood's Hotel, York (Edwin came from Yorkshire: he had been born in Doncaster).

Dear Mother:

This is the first letter you have ever received from me—and although I have tried for a great number of years in order to be qualified and admitted into your family—I trust the appellation is pleasing to you.

We arrived here last night, all safe, thank God, but as you may very well conceive, completely tired out …

We hope that the day passed off in every way that you could wish after we left—and that the company departed with happy faces and kind wishes. Eliza is very well and happy and sends her dear, dear love …

Eliza and Edwin spent this first married day "looking at the Cathedral". On their return to Manchester they took rooms at 30 Moreton Street, Cheetham, where on 20th February 1846 their first son, Herbert Edwin, was born. When Eliza was preg-nant again they moved to 141 York Street, Cheetham, which now seems to be 141 Cheetham Hill Road. This part of the street was then called York Place. There were three boarding houses in the terrace and the Hodgsons' other neighbours included a silk manufacturer, a copper-roller manufacturer, a warehouseman, a dyer, a corn-factor, a wool-draper and a card-maker.

John George, the second child, arrived on 24th July 1847 and on 2 November 1849, Frances Eliza was born. Not far away, Mrs Gaskell was writing a letter to Charlotte Brontë, congratulating her on *Shirley*. Her own *Mary Barton* had been published the previous year; the Manchester operatives Mrs Gaskell wrote of were the same people who were soon to fascinate the young Frances, in spite of her family's efforts to protect her from them.

In the 1851 census, Edwin Hodgson had in his employ at the house in York Street, two servants: Ellen Parry, a "house-servant" of twenty-eight from Anglesey, and Elizabeth Mottram, a nineteen-year-old nurse from Frodsham, not far away in Cheshire. According to *A Manual of Domestic Economy* published in 1857, the total annual wage bill for the two young women was likely to be only £18. 15s. and the income of someone employing two servants not more than about £250 a year.

The others who "abode in the house on the night of March 30, 1851" were the "Fancy Where Ironmonger" head of the house, Edwin Hodgson aged thirty-five, his wife, Eliza, aged thirty-six, and their three children: Herbert Edwin, aged five ("scholar"), John George, aged three, and Frances Eliza, aged one.

Frances was auburn-haired and always inclined to be plump. A brother once joked that when she fell she bounced like a rubber ball. Later in life she was described by one of the many journalists who interviewed her as "disappointingly short" but with "perfect lips"—"firm, full and well-chiselled".

There is no photograph of Frances as a child. In 1892 she said this was because "she belonged to an era when photography was not as advanced an art as it is today". There were, however, a number of Photographic Studios in Manchester at this time, offering first-class portraits, and their advertisements in the *City Trade Directory* were alongside Mr Hodgson's own and those of the hat-lining-cutters, the japanners, the bonnet-box-makers, the heald-knitters, mangle-makers, ostrich-plume-manufacturers, gutta-percha-suppliers and dealers in live turtles. It is probable that Mr Hodgson's budget did not run to the cost of the new-fangled photographers, even though they claimed to provide their first-class portraits at most reasonable charges. Mr Hodgson was not one for conspicuous expenditure. His advertisement in the *Trade Directory* was one of the smallest.

But life was comfortable enough. Travelling to Deansgate on a horse-bus, it was easy to ignore the fact that, not far away, were places that were an offence to eye and nostril, "the homes of vice and poverty which surround the huge palaces of industry and clasp them in their hideous folds".

The Directory of 1852 was able to exclaim ecstatically at the sight of eighty-six thousand Manchester Sunday School children, the Hodgson boys almost certainly among them, gathered in Peel Park on 10th October 1851 to greet Queen Victoria.

"Honour to the Monarch whose auspicious reign is productive of such a blessed sight! Honour to the town that can present it!" But the Queen herself, while gratified by the cheering enthusiasm of the crowds, and their good behaviour, noted in her diary "a painfully unhealthy-looking population".

Edwin was determined to give his children a healthy life. The little house in York Street was becoming crowded and the aspect no longer as rural as it had been only three years earlier. The population of Manchester had increased by sixty thousand in the last ten years. The Hodgson family was increasing too. Early in 1852, shortly before the fourth child was born, they moved a mile or so further out along Cheetham Hill Road into a brand-new terrace opposite St Luke's Church. The house, destroyed quite recently, had the words ERECTED 1852 on the garden wall. It was one of a row of seven, of brick, double-fronted, with rather attractive doorways. Each had two main floors, with basement and attic.

Certainly 9 St Luke's Terrace, as it was then called, was a good step up from the house in York Place. Edwin Hodgson was prospering. But the front garden is small (and we know it has not been altered because of that dated wall) and the whole house bears little resemblance to the "imposing mansion ensconced in trees" which Vivian Burnett described in his life of his mother. He called the house "Seedley Grove" but this seems to have been, not Edwin's house, but a part of Tanners' Lane, Pendleton, several miles west of Cheetham Hill, where Frances stayed later.

The real joy of St Luke's Terrace was that it backed on to fields belonging to the Earl of Derby, and that the lake and beautiful grounds of Temple House were close by. Frances' first memories were of St Luke's Terrace in February 1852 when she was two years and three months old. The memory can be dated with this precision because Edith Mary had just been born. It is rather fitting that the first memory should be of this younger sister, for Edith was to provide Frances during much of her life with what she most needed—not only love but an audience, not only a friend but an admirer.

But on this first occasion Frances was the admiring audience and she already knew her own mind. She wanted to hold the new baby. The nurse, not having much confidence in the arms of a two-year-old, held

the white-robed new baby in her own arms and amiably pre-tended to place it in the short arms and on the tiny knees while she was really supporting it herself.

"There," she said. "Now she is on your knee." She thought she had made it all right, but she was gravely mistaken.

"But I want to hold her *myself* …"

"You are holding her," answered the Nurse, cheerfully. "What a big girl to be holding the new baby just like a grown up lady."

But Frances was not deceived.

"I am *not* holding her," she said. "You are holding her."

Looking back on it many years later, Frances said she could still feel this first realization that people who were grown-up could do what they chose—hold babies, come and go as they pleased. Moreover, that they could always stop children doing what they wanted, that there was no appeal against their omnipotence. Another early memory dates from this same month, and it has to do with various important matters, such as a feeling for language and the necessity of not hurting people. A visitor had called to see the new baby.

"What is your new baby's name to be?" the lady asked.

"Edith," was the answer.

"That is a pretty name," said the visitor. "I have a new baby, and I have called it Eleanor. Is not that a pretty name?"

Frances apparently went through agonies of indecision, before she finally came out with her honest and yet tactful answer. For some reason, she did *not* think Eleanor was a pretty name.

She thought it was an *ugly* name; that was the anguish of it. She could not bear to reveal to the new mother just what she had done. She could not bear to think of the poor new baby saddled for life with an ugly name. The visitor thought she was shy or too small to have any opinions on the subject of names. "Don't you think it's pretty?" she coaxed. "Don't you like it?" Frances swallowed. She already had strong feelings that it was wrong to be unkind. "I don't think," she finally muttered, "I don't think it is—as pretty—as Edith."

And everyone laughed and smiled and petted her. No one realized how much thought had gone into the reply. It did not occur to anyone in those days that two-year-olds could think. Children were considered to be "either comic, adorable, tiresome or intolerable". They were not regarded as embryo intellects, whose growth it is the pleasure and duty of intelligent maturity to foster and protect. Morals and manners were attended to, desperate efforts were made to conquer their natural disinclination to wash their hands and faces. It was a time-honoured custom to tell them to "make less noise", and everyone knelt down in his nightgown and said his prayers every night and morning.

The creed went like this:

> *Speak when you're spoken to,*
> *Come when you're called,*
> *Shut the door after you,*
> *And do as you're told.*

On this occasion, Frances had spoken, eventually, when she had been spoken to. So she was praised and cuddled. No one had realized she was obeying her mother's advice in a far more funda-mental manner. She had been kind. This was her mother's constant teaching. "Be kind, my dear, be kind. Try not to be thoughtless of other people. Be very respectful to people who are poor. Never be rude or vulgar. Remember to be always a little lady."

There is no one more anxious or concerned to be ladylike than the person who needs to reassure herself that she is indeed a lady. The Revd R. Parkinson, Canon of the Collegiate Church, looked at Manchester in 1841 and wrote: "There is no town in the world where the distance between the rich and the poor is so great, or the barrier between them so difficult to be crossed." It was immensely important to stay on the right side of the barrier.

It was also extremely important to stay on the right side of the law. Frances was peace-loving and pleasure-loving. She liked to do what was right and to please everyone. Throughout her life she wanted most to please. She could not bear to offend. One of the most vivid memories of her childhood again made her feel how little adults remember what it is like to be a child, something she never forgot.

One day Frances was sitting on a bench in a park studded with notices saying KEEP OFF THE GRASS. She was three and just learning to read. (She had learned her capital letters, with her brother Herbert's help, from the advertisement columns of the newspapers.) She was so small that she was worried she might fall through the back of the bench and on to the forbidden grass. A policeman came to sit beside her and she plucked up enough courage to ask him a question.

"If anyone treads on the grass must you take them up? Would you have to take me up if I went on it?"

"Yes," said the policeman solemnly. "I should have to take you to prison."

"But," Frances said, "I am so little I might fall through the back of this seat. If I was to *fall* through on to the grass, should you take me to prison?"

How much it mattered to her must have shown on her face but the policeman stuck to his facetious point. "Yes," he said, "I should have to pick you up and carry you at once to prison."

Frances did not say anything more but at night, for a long time afterwards, she awoke shivering with terror. Only on one other occasion in her childhood was she teased so cruelly by an adult. She never forgot that either. It was four years later. She and her best friend, both regular admirers of new babies, saw one particularly attractive specimen taking the air in the arms of an elderly person, who noticed their admiration.

"Are you so very fond of babies?" she enquired. On being told that they were indeed, she calmly offered to give them this one, assuring them that its mother had more than enough already. Frances gasped at the thought of such a riotous superfluity of new babies and fell for the proposal. The elderly woman promised to return with the baby and some of its clothes and equipment the following evening. They were to meet her at a certain corner at quarter past seven. The little girls waited and waited in a fever of anticipation but they never saw the elderly woman or the baby again. One hundred and twelve years later, someone who had known Frances said to me, "She never was a good judge of people."

The Keep off the Grass incident made more impression on the child than the death of her father. How close she had come to prison! She woke trembling in the night. Her father's death was much less frightening. He died that same year, on 1st September 1853, of apoplexy, they said. Frances was not yet four. She was taken in to see him, laid out on the crimson-draped four-poster bed. "Papa has gone to heaven," someone said and she looked down at him with interest and without fear.

His death, of course, made a great difference to their lives. He died intestate. Eliza Hodgon, pregnant with the fifth child, signed the deed of administration as his relict. It was witnessed by her brother, John Clegg Boond, warehouseman, and her mother, Hannah. "The Personal Estate and Effects of the intestate were under the value of five thousand pounds"—all the evidence suggests that it was probably considerably under.

The fifth child, a third daughter, was born on 6th January 1854 and christened in St Luke's Church on 8th March. She was called Edwina, after her father, whose trade before his death was given in the church register as silversmith. Mrs Hodgson, recovering from the shocks of death and birth, decided to run the family business herself. Other women did it and so would she. There was a Margaret Rogerson in the 1854 Directory, "basket, skip and hamper manufacturer", and another woman, Anne Cowburn, who had taken over a "carriage manufactory", and thanked "the Nobility, Gentry and Public generally, of Manchester and its vicinity for the liberal patronage and support received since the death of her Husband."

The two servants were busy with the house, the new baby and two-year-old Edith that spring of 1854. John and Herbert were at school and Frances was left more and more to her own devices and to the occasional attentions of her grandmother. It was her grandmother who bought Frances her first book. Which grandmother it was, is not clear. Hannah Boond lived not far away and Mary Hodgson, Edwin's mother (born in Stafford in 1782), at some stage came to live with her son's family. Frances' description of the book-buying grandmother has much in common with that of Miss Alicia Temple Barholm in a book she wrote fifty years after her grandmother's death. Grandmamma "had silver-white hair, wore a cap with a full white net border" and carried sweets in a silver snuff-box. They bought the book in a tiny shop with a window crammed with toys and delights in glass jars.

"In a life founded and formed upon books," Frances wrote, "one naturally looks back with affection to the first book one possessed." It was called *The Little Flower Book*. A stood for Apple Blossom, C for Carnation and R for Rose. Each page was divided into two and, under the picture of the flower, splendidly coloured on a black background, there was an appropriate verse. In children's books in those days, of course "no well-regulated person ever mentioned the poppy without calling it 'flaunting' or 'gaudy'". The violet was modest, the rose sweet.

It was not only in her book that Frances liked flowers. She writes in her autobiography of her childhood of "that enchanted garden which, out of a whole world, has remained, throughout a lifetime, the Garden of Eden". In his book, Vivian Burnett takes this to be the Hodgsons' own garden. But Frances said, "I do not know with any exactness where it was situated. I imagine it was a comfortable countrified house with a big garden round it and fields and trees before and behind it." This was certainly not 9 St Luke's Terrace, Cheetham Hill Road. It seems that in this year after Edwin's death, Eliza felt she could no longer keep on the house. The family moved temporarily to Seedley Grove, Tanner's Lane, Pendleton. There were Cleggs in Seedley Grove in the 1854 Directory. Eliza's mother had been a Clegg and it is likely that the widow and her five young children (Herbert, the eldest, was only just eight) took refuge with better-off relatives while trying to find a house they could afford.

They were there for less than a year but it was an important year for Frances. She discovered the garden that was to be with her for the rest of her life. It was certainly one of the ingredients of "the Secret Garden", though there were other and more important ones. The second garden which contributed to that book written fifty years later, she was to see later in Salford. It was a poor, abandoned garden behind a "little green door in a high wall … It had been a garden once—and there were the high brick walls around it—and the little door so long unopened, and once there had been flowers and trees in it." Frances "bent down and looked the weeds in their faces and touched them tenderly. 'Suppose they were roses and pansies and lilies and violets.'" Frances imagined everything carpeted with flowers and wondered whether "the long dead Garden—the poor, old forgotten, deserted garden—did it know that suddenly it had bloomed again?" The third garden was at Rolvenden in Kent.

Frances once told a story of Watts, the painter. "He had painted a picture of Covent Garden Market, which was a marvel of picturesque art and meaning. One of his many visitors, a lady, looked at it rather doubtfully. 'Well, Mr Watts,' she said, 'this is all very beautiful, of course, but I know Covent Garden Market and I must confess I have never seen it look like this.' 'No,' replied Watts. And then, looking at her thoughtfully, 'Don't you wish you could!'"

Frances, herself, had this ability to transform things beyond their reality. She could make the Salford garden bloom again in her imagination. She could remember the Seedley Grove garden, flooded with perpetual sunshine and filled with the scent of roses and mignonette and new-mown hay, apple blossom and strawberries. She never remembered it in winter—perhaps she was not there in winter.

There was a jungle of flowering shrubs there and a warm, scented alley of sweet briar, which led down to the Rimmers' cottage. The Rimmers were important too. Frances' contact with Emma Rimmer was her first real contact with the outside world, the world beyond the family, with its stress on ladylike behaviour and the keeping-up of appearances. There was nothing ladylike about Emma Rimmer. She lived in a whitewashed cottage beyond the garden of Seedley Grove. Mr Rimmer kept pigs and Emma knew all about pigs. This meant a great deal to Frances; she always cherished the acquaintance of people who knew about things. Years later, when asked what characteristics she considered the cause of her success, she replied, "The fact that I was interested in everything in the world—from emperors and prime ministers to swineherds and cats and dogs and every smallest blade of grass that grows."

Emma Rimmer was Frances' first swineherd, and, as well as knowing about pigs, she had the advantage of not having been banned by Mrs Hodgson, as had the tollgate-keeper's daughter, who was said to be a "rude little girl". Emma was not rude, but it was through Emma that Frances committed her first "crime". The girls were playing together when Frances suddenly felt hungry.

It happened that Mrs Rimmer displayed a cardboard notice in her cottage window:

> Pop. A penny a bottle
> Ginger beer.
> Sold here.
> Also nettle beer.

There were glass bottles of raspberry drops, bulls' eyes and hum-bugs. There were real Eccles cakes at a penny each and pieces of parkin for a halfpenny.

"I wish I had a halfpenny," said Frances. "If I had a halfpenny, I would get a halfpenny parkin."

Emma stopped jumping. "Why does'na tha go an' get a parkin on trust?" she said. "My mither'd trust thee for a ha'p'ny. Tha could just get thy parkin an' pay next toime tha had a ha'p'ny. A moit of people does that way. I'll go an' ax Mither fur thee now."

To Frances, imbued with the idea that debt was dishonour-able, the suggestion was far from respectable. "Mamma would be angry," she said.

"Tha needn't say nowt about it," said Emma. She went for the parkin.

After the first bite, the enormity of what she had done struck Frances. What if she *never* had a halfpenny and her family were involved in her dishonour. She could not eat the parkin. Nor could she return it to Mrs Rimmer with a semi-circular piece taken out of its roundness and the marks of her teeth on the edge. What should she do with the evidence of her guilt? In later years she said she knew exactly what a murderer felt like with a body to dispose of. Again she could not sleep at nights, this time for worrying about the parkin, which, for some reason, she had hidden in the dining-room sideboard. In desperation she con-fided in seven-year-old John George. Fortunately he possessed a penny. He went to Mrs Rimmer's cottage and paid for the parkin. Frances breathed again.

This story, like the Keep off the Grass one, makes Frances sound excessively law-abiding. But it was her lively imagination, not a lack of spirit, that made her suffer. As she read more and more, her whole life became coloured by drama.

Storytelling was not part of the pattern of her life. Her mother was too busy. The young nurse was busy too with Edith and Edwina, and she lacked imagination—though it was she who first sang "Alice Benbolt" to Frances with its mournful last verse:

> *In the little churchyard in the valley Benbolt*
> *In a corner obscure and alone*
> *They have fitted a slab of the granite so grey*
> *And sweet Alice lies under the stone.*

Betty Mottram knew nothing more, of course, than the words she had learned. She did not know nor care why sweet Alice died. But Frances worried and puzzled over it. One day she buried a doll, though she was not called Alice, under a slab of cardboard and strewed flowers over the grave. She never dug it up. The song, like the gardens, was with her for the rest of her life, cropping up again and again in her books. But Betty Mottram was useless as a storyteller.

Grandmamma at least encouraged an interest in the Bible. Frances recalled standing at her knee, picking out the words "When Jesus was born in Bethlehem of Judea", when she was only three. It was probably her grandmother who told Frances the story of the Slaughter of the Innocents, the first story which made much impression on her. "A little illustrated scripture history afforded a picture of Jewish mothers rushing madly down broad stone stairways, clasping babies to their breasts, of others, huddling under the shadow of high walls, clutching their little ones and of fierce men slashing with swords."

The dolls belonging to Frances were up till this time mere things stuffed with sawdust. In later years she lamented the lack of realism in the dolls of her childhood and envied her grandchildren. Her first doll had a black skull-cap with two ringlets attached, instead of real hair. Her eyes were staring, with painted eyebrows and eyelashes. Her mouth was carved and her teeth painted on. Her limbs were rag things, hanging, and her skin was white calico.

It was only when Frances could read to herself that the poor dolls came to life. Then they became involved in every sort of battle, murder and sudden death. No sedate tea-parties for them. If they were not being slaughtered as innocents, they were being executed as Mary, Queen of Scots, shipwrecked in the Pacific, or pursued by tribes of Red Indians. It was in Islington Square, Salford, that most of these games were played. But it was while the Hodgsons were still at Seedley Grove that Frances first went to school.

The school belonged to the Misses Mary and Alice Hague, the daughters of a clergyman. Twenty years earlier, the Manchester Statistical Society had reported the fact that a third of all Manchester children received no education whatsoever. It also lamented the fact that the majority of children who attended dame schools "derived little or no benefit from their attendance". The Miss Hagues' school was certainly a dame school—and so was the Miss Hadfields' in Islington Square. But Frances was lucky in her schools.

Not, of course, that the Miss Hagues had much belief in the educational benefits of fiction. When Frances was to have a reward "for politeness and good behaviour", they were fortunately in rather a hurry. They picked up *Granny's Wonderful Chair* in the bookshop without looking at it very carefully. "I'm afraid," they told Frances, "it is a very silly book. It is all about fairies." Frances felt a thrill of guilty joy. The landscape of this book, like that of the garden at Seedley Grove, became a permanent part of her mental furniture. There was "a broad pasture where violets grew thick in the grass and thousands of snow-white sheep were feeding", there were rose-trees and nightingales and lilies, and the inhabitants fed on deer's milk and cakes of nut-flour.

In 1855, with her head full of roses and nightingales, Frances looked out of new windows on to a different view. Mrs Hodgson had found the house they were to live in for the next nine years—16 Islington Square, Salford, across the River Irwell, the coal-black, foul-smelling River Irwell. For the next nine years, the real flowers Frances saw were "the daisies and buttercups of the public park, always slightly soiled with a soft drift of smuts". Even the park was some distance away. The story went that the sooty square had once been an ornamental lake with swans and lilies, but it seemed impossible.

Islington Square, like the Hodgsons, had seen better days. It was a closed square, shut in by a large and quite imposing iron gateway. Only these gates separated the Square people from the Backstreet people. The Square retained an atmosphere of faded gentility. The houses were mostly occupied "by widowed ladies with small incomes and unwidowed gentlemen with large families". Several of the houses were empty and those that were not were generally let out in rooms or had a dilapidated air. The lodgers at Number 21, for instance, included a railway porter, and a prison warder—it was not far from New Bailey Prison—called Ezekiel Gilbody.

They were the sort of houses that needed large numbers of servants to run them easily, but the sort of people who could afford large numbers of servants no longer lived in Islington Square, with the back-to-back houses of the mill-workers, twenty-five to the acre, crowding in on every side—those hovels and huts that even Engels said "defied description". There was a dirty and violent world just beyond the iron gates. Frances could see it from the windows of the nursery.

If at Seedley Grove it had always seemed to be sunny, so in Islington Square "it seemed always to be raining on stone pavements and slate roofs, shining with wet". The backyards of the houses of the Square were divided by a long flagged passage from the backyards of some Backstreet houses. It was a sad grey sight. What Frances saw from her windows had a profound effect on her whole life. It was the nearness of squalor, of dire poverty. At one time, when she was sleeping at the back of the house, she woke to see, by a trick of light, people in the house behind reflected on her ceiling. It was four o'clock in morning and the man and woman were getting themselves a bite to eat before leaving for their day's work. "There are Backstreet people on our ceiling," Frances said to Edith, waking her to see them. The man might have been the rag-gatherer, the twister-in of cotton or the spade labourer, who all lived in that backstreet. They were so near, the poor. They were there, just beyond the windows, even on the ceiling. The only thing that kept squalor away was money. Mrs Hodgson did not talk about money. But Frances already knew that this was so.

In Cheetham Hill and Pendleton, the Hodgson children had been protected from the poor. Now they were rather poor themselves but rich compared with those around them. Mrs Gaskell's great "prevailing thought"—"the seeming injustice of the inequalities of fortune"—was already evident to the small Frances. Mrs Hodgson kept her business worries from her children. Frances still had ankle-strap shoes and a party-frock and *Peter Parley's Annual* for Christmas and as much as she wanted to eat. Outside, beyond the windows, many of the children went barefoot, even in the snow. In one street there was 'only one privy for three hundred and eighty inhabitants'. Pigs rooted among the putrescent garbage in the streets. It was normal for workers in the mills to toil from five in the morning until seven or eight in the evening, although, since the Ten Hours Bill of 1847, children's working hours had been restricted.

Things *were* improving. More roads were paved; more sewers constructed. The building of back-to-back houses had stopped in 1844. In 1858 better provision was to be made for the burial of the dead. The water supply, which had been largely blamed for the high mortality rate, was safer. Public health was the main preoccupation of Manchester in the 1850s. Too many people were dying. Nearly half the children died before they were five.

It was not only the barefoot children who died. Frances had vivid memories of the deaths of children in her own school. Alfie Burns was the first dead child she saw. His death was not unexpected.

He had bluish-purple lips; he was said to have heart disease. Frances had once given him a new slate pencil because she had been told he might die suddenly. And he did. It was difficult to imagine him surrounded by walls of chalcedony and sardonyx, chrysolite and beryl. It was difficult to believe that Alfie Burns had overnight exchanged a world of inkstands and copy-books for one full of horses with the heads of lions and breast-plates of fire and jacinth and brimstone. Grandmamma had been reading *Revelations* to her. What is interesting, Frances thought years later, is that we know no more about it all when we are seventy than Frances knew at seven.

Frances was taken to see the body of Alfie Burns by Annie Hadfield, who lived at 19 Islington Square. (Frances was always *taken*. Her strength was in a certain steadiness of purpose, in a care and concern for everything she saw. But she never led the way.) It was the custom to visit the dead. Death was not something to keep out of sight. Frances was sad that Alfie was not transformed. "This is only dust," she kept telling herself. "Alfie has gone to heaven. He is an angel." But he did not look like an angel in his frilled muslin nightcap. Frances put out her hand and touched his cheek. It was the thing to do. If you touched the dead one, you did not dream about it. "As cold as death!" It was a soft chill which held no possibility of ever being warmed. "Poor little Alfie," Annie Hadfield said, "I'm very sorry for him, but he's better off." This was the general opinion and Frances did not question it.

But she did question Mrs Alexander's adage—or at least her mother's interpretation of it. Mrs Hodgson believed that the rich man in his castle—or rather, the genteel in Islington Square—should keep their distance from the poor at the gate. Mrs Hodgson worried about her children's accents, as many mothers have worried since. If she could not protect them entirely from glimpses of "the most disgusting and loathsome forms of destitution" (which appalled the American visitor, Henry Colman in 1845), at least she would try to see that they spoke nicely. Was it really true that the pronunciation of the word "I" alone could settle the whole question of a man's rank and education? It seemed very like it.

But Frances loved the Backstreet children and the strange way they spoke. She had loved the way Emma Rimmer spoke. To stray into a forbidden backstreet and lure a dirty little factory-child into conversation was a real delight. And she and her friends would stand at the iron gateway of the Square and listen to the factory people as they streamed past at twelve o'clock for their brief midday break.

The little girls, their heads pressed against the iron bars, watched the women with their aprons tied back and shawls over their heads and the men and boys in their corduroys, great throngs of them clattering past in their wooden clogs, gossiping and swearing, with bold, unwashed faces.

One day when Frances was sitting at a window, supposed to be learning her lessons for the next day, she was surprised to see half a dozen factory-girls gathered about the lamp-post in the middle of the Square. Frances had proprietorial feelings about this lamp-post. It was directly opposite Number 16 and when she lay in bed at night—in the big crimson-draped four-poster bed she often shared with her mother—the gaslight made a bright patch on the wall and kept her company. Moreover the lamp-post had a solid base of stone, on which Frances and her friends used to sit. It was their property. And, anyway, what were the factory-girls doing in the Square? It was not a thoroughfare.

They were talking loudly, pushing each other, glad to be free. But there was one who was not fooling around. She was knitting a coarse blue worsted stocking. There was something strong and special about her. Frances could not explain it. As she watched, a man came into the Square—a tough-looking man with a mole-skin cap pulled over his brow.

"Here's thy feyther!" one of the girls exclaimed. The group stopped laughing and broke up. But the girl who was knitting went on knitting. When the man swore at her and bullied her and threatened her with his fist, she went on knitting but started to walk slowly out of the Square.

"Dom tha brazent impidence!" Frances heard him say. Frances never forgot this girl. Fifteen years later, changed into a pit-girl, she was the heroine of Frances' first novel, *That Lass o' Lowrie's*. Up till this moment, heroines in Frances' eyes had worn diamonds and silks. They had "luxuriant ringlets, brows of ivory, pink ears like ocean shells and the tiniest feet in the world". Many later heroines would too. But this one was different.

Frances learnt to speak the dialect as well as anyone, though Mrs Hodgson did not realize it. Frances and her friends used to speak it when they were alone. There was a small boy called Tommy, whose family lived rent-free as caretakers in one of the big empty houses. "Eh," he would say, "tha should heer my Grandfeyther sweer when he's drunk. Tha never heard nothing like it—tha didn't." When Frances' curiosity was sufficiently aroused, he would oblige with a repetition of his grandfather's choicest phrases. Frances was no longer the innocent small girl she had once been. Fighting was no longer something she read about in books. It was there on the streets, just beyond the iron gates. Black eyes, beer jugs broken over heads, they were common. "A row in Islington Court!" "There's a man beating his wife in Back Sydney Street!" The cry would go up and the little girls would hover by the iron gates, hoping to see a policeman march by with somebody in custody. Occasionally they would see, as they stood at the gates, a stretcher party going by—carrying a weaver, caught and crushed by a loom as Frances' hero, Surly Tim, was to be crushed years later.

But the outside world was not so exciting that it kept Frances away from books. She read voraciously, often getting into trouble for reading when they had visitors, for wanting—dreadful thought—to read at meals, for reading when out visiting. She discovered, in a desperate search for stories, the contents of her mother's secretaire. On one occasion, she called this discovery of shelves full of books that were "not too old to read … the greatest event of her entire life". Some of the books annoyed her intensely—gift books of verses called *The Keepsake* and *The Final Tribute*, with engravings of smooth-shouldered ladies with "snowy bosoms" and "ruby lips". The phrases might come in useful but there were no stories there. She felt like kicking *The Keepsake* all over the room. The pretty binding was a cheat. But there were stories in some of the books of poetry. She found *The Ancient Mariner* and *The Eve of St Agnes* and *Don Juan*. She read Shakespeare and Scott. But it was Dickens and Thackeray who impressed her more, and they were the writers most often quoted and referred to in her own books.

And she used them all as fuel in her private games. She was conscious that other people thought her odd for talking to herself, and she normally whispered as she played and kept to an inconspicuous corner of the nursery, stopping in mid-sentence if she thought Edwina and Edith were listening. It was only later she developed her taste for an audience. But one day she was playing in the hall as she badly needed the candelabra stand at the bottom of the stairs—a product of the family firm—as a prop. She tied a black gutta-percha doll to the iron stand and lashed it with one of her brother's toy whips. Her mother, the kind and gentle woman, was dismayed to come down the stairs and see the violent and furious child.

"I was only playing," Frances said. "I was only pretending something."

"It really quite distressed me," her mother said afterwards to a friend. "I don't think she is really a cruel child. I always thought her rather kind-hearted, but she was lashing that poor black doll and talking to herself like a little fury. She looked quite wicked. She said she was 'pretending'. You know that is her way of playing. She does not play as Edith and Edwina do. She pretends her doll is somebody out of a story and she is somebody else. She is very romantic."

It was only years later that Mrs Hodgson discovered that the black doll was Uncle Tom and that the violent Frances was the godless and cruel Simon Legree. Frances had been reading *Uncle Tom's Cabin*, which was published the year she was three. It was her first impression of America and she became a fervent abolitionist. If the lot of the Backstreet children was a sad one, how much worse off were the Negroes of the South. At least "the English labourer is not sold, traded, parted from his family, whipped". But the Negroes were far away. Frances had no idea she would ever see them. The Backstreet people were outside the iron gates, beyond the windows, even on the ceiling of her room. They could not be ignored.

As important to Frances' development as this knowledge of another world was the presence in Islington Square of the Hadfield family at Number 19. Henry Hadfield was a remarkable man and his story, as well as his character and interests, affected Frances. His obituary in the *Manchester Guardian* in 1887 called him "a well-known drawing master and painter". "In early life it had been anticipated that he would share in the final disposition of the fortune of his wealthy relative (the founder of Henshaw's Blind Asylum) but these great expectations were not realized and much was also lost in fruitless litigation." Hadfield was a drawing master at the Mechanics' Institute for nearly fifty years. He had a "genuine enthusiasm for popular education and advocated it in days when its propriety and necessity were by no means universally allowed". The *Guardian* spoke of "the sterling quality of the man" and recorded the fact that "among those who came within his influence was Mrs Hodgson Burnett".

Two years after the Hodgsons moved to Islington Square, Henry Hadfield published *A Treatise on Perspective* and in 1860, when Frances was eleven, a long dialect poem called, "The Triumph o' Proide or th' history o' Jim Boardman an' Ailse Sidewell, afore an' after they 'en wed". It seems likely that he encouraged Frances' interest in dialect which she was to use with such effect in her first novels and again, much later, in *The Secret Garden*.

Frances, Edith and eventually Edwina all went to school in Henry Hadfield's house where there was a "Select Seminary for Young Ladies and Gentlemen". Years later Frances was to give a vivid picture of another "select seminary", attended by Sara Crewe. But the Miss Minchins of *Sara Crewe* were very different from the Hadfield girls, Sarah, Jane and Alice. When the

Hodgsons arrived in 1855, the school must have been new, for even Sarah was only nineteen. There were six other children— George, Susette, Edward, Annie (already referred to as Frances' best friend), Henrietta and Eliza. Edward was the same age as John Hodgson; Henrietta and Eliza played with Edith and Edwina. The children were in and out of each other's houses the whole time and it was through the Hadfields that Frances first saw a grander, richer world which was to fascinate her as much as the Backstreet one.

Annie kept Frances well supplied with stories of her cousins at Grantham Hall and sometimes Miss Eliza was actually to be seen, coming to call in her lavender silk frock and lace parasol. When Sarah and Jane were bridesmaids at a Grantham Hall wedding, Frances and some of the other school children went to the church. "I wonder if they like each other very much," Frances asked, looking at the newly married couple, but nobody seemed to know. Jane and Sarah sometimes went to balls at Grantham Hall. Annie took Frances in to see the pink silk dresses they were to wear on one of these splendid occasions. Frances imagined their conversation as "at once sparkling, polished and intellectual beyond measure, something like grammar, geography and arithmetic set with jewels of noble sentiment and brilliant repartee". Dancing in their pink dresses, did they lift their dark eyes to their partners and ask "What is Macclesfield noted for?" or "Fifteen from fifty-seven and how many remain?"

The children danced too at their Christmas parties. They danced polkas and schottisches and quadrilles. They ate tipsy cake and Sally Lunns; they drank negus and cowslip wine. Frances looked forward to these parties with rapture. She longed for the party. But then, when she was there, even as she danced and the music and laughter surrounded her, she could not quite believe that this was the joy she had anticipated. She found she was asking the questions: "Is *this* the Party? Is this really the Party?"

Frances found that it was like this all through her life. What actually happened was never quite as good as it was in her imagination. "One does it all one's life," she wrote in 1892. "Everybody dances, everybody hears the music, everybody sometimes wears a sash and a necklace and watches other White Frocks whirling by—but was there ever anyone who really went to the Party?"

Arithmetic was different. At least one expected nothing from arithmetic. "Fifteen from fifty-seven and how many remain?" At least there was a definite answer, even if you got it wrong. Frances often did get the answers wrong. In 1895 she was still getting them wrong. "It is known to my entire world that I cannot add up," she wrote to Charles Scribner, her publisher. Her teacher, Sarah Hadfield, had put it tactfully: "Frances had no taste for arithmetic. And she had but a poor memory for dates and geographical particulars. Grammatical construction and analysis seemed to present no difficulties and she remembered clearly and readily historical events and incidents. She had a passion for reading and was not deterred by 'dryness'. Her powers as a story-teller were early developed and at school the children would stand spellbound around her while she improvised for their amusement some story of wonder and adventure."

The story of "Edith Somerville" went on for weeks. "Tell a little 'Edith Somerville'", someone would say if Miss Hadfield was a few minutes late for a lesson. It started as a school story but went on and on until Edith Somerville was loved by Cecil Castleton. Drinks of cold water (forbidden in the schoolroom) and green apples were part of these story-telling sessions. When the apple season was over, they chewed raw turnip. Frances hated the flavour of raw turnip but would not admit it. "In life itself," she wrote years later, "agreeable situations are often flavoured by raw turnip." It needed that steadiness of purpose which Frances was cultivating to close one's eyes to the fact that the turnip was not a sun-warmed peach. The situation itself was certainly agreeable. Frances was giving; the audience was happy.

Her sister Edith, always the listener, the receiver, recalled, "She was just like her own Sara Crewe. These stories were very romantic. Someone in them would be forlorn, sickly or miserable—

pitiful in one way or another. And there would be someone else, who was brave and strong and helpful. The strong one would have to go through all sorts of trials and tribulations. But in the end things would come out right for everybody in a fairy tale sort of way." Frances always wanted everything to come out right for everybody. And in her stories she could make that happen.

In life you often had to learn to put up with things as they were. But she was already discovering in herself a strength of character, a toughness which she said, in a letter to Israel Zangwill in 1895, was the thing she had cared for most all her life—"the refusal to be overpowered by circumstances". In this letter, she recalled an incident left out of the autobiography of her childhood. "An insensate person in authority struck me across the upper part of my arm with a riding whip and, after regarding the livid cut in the soft flesh for a moment or so, I looked up at the person who had done it, and laughed." She was eight at the time.

There was something else she did not mention in her book. "I shall not touch upon that," she said in a letter to her editor, E.L. Burlingame, in 1892. "That" was "the only really sentimental episode of her life". At nine years old she had apparently fallen "in love with a man of thirty who regarded her as a nice little kitten". This was probably the William Henry Ball mentioned in her son's book. "He was willing to discuss books with her. He aroused in her an admiration that was akin to adoration." The interesting thing about Frances' own reference in her letter to Burlingame is the use of the word "only". Sentimental was of course not a derogatory word. But she did not show the stories she was writing to William Henry Ball.

At first she wrote them down on her slate but was annoyed at having to rub them out when she got to the bottom. Then she searched for paper. She found some old notebooks, belonging to the young Welsh cook, Mary Bury. They still kept a cook, for Mrs Hodgson was occupied with the business and her mother-in-law was getting very old. There was also a general servant, an Irish girl, who had too much to do. The "governess" referred to in Frances' book about her childhood seems to have actually been a lodger. Hannah Hartley is down as "visitor" in the 1861 census, but she was there a long time.

The cook's notebooks were useful, though she would not part with them until they were greasy. Frances' words jostled with the shopping lists. "Sir Marmaduke turned his anguished eyes upon her, and cried in heart-wrung tones: 'Ethelberta—my darling—oh, that it should be so!' ONIONS 1*d*. SHOULDER OF MUTTON 10*s*." Frances never showed anyone the written-down stories. She was particularly keen to keep them away from the boys, who thought writing stories was the silliest possible way of passing the time, even for girls who could not play cricket.

She also wrote poetry and that had to be hidden even more carefully from the boys, though their father was reputed to have written poetry, as well as letters to the papers signed Pro Bono Publico or Irate Citizen. The poetry still came as a shock to Mrs Hodgson. The first poem of all is lost. Frances remembered it was about church bells. There were plenty of possibly appropriate rhyme words—Bells, Shells, Tells, Sells and Ring, Sing, Fling, Wing—which made the whole thing surprisingly easy. A verse of the second poem survives. Frances was alone on a Sunday evening, her mother was at church with the boys, Edith and Edwina asleep upstairs. She was about ten.

Alone—alone! The wind shrieks "Alone!"
And mocks my lonely sorrow,
"Alone—alone!" The trees seem to moan,
"For thee there's no bright tomorrow."

There were no trees and the only sorrow was that tomorrow was Monday and school again. But Frances was rather pleased with the verse, as she was so often to be pleased with what she had written. Yes, she definitely liked it. But, try as she might, she could not write a second verse in the same vein. She decided to make it funny. She had been reading humorous poems in *Punch*, and really it was rather funny to be trying so hard to think of something sorrowful.

When her mother got home, she showed the poem to her and she laughed a lot at it, thinking it was something Frances had copied out. Mrs Hodgson did not laugh very much these days, but she stood there, in the mourning she still wore, and laughed. When she discovered Frances had written the poem herself, Mrs Hodgson was amazed. None of the other children she knew wrote poetry. How extraordinary it was, and how clever.

Two other childhood poems survive. One carries the note "Composed by Fannie E. Hodgson at the age of twelve" and shows that Frances was not over-awed by Lemprière's *Classical Dictionary*, which she always kept in her desk at school to offset the effects of arithmetic:

> *King Jove had given a dinner*
> *To his courtiers handsome and bold,*
> *And as his friend, Bacchus, had sat by his side,*
> *He took too much wine, I am told.*
> *For such a sweet Goddess attended him*
> *So brightly bewitching and clever,*
> *A sort of compound of Venus*
> *Aurora, Clyte and Minerva …*

And so on, for verse after verse.

The other poem is worth quoting in full, for it commemorates a controversy and is attractively personal. "The Illuminations" celebrated the marriage of the Prince of Wales to Princess Alexandra of Denmark on 5th March 1863. Frances was then thirteen. She sent these verses to her cousin:

> *My dear Emily White—did you see the sight?*
> *On that day of joy to our nation.*
> *Did you go into town and see Feathers and Crown*
> *On the night of the Illumination?*

We went in a cart, which I assure you looked smart
On that day of joy to our nation.
There were blossoms and favours near the hearts of young shavers,
On the night of the Illumination.

We nearly got teemed, oh, how Carrie Boond screamed!
In that vast deal of conglomeration.
Our charger so fleet rushed down a back street
On the night of the Illumination.

Some very fine day I will step up your way,
At least, if to it you agree.
With two tales I've been writing, full of murders and fighting—.
So I hope you'll be glad to see me.

The controversy was over the spending of public money on illuminations at a time when Manchester was still "wrestling with gaunt distress", as the Manchester *Courier* put it. The papers were full of the meetings of Relief Committees. On the day of the wedding, two hundred and eighty-six individuals were new applicants for relief in Salford. A man was sent to prison for three months for stealing rags.

The war in America was having a disastrous effect on the cotton industry, dependent as it was on the shipments of raw cotton from the Southern States. The previous year, 1862, no fewer than 52,477 people in Manchester, and a further 16,663 in Salford, were receiving relief. The number of work-people without jobs was more than twice the number still in employment. The cotton famine was said to have destroyed one half of Manchester's principal industry.

It seemed to Frances that for years and years everyone had been living under the shadow of a cloud spoken of as "the war in America". "All the human framework of the great, dirty city depended upon it for bread, all the middle classes for employment, all the rich for luxury." The papers reported terrible stories from

America. People who had hardly heard of America before became familiar with the names of the bloody battlefields.

There were terrible stories from closer to home, too. And then, in the midst of "the Lancashire Distress", as it had been called, they decided to celebrate Prince Edward's wedding. Fifteen members of the City Council voted against the expenditure of public money on illuminations, but it was approved by a majority of twenty-six. There were strings of lights a hundred yards long, ten-feet plumes and mottos (such as GOD BLESS THEM) picked out in lights. The Wholesale Fish Market in Great Ducie Street had the words LONG LIVE THE PRINCE AND PRINCESS in letters three feet high.

"In the evening the illuminations were very brilliant and pretty general—though some persons and firms preferred, on the present occasion, to devote what would otherwise have been expended on illuminations and fireworks, to entertainments for their employees ... We are sorry to say that in the crowd of persons who flocked to see the illuminations, one man was killed and several injured—entirely in consequence of their own impudence and eagerness." The Manchester *Courier* confirmed more staidly Frances' description of the "vast deal of conglomeration". It was all very well for the employees enjoying their alternative entertainments. The unemployed looked up at the bright lights and were not fed.

Things were still very hard in the winter of 1863. John Ward, a mill-worker from nearby Clitheroe, wrote painstakingly in his journal: "It has been a very poor time for me all the time owing to the American war which seems as far off being settled as ever. The Mill I work in was stopped all last winter during which time I had three shillings per week allowed by the relief committee which barely kept me alive ... My clothes and bedding is wearing out very fast and I have no means of getting any more ... If things do not mend this summer I will try somewhere else or something else, for I cant go much further with what I am at."

Mrs Hodgson was beginning to feel the same. The middle classes, who had flourished on the cotton trade, had built themselves fine houses and bought candelabra and silverware, plated goods and door furniture made by Edwin Hodgson's of 62 King Street. Now no more houses were being built. Between 1861 and 1864, 1,193 petitions were filed in Manchester Bankruptcy Court. Three hundred and thirty-eight mills disappeared for ever. Mrs Hodgson's account books were more and more discouraging. Frances often found her looking tired and depressed, as she took off her black bonnet on returning from King Street. Years after, Frances recalled how her mother's hands trembled, as she took off her bonnet and said, "I am afraid I am not a good business woman." But she did not go bankrupt. She sold the business to Penman and Butt, who, long afterwards, were still flourishing at that address.

Islington Square was dirtier and more depressing than ever. The big houses at one side of the Square, which had stood empty for years, were being demolished to make way for smaller ones. The Hadfields moved out to pleasanter air at Strawberry Hill. Mrs Hodgson took a smaller house at 1 Gore Street, Greenheys, Chorlton on Medlock. She was glad to be listed in the Directory as a "householder" at last. She had not enjoyed her years as an "ironmonger". But the interest on the proceeds of the sale of the business was not really sufficient to live on. They would have to try "somewhere else or something else".

Then the letter came from America. William Boond, Eliza Hodgson's brother, had gone to Tennessee years before. He suggested that the family join him. He had a dry-goods store in Knoxville. The Knoxville *Whig* of 16th November 1864 carries his advertisement—"William Boond, Grocer, Provision Dealer and Commission Merchant, Corner of Gay and Union Streets". He had prospered during the war. He believed he could find work for the boys. It was a cheerful letter and it came at a cheerless time.

It was several years since the peak period of emigration to America, but the war had stimulated rather than suppressed interest in the New World. John Ward of Clitheroe was not alone in following every move in the Civil War and in the election of November 1864. The violent effect of American affairs on the economy of Lancashire at least made America seem nearer. The new screw-steamers were crossing the Atlantic in between ten and fourteen days. The prospect did not seem too daunting, though the Hodgson children had travelled no further than Rhyl, and Eliza no further than York, on that honeymoon visit exactly twenty years before. A poet in the *Illustrated London News* had compared going to America with going to Heaven. All sorts of joyful things would await them "once landed on that other shore". It seemed possible.

They took passages on the *SS Moravian*, a first-class, powerful screw-steamer, owned by the Montreal Ocean Steam-Ship Company, sailing from Liverpool on Thursday, 11th May 1865, for Quebec. The journey was four hundred miles shorter and cheaper than to New York, and the Company guaranteed to convey them, at very moderate rates, to most of the principal towns in Canada and the United States, by arrangement with the Grand Trunk Railway Company of Canada.

The Liverpool newspapers on the day they sailed carried the report of Lincoln's assassination on 15th April. They also carried the news of a FRIGHTFUL STEAMBOAT DISASTER. Fifteen thousand Federal prisoners had drowned in the Mississippi, following a boiler explosion. More encouragingly, they announced: "General Johnston has surrendered to Sherman and at length the war may be definitely pronounced at an end."

What definitely was at an end was Frances' childhood. She was fifteen and a half and her character was formed. The characteristics she showed then, so she herself maintained, were to stay with her for the rest of her life. She was curious, romantic, buoyant, compassionate, generous, restless and not very wise. Thirty years later she said that she could not see she was much wiser than she had been on that cold spring day when she left England for the first time.

2

My Object is Remuneration
1865–1873

The Hodgson family reached Tennessee in June, after two weeks of travelling by train through Canada and the United States. The inside of the train was plushy and thickly tasselled, with fancy mirrors and brass cuspidors. Not long before, Robert Chambers in his *Edinburgh Journal* had recorded his disturbance that American railway conductors "affected a dash of the gentleman and, off duty, passed for respectable personages at any of the hotels". But Frances was delighted with everything, and most of all with the view from the windows of hundreds upon hundreds of miles of American forest—a fertile wilderness such as England had not been since it was a Roman province. In Islington Square there had not been one tree.

But there was more to Tennessee than trees. Three months earlier, Andrew Jackson, the Military Governor, announced to the people that "the shackles have been formally stricken from the links of more than 275,000 slaves in the state". The decision was bitterly disputed, of course. One slave-owner spoke of "the nigger" as "that dark fountain from which has flowed all our woes". If the slaves had to be freed, he wanted a fair price for his belongings and the coloured population removed beyond the limits of the state. He feared for his life if the Freedmen remained in Tennessee.

In this divided state, it was not only the slave-owners who feared for their lives. While the Confederates controlled East Tennessee, the Unionists had suffered. Some had been executed for bridge-burning, many had been imprisoned and some had died in prison. Unionist property had been confiscated for military use. Cruelties had been committed "to gratify old party and private animosities". Now the Unionists had their revenge. "I love East Tennessee and I sorrow for her now," wrote an ex-Confederate to a Unionist friend in December 1865. "Would to God that something could be done to assuage this bitterness and restore East Tennessee to peace and harmony."

Ruin and destruction were evident on every hand: burned houses, ravaged land, the detritus of war. The armies had left the land barren. There were deaths from starvation. Many Confederates, even after taking the Oath of Allegiance, were kept prisoner in the North. Those who did return, both Unionist and Confederate, were weakened by war. Amputation, the only cure for infected wounds, was common. In addition to the war casualties, which had reduced manpower sharply, there was a whole sale desertion of rural areas by the Negroes, who thought their new freedom meant freedom from work. How could they settle down and work quietly for men they hated? They longed for their own forty acres and a mule. When there seemed little hope of that, the towns were packed with vagrant Negroes. On 23rd August 1865 the Knoxville *Whig* commented: "This congestion in cities and towns of such crowds of colored folks, to live in idleness and on rations furnished by the government, is all wrong. It is doing the blacks an injury that will show itself after a while. All sorts of depredations are committed by the blacks." Released slaves and under-employed soldiers roamed the country in bands. Murders and robberies were so common that few people went out at night. From all over the state came reports of atrocities. A typical one was dated 12th May 1865 (the day after the Hodgson family left England), relating how three men of the Second Tennessee United States Mounted Infantry forced their way into a home in Hardin Country, West

Tennessee, violated a mother and her two daughters and hanged them until they were almost dead, in an attempt to find some money they were supposed to have hidden.

No one had money—least of all William Boond, Eliza Hodgson's brother, Grocer, Provision Dealer and Commission Merchant, whose cheerful letter had started the family on their long journey. That letter had been written the year before, when his store had been flourishing on the liberal spending of men who knew they might soon be dead. Now the war was over; spending was reduced to necessities and there were few enough of those. Uncle William said he could employ Herbert, who was now nineteen, but there was no work in Knoxville for John George and nowhere for the family to live.

Having seen Knoxville, Frances was not altogether sorry. Both armies had swept through it and Knoxville in 1865 was a sad place. Years later Frances described it as Delisleville in her novel, *In Connection with the De Willoughby Claim*:

Delisleville had never been a practical place and now its day seemed utterly over. Its gentlemanly pretence at business had received blows too heavy to recover from until time had lapsed. Its broad-verandahed houses had seen hard usage, its pavements were worn and broken, and, in many streets, tufted with weeds; its fences were dilapidated, its rich families had lost their possessions, and those who had not been driven away by their necessities were gazing aghast at a future to which it seemed impossible to adjust their ease-loving, slave-attended, luxurious habits of the past. Houses built of wood after the Southern fashion, do not well withstand neglect and ill fortune. Porticos and pillars and trellis-work, which had been picturesque and imposing when they had been well cared for and gleamed white among creepers and trees, lost their charm drearily when paint peeled off, trees were cut down and vines were dragged away and died. Over the whole of the gay little place there had fallen an air of discouragement, desolation and decay.

Uncle William, however, remained cheerful and full of suggestions. He had a grist-mill in Dandridge. John George could work
there, and there was a little log-cabin the Hodgsons could have
in New Market, just twenty-five miles from Knoxville and only a
few miles from Dandridge. It was not what Frances had imagined
when she had first heard they were coming to America and she
had remembered the plantation life of *Uncle Tom's Cabin*, with
people dressed in white sitting on verandahs covered in vines.

They left Herbert in Knoxville and went to New Market, hoping
for the best. Most of New Market had been intensely loyal to the
Government in the war. It was the home of Russell Thornburgh,
the senior major of the First Regiment of the Tennessee Volunteer
Cavalry. Violent anti-Confederate feeling expressed itself in open
letters nailed to trees. This one is dated the very month that the
Hodgsons arrived in New Market:

> Spetial Order No 1
> In the Woods near New Market Tenn
> July the 24th 65
> All damed Rebels are hereby notified to lieve at wonce, if found
> her at the expiration of ten days from the date of this order and no
> preparation to lieve Thrashing mashiens will sit at wonce enough
> to thrash all crops with the usual tole hickry withs and cowhides or
> anything els that may be required on the occasion. We are working
> by the order that you theving God forsaken helldeserving Rebels
> issued four years ago Union men and Rebels cannot live together
> which we find not altogether bogus
>
> > We are vary
> > respectively
> > Old Soldier

Perhaps the empty log-cabin Willliam Boond found for his sister
and her family was one deserted by some "God forsaken helld-
eserving Rebels", frightened from their home. It was a simple
building in a simple place.

There was one unpaved street, splashed with tobacco spittle—that "detestable yellow dye which mars everything in this country". The street was lined with wooden houses, some of boards painted white and some made of rough logs. At one end of it there was a tannery and the Baptist Church, at the other a blacksmith's and the Methodist Church. There was a narrow winding stream beside the street, and trees everywhere. The surrounding forest and hills shut New Market off from the outside world. A log-cabin was appropriate. It was quite like Fenimore Cooper, except that, whatever anyone else might be up to, the Indians were no longer on the warpath. Frances asked about the Indians and the answers did not sound like Fenimore Cooper. "They gener'ly come a beggin' somepn good to eat," one of their neighbours told her. "Vittles or a chaw er terbacker or a dram er whisky is what they're arter."

The New Market villagers might not have victuals to spare for the Indians but they were very good to the Hodgsons. They found it pleasant to talk to people who had nothing to do with old quarrels or current controversies. Their peculiar situation aroused a good deal of friendly gossip, and gossip was the basic entertainment of New Market. The Hodgsons' situation was peculiar. They were in the meanest and smallest house in the village. It was known that most of the time they had scarcely enough to eat. But "in a community where shoes and even under garments were not always possible, the girls appeared in the neatest of sprigged muslin dresses, white stockings and ankle-strap shoes". The normal dress of the New Market girls was an unwaisted and ankle-length sack of coarse linen or, in the winter, linsey-woolsey, with a poncho-type of hole for the head, secured by a drawstring at the neck.

Mrs Hodgson had, of course, brought their wardrobes from Manchester, and not only their clothes but several barrels of treasured household effects. The floorboards might be bare and the table rough, but Mrs Hodgson still had some fine linen and silver from more prosperous days, and she would not sell it. John came down from the mill once a week, bringing corn-meal, hominy, bacon and molasses. Herbert sent as much as he could from Knoxville, but they were often hungry—and grateful when Mrs Jenkins, from down the road, thought they might like a taste of some "biskits" she had just baked, or Bill Peters passed the time of day and presented Mrs Hodgson with some cuts from a pig he had just slaughtered. Frances remembered such acts of kindness all her life. "New Market was full of graduating angels of a simple gentle kind," she wrote in a letter in 1922. "I am sure they are all in Heaven now."

Their nearest and kindest neighbours were the local doctor and his family. The Burnetts lived in "a wooden structure, fairly comfortable in a primitive sort of way", which stood across a clearing from the Hodgsons' cabin. Dr John Burnett was the only doctor for many miles. He would ride off to his patients among the hills, his saddle bags full of medicines and instruments. He was often away for days at a time. In his scant leisure, he liked to read and he liked to talk. He was a kindly man, warm and approachable. It may well be that the devoted Southern fathers of Frances' stories *Esmeralda* and *Louisiana* owe something to John Burnett. He had four children: three girls, Joe, Ann and May, and a boy, Swan. Swan was also a reader but mainly, until Frances came, of his father's medical books. Seven years before he had been walking in the fields and slashing at the heads of corn with his knife, when it had slipped and wounded his leg. After that he always limped, and read because he could not run. Now he was eighteen. Frances introduced him to Dickens and Tennyson and Thackeray, and he began to love her.

In some moods, later on in life, Frances spoke of "those awful starving days in New Market" when they "went without—food, clothes and fire". In other moods, and more often, she remembered the good things. Swan Burnett did not count for much, the limping, pale, adoring boy, but there was a great deal that was good, that first summer in Tennessee. They rarely saw a newspaper. It was only when Herbert managed the occasional journey from

Knoxville that they heard of the violence and lawlessness that were sweeping the State. There was only one train a day and it was rare for anyone to get off or get on. The girls used to go down to the station sometimes to see the train go through. One day a Unionist private soldier leaned his prison-clipped bald head out of the window and said, "Say, gals, don't you want a lock o' my har." Frances never forgot his face.

But for the most part the outside world was outside, beyond the hills. All you could see were the hills and the forests and the vast clear blue sky. A field sloped upwards beyond the log-cabin. There were green aisles of tall, broad-leaved Indian corn, and beyond the cornfield, the forest. "There is a wide, wide distance—a distance which is more than a matter of mere space between a great, murky, manufacturing town in England, and the mountains and forests in Tennessee—forests which seemed endlessly deep, mountains covered with their depths of greenness, their pines and laurels, swaying and blooming, vines of wild grape and scarlet trumpet-flowers swaying and blooming among them, tangled with the branches of sumach and sassafras." Frances stopped pretending in the old way. "There was no need to pretend. There were real things enough." She still wrote but the stories took a new tone. "Sir Marmaduke Maxwelton was less prominent, and the hair of Edith Somerville flowed less freely over the pages. Hair and eyes seemed less satisfying and less necessary. She began to deal with emotions … In Islingon Square she had imagined—in the forests she began to feel."

Frances spent a great deal of time in the forest, but she and Edith knew how worried their mother was and that they must try and earn some money. They tried everything in those early days. Embroidery—and people didn't want it. Music lessons—and people thought them too young. Chickens—and they wouldn't hatch, and when they did they died of the gapes. There was the awful problem, too, of having to sit on the hen to make her sit on the nest. They tried setting goose eggs and only one hatched and that wasn't a goose. It was a gander, and a plank fell on it and killed it. Late in 1865, soon after her sixteenth birthday, Frances set up her own "Select Seminary". Actually it was not very select. She would take any pupils who were available. She managed to attract eight children, who paid their fees in cabbages, carrots, beets, potatoes and eggs.

It did not last long. In 1866 William Boond's business finally closed down and Herbert, now twenty, got himself a better-paid job with Knoxville's leading jeweller, watch-maker and mender. John was tired of Dandridge; he wanted to go to town too. The whole family moved to a frame-house a few miles outside Knoxville on the Clinton Pike. The daughter of their Knoxville doctor described the house like this: "It was a planked-up arrangement with crude windows and doorways that were practically covered with morning glory vines. It was the ordinary cabin home but it was neat and home-like and nestled among pines." Swan Burnett was sad that they were leaving New Market but he was, in any case, due to begin his studies at the Miami Medical College, Cincinnati, Ohio. From there, he wrote adoring letters to the house on Clinton Pike and Frances answered them, imagining as she wrote, not Swan, but one of the heroes of her own stories with a more romantic name. (For some reason she never could accept Swan's name and never used it.)

Frances spent more and more time out of doors during the summers of 1866 and 1867. Though closer to Knoxville, the new home was even more deeply rural than New Market. It was very small and perched on a small hill, as if some flood, receding, had left it there. They called it Noah's Ark. "One stood on the little porch of Noah's Ark and looked out over undergrowth and woods and slopes and hills, which ended in three ranges of mountains, one behind the other. The farthest was the Alleghenies ... There were no neighbours but the woods. There was no village. The town was too far away to be often visited by people who must walk. There was nothing to distract."

Frances made herself a place she called the "Bower", in among the sassafras, sumach and dogwood. A wild grapevine made the roof. The floor was moss and grass and pine-needles. For one of the few times in her life, perhaps, as she lay there, she was really happy. She didn't feel that she was missing anything. She felt she was at the Party, that this was what life was all about. She wrote there and she read there, a new book when she could get hold of one, which was rarely. She got to know the small animals and insects and the bright birds—but there was no one to tell her what they were called. There had been only sparrows in Manchester. She gathered wild flowers, but she did not know their names. She felt herself under a strong personal obligation to Christopher Columbus—although, when she wrote, she still wrote of England and of its people.

And she couldn't spend her whole life in the Bower. She had to come home for dinner and for bed. Money seemed scarcer than ever. Everything was wearing out. John, mysteriously, was bringing home less than ever. Frances exaggerated their predicament until she made them all laugh. "I laugh instead of crying," she used to say. "There is some fun in laughing and there is none in crying." But the sprigged muslins were shabby and laughing made them feel even tighter under the arms. Someone lent Mrs Hodgson a copy of *Godey's Lady's Book* and Frances, Edith and Edwina pored over the coloured engravings on fold-out sheets. They could not imagine Bert or John wanting a shooting scene embroidered on their handkerchiefs and they were not taken with the designs for a pen wiper ("finished off in tassels of brown silk soutache") or the "square in Guipure Netting, suitable for doyleys"—but the vandyke lappets and fernando mantles were delightful. They longed for the latest fashions, although the voluminous skirts over waist-pinching stays would not have been very comfortable for bird-watching. And it was some consolation for their deprivation to read of the increase in the number of deaths by burning "by the fashion of wearing crinolines".

There was no chance of starting another school. There were no children near enough at hand; and, anyway, was it really fair to set yourself up as a teacher if your arithmetic was so bad? Frances went on reading *Godey's Lady's Book*. This was the dominant woman's magazine of the time and claimed to provide "honeyed delights for a lady's vacant hours". It is worth examining in some detail, for its values and standards were to have a considerable influence on Frances and her early writing. "A new spirit was at work in middle-class America. A new prosperity" (and even Tennessee was rapidly becoming more prosperous) "was feeding aspirations for what was popularly called culture, a notion vaguely associated with the printed page." American publishing was flourishing, with more and more steam-power presses in use. There was no international copyright, so publishers could print any British writer they fancied and not pay him a single cent. It was not only the long dead who were produced in vast cheap editions. Beside the "Beauties and Gems" and "Pithy Extracts" from Shakespeare, there were uniform volumes of Scott and Dickens and Edward Bulwer-Lytton on every bookshelf.

Mere amusement was not enough; it took moral purpose as well to run a successful magazine. *Godey's* editor was Sarah Josepha Hale. She sympathized with unpopular causes, such as women's right to participate in charity fairs or collect funds for the Bunker Hill monument. She steered a careful course between two extremes. One was a belated eighteenth-century view of the elegant female who had wept, fainted and clung through the lesser fiction of the last two generations—the other the contemporary concept of the "new" woman who cultivated her mind, had opinions and pronounced hard words correctly. Mrs Hale printed many sops to her readers but her own message always was "you have a mind; cultivate it. Home is woman's proper sphere; stay in it. Woman's influence is profound; use it. Watch your diet, get plenty of fresh air and exercise and wear your India rubbers when it rains." Women would be better wives and mothers if they used their minds. It was all very well for young girls to love the moon, write in a Lilliputian handwriting and read Byron (though they were not to think of his sins). After twenty-one, a girl should value common sense. The stories in the magazine were romantic, of course. Seamstresses and governesses married the only sons of their mistresses, widows of the town millionaires. But young women also gave up everything to go as missionaries to foreign lands or found themselves married to rakes and drunkards, whom they usually reformed. With the opening up of the West, the etiquette columns were no longer so likely to have advice about stepping into a carriage "with measured action and premeditated grace". There was a new feeling for reality in the air. Frances' favourite names, Kathleen, Rowena, Clarence and Gerald, were still in abundant use. But Effie and Emmie and Joe had arrived.

The thing that really interested Frances was the column of Answers to Correspondents:

> *Elaine the Fair*—Your story has merit, but is not quite suited to our columns. Never write on both sides of your paper.
> *Christabel*—We do not return rejected manuscript unless stamps are enclosed for postage.
> *Blair of Athol*—We accept your poem "The Knight's Token". Shall be glad to hear from you again.

Was it possible that if Frances sent them one of her stories, they would be glad to hear from her again, provided she remembered about not writing on both sides of the paper? She wondered, it had never occurred to her before, how much they paid for stories in magazines.

There were all sorts of problems. Another "answer" bothered her.

> *March Hare*—We cannot receive MSS on which insufficient postage has been paid.

How did one find out what the correct postage was? Herbert had always taken into Knoxville her letters to the Hadfields and the cousins in Manchester, Emily White and Carrie Boond. But she didn't want him to know she was sending stories to the magazines. He would be sure to laugh and tease her. He was always asking her how she was getting on with her tale of "The Gory Milkman and the Blood-stained Pump". It seemed to amuse him. Then there was the paper. *Airy Fairy Lilian* was told to "write in a clear hand on ordinary foolscap paper". What was ordinary foolscap paper? If the magazine had demanded extraordinary foolscap she would have felt it no more surprising. And how to pay for it, ordinary or extraordinary? The problems were enormous. It was only the real wish, the necessity, of contributing to the family income that made her overcome them.

One day Edwina came in and said: "Aunt Cynthy's two girls made a dollar yesterday by selling wild grapes in the market." Aunt Cynthy was the Negro woman who helped with the Hodgson washing.

"It's a good thing we are not living in Islington Square," Frances said. "We couldn't go and gather wild grapes in Back Sydney Street." Aunt Cynthy's girls took them to the place where the grapes grew in abundance. They picked all day, sold them in the market, bought paper with the money and had enough left over for the stamps. Frances wrote the story out carefully. It was called "Miss Carruther's Engagement". And then she panicked at the thought of the Editor of *Godey's Lady's Book*. She imagined him as a mad bull or a tiger with hydrophobia, raging and foaming at the mouth, in consequence of an inadequacy of stamps or a fault in punctuation or handwriting on both sides of the paper. She thought he would return the manuscript with withering comment ("We do not want the hasty composition which needs to be corrected"), or perhaps not return it at all and keep all the stamps.

There was a copy of another less impressive woman's magazine in the house; *Ballou's Magazine* it was called. Frances decided to try that. The stories were not quite so polished. She was sure hers were better.

This is the letter she sent with her story:

> *Sir:* I enclose stamps for the return of the accompanying MS
> "Miss Carruther's Engagement", if you do not find it suitable for
> publication in your magazine. My object is remuneration.
>
> > Yours respectfully,
> > F. Hodgson

A Knoxville schoolmaster sometimes called at the house to talk to
Frances. Edwina and Edith would crouch at the top of the stairs
listening. Edith remembered wishing she could "go to school
again and study history and philosophy just to be able to talk
to Mr S. the way Frances did". So now Frances was engaging
in that conversation, "sparkling, polished and intellectual beyond
measure", which she had imagined for the Miss Hadfields in
Islington Square. And the schoolmaster had another use. He was
pressed into service. He would take the package into Knoxville,
buy the stamps with the wild-grape money and lend his address
so that the reply would avoid the boys.

Frances swung from optimism to despair and back to optimism
again. She had no idea how much magazines paid. "Suppose it's
only about a dollar. I'm sure it's worth more but they might be
very stingy." She started to make calculations. "The magazine
costs two dollars a year. And if they have fifty thousand subscrib-
ers, they haven't many stories in each number, it would be a
thousand dollars!" When the letter came, it was very puzzling.
It began by praising the story. Its sole criticism was that it was
rather long. It did not say it was rejected, nor that it was accepted,
and it said nothing about remuneration. Frances, with the sound
business sense she was to show all her life, asked for the story
back. She claimed that she never had a story rejected in all her
sixty years of writing except for reasons of length. But this story
she asked the editor to return. And she then sent it to the editor
of *Godey's Lady's Book*.

Mrs Hale replied: "Sir, Your story—'Miss Carruther's
Engagement'—is so distinctly English that our reader is not sure
of its having been written by an American. We see that the name

[it was the schoolmaster's] given us for the address is not that of the writer. Will you kindly inform us if the story is original?"

Frances replied: "The story is original. I am English myself and have been only a short time in America."

Mrs Hale was still not convinced. It was one thing for magazines and book publishers to use English material without payment. It was quite another if a Tennessee girl was trying to get money under false pretences. "Before we decide will you send us another story?"

Frances sat down and wrote a story called "Hearts and Diamonds". Remembering *Ballou's* editor had complained of length, she made the new story exactly half as long. And then, at last: "Sir, We have decided to accept your two stories, and enclose payment. Fifteen dollars for 'Hearts and Diamonds' and twenty dollars for 'Miss Carruther's Engagement'. We shall be glad to hear from you again."

"Hearts and Diamonds" finally appeared in *Godey's Lady's Book* for June 1868 and the other story the following October. Frances, at eighteen, was a published writer—though the stories appeared under a nom de plume: THE SECOND. The first story appears as five solid pages of print without a single illustration, but it is far from dull. There are some sound, if romantic, democratic sentiments. "I am happy to say I am not ashamed of my forefathers. I believe one of my grandmothers was washerwoman to a nobleman's wife; in my opinion an infinitely more exciting position than that held by the lady herself. Imagine the fun on scrubbing days!" There are some pleasant interjections from the author, most of them beginning with the word "apropos". The setting is a "watering place". When Valerie Belaire vows to make Pendennis Charrington propose to her, the author interposes, "Very wrong and foolish, was it not? Still I have nothing to do with that, I am only telling a story." It ends with the sentence: "Hearts proved the winning card in this game, at least."

After this success—thirty-five dollars was a tremendous help to the family's financial position—there was no stopping Frances from telling stories. What had seemed to be pleasure and self-indulgence now took on quite a different aspect. Part of the cheque (as seemed only right, after all the fashion plates in *Godey's Lady's Book*) went on alpaca—"shiny, silky stuff. Mama, who was an excellent needlewoman," wrote Edith, "helped us make the frocks. Fannie's was straw-color with blue scallops and mine was blue with straw-color scallops."

It was exciting, this summer of 1868, seeing that first story in print. What was not quite so exciting was to sit down to the writing of light romance when nothing romantic ever happened in your own life. Noah's Ark which had seemed so perfectly situated—with the view of the Allegheny mountains beyond the pine trees—now seemed unbearably isolated. Life was somewhere else. The Party was in another room.

In 1869 the Hodgson family moved into Knoxville itself. John was not often there. His nephew Vivian years later said: "Fate did not deal kindly with him." To his mother's horror—the fact was never mentioned in the family—he had taken a job as bartender with John Scherf at Lamar House. Herbert, good steady Bert, was still working for J. Wood, the watch-maker. But John was behind the bar at Lamar House. It was all very well in a story to celebrate the fact that your grandmother was a noblewoman's washerwoman, but to have a brother pouring drinks at Lamar House was hard to bear. When she was over seventy, Frances recalled Lamar House, "where I think at that time *all* the balls were given". But she never mentioned John George. He goes out of the story for ever.

Mrs Hodgson goes out too. She died on 17th March 1870, aged fifty-five. Frances, aged twenty, was left in charge of the family in the roomy but dilapidated house, called Vagabondia, with its yard running down to the Tennessee River. Frances' occupation in the 1870 census was given as music teacher. Swan Burnett was in Knoxville too now. The Tennessee State Guards were busy suppressing the first Ku Klux Klans and Swan was appointed to the State Guards' Hospital.

There is a vivid picture of Frances and Swan and of the life in the house on the Tennessee River in Frances' book *Dolly* or *Vagabondia*, which was first published as a serial in *Peterson's Magazine* in 1873, but not until 1877 as a book. The story is set in London, in Bloomsbury Place, but there is no doubt that it reflects a good deal of the atmosphere in Knoxville after Mrs Hodgson's death. The family in the story is a "Bohemian" one—the brother an artist (so much more romantic than a watch-maker). There is a guitar hanging on the wall, and the idea is that feelings of freedom and unconventionality do a great deal to compensate for lack of money.

Bert, like Philip in the story, also had a young wife by this time. The 1870 census records her as Ann, aged eighteen, born in Tennessee. The Crewes in the story, like the Hodgsons, are extremely hard-up. The girls spend a great deal of time unpicking bodices and renovating skirts in order to appear reasonably respectable in the eyes of the Philistines. Claud Cockburn once described the Bohemian in literature as "a kind of cultural bank-robber engaged by the author to attack the intellectual strong-rooms of the bourgeoisie". The trouble with Frances' Bohemians is that one feels their Bohemianism is only skin-deep. Given a decent bank-balance, they would happily knuckle down as insiders.

Griffith Donne, who is certainly Swan Burnett, is not a Bohemian. He is patient, jealous, longing to marry. His idea of bliss, like that of T. Tembarom (another unlikely hero, fifty years later), is a little house in the suburbs. Reading Griffith's words, one seems to be overhearing Swan talking to Frances. "It was just the very thing we should want if we were married. Six rooms and kitchen and cupboard and those sort of contrivances ... There is a garden of a few yards in the front and one or two rose bushes. I don't know whether they ever bloom but, if they do, you could wear them in your hair ... And, by the way, I saw a small sofa at a place in town which was the right size to fit into a sort of alcove there is in the front parlour—a comfortable, plump little affair, covered with green—the sort of thing I should like to have in our house, when we have one."

Dolly, like Frances, is not in the least interested in green sofas. Dolly's weakness, like Frances', "lies in wanting everybody to like her—men, women and children; yes, down to babies and dogs and cats ... She can't help doing odd things and making odd speeches that rouse people and tempt them into liking her." Dolly, like Frances, knows that "nervous headaches are useful things". Griffith, like Swan, has to wait for seven years before he persuades the girl he loves to marry him. Swan had waited four when he went away again—to Bellevue Hospital Medical College in New York. He began to specialize in what was to be his life's work, the study of the eye, at this time combined with the study of the ear.

On the surface, life in Vagabondia was pleasant enough. Knoxville, five years after the end of the Civil War, was a very different place from the decaying, discouraging small town they had first seen on their arrival from England. Edward Dicey, the English journalist who was soon to become editor of the London *Observer*, gives a picture of small-town American life at this period. "Probably there is as much scandal and gossip here as in the Old World country town but there are not, as yet, the social divisions which exist with us. If you inquire the names of the owners of the handsomest houses, you will find that one, perhaps, began life as a stable boy, another was a waiter a few years ago in a hotel of the town and a third was a bricklayer in early life. On the other hand, some of the poorest people in the place are persons who were of good family and good education in the Old World. This very mixture of all classes ... gives a freedom, and also an originality, to the society in small towns, which you would not find under similar circumstances in England."

Frances seemed to enjoy Knoxville's small pleasures as much as anyone. There was music-making and sing-songs round the piano—Bert played and so did Frances. A cousin, Fred Boond (was he William's son?) played the bass viol. Charlie Haynes played the violin and Frank Bridges, the flute. Pleasant Fahnestock, who married Edith, was an indifferent performer on the clarinet. There was boating on the river; there were picnics, church socials, those "balls" at Lamar House, candy-pulls and parties. But it was hardly stimulating intellectually. The census reveals that Fahnestock was a carpenter and Bridges a house-painter. Perhaps they would one day own the handsomest houses in town but for the moment there was always, for all of them, a nagging shortage of money. And, unlike the characters in *Dolly*, none of the real inhabitants of Vagabondia or their friends had rich relatives waiting in the wings. The only way out and up was by hard work.

Frances worked. She had stories published at this time in every magazine in America, "except *Harper's*, *Scribner's* and the *Atlantic*. I was not sufficiently certain of my powers," she wrote years later, "to send anything to them. It would have seemed to me a kind of presumption to aspire to entering the world of actual literature." Her stories at this time were pot-boilers in the literal sense. Her object was remuneration and nothing else. But she wrote so much ("five or six little ten or twelve dollar stories a month") that she was able to start putting some money aside for a visit to England.

Swan, in New York, received the full impact of her frustration with life in Knoxville. She was calling him Jerome at this time.

My dear Jerome:

... There is a very strong feeling deep in my heart, telling me that something must be done to raise us all a little from the dust, and the very strength of that feeling lies in the fact that I am *sure, sure, sure* I must do it. You have no need to smile. Nobody else will do it, because nobody else cares a cent whether we drag through our wretched lives as shabby, genteel beggars, or not. We are not shabby, genteel beggars, says Bert, when I fire up a little—but we are shabby, genteel beggars, I say. We are not respectable people in our own eyes, whatever we may be in any one else's. I would as soon be a thief as feel like one, and I do feel like one ...

Respectability doesn't only mean food and a house—it means pretty, graceful things; a front street *not* close to the gas works; an occasional new book to provide against mental starvation; a chance to see the world; a piano and fifteen cents spending money (not to be squandered recklessly of course). "Man cannot live by bread alone," said the minister to his drunken old parishioner. "No," said the apt non-convert, "He mun hae' a few wedgetables," which is my opinion. What I want is a "few wedgetables".

What is there to feed my poor, little, busy brain in this useless, weary, threadbare life? I can't eat my own heart forever. I can't write things that are worth reading if I never see things which are worth seeing, or speak to people who are worth hearing. I cannot weave silk if I see nothing but calico—calico—calico. It is all calico, it seems to me. Ah, me! Ah, me! see what a tangled skein of thread for one poor little woman to unwind.

The last phrase was overdoing it, besides being a confusing mixed metaphor. Frances never considered herself a "poor little woman". Swan would write back, of course, and say he cared; it was nonsense for her to say nobody else cared a cent. But Frances didn't want his help. She wanted to be the one to do the raising. Swan should have been warned. And although Frances' desires in this letter are impeccable—books, travel, music—and the homely "wedgetables" enforces the wholesomeness of her longings, her stories at this time show that she already knew the temptations of "luxurious gayety", of selfishness and scheming ambition. She protests too much about how horrible it is to marry for money. If she had been beautiful and had had no talent … But she was not, and she had. She was also extremely hard-working, though naturally, she insisted, lazy.

The editor who was receiving most of her work in 1871 was Charles Peterson, owner and editor of *Peterson's Ladies Magazine*. Like *Godey's, Peterson's* contained fashions and recipes but Mr Peterson himself was a cultivated man with a real concern for literature.

Mr. Peterson began by paying me as the rest did but after I had sent him a few stories he wrote me a letter I could not easily forget. He told me that my work was worth more to him than that of his other contributors and that this being the case, he felt it only fair that he should pay me more … He sent me a check which was almost double what I had received before … This was only the initial act of a series of most generous kindnesses. I was so young and so unprotected by any worldly knowledge, and he protected me against my own simplicity.

He actually encouraged her to aim higher and try the literary magazines which she had thought beyond her abilities. The contrast between early stories like "Kathleen Mavourneen" and "Pretty Polly Pemberton" and the others, such as "Surly Tim" and "Seth", is a striking one. It is not that the first type are clumsy or amateurish. Certainly Frances was writing about a world she did not know, but she was a lot older than Daisy Ashford and the gaffes are few. She has the air of being a confident young writer. If the ideas are commonplace, limited to the conventions of the women's magazine stories of the time, and the language dull, there is a lightness of touch in the telling and enough humour to distinguish them from most of their companions in *Peterson's* or *Godey's*.

Frances always had a weakness for physical beauty (her obsession with Cedric's beauty is one of the flaws in *Little Lord Fauntleroy*), and in these stories *all* the girls are beautiful, with pretty, innocent faces and lovely figures. Their heads are set on their charming throats like lilies on their stems. She also indulges her weakness for romantic names: Gaston Framleigh and Diana Dalrymple are the sort of people who move in this world. The two particular stories I have mentioned, "Polly Pemberton" and "Kathleen Mavourneen", illustrate how repetitive she could be (which is not surprising, remembering how she was churning them out). Both stories use Frances' favourite theme throughout her life—that of a sudden reversal of fortune. Polly's great-aunt dies, Kathleen's uncle dies. They both leave vast sums of money to these penniless young women, one an actress, the other a governess. Both girls know money won't buy happiness, both have misunderstandings with their lovers, and both end happily. Frances had admonished her character: "Stick to your jackdaw's feathers, Polly Pemberton, and don't let yourself dream—even dream—of peacock's plumes." But Polly gets her peacock plumes all right in the end.

Frances' own path to similar adornment was not through romantic women's magazine stories but through much more impressive fiction, a new realism. In September 1871—she was then nearly twenty-two—Frances decided to approach the prestigious *Scribner's Monthly* in New York. It was a new magazine; its first issue had appeared the previous November. It was the first quality magazine to carry advertising, it paid well and it at once fulfilled Charles Scribner's ambitions for it: "I want to issue a magazine that is handsomely illustrated, beautifully printed and that shall have as contributors the best writers of the day." This is the reply Frances received when she sent off her first story:

> October 3 1871
>
> F. Hodgson or Dr Burnett:
>
> The story of "The Woman who Saved me" is declined on account of its length. It would make nearly 16 of our pages which is too much for a "short story" and we don't want any more serials.
>
> Who are you? You write with a practised hand and we shall always be glad to hear from you. Stories should not be more than eight or ten pages in length.
>
> R. W. Gilder

Swan Burnett had returned to Knoxville from New York and had taken a small office in Gay Street and was trying to establish himself as a specialist in the eye and ear. When not working, he spent a good deal of time, as he was to do for many years, writing Frances' business letters for her. He was also still spending a good deal of time trying to persuade her to marry him.

Frances was a little hurt that none of the numerous stories she had contributed to other magazines had made any impression on the editorial staff of *Scribner's*, for she had long ago discarded her nom de plume and had been writing as "Fannie Hodgson". But she was not put off, and when, soon after, she found herself weeping as she finished "Surly Tim", she decided to try *Scribner's* again. The editor-in-chief was Dr J.G. Holland, who, under the name of Timothy Titcomb, was at this time in the middle of waging a campaign against the "literary buffoon", Mark Twain; R.W. Gilder was the assistant editor, then aged twenty-seven. This rather unconventional acceptance eventually arrived from New York:

> Feb 23 1872
>
> My dear Miss Hodgson:
>
> Dr Holland, Dr Holland's daughter (Miss Annie) and Dr Holland's right-hand man (myself) have all wept sore over "Surly Tim". Hope to weep again over MSS from you.
>
> Very sincerely and tearfully,
> Watson Gilder

This was the beginning of a long working relationship and friendship with Richard Watson Gilder. Throughout her life, Frances was to regard him affectionately as a sort of "cherished relative", though, in later years, they rarely met. He was the one person she would really trust to read her proofs or cut with his blue pencil. At one stage, in 1881, their relationship was dangerously unbusinesslike and did much to weaken her marriage, but in the first few years he was the ideal editor, encouraging her, listening to her and making sure she did justice to the talent he had recognized in this first story, "Surly Tim". After his death in 1909, she wrote: "I could imagine no pleasure more keen to one born with the storytelling habit than to sit and tell a growing story to Richard Gilder, led on and on by the mere luring gleam in the extraordinary eyes no-one who knew him well will ever forget."

"Surly Tim" is sub-titled "a Lancashire Story". Most of the tragic story—and it has the true ring of tragedy, so much so that Gilder's acceptance letter seems unbearably flippant—is told in the words of Tim Hibblethwaite himself. It was more than six years since Frances had left Lancashire but the dialect was still in her ears, and Tim's story is the real thing, in quite a different category from the tales of watering-places and society with which Frances had boiled her pots. So is the story "Seth"—set in a Tennessee mining village called Black Creek but with the main characters all Lancashire people. There were indeed numbers of Lancashire immigrants mining in East Tennessee at that time. The story is beautifully controlled from its first plain sentence: "He came in one evening at sunset with the empty coal-train—his dull young face pale and heavy-eyed with weariness." Much of the final effect of the story depends on the revelation that the young miner, Seth, is in fact a girl, but again the feeling is a truly tragic one. There is nothing sensational about it.

From now on Frances found "it was not necessary to write six stories a month when she wanted to cross the Atlantic". She wanted to return to England for a visit and she had money enough to do so. She was determined to go, and nothing Swan Burnett could say would stop her. But she agreed to marry him on her return. Swan wondered whether she would ever come back. He concentrated on the eyes and ears of Knoxville with despair. But in fact Frances' feelings flourished on their separation and the regular diet of love-letters. Seen from the other side of the Atlantic, Swan became a more romantic figure than he had ever been when readily available. Frances enjoyed the rôle of separated lover.

She left Tennessee for the first time in nearly seven years and, at the age of twenty-two, met for the first time some literary people. It was five years since Frances had imagined editors as tigers with hydrophobia foaming at the sight of an untidy manuscript or an insufficiency of stamps, but it was still with a certain amount of trepidation that she arrived in New York on her way to

England. There is only one story of her days in New York; she was apparently whisked off by a rival editor—a woman considered "advanced" in her thinking—from under the nose of R. W. Gilder. Gilder waited at her hotel until the two women finally returned after midnight. However, he was not deterred and accepted a revised version of "The Woman who Saved me", the story he had sent back, because of its length, a few months before. The payment was a hundred dollars. He also gave her a list of books she should read. Her self-education continued.

Frances arrived in England late in the spring of 1872. She had evidently made some arrangement with the Knoxville *Daily Chronicle*, for the first news of her is a piece in that paper by-lined "Chester, August 1st 1872" telling of some of the hazards of an American tourist in England. It is interesting to realize that these rather familiar activities were going on more than a hundred years ago:

> Of course we were prowling you know. It means going to a place as tourists always do go to places, wandering from one end of it to the other, appearing in groups in all sorts of impossible corners that are remarkably hard to get at, and not much to look at when they are reached. It means snatching a ghost of a dinner at a fashionable restaurant, and then rushing off again and goad-ing one's unfortunate guide to madness by insisting on being led into mouldy places in damp situations for the express purpose of seeing nothing in particular.

Sightseeing was a new experience for Frances and she probably enjoyed it a good deal more than she thought it proper to express in a column for the local paper in Tennessee. A letter to Rosie Campbell, the small daughter of their Knoxville doctor, is more typical. All her life Frances was really fond of the company of chil-dren. She had often walked along the banks of the Tennessee River with Anne and Ada and Rosie Campbell and told them stories of the days when the Cherokee Indians were camped near Knoxville.

Now she wrote to Rosie from England. The letter is dated New Year's Day 1873, and Frances was staying at Clifton Hall, the home of the sister-in-law of her old friend, Henry Hadfield. Nearly all the Hadfields were there and it was a happy time. Frances wrote for the "amateur theatricals" a burlesque called *The Fool of the Family*, but her great personal success was as Bo Peep, though it is difficult to believe the children thought she was beautiful when we see the moon-faced girl whose portrait appeared that Christmas, with others, on the title-page of *Peterson's Magazine*. Frances nearly always disliked the photographs that were taken of her and she had good reason to dislike this one.

She wrote to Rosie:

> I have been very sick for a long time, but I am quite well again. I have been having a very merry Christmas. Just before Christmas day the ladies I am visiting gave a grand party for little children and twenty nice little girls and boys came, all beautifully dressed, and danced and had cake and wine and almonds and raisins and all sorts of good things.
>
> And besides that we grown-up people acted a little piece on a stage for them like people do at the theater. I had a very pretty dress made on purpose to wear while I sung them a little song called "Little Bo Peep". I was the little Bo Peep and my dress was made of rose-colored silk and had flowers and lace and satin bows on it and the children thought I was beautiful. After I had sung the song I came off the stage onto their dancing room and they all crowded round me and begged me to dance with them. And I did dance with them, one after the other and you should have seen how sweet they were and how prettily they behaved. I wish my Rosie had been there to dance with little Bo Peep too.

Frances also told Rosie that she had some presents for her and would bring them when she came home in the summer. It is the first record of a pleasure she was to give herself all through her life, the buying of dolls'-house furniture and equipment:

In the first place there is a whole dinner service for your doll, plates and dishes and sauce boat and vegetable dishes and bread plates and everything else.

There is a set of doll's chairs covered with rose-colored silk and edged with gilt and then there is a doll's center table with a real marble top and a little decanter stand with pink bottles on it to put on the table. And then there is a bureau and a sideboard with real marble tops and mirrors over them and all of these things I am saving for you, my love. Give my love to Anne and Ada and tell them I shall have something too, for them. Don't forget to be a good little girl and help mamma.

Your affectionate, Fannie.

Rosie remembered them as the best present she had ever had.

Frances spent most of her time in England with the Boonds, her Uncle John's family, but she also stayed with friends in Cheetham Hill and with the Hadfields at Strawberry Hill, just outside Manchester. Henry Hadfield recorded: "She spent several weeks with us, making herself completely one of the family. She wrote a good deal, but was seldom absent from the family circle for long."

Frances did not try the English magazines but she sent stories back to America regularly. Stories appeared almost monthly in *Scribner's*, *Harper's*, *Peterson's*, *Leslie's* and *Godey's Lady's Book*. The Editor of *Harper's*, in accepting "One Quiet Episode", predicted that a brilliant career lay before her.

She returned to Tennessee in August and the wedding was fixed to take place in the Burnett family home in New Market on 19th September 1873. Frances wanted to delay the wedding, because the wedding dress she had ordered in England had not yet arrived. But Swan was not having it. He said he had waited seven years and he was not waiting any longer—any more waiting would have to be after the wedding: "and this in face of all my prayers, tears and agonised appeals", Frances wrote to the Hadfield girls in Manchester. "Men are so shallow—they have no idea of the solemnity of things! I am fully convinced that today he does not know the vital importance of the difference between white satin and tulle, and cream-colored brocade. He thinks that one did quite as well as the other and that neither could have much to do with the seriousness of the marriage ceremony."

Edith and Edwina were both already married and they came to the wedding from Knoxville, each with a baby in arms. Edith described the occasion briefly: "The old-fashioned living-room, lit with candles, had a sort of plain dignity, and after the simple ceremony we went into the dining-room for supper."

Frances and Swan went to New York for the honeymoon. Through Richard Gilder they met George MacDonald and Bret Harte. W.H. Auden called MacDonald "one of the most remarkable writers of the nineteenth century". Mark Twain had said that Harte was "the most celebrated man in America—the man whose name is on every single tongue from one end of the continent to the other". Frances rejoiced, in a letter to Manchester, at the noise of "literary lions roaring in the drawing-rooms". It was a sound well calculated to send a chill down Swan's spine.

3

Chestnuts off a Higher Bough
1874–1881

From the beginning, Frances was restless. Knoxville was impossible, that first summer of her marriage. It was unbearably hot. Whenever she could, she got out of town and visited friends where the air was cooler and fresher: her particular friend was a seven-year-old girl called Birdie, whose father had been a Confederate officer in the war and was now a teacher. Frances claimed later "she was the only very intimate acquaintance I had, though I knew a good many people". Frances took Birdie's doll home to Knoxville with her, as she was said to need convalescence after measles. She made her a new outfit and sent her small owner letters, purporting to tell of the delights of recuperation at Montvale and White Sulphur. It was for Birdie that Frances wrote her first children's story—"Behind the White Brick". She sent it to her to put in a paper that Birdie and her brothers and sisters published. Frances always had time for children.

And now, in this first year of her marriage, she was expecting one of her own. She felt extremely unwell and Swan's energy seemed to make her feel worse. "He is positively *aggressively* healthy and is always confiding to me that he never was so well in his life as he has been since he was married." Writing to Manchester in the July of 1874, when she was seven months pregnant, she said: "I have suffered fearfully from the intense heat of this summer.

I do not think I shall ever sing the praises of a summer in the sunny south again—I have positively gasped through the last two months and I shudder at the thought of August. I spend two or three hours every afternoon lying on the bed in the loosest and thinnest of wrappers fanning with a palm leaf fan and panting and longing for rain. I can't sleep and I can't rest—in fact, I can't do anything but feel profane."

Already, after ten months of marriage, she was longing to get away. "I am trying to persuade my husband to give me six months' leave of absence next year, and if he will, I intend to come to England. I wish his friends in Washington would make him consul to somewhere in Europe. I am tired of the south." There is a mysterious reference to the sort of activities she explored in her later Washington novel, *Through One Administration*: "It is possible we may go to Washington this winter—that is, if a certain geological, political, official friend gets a certain Bill through—and if so, I am going to plunge into politics like the rest of the feminine Washingtonians and be an active lobbyist and exert my influence on the affairs of the nation. I begin to think political life would suit me. Don't you think I could do myself justice on civil right or protective Tariff? If I should ever distinguish myself, you can write a book entitled *Half-hours with Immortal Females.*"

But Frances knew perfectly well that the way she was to do justice to herself was not by playing at politics but through her writing. Her long visit to Manchester the year before had stirred her memories of the Back-street People, who had held her imagination as a child in Islington Square. In particular, she kept remembering the face of the girl who had knitted the blue worsted stocking and who had refused to be daunted by her father's raised fist and angry words. This girl had been an operative in one of the cotton-mills, but Mrs Gaskell, whose novels had been much discussed in Manchester, had already explored the lot of the distressed mill-workers. Frances decided to make her heroine a pit-girl. When she had been staying with the Boonds, the *Manchester Guardian* had carried "some facts about the Lancashire coal mines". And it seems quite likely that her interest in dialect had been further stimulated by the Reverend William Gaskell's "Lectures on the Lancashire Dialect" which had been appended to later editions of *Mary Barton*. Most of the material for *That Lass o' Lowrie's* undoubtedly came from real life but it is possible that Frances had seen Kay-Shuttleworth's pamphlet on "The Moral and Physical Condition of the Working Classes Employed in the Cotton Manufacture in Manchester". Dan Lowrie is certainly a portrait of the typical working man described in it: "He lives in squalid wretchedness, on meagre food and expends his superfluous gains in debauchery."

The old questions of social inequality and injustice had struck Frances even more forcibly on her return to England from the comparative democracy of Tennessee: what right have we to be more fortunate? Like Mrs Gaskell, Frances believed in charity and opportunity rather than revolutionary change. The division in the established Church between the old clergyman (smugly confident in the benefits of his orthodox encouragements and rebukes) and the new young curate, labouring for literacy and social justice, was also one that must have been brought home to her on that visit. The reception of her Lancashire stories in the literary magazines and Richard Gilder's warm approval of her ideas gave her the confidence to start work on her first major novel.

It was not easy. Lionel was born in a small house on Temperance Hill, Knoxville, on 20th September 1874. She engaged an elderly Negro woman called Prissie, who had been a slave, to help her look after the child. Edith described her as "fine and upstanding, with pipe, bandanna, a deep voice and a heart of gold". From the first, Frances invested a good deal of emotion in her son. Before the birth, she had apparently knelt to pray for the unborn child: "Let it be happy, oh God! I pray you let it be happy! It does not matter what you do to me, but let it be happy!"

When Frances was trying to write and the baby was crying and the patients were not coming to Swan's surgery, it was not easy to thank God. Knoxville was really too small to support an eye and ear specialist. The family depended more and more on Frances' pen. Swan thought if only he could further his studies in Paris, he would on his return find it easier to establish himself in Washington.

But how on earth could they afford to live in France? Frances had some money saved but it would not keep them long. There were four fares to be paid, as Prissie would certainly have to go too, to cook and look after Lionel, if Frances was to be able to write. There were no rich relatives as there were so conveniently in so many of Frances' stories. But there was a sort of fairy god-father. Charles Peterson, of *Peterson's Ladies Magazine*, agreed to advance to the couple one hundred dollars a month, to be paid back by Frances in the form of stories for his magazine.

They left Knoxville in the spring of 1875, when Lionel was six months old. Frances wrote to tell Edith that they had found a flat at 3 Rue Pauquet, close to the Champs Elysées, at a rent of "$34 a month for five rooms: two bedrooms, kitchen, dining-room and parlor, quite nicely furnished. Prissie does our cooking and you know how economical she is, so be sure that nothing is wasted … Paris is an awfully tempting place to poor people but we are so poor as to be almost beyond temptation … You may imagine how busy I have been when I tell you I have seen nothing of Paris yet but the streets. I have not been to any of the churches or palaces or galleries, though of course I have seen the outsides of them. We have to pass the Madeleine and the Tuileries and the Palace of the Louvre on the way to the Bon Marché."

Frances had to write two stories a month for *Peterson's* in return for the regular cheque, but she was also trying to get on with the book, *That Lass o' Lowrie's*. On the strength of the first couple of chapters, Gilder had promised to start serializing it in *Scribner's Monthly* the following year, 1876. Edith gives some idea of the difficulties Frances had to contend with: "When Sister wanted quiet for her writing, Prissie would shout to Lionel, 'You come here! You keep away from yoh Ma, you little rascal or Ah'll flay you alive!' And the child would dance and shout for glee, as if to be flayed alive was the sweetest thing that could happen to a child."

That winter in Paris, Frances described Lionel like this: "the roughest, biggest, tearingest rascal the family has ever known. He grubs and scrubs and a new dress lasts him just half a day. If you could see how he looks sometimes, you would not wonder that I found a gray hair on my head last week. I can only fold my hands resignedly and give him up as a bad job … If I kept him clean, he would not only have his cuticles washed off, he would pine away and die. Sometimes I don't see him for weeks for all the dirt on him." It is worth quoting at length these passages about her small son, for it is sometimes suggested, by those influenced by the associations of the phrase "Little Lord Fauntleroy", that Frances' view of children was a totally unrealistic one.

Lionel's toys and his treatment of them are also reassuringly familiar.

They are confined to a lamb without legs and a three-sous doll without either arms or legs, which doll he calls Gutter. Gutter's trials are numerous. She was used to stir up the charcoal pile; she was dragged round the house with a string; she was beaten and severely admonished because she refused to eat crusts, and then her head was split open and filled with tobacco-smoke from Prissie's pipe. And I think when standing in a corner with the smoke issuing from her cranium, and a mournful smile upon her battered countenance, she gave for the moment supreme satisfaction. The lamb, who is used principally to scrub the floor, wears a constant expression of long-suffering painful to behold. His Ba-a was broken off early in life, and then he got into difficulties about crusts. It seems there is something radically wrong with the moral nature of a lamb who refuses crusts. The owner of this recreant flock of one has got a double-tooth and is the most engaging little sinner out.

Swan was making the most of his time in Paris but was acutely aware that it was Frances who was supporting the family. Frances wrote to Edith: "You must not think I begrudge my struggle

… When I am the wife of the greatest ophthalmologist in two hemispheres, I shall forget my present troubles." Frances called Swan "Doro" now, which was something to do with the fact that he had called her Dora Copperfield when they were first married because she was so hopeless at cooking. Like the Copperfields, the Burnetts' joints had seemed to come from deformed sheep and had never hit any medium between redness and cinders. Fortunately Prissie was taking care of that side of things now. "D. is just as busy in his way as I am in mine—studying all morning, at the hospitals all evening and studying again at night. D. feels he is reaping great benefit from his stay here, and if he does, my end will be accomplished to a great extent." And again in another letter: "D. is getting along splendidly. He is drawing and painting eyes, and says he would not have missed these opportunities for anything. He has met so many celebrated men…"

Frances met no one. She stayed at home and wrote, and when she was not writing she sewed. There was no money to spend on clothes. She wrote to Edith: "I never worked so hard in all my life as I am doing this winter. I have just made myself a black velvet hat, remade my black velvet basque, made Lionel two outdoor suits: one black velvet trimmed with white fur, the other gray and blue flannelette; made him two under-dresses and a warm skirt and bodice; made Aunt Prissie a black cashmere dress and basque, and cleaned and entirely made over my black silk, which was as much trouble as ten dresses. We dine at six, and last night after dinner I made flannel underclothing, and the night before hemmed half-a-dozen large handkerchiefs …" For weeks she had either a needle or a pen in her hand.

And she found she was expecting another child. They had planned to travel a good deal on the continent that year of 1876, and it seems they did get to Rome for, writing to her second son in 1895, Frances recalled the time when she was expecting him:

I *love* your love for your music. It was I who did it anyway. Before you were born, I used to go and sit in St Peter's in Rome and listen to the music and lift up my little soul praying for you in a sort of trance of love, and I used to look always at a lovely little marble angel with a scroll of music in its hand and an instrument on its knee.

This may have been one of the winged cherubs carved by the baroque sculptors of the eighteenth century working in Bernini's tradition. It was, of course, a common idea in the nineteenth century that women could affect their children's lives by their thoughts and attitudes during pregnancy. Whether Frances actually believed this seems doubtful to me. It sounds more like the sort of charming thought which occurred to her in middle age, with little real feeling behind it, though her attitude to music throughout her life was genuine enough. In the character of Judge Rutherford in *In Connection with the De Willoughby Claim* she put the matter more cogently: "There's a mean streak in a man that don't care for music. I wouldn't trust him behind a broomstraw." It's amusing to speculate how different Frances' attitude to Vivian might have been if she had thought of herself gazing, not at the music angel, but at one of the marvellous lions on Canova's monument to Clement XII.

What is certain is that Frances had little time for gazing during her pregnancy and she was not full of joyful anticipation. A poem dated 7th March 1876, four weeks before Vivian was born, gives some idea of her state of mind. It is dangerous, of course, to take biographical evidence from creative writing but the mood of this poem fits in with other evidence in her letters. She was not suicidal but she was tired and she often felt very much alone, as Swan rushed off happily to his hospitals:

> *When I am dead and lie before you low*
> *With folded hands and cheek and lip of snow,*
> *As you stand looking downward*
> *Will you know*
> *Why the end came and why I wearied so?*

I think you will remember as you gaze
Another look you saw in other days
A brighter look you used to love and praise.
But will you know
Why the change came and why I wearied so?

Perhaps a hot, impassioned, useless tear
Will fall upon the face you once held dear
And you will utter words I cannot hear
But will you know
Why the end came and why I wearied so?

I think you will remember something done
By the hands chilled to Death's responseless stone,
Something to give to thought a tenderer tone.
But will you know
Why my heart failed and why I wearied so?

You cannot mourn me long—Why weep for Death?
Rather let Death weep for Life's laboring breath
And the sharp pangs Life's labor ever hath!
But will you know
What mine have been and why I wearied so?

The world—your world will be before you yet—
E'en while my grave grass with Spring rain is wet
You will have found it easy to forget
But will you know
Why my heart failed and why I wearied so?

But I—the Dead—shall lie so low—so low
And soft above me the Spring winds will blow
And Summer rose will pale to Winter snow
And—No, you will not know
Why the end came and why I wearied so.

There was one great excitement to sustain her. In spite of all the difficulties, *That Lass o' Lowrie's* had been completed on time and began to appear in monthly instalments in *Scribner's*, starting in the February issue. It reached Frances just before the baby arrived and she was amused to see an announcement which grouped her with Bret Harte and Edward Everett Hale as authors of "three remarkable serials by American writers".

The baby was born on 5th April 1876 in the apartment on the Rue Pauquet. Frances "passed through every conceivable agony" and the baby disappointed her by being a boy. Lionel, just talking, suggested they should throw it in the fire. But, fortunately, the infant was a "sweet, gentle little thing, just nurses and sleeps and nestles and grows fat". He seemed determined to make himself welcome. "From his first hour, his actions seemed regulated by the peaceful resolve never to be in the way." The daughter was to have been called Vivien (after Merlin's seducer in one of the *Idylls of the King*). Disraeli's novel showed it would, with a letter's alteration, do for a boy too. So Vivian it was.

Frances was exhausted. "I have worked like a slave when I ought to have been resting," she wrote to Edith. "I have earned a great deal but it takes it all barely to live. It seems as if the more I make, the less I get. I have been under heavy expenses for my confinement. I had to have a nurse for two weeks."

They felt the time had come to return to America. In spite of Frances' incessant work there was only enough money for their return passages. "We shall not have enough to live on, even in Knoxville. I am all at sea just now, but perhaps it will come out right. And, in spite of all my anxiety, I cannot wish I had not spent my money. Three thousand dollars would certainly have bought a house in Knoxville, but then, you see, I did not want a house in Knoxville; that is not what I have aimed at. I want my chestnuts off a higher bough.

> I want a rest. Oh, if I could just
> Lay down de shovel an' de hoe,
> Hang up de fiddle an' de bow!

I think this is a tired world altogether. But this seems like grumbling, and I don't want to grumble because, after all, I have not been beaten in this fight yet."

Before returning to Tennessee, Frances took her family to Manchester. They had stayed there briefly on the way to Paris the previous year. Henry Hadfield recorded his impressions of Frances at this time. "Mrs Burnett has nothing about her of the supposed typical authoress ... She seemed much like many thousands of other young English wives and mothers, but, though more disposed to chat of her little family than any other topic, she was at the same time a bright intelligent woman, capable of quietly noting types of character and modes of life without betraying the process." Mr Traice, of Leamington, who was visiting the Hadfields at the same time, had not read any of Mrs Burnett's work. "If we had not been told she was a writer," Mr Traice wrote to Mr Hadfield on his return to Leamington, "we might have departed with the feeling of having passed the evening with a frank, unpretentious wife of a husband eager to explore all the depths of physiology."

Frances was obviously trying her best, at least on such social occasions, to appear as the nineteenth century's ideal type of womanhood. A girl was "trained to fetch slippers as retrievers to go into the water after sticks", she wrote later in *The Shuttle*. She was supposed to be submissive, quiet, gentle, to identify herself with her husband's will and interests, bear his children and keep to his house. Frances was already well aware that her nature did not fit her for this, but that any other path was likely to be a thorny one. The two types of womanhood are neatly contrasted in Hawthorne's *The Blithedale Romance*, which it is reasonable to assume Frances had read, for the heroine (and I don't think this has ever been pointed out) was called Zenobia Fauntleroy. Zenobia says:"The whole Universe ... and Providence or Destiny, to boot, make common cause against the woman who swerves one hair's breadth out of the beaten track." Zenobia, passionate, active, has been foolish enough to set a woman's independent judgment against a man's. It is Priscilla, gentle, passive, whose life had only one purpose, identification with a man's will, who secures happiness. Zenobia drowns herself—just as Cleo does in "Jarl's Daughter" and as Lina Clangarthe does in "The Tide on the Moaning Bar", both stories Frances wrote at this period. Whatever happened, Frances would never drown herself; but nor would she conform, or deny herself the right to make her own life. "I have not been beaten in this fight yet," she had written. The fight was for what Henry James once called "laurels and shekels", the two inextricably entwined. But could any victory bring happiness as well? It seemed unlikely.

They returned to Tennessee in the autumn of 1876. Frances and the children took refuge with Swan's parents in New Market while Swan went to Washington to try to establish himself. In a letter to Edith in 1881, Swan looked back at this time.

> I have had in many particulars a hard fight. We came back from Europe not only penniless but in debt, and I came to Washington without money or friends or even acquaintances to establish myself in my profession—As I look back at it now I don't see how I had the courage to attempt it. But I had determined that I would and I came. I won't tell you how I suffered and almost starved—of the dreary months of loneliness and despair, but still I would not give up. Finally patients began to come in—very slowly—but they came and have continued to come in slowly increasing quantities all the time since.

In writing in this same letter of their time in Paris, he did not refer to Frances or pay any tribute to the fact that it was her work which had made it possible for him to study there. He found their reversal of rôles difficult to accept. Many men find it difficult even now to tolerate a breadwinning wife. In the 1870s the position was so extraordinary as to be unmentionable.

In New Market, Frances kept herself sane with a correspondence with Richard Gilder. She was proof-reading the final chapters of the serial of *That Lass o' Lowrie's*.

New Market

Dear Mr Gilder:

… If you are sure it will be best all round, leave out that final paragraph. Let me tell you it cost me a pang to write it—for me the book ended with Joan and Derrick in the garden, but I felt as if I must drag the rest in, and I will wager you all the immense profits the book will eventually bring me, that if it is left out I shall be promptly set upon by fifty thousand ghastly people who will ask me why I did not "do something" with Anice, and also if "it isn't rather incomplete".

The question suggests itself, however, as to whether I am writing for these people. I would rather not—but must I?

Sometimes I hate that girl, too. She seems too Sunday Schooly. She is not what I meant her to be, but everybody won't dislike her as much as you do. Thank you for saying I shall not make such a mistake again. I don't think I shall …

And from another letter:

… Thank you for the kind things you said. They help me to believe more in myself and when I can do that it makes such a difference. And there is no danger of my becoming vain.

… The fact is I work very hard, but just now it is impossible that I should do the work I like best. I don't mean, you know, to urge that threadbare old plea, "I must live," I should not consider that necessary, or even desirable, but then you see there are four of us, so the miserable, obtrusive pot must boil.

On 30th October 1876, Mr Scribner sent her a proposal for the publication of *That Lass o' Lowrie's* as a book. "We have read with interest that portion of your story which has thus far appeared in *Scribner's Monthly* … We will bring out the book in handsome style and bear all expenses attendant to its appearance and will allow you a copyright of 10% on all copies sold after the first one thousand. We ask you not to require any copyright on the sale of one thousand copies in order that we may thus be able to reimburse ourselves for the outlay (a considerable sum) in making the stereotype plates. This arrangement is one we frequently make with an author. Hoping that it will prove satisfactory to you …"

The formal contract was sent on 10th January 1877. "The formidable appearance of the document need not alarm you," Charles Scribner wrote reassuringly, "it is one of our regular forms." Frances, full of the fact that, at nine months, Vivian had just taken his first steps, sent the contract to Swan in Washington and he intervened to ask the price the book would sell at. He also asked about complimentary copies. Scribner's said they had "no regular custom in regard to presentation copies but in this case will with pleasure put aside a dozen copies for Mrs Burnett and make no charge whatever for them".

Scribner's knew they were on to a good thing. On 22nd March, J. Blair Scribner wrote to his agent, Charles Welford, in England: "I send by post the early sheets of a new novel by a *new* novelist, one for which we expect a large sale and a decided success. The book will be published by us early in April. The story has been running as a serial through our Magazine and has attracted a great deal of attention. Now we are anxious to see the book published in England and will sell a duplicate set of sheets … for half the cost … and with the understanding that, should the book prove a success in England, the author is to receive a fair consideration in the profits. It is our opinion that the author has a brilliant future before her. The story is original and powerful and the scene is laid in the Old Country and therefore particularly suited to an English Audience … Please give Mr Warne the first chance." Business was unsatisfactory, "owing almost entirely to the dull times". They badly needed a best seller.

In March, Frances, still in New Market, wrote to Richard Gilder. She had agreed he should read the final proofs—she had already read them for the serial—and make any cuts that were necessary.

New Market, March 3 1877

My dear Mr Gilder:

I am glad the book is to be published soon. In a few months I suppose I shall have the satisfaction of knowing whether or not I can do work worth money.

Standing as I do upon the low level of those debased persons to whom money must be the first object, I am degradingly anxious to know that.

... If you have cut the rest of the story only as you have the chapters already published, it can only have been to their improvement. In writing it, I made the mistake of forcing myself to write when I had nothing to say.

The book was published in the first week of April 1877. On 28th April Mr Scribner wrote to Frances: "We take pleasure in informing you that your story is meeting with very fair success with the public." And, showing how incredibly fast publishers could work in those days, he added, just five weeks after he had written to Welford, "We have also to inform you that *That Lass o' Lowrie's* has already been published in England by Messrs F. Warne and Co—and we send you by mail a copy of the English edition." Scribner told Frances that he had said to Warne "if anything is made out of the Book he must share it with the author, otherwise he may not get Mrs Burnett's next story and she is considered by good judges as the 'Coming Woman' in literature". Warne's were not, of course, as copyright law then stood, obliged to pay more than the initial sum for the sheets they had bought from Scribner's—and it seems that they did not, for Scribner, writing to Welford the following October about the English edition of *Surly Tim and other Stories*, said: "Do not give Warne any particular advantage for he has acted very shabbily about *That Lass o' Lowrie's*. Put them up to the highest bidder." (Chatto and Windus seem to have won, although there was also a Ward Lock edition.)

In America Scribner's had ready the third edition of *That Lass o' Lowrie's*, three weeks after the first. The American public loved it.

They liked their squalor at a distance. The history of *Scribner's Magazine* tells how later, in the nineties, the reading public would permit Kipling a licence they would not tolerate in an American. Certain magazines would publish Arthur Morrison's realistic stories of slum life in London, but not Stephen Crane's realistic stories of slum life in New York.

The critics were unanimous in their praise. The *New York Herald* had "no hesitation in saying that there is no living writer (man or woman) who has Mrs Burnett's dramatic power in telling a story … The publication of *That Lass o' Lowrie's* is a red letter day in the world of literature." The *New York Times*, in a column-length review of considerable perception, wrote: "For a first novel, by a young author, as it is said to be, *That Lass o' Lowrie's* is a work of remarkable promise. The tone set in the first chapter is adhered to throughout; the place is a mining village of Lancashire … There is no cant in the religion of this book; what lesson it teaches is that good works do not consist in tracts and sage advice, but sympathy and kindliness offered from a footing of equality between giver and receiver." The theological wars between Craddock and the Rector are "fine pieces of writing, exhibiting a most unusual combination of humour and strength in the author … A remarkable point about these characters drawn by Mrs Burnett is their sharpness, their relief. Each is distinct and individual." The reviewer discovered the weakness in Anice which Frances had expressed in her letter to Richard Gilder: "The difficulty with her characterization is that she is made an admirable character—one to be imitated—whereas, in truth, she is a wretched, dwarfed personality … It has a broad North Country dialect which interferes very little with the understanding of the text and after a little becomes positively pleasing." The *Springfield Republican*, a much respected paper, called it "wonderfully fresh, clear and strong", and talked of "the masterly portraiture of one of the finest creatures of fiction—Joan Lowrie". And, most amazing and exciting of all, the *Boston Transcript* declared: "We know of no more powerful work from a woman's hand in the English language, not even excepting the best of George Eliot."

Frances gave Vivian's baby carriage to some people called Snoddy (it can now be seen at the University of Tennessee) and joined Swan in Washington, in a little brick house he had found in M Street, N.W. She wrote to New York:

Washington, April 30 1877

My dear Mr Gilder:

Having read about fifteen reviews, I sat down and gave a sigh of relief. The throwing up of hats I defer until the sale of the tenth thousand.—Until then I can't afford it, unless I could borrow a hat from some bloated aristocrat with two.

… Don't you wish you could see the sonnet I received the other day, beginning, "Fame sits upon her lofty pinnacle, etc." Source, Melledgeville, Georgia. Doro alternately reads notices in a sonorous voice and snubs me to reduce me to submission, but secretly he quails before the eagle eye of the "Coming Woman".

Very sincerely,
F.H. Burnett

Washington in 1877 had broad avenues but the streets were ill paved. Frances describes it in her novel *In Connection with the De Willoughby Claim*: "The public buildings alone had dignity; for the rest it wore a singularly provincial and uncompleted aspect. Its plan was simple and splendid in its vistas and noble spaces, but the houses were irregular and without beauty of form; Negro shanties huddled against some of the most respectable." Frances mentions this characteristic in another story: "In almost every wide street one saw small shabby cottages or tumble-down shanties side by side with the largest and most comfortable homes. It was the means of showing one contrasts in life." It was like a symbolic illustration to one of Frances' stories, though, strangely enough, her Washington novel, *Through One Administration*, is perhaps the only book Frances wrote in which all the characters are in more or less the same social circumstances.

The M Street house looked across empty lots to the British Legation, then a sort of outpost in the sparsely settled area between Washington and Georgetown. The first months in Washington were not good in spite of the reception of *That Lass*. The house was uncomfortable. Both Frances and Vivian were ill. They had a short holiday that summer at Point Pleasant, New Jersey, but it was rather overshadowed by the vexed question of the unauthorized publication of some of her early stories. Peterson's, anxious to cash in on the sweeping success of *That Lass*, prepared several volumes of stories. Frances had retained no rights in the stories and there was nothing to stop them—but she asked that they should make it clear that they were reprinting stories from earlier years. This they did not do, and Frances was unjustly accused by a New York paper of "engaging in the speculative enterprise of selling chaff after wheat … 'Theo' bears all the marks of a tentative, crude essay and is to *That Lass o' Lowrie's* as a tyro's stiff pale etching to the broad, glowing performance of an experienced hand." Frances was much hurt and Scribner's agreed to circulate a card explaining the position. The statement specifically exonerated her old friend Charles Peterson. "He was my earliest and best friend and to his thoughtful generosity I owe more than I can ever repay."

"Theo" was, moreover, as Frances told Gilder in a letter in September 1877, "full of the most ridiculous typographical errors—'Bacon' for 'Byron', 'wild' for 'mild', 'viante' for 'riant' etc. etc. It is a pathetic sort of thing to me now. It is such a nice, idiotic, sixteeny little thing. I was a much nicer girl when I wrote that than I am now. I did not know whether to laugh or cry last night when I went over it." Swan raged at seeing a Peterson advertisement announcing "five new books by Mrs Burnett" on the same page as the one thousand and two novels by Mrs Southworth.

In the following years, 1878 and 1879, Scribner's themselves issued a number of volumes of the early stories. If the "youthful stories" were to appear in book form, it was surely better that Frances should revise them and make clear how young she had been when she wrote them. "They are the children of her brain," Swan wrote to Scribner, "and she has a natural affection for them and does not like them wandering around as outcasts. They have done all the harm they are capable of doing her and a revised and authorized edition may undo some of the harm already effected." Frances herself, in a preface to two of the most interesting "novelettes"—"The Tide on the Moaning Bar" and "A Quiet Life"—called them "these small waifs and strays". But not everyone was disarmed. In my copy of *Earlier Stories, First Series*, someone has written in pencil "A decidedly mediocre authoress—her idea of experience is cynical worldliness."

Surly Tim and Other Stories was published by Scribner's on 16th October 1877. Frances prefaced them with a note that these were the early stories which she thought "most worthy of preservation" in book form. But her main preoccupation that autumn, as they moved into a more satisfactory house at 813 13th Street, was her new novel, *Haworth's*. She was conscious of looking at the critics over her shoulder this time—just as Mrs Gaskell had been when following *Mary Barton* with *North and South*. "The difference between this and the *Lass*," she wrote to Gilder, "is that then I was simply writing a story, and now I am trying to please the critics. It is a fatal kind of thing and I am trying desperately to overcome the feeling, and perhaps I shall in time. It would do your heart good to see me write and cut out, and brood and groan and get up and lead myself round the room by the bang. Tell my dear H de K [Helena de Kay was Mrs Gilder's maiden name] that her pet abomination is nearly pulled up by the roots and that it seems likely I shall write *Finis* to it and the new book at the same time …"

Frances thought it might be good. "I enjoy it very much and seem always ready for it," she told Gilder. "When I have ten chapters you will see them." On 23rd October she wrote from the house on 13th Street:

My dear R.W.G.:

... You will rejoice to hear that "Haworth's" progresses gorgeously. I wrote a scene this morning which I believe will make you quiver. And the sole object of my literary existence is to make R.W.G. quiver. I am not afraid of you now as I was in the first six chapters which I wrote and re-wrote five times.

I am *stronger* than you now, vile tyrant, and have cast off your yoke and trampled it under foot, but I like to try things on you in spirit as upon a many-stringed and sensitive instrument.

I write something and then gloat over it. "Possible effect on R.W.G.?" I say, "He will quiver." And then I gloat again and proceed. This scene is a queer thing. It is not a loud scene and it wrote itself. Before I knew anything about it a woman came to a certain door and stood there. I did not have an idea of what she was going to say and once I stopped to turn her back. But she walked in herself and said and did some things which caused me to come downstairs afterwards and sing—sing at the top of my voice.

And then on 5th February 1878:

My dear R.W.G.:

... I am in a queer sort of mood. (I ought to have begun by saying that Doro sends you the first instalment tomorrow.) After working and going through agonies untold, and raving and tearing and hating myself and every word I ever wrote, I have suddenly walked out into a cool place and begun to soar, and have soared and soared until I don't think I shall ever return to earth again.

How it happens—how, after loathing a thing and slaving over it and writing every chapter of it over again and over again and over again, and slashing into it, and cutting out of it, I can suddenly stand apart from it in cold blood and say, "It is—*stunning*,"—I don't see.

... I believe some of it is just terrible. There is a dead man in it who is the most *living* creature I ever made—just a simple, gentle, working man whose life was a failure and who died and lies out

under the grass in a little country graveyard—and who yet lives
and *lives* and *lives*—!

Gilder responded just as she wished. "Somehow," she told him,
"you are always in tune. It is so grand that, when I have been
roused desperately by anything, it never passes you by."

The gossip column of the *New York Tribune* on 22nd February
1878 told the public they might soon expect a new book. Mrs
Burnett "is an industrious and domestic person of whom her husband said enthusiastically, 'she can do anything'." Serialization of
Haworth's was to start in *Scribner's* in November. When the proofs
arrived, Swan read them "with raptures for the five hundredth
time". If he was jealous of her talent at this stage, he certainly
didn't show it. Scribner was enthusiastic too. He predicted sales
of *Haworth's* would far surpass even those of *That Lass o' Lowrie's*.
He suggested a 12½% royalty on all copies sold. "This is the same
copyright that we give to our most popular authors." Publication
in book form in America was fixed for 6th September 1879.
Macmillan in England would publish ten days earlier.

Macmillan did not "care about having the illustrations". Frances
was not very keen on them either. Henry James considered
illustration an affront to the written word. He would send the
illustrated magazines—*Scribner's* and later the *Century*—only what
he regarded as his poorer efforts. Frances did not feel as strongly
as that. But "the pictures of Murdoch are not at all like him",
she wrote to Gilder. "They are too boyish and conventional. He
ought to be dark and tall and gaunt. He seems to me more like
you in the face …" She suggested, rather naïvely, that the artist
should think of Gilder's face as he worked on Murdoch's.

But there were more worrying problems than the illustrations.
Macmillan wrote in June to say "some publishers in London
contemplate reprinting *Haworth's* for the purpose of testing how
far an American author's books can be protected in England. We
are of course sorry that any book of ours should be chosen for a
test as we are peaceable people and don't like lawsuits but, if we

find ourselves being robbed, we shall do what we can to protect ourselves." It was decided that, to secure a legal copyright in England, it would be necessary for Frances to stand on the soil of a British dominion on the day of publication. On 31st August, Swan wrote a postcard to Scribner: "We returned from Canada a.m. yesterday. Mrs Burnett will therefore be in the United States for publication here."

Ten days after publication, *Haworth's* went into a third edition. Ten thousand copies were already in circulation in America. A *Philadelphia Press* reviewer wrote to Scribner that he was very much pleased with Mrs Burnett's new work but wanted to make a suggestion. "If she can (and I don't see why a woman of genius cannot), she should get out of Lancashire and its dialect and give us an American story, but without any yankee or nigger talk." There were plenty of English novels already, weren't there?

Washington society was beginning to notice Frances. "I find myself obliged to go out very often," she wrote to Gilder, "and if I were to tell you what happened to me, you would think my head was turned … I have a very exciting time. I dare say if I stayed here long enough, I might have a boiled senator for dinner every day. I wonder how they would taste." People were not quite sure what to make of Frances. She was very unpredictable. Julia Schayer—widow of a German count and wife of the Recorder of Deeds of the District of Columbia—recorded her impressions at this time: "There are those who call Mrs Burnett plain and those who call her beautiful. Some have found her cold, and an indifferent talker, while others have left her presence in a state of wild enthusiasm over her vivacity and brilliancy …. She is as one happens to find her—gay, amusing, fascinating or reserved, distrait, even haughty as the case may be."

There were not many people she was anxious to impress. Someone who knew her in these days recalled the embarrassment of her neighbour, Miss Brandt, keen to show off her celebrated friend to visitors from Paris. Frances was detached and reserved. The visitors leaned forward eagerly to hang upon her words, but the words were few and unimpressive. Then a group of children at the other end of the room—Miss Brandt's nieces and nephews—begged Frances to tell them a story. "Her face changed … She sat down upon the floor … and in a moment she was deep in all kinds of elfish, childish talk … Her face, her whole figure, radiant, absorbed, the expressions of humor, of fear, of mystery flitting across it, reaching out to them and each expression reflected in the small faces about her."

Frances' name was becoming known in England too. There had been excellent reviews of *That Lass o' Lowrie's*, and thirty thousand copies had gone very quickly. The sheets of the *Surly Tim* stories had been sold to Chatto and Windus, and Macmillan, as we have seen, were publishing *Haworth's*. Of Chatto, Scribner wrote to Swan, "You open connection with a good and enterprising firm than whom none are better." He added, "W.H. Smith, the great newsman and member of parliament, took 1000 copies of the first edition of *Surly Tim*. This item alone is certainly indicative that Mrs Burnett's reputation is rapidly growing in England." She would be able to "command her own price" for a future book. Recent issues of *Punch* had contained a burlesque of *That Lass o' Lowrie's*. "It will afford you and Mrs Burnett a good deal of amusement." It was excellent publicity if they could take a joke. "Mr Punch" maintained he had been approached by the New Provincial Novel Company and had been chided for never having exhibited "Life in the North with the real dialect of the northern provinces as it is spoken by the local yokel". In his hands, Joan Lowrie becomes Em Beerie (or "Towery Beerie", as she is known on account of her great height) and her accurate Lancashire becomes "Luke ere yo stewp'd foo' ar a yo! Yo deed na nok th'ar tiddle-pops o' ar Parson int' ar kole-p't, yar did na; bart oi deed, oi deed …" "Mr Punch" obviously thought it was a very good joke, for it went on for page after page, in issue after issue. But there was more irritating news from England. No fewer than four people had dramatized *That Lass o' Lowrie's* without consulting Frances. This was the second (Peterson's treatment of her early stories had been the first) of many tedious skirmishes caused by the fluid and uncertain state of the copyright laws.

Adapters could and did do the most extraordinary things with the books they adapted. A review of *Liz or That Lass o' Lowrie's* at the Royal Amphitheatre, Liverpool, in the *Era* of 15th July 1877 points instantly to one of them. The character Liz in the book—the poor wronged girl with the bastard child—was obviously considered too strong meat for the stage, but Joan in the book is now called Liz. "Few modern stories have so secured the attention and approval of the public as Mrs Burnett's *That Lass o' Lowrie's* and it is therefore no matter for surprise that the keen eye of the dramatic author should have seen its adaptability for stage purposes," wrote the *Era* reviewer. "The mine explosion was managed with realistic success" and the whole production was highly recommended. This was a version by Joseph Hatton and Arthur Mathison.

Another dramatizer was Charles Reade. Reade is now scarcely remembered except for *The Cloister and the Hearth*, which everyone has heard of and few have read. He was an extremely prolific novelist and dramatist, specializing in adaptations. It was with some asperity that he replied to the *Manchester Examiner's* charges that he had treated Mrs Burnett unfairly.

Suppose a man has an unenclosed meadow and imperfect law permits people to graze cows there gratis and suppose a dozen men do graze their cows there gratis, but one honest fellow says "I'll graze my cows there, for I have a legal right, but I'll pay you, because you have a moral right", is not his morality higher than the world's, higher than Manchester morality and higher still than American morality in its public dealing with foreign authors? Well, the above is the exact position I took, even when I doubted Mrs Burnett's legal right. So much for my words misrepresented by Yankee anonymuncula—I might say skunkula ... "Joan" was never played in the United States with my consent. But this Spring it *was* played four nights in some out-of-the-way part of that country.

Those who played it forwarded me just £20. What did I do with it? Pocket it all or share it with Mrs Burnett? I sent her every cent of it and I forward you the voucher. Will you be so kind as to examine it and the endorsements and say whether I am or I am not punctilious in dealing with that gifted woman and her rights?

The controversy was the subject of a leader in the *New York Times* on 31st October 1878. Charles Reade had written to say that he had himself suffered by having his novels dramatized in the States: "I cannot be divinely just to American citizens in a business where they never show me one grain of human justice or even mercy; and so long as your nation is a literary thief, you must expect occasional reprisals." "The only way for a novelist to protect a book," wrote the *New York Times*, "is to dramatize it himself and copyright the play before he publishes the novel. If the latter is published first the author cannot prevent any person from adapting it for the stage, even though he should himself dramatize it ... The Copyright Commissioners have recommended that the law be amended." Joseph Hatton actually wrote to the paper saying that, but for his play, people would never have heard of the book.

The immediate result of all this as far as Frances was concerned was that she put aside her other work, sat down and plunged into dramatizing *That Lass* herself. "I never was so excited about anything in my life," she wrote to Gilder. "I have rewritten the whole of the first act and am going on like wild fire. I can't stop a moment," but she could always find time to write to Gilder. "Doro keeps saying 'Now, don't get excited, don't get excited,' but I am and I will be ... I make Dan talk Dan Lowrie and Joan talk Joan instead of drivelling about her broken heart as Hatton has her do. I am wild to finish it and have you compare the two. Hatton's play shall *not* be played to spoil my reputation. Oh! if I could see you! Doro suggests pounded ice. Yours frantically, The Dramatist."

Frances' version was played in New York in the autumn of 1878. She evidently had to accept the help of a collaborator, as the name of Julian Magnus appears with hers on the Booth Theatre playbills. As in nearly all the later productions of her plays, Frances involved herself in rehearsals. One night in New York she and Marie Gordon, who played Joan, were bemoaning the weakness of an actress in one of the minor parts: "Oh, how I wish I could take it!" Frances said, perhaps remembering her success as Bo Peep in the amateur theatricals in Lancashire. Marie Gordon clutched her and almost shrieked, "Oh, if you only would. I would give the world if you would. If you would only try it once in some little town." "Of course," wrote Frances to Julia Schayer, "of course, I told her it was impossible, but wouldn't it be a lark? However, I have a husband, also offspring and consequently rather shall my right hand cleave to the roof of my mouth." It was bad enough being a writer. She was continually stepping off that beaten track that woman were supposed to keep their feet on. Actresses, like Polly Pemberton in her early story, were considered to have a "horrid demoralizing life" and to be "tawdry and disreputable ... painted and fast". They could not be ladies—and Frances could still sometimes hear her mother's voice in her ear: "Remember to be always a little lady."

What indeed would Eliza Hodgson have thought if she had been able to see Frances in the stalls at the Booth Theatre watching her play, miles away from her place beside her husband and children? Was it true, as Frances had suggested ruefully to Richard Gilder, that she had been a much nicer person in those early Knoxville days? Those quiet days flourished in her memory; the frustrations and limitations she was beginning to forget. She had certainly succumbed to the attractions of the theatre, but the production of *That Lass o' Lowrie's* was not a success. When it was on tour in Philadelphia, the critic of the *Daily Sun* lamented that Marie Gordon "moved through the scenes in a dreamy and disagreeable manner"; "Mr J.B. Booth as Dan Lowrie looked villainous" but "Mr Harry Dalton as Fergus Derrick was very heroic, rolled his eyes, sighed and made altogether a very sickly lover". It was discouraging; but "Esmeralda"—one of her Paris stories—was soon to be a triumph on the stage. Frances could persuade herself that there was nothing actually sinful about the theatre, though it did take her away from her children, and that gave her a bad conscience when she remembered to think about it.

There were things besides the theatre which took her away from the children. In February 1879, for instance, she was invited to dine with the Papyrus Club of Boston. She wrote to Gilder to ask his advice: "Please tell me frankly in confidence if you think I should like it. It startles me just at first to be brought before the world by people who have entertained Longfellow and Holmes and other distinguished persons. Would I be simply expected to beam my little beam as I do in Washington and murmur gently, 'Thanks. You are very kind to say so'. 'You are very good, etc. etc.' ..."

Gilder evidently encouraged her, and she had a helpful letter too from Mary Mapes Dodge, editor of *St Nicholas*, Scribner's children's magazine, and author of *Hans Brinker and the Silver Skates*: "Perhaps, if you have no escort, you may like to go to the Revere House, where I shall settle for a day or two, because the dinner is to be at that house, and it will be 'handy' for unprotected females to step downstairs to the dining room."

Frances arrived in Boston in good time. Vivian Burnett tells what happened next: "A kindly young Harvard professor invited her to go with him to Concord, to see the historic town and meet Emerson, the trip to be made in the afternoon, before the banquet in her honor. The dear old Sage of Concord was met and an excursion about the town was being considered when the escort suddenly awoke to the important fact that there was no train running to Boston from Concord which would get his confiding guest back in time for the banquet ... It was a piteously painful moment for a diffident young writer who had come a long distance, with much misgiving, to be honoured by a gathering of literary notables." They were very late indeed for the dinner—but all was not lost. John Boyle O'Reilly wrote afterwards: "Do you know how you charmed everyone in Boston, Mrs Burnett? Oh, of course not; but you did ...." One of the company was

Louisa M. Alcott: *Little Women* had been published eleven years before. Should Frances be spending the time with her own children, rather than being fêted by the authors of children's books? She genuinely loved her children and was charmed and fascinated by them—but she found her own image of goodness, which occurs a number of times in different books, of the young mother in the nursery with her baby on her knee, a peculiarly testing one. The idea of it was delightful but the reality not attractive for very long, unless there was someone gazing in from outside that nursery door, admiring and appreciating the image.

Was she becoming too self-conscious altogether? She was working on *Louisiana*, her first American novel. Olivia Ferrol, a New York girl holidaying in a North Carolina mountain resort, writes to her literary brother: "You see how I have fallen a victim to that dreadful habit of looking at everything in the light of material. A man is no longer a man—he is 'material'; Sorrow is not sorrow, joy is not joy—it is 'material', there is something rather ghoulish about it." In a letter to Gilder, Frances had seen herself as a "species of ghoul"; "I take a slice off somebody almost every day. I wonder if it is quite fair."

The habit might make life difficult but it worked well from a literary point of view. *Louisiana* is an exploration of Frances' favourite theme. It is a Pygmalion story. Olivia decides to take Louisiana, the simple farmer's daughter, in hand. "If you were dressed as I am ..." she muses. There is a marvellous scene where she questions Louisiana and reveals her absolute ignorance:

"You never read *The Scarlet Letter*?"

She flushed guiltily. "No," she answered. "Nor—nor any of the others."

Miss Ferrol gazed at her silently for a few moments. Then she asked her a question in a low voice, specially mellowed, so that it might not alarm her.

"Do you know who John Stuart Mill is?" she said.

"No," she replied from the dust of humiliation.

"Have you never heard—just heard—of Ruskin?"

"No."

"Nor of Michael Angelo?"

"N—no—ye—es, I think so—perhaps, but I don't know what he did."

"Do you," she continued, very slowly, "do—you—know—any-thing—about Worth?"

"No, nothing."

"Oh," she cried, "how—how you have been neglected!" She was really depressed.

Olivia determines to train Louisiana's young mind in the path of learning and literature but realizes she has almost betrayed her own frivolous nature:

"If you wish to—to acquire anything, you must read conscien-tiously and—and with a purpose." She was rather proud of that last clause.

"Must I?" inquired Louise, humbly. "I should like to—if I knew where to begin. Who was Worth? Was he a poet?"

Miss Ferrol acquired a fine, high color very suddenly.

"Oh," she answered, with some uneasiness, "you—you have no need to begin with Worth. He doesn't matter so much—really."

But it is the Worth dresses in Olivia's trunk, rather than any rap-idly acquired literary small talk, which transform Louisiana and encourage Laurence, Olivia's literary brother, to fall in love with her. The story is far more than a gentle satire on the pretensions of literary New York; it is a passionate defence of the simple, unsophisticated values, of the quiet life Frances had herself known in New Market.

Washington life was delightful, of course, on the surface. But Frances could feel a part of herself disappearing. "I was a much nicer girl when I wrote that than I am now." Tennessee was so far away. Was she herself exchanging old Dr Burnett's values (as I said earlier, Louisiana's father was probably based on Swan's father) for those of a world which pretended to admire Ruskin but secretly put more value on Worth?

Swan saw the changes in Frances with misgiving. He wrote sadly to Edith on 24th August 1881, when Frances was away from home, as she was so often away.

"There are a few old-fashioned notions which I had when we all lived together in Vagabondia which I am not yet ready to give up. I learned in those old days the value of love, and faithfulness and unselfishness and my more extended experience has only taught me to value them still more highly. It has taught me moreover that happiness comes from *within* and not from *without*. And do you know there have been times when I would have been glad to have gone back to the old days with all its hardness and uncertainty? It held at least hope and confidence and it has not always been thus since we last met." He went on to tell of his struggles on coming to Washington (already quoted on page 83). "Now! Don't you think I have talked a good deal about myself? As regards the others, they were well a day or two ago—Frances has frnished her play [*Esmeralda*] and it will be put on the stage at the Madison Square Theater, New York about the 1st of October. I hope it may be a success. It has cost her enough in various ways to make it."

All her work in these four years since coming to Washington had been done at great cost. She had pushed herself—or been pushed—too hard. She had written four novels, two plays and numerous short stories. She had moved house three times, run a home and concerned herself fully in the lives of her two small sons. She had entertained and been entertained. And—conscious of her lack of formal education—she had read a great deal. David Hutchinson, superintendent of the Congressional Library, had outlined a reading course for her. It had all been too much. As she put it herself in a letter to Gilder, "I seemed to arrive at my break-down. My backbone disappeared and my brain; when I found they were really gone, I missed them. Their defection seemed so curious that I began to try to account for it and finally rambled weakly round to the conclusion that it might be because I had written ten books in six years and done two or three other little things. You have to have a reason, you know, and even a poor one is better than none … I lie on my back and despise myself."

There were other effects than purely physical ones. Swan had suffered; their marriage had suffered. Frances herself, though more often buoyant and optimistic, had days of deep depression. There is chilling evidence of this in an undated fragment in her own writing:

I wonder if it ever occurs to any one that it is possible that I should be tired. I don't think it does, in even the faintest manner. "How did you get on this morning? How much did you do? Is your story nearly finished? How much longer will it take you?" That is what they say to me.

I am a kind of pen-driving machine, warranted not to wear out, that is all. And if I show signs of doing so, it is certainly astonishing and uncalled for. I have somehow begun to feel myself held by a remorseless, silent Fate.

Write—write—write. Be sick, be tired, be weak and out of ideas, if you choose; but write! There are people who are saying that to me always, even when they don't utter a word. I am ashamed to look them in the face, if I have not done my usual task. If they beat me with whips, they could not drive me more than they do by their thoughts and eagerness for my work, which communicate themselves to me without need for speech.

Does anyone ever think that I ought to be happy?… I should be ashamed to write down upon paper, even in secret, the thoughts that are *forced* upon me, in spite of my efforts to crush them back every day of my disappointed life … I wonder if I shall ever understand—after I die—if there is an "after". But if there is not, and I am only a straw after all, and all this passion and misery is nothing but the wind that twists me! If I was sure of that, *then* the world should be mine as well.

I am so tired this morning that my arms and hands tremble as I write, and every nerve in my body seems unstrung. I can see my weariness in my face when I look in the glass; my eyes are bloodshot and heavy. I could see it in the face of a man or woman I had never met before, but no one sees it in me—and who would care, if they did? and if I were to die tonight—what would that matter?

It is a poor revenge—this dying. My dying would be a poorer revenge than any other. It would be a surprise, because I have nothing to die for, but I have even at last reached a stage of psychology which teaches me that it would be nothing more. People die every day and always have died. Who would remember me a week after the earth lay on me? Not one, *I swear*, of those who are nearest to me. Edith would care, and that would be all. And not *one* thought would rise with power enough to influence the future of the children I have almost given my soul for ... God give me my life for my children's sakes!

It was ironic that whereas most nineteenth-century husbands would have resented having a working wife—and there were times when Swan did—sometimes it seemed to Frances that he cared more about her books than he did about her. There were those moments when Frances felt Swan would not remember her "a week after the earth lay on me", echoing the earlier poem: "E'en while my grave grass with Spring rain is wet, you will have found it easy to forget." He might forget her but he would go on writing to her publishers.

It is an interesting reversal of the situation Henry James describes in "The Lesson of the Master", where the writer is forced by his marriage into the market-place: "My wife makes all my bargains with my publishers for me, and she has done so for twenty years. She does it consummately well; that's why I'm really pretty well off." But the lesson is that "marriage interferes". All through these years, while Frances wrote to Gilder about the stories themselves, it was Swan who wrote the business letters to Scribner's. More than twenty years later, during her second marriage, Frances was to confide to Ella Hepworth Dixon how much she could have loved "an unbusiness-like husband", one who did not urge her to finish Chapter Ten that morning. In January 1880, asking for the contract for *Louisiana*, Swan appended his first critical P.S. "Why is it that you abandoned the idea of advertising Haworth's 'extensively' as you wrote us you intended doing?" Charles Scribner sent the contract and assured Swan that *Haworth's* was advertised "more extensively than any of the autumn publications" and would be again in the spring. In April *Louisiana* was published in both countries and Frances went north to Canada again to be on British soil on British publication day. Swan liked the appearance of the book but had "serious doubts about the advisability of making it a $1.25 book". He wishes they had adhered to their "first intention of making it a $1.00 book. I suppose, of course, the recent advance in paper has influenced you largely but I think the public would rather have a less expensive paper and pay less for the book." Scribner replied very politely that he did not think they had made a mistake about the price. There must have been times when he wished Swan would confine his energies to ophthalmology.

For Swan was himself forging ahead in his profession. He had established a dispensary for treating the diseases of the eye, the first in Washington. After the slow start, patients were now coming in large numbers (between twenty and forty each day it was open) and providing him with ample opportunities for research. His writings contain diagnostic and therapeutic points concerning the eye of the Negro (physiologically, somewhat different from that of the Caucasian), which had not been previously recorded. In 1878 he had become a lecturer in ophthalmology and otology at the Medical School of Georgetown University and in 1883 he was to become a clinical professor. The British Museum has a copy of his translation of *The Introduction of the Metrical System into Ophthalmology* dated 1876, when they were in Paris. In 1879 he published another translation and in 1883 an original work

Refraction in the Principal Meridians of a Traxial Ellipsoid. An 1882 lecture at the Smithsonian was published under the beguilingly simple title "How We See".

It was not for want of other occupations that Swan bombarded Scribner's with letters and finally decided to accept an offer from James R. Osgood and Company of Boston for Frances' new book *A Fair Barbarian*, which had begun to appear in *Scribner's Monthly* in January 1881. Swan was apparently unaware of Osgood's reputation. Bret Harte and Harriet Beecher Stowe had complained loudly about his carelessness and flickering application. In fact, he had been heading for bankruptcy for ten years. But in 1881 he was campaigning strenuously to attract not only Frances but William Dean Howells and Mark Twain. Scribner's brought out a new uniform edition of *That Lass o' Lowrie's*, *Haworth's* and *Louisiana* in June. "It has been a matter of great regret to us that the publication of *A Fair Barbarian* was not confided to us. Without forcing ourselves upon your notice, or claiming any special attention, may we inquire whether we may expect to be the publishers of other writings of Mrs Burnett? We trust that an opportunity will be given to us of competing with other Publishers for that honor."

Poor Scribner's had behaved impeccably, but apparently there was no clause in their contracts about future books and the Burnetts felt no loyalty. Swan wrote coldly, "As regards Mrs Burnett's future books … she is always open to any proposition which is likely to further her interests from a business point of view." The following February he actually asked Scribner's in a curt letter if they would dispose of the plates and stock on hand of all Mrs Burnett's books—"and if so, at what price?" Scribner's naturally refused. "We have spent a large amount of money in advertising them and bringing them to the attention of the public and we would prefer to keep any profit there may be from their sales."

In March 1881, Emily Dickinson wrote to Mrs Holland: "The neighbourhood are much amused by *A Fair Barbarian* and Emily's *Scribner* is perused by all the Boys and Girls—even the cynic

Austin [her brother] confessed himself amused ..." Frances had visited the Dickinsons in Amherst the previous May. "In the midst of luncheon," Frances recalled, "there was brought to me a strange wonderful little poem lying on a bed of exquisite hearts-ease in a bow." Unfortunately, we don't know which poem Emily sent her.

In *A Fair Barbarian* Frances looked again at a confrontation which was, inevitably, to obsess her all her life. In *Haworth's* the young American, Hilary Murdoch, returns to the industrial Lancashire his father had left thirty years before. In *A Fair Barbarian* the atmosphere is more that of *Cranford* than of *Mary Barton*, the setting a village in which "it is not our intention or desire to be exciting, my dear". Octavia, Belinda Bassett's American niece, is in every way calculated to upset the village. She is unaffected, good-natured, generous, but she is also careless of the conventions, decidedly "forward", and she does not play the piano. It is a light undemanding book but the relationship between Octavia and Francis Barold is more complex than in the usual romantic novel and Octavia is an extremely convincing character. It is tempting to see her adventures as a gloss on Frances' own visit to England in 1872. But Eliza Hodgson had made sure that Frances knew the conventions. If she was at heart an Octavia, on that English visit anyway Frances had appeared convincingly enough as an English girl. Frances was to use the theme of the American in England in *Little Lord Fauntleroy*, of course, and in two of her major adult novels—*The Shuttle* and *T. Tembarom*. It was to earn her, from Marghanita Laski, the appellation "poor man's James".

Frances was already reading Henry James. She had bought *The Europeans* on its publication in 1878 and wrote to Gilder: "What a *neat* imagination that man has ... He does not make me glad or sorry or triumphant. All the time I am admiring Henry James and thinking how beautifully he goes all round a thing and what excellent order he leaves it in—with no ends straggling—no gaps—no thin places. 'How clever you are,' I keep saying, 'and how neat.'" But she did not seem to fear comparison with *Daisy*

Miller, which had been published just the year before *A Fair Barbarian*. She did not meet James on his visit to Washington in 1882. But both Frances and James met Oscar Wilde.

Wilde was in the middle of his extraordinary lecture tour, weary of such questions as "Is it true you colour your bathwater with essence of verbena?" At Yale three hundred students had turned up at a lecture wearing red neckties and carrying sunflowers. At Rochester the manager had had to send for the police. Locks of Wilde's hair were in great demand. He was paid $1,000 for an hour's lecture. James spent the evening of 22nd January 1882 with the Lorings in Washington "and found there the repulsive and fatuous Oscar Wilde, whom, I am happy to say, no-one was looking at". James' friend Henry Adams refused an invitation to receive at a reception at the British Legation in honour of Wilde. But Frances was delighted with him.

He came to her house on I Street wearing "a black silk claw-hammer coat, fancily flowered dark waistcoat, knee breeches, silk stockings and patent leather pumps with broad buckles, an inconspicuous flower in his button-hole". It is tempting to assume that the Burnett boys' clothes, to be immortalized by *Little Lord Fauntleroy*, were influenced by this visit. The story goes that Frances, instead of introducing Wilde to her other guests, as a good hostess should, spent most of the afternoon talking to him in a corner. Chided for this later, she said, "What would you? I can see the rest of you at other times."

Frances was not a member of Henry Adams' circle. As James said, it "left out, on the whole, more people than it took in", and Adams tended to want beauty in women. Frances was not beautiful. She had once paid a social call on Mrs Adams but it was never returned. Adams had been careful when his novel *Democracy* was published anonymously in 1880 to deny its authorship. "The secret had to be kept if the Adamses were to hold up their heads in Washington. Only a short time later," wrote Adams' biographer, "two women novelists satirized Washington society and paid the extreme penalty." The first was Mrs Dahlgren, whose book was called *A Washington Winter*; the second was Frances Hodgson Burnett, the book *Through One Administration*.

Frances had begun another large novel in 1880. She had written to Gilder, "I have about three hundred pages of a book done and generally I don't seem to care about it." It was *In Connection with the De Willoughby Claim* and was not completed and published until 1899. She spent the summer of 1880 at Nook Farm, just west of Hartford, Connecticut, the community founded in 1851 by John Hooker and his wife, Isabella Beecher Hooker. Nook Farm's inhabitants included Hooker's brother-in-law, Francis Gillette, United States Senator, abolitionist and temperance reformer, Harriet Beecher Stowe, author of Frances' admired *Uncle Tom's Cabin* and Isabella's sister, Charles Dudley Warner, Mark Twain's collaborator on *The Gilded Age*, and a whole network of writers and their relatives. Twain himself lived there but he was spending this summer of 1880 in Elmira while his Nook Farm house, turreted and extraordinary enough already, had thirty thousand dollars spent on its further embellishment. The next year Twain was to send Frances an inscribed copy of *The Prince and the Pauper* and it seems likely they had met by this time. Frances was at Nook Farm principally to work with William Gillette, Hooker's nephew, who had been encouraged by Mark Twain to write for the theatre. Frances had met him on her visit to Boston. He had had a great success with his play *The Professor* and he had promised to help her dramatize her story "Esmeralda".

Frances returned to Washington in time for the excitement of the Presidental election. General Garfield, the Republican Presidential candidate, was a neighbour and family friend. The Burnetts had moved to 1215 I Street in 1879. A plaque on the wall there now, put up in 1936 by David O. Selznick, commemorates the fact that ON THIS SITE FIFTY YEARS AGO THE DEATHLESS CLASSIC LITTLE LORD FAUNTLEROY WAS WRITTEN. The houses must have been renumbered for the plaque is a few doors below the present number 1215. The plaque includes a quotation from a letter written by Oliver Wendell Holmes (see page 166). The house belonged to General Grant, to whom it had been presented by some of his admirers. He had never lived there and the Burnetts rented it from him. The Garfields lived on the corner, opposite the dressmaker. They had three children—Abe, Irving and Molly—and the four boys played together a good deal. During the campaign, Vivian and Lionel became passionately involved. If they heard "Rah for Hancock!" in the street, they would fling open the windows, lean out precariously and shout, "Rah for Garfield!" There was in fact, at this period, very little to choose between the two parties: "In a sense, parties became ends in themselves, with Democrats existing to battle Republicans, Republican existing to oppose Democrats." But "how could one disown the party of the martyred Lincoln?" Garfield's background, apart from his propinquity, appealed enormously to Frances. His experiences had in some ways paralleled her own. His father had died when Garfield was two and the widowed mother had struggled to bring up her four children in a log-cabin in rural Ohio. The boys thrilled at the story of the hero of Chickamauga.

There was a pleasant letter from Mrs Garfield in reply to Frances' congratulations on the General's nomination:

Mentor, Ohio,

November 13 1880

My dear Mrs Burnett,

... Tell the small boys that the account of their patriotic exploits has been read at our table, and while the voters at the table all regard them as deserving great merit for their heroic efforts to endanger their lives, Mrs Garfield is compelled to admit that her admiration is nearly all lost in sympathy for their afflicted mother, watching with terrified eyes the third story windows.

Thanks for your congratulations. General Garfield joins me in kind regards to yourself and to Doctor Burnett, and the whole family join in a round-robin of kisses to the young Republicans.

Very truly yours,
Lucretia Randolph Garfield

Garfield got to the White House by an extremely narrow margin. But he was there. Frances wrote gaily to Gilder:"Would you like any little thing in foreign missions? Say—Court of St James? If so, mention per postal." The Burnett boys, as Vivian remembered it, rode "their newly acquired bicycles in the porches and halls [of the White House], colliding with sluggish senators and cabinet officials." This idyllic state of affairs did not last long. On 2nd July 1881, President Garfield stood on Washington Railroad Station with Secretary Blaine and was shot by a disappointed office-seeker called Guiteau. By a strange coincidence, only a few days before, Guiteau had threatened to kill E.L. Burlingame, the Scribner editor, for turning down a manuscript he had submitted. For Garfield, it was bullets not threats. Two lodged in his body. It took him more than two months to die. Henry Adams was curiously unmoved by his friend's death. He thought of Thackeray and Balzac. They had "never invented anything as lurid as Garfield, Guiteau and Blaine". But Frances thought of Garfield himself, and of the extraordinary fact that she, the girl from Islington Square, had known the assassinated President. She wrote a poem and read it at a memorial meeting held by the Washington Literary Society:

> … *Watchman! How goes the night?*
> *In tears, my friend, and praise*
> *Of his high truth and generous trusting ways.*
> *Of which warm love and buoyant hope and faith*
> *Which passed life's fires, free from all blight or scathe.*
> *Strange! We forget the laurel wreath we gave,*
> *And only love him—standing near his grave…*

It was at this same society, a few years before when she had first come to Washington, that the president of the society had walked her round and patted her hand, saying, "Why, you little childish young thing. What do you mean by writing books like that?" Frances was no longer a young thing. She was nearly thirty-two—and Washington, for all its charms, was as much of a jungle as any mining town in Lancashire.

She had been exploring it all that summer in her new book *Through One Administration*, having finally put aside *In Connection with the De Willoughby Claim*, "the fiend" which had dragged at her for months. She wrote to Gilder in raptures. The new book interested her as she had never expected to be interested in anything again. "As it develops, it pays the subtle compliment to my intelligence of proving to me that I know ever so many things I scarcely thought I knew. I don't think I ever wrote anything which seemed so to write itself … I hate and detest love stories," she added, surprisingly perhaps for one who had written so many. "But it seems that you must have their grinning sentimental skeletons to hang your respectable humanity and drapery upon." It was undoubtedly true that Frances put no special value in many of her books on the love between man and woman, the sexual relationship. Many of the most strongly loving relationships are between mother and son, father and daughter, between sisters, between friends. It was true of her, in the phrase James used of Stevenson, that "the idea of making believe appeals much more than the idea of making love".

It was not the love between Bertha Amory and Tredennis that interested her; it was the lack of love between Bertha and Richard Amory. *Through One Administration* has been called a political novel, and indeed it is partly that. Its picture of lobbying, of machinations and intrigues, is vivid and convincing. Frances' portrait of Washington is confirmed by Henry Adams' biographer: "The political tension never relaxed for a moment. A kind of breathlessness was always in the air. Each day during the Washington season some new disclosure, some overwhelming turn, seemed always to lie beyond the corner." Adams reported that Henry James was revolted by the intrigues. Dubious dealings were then, as now, always coming to light. Secretary of State Blaine was reviled as "the continental liar from the State of Maine", when he was found to have been involved in profitable but shady railroad deals. *Through One Administration* examines a "struggling, manoeuvring, over-reaching, ambitious world". It also examines a failed marriage, the consequences of marrying the wrong person.

Bertha Amory has made the mistake of "merely marrying the man who loves *her*". The story is her tragedy written not solemnly, but lightly. "There is a fashion in emotions as in everything else," said Bertha. "And sentiment is 'out'. So is stateliness ... Griefs are as much out of fashion as stateliness ... Making light of things ... is a kind of fashion nowadays." But Bertha, like Frances, has a hunger in herself to be more serious. The sadness is that "we have obliged ourselves to be trivial for so long that we are incapable of seriousness". For a time, it is possible to deceive oneself, to think that nothing matters, to amuse oneself continually, to enjoy excitement and diversion.

Bertha admits, as Frances could never admit: "I am not very fond of anything or anyone. Not so fond even of Richard and the children, as I seem. I know that, they do not. If they were not attractive and amiable, or if they interfered with my pleasures, my affection would not stand many shocks." The men, though each one is distinct from the others, are shadowy compared with Bertha. The plot is complex and would be impossible to summarize, but as a portrait of a woman in her time, *Through One Administration* is a rich achievement.

R.O. Beard in an article in the *Dial* for October 1882 worried about "A Certain Dangerous Tendency in Novels". *Through One Administration*, like Thomas Hardy's *Two on a Tower*, which had also just been published, was "stained by a covert but unmistakable depreciation of the most sacred vows". Beard pleaded for "a purer type of fiction, which shall leave untouched by the faintest breath of dishonour the sanctity of wedded lives, and which can be placed in the hands of youth, with the assurance that an active sense of virtue and honor will be fostered by its influence". This attack, ludicrous as it now seems to us, is surprising even in context, for there is no happy ending for Bertha. If one must find a moral, it is surely to have *more* respect for the marriage vows, to take much more thought before making them. What really angered critics like Beard was Bertha herself—this woman created by their own society, for Washington and Bertha are inextricable. They wanted women to be quiet, honest and innocent, concerned with fashion and not with power, affectionate and not passionate. It was not a woman's job to throw out phrases, such as "All men are born free and some equal", "I make a practice of recognizing my children when I meet them on the street", or "The worst punishments in life are the punishments of ignorance".

But for every reader like Beard, there were twenty who relished the book. A contemporary critic in *Literary News* drew attention to the way the author had "lived and learned and suffered" in the ten years since *That Lass o' Lowrie's*. Another called it "a scathing attack on corruption in government". It was one of Frances' most successful books. A more recent critic wrote that Mrs Burnett showed how "a natural storyteller could use the complicated inter-relations of the social, financial and political life of Washington for their proper function of developing character … The tragic ending … gives Mrs Burnett a right to claim a place with the most logical of realists."

It was a fact that Frances found difficult to accept—that critics take writers more seriously if their books end unhappily. She preferred happy endings. "There ought to be a tremendous lot of natural splendid happiness in the life of every human being," she once wrote to Vivian. "The acceptance of the belief that this is only a world of sorrows is hideous and ought to be exterminated." She once said, "I do not think anyone has ever existed who so strenuously, passionately insisted that people should be happy as I do." "Good God!" Tom says, almost in exasperation, in *The De Willoughby Claim*, "Why can't people be happy—I want people to be happy." In life, the problems involved in making people happy are often immense, things get out of hand, so much is out of our control. In art, Frances could have her own way; and all her other books end happily. *Through One Administration* was too near the bone for her to be able to deceive herself. There could be no easy romantic solution for Bertha Amory, nor indeed for Frances Hodgson Burnett. It was not possible for her to be happy in making others unhappy.

We know, from his letter to Edith, that Swan Burnett was not happy in 1881 when Frances, having sent the boys down to old Mrs Burnett in New Market, went off to Long Island with most of *Through One Administration* in her luggage. It was due to begin serialization in the *Century*, the successor to *Scribner's* under Gilder's editorship, the following November. Also in her luggage was the draft dramatization of "Esmeralda". "I hope it may be a success," Swan wrote to Edith, as we have seen. "It has cost her enough in various ways to make it." It had probably cost Swan more. Frances wrote to him jestingly to tell him he "might fill my place with another person of equal attractions" if he could find one. Was it a very good joke—when it really did seem she was happier away from Swan and Washington?

Years later, Frances made Lady Maria say in *The Making of a Marchioness*: "If people will marry, they should choose the persons least likely to interfere with them." Swan seems to have had this negative virtue. He never tried to stop her doing what she wanted to do. At Long Beach she and William Gillette were working on the "Esmeralda" play, which they had begun at Nook Farm the previous summer. At least, they were supposed to be working. She wrote to Julia Schayer:

> Mr Gillette comes out to me and we are convinced that we are working on the play—only the sea and the sand and the sky and things, don't you know? This morning we simply played with sand and he said it rested him to look at my tennis suit, which he is amiable enough to think one of the prettiest things he ever saw. Yes, dearest, I know what you are saying in your little mind, but when I tell you in confidence that he is engaged to be married and things, and is supposed to be densely in love, you will know he is quite safe and accusations are quite needless.

There were other attractions: "Yesterday … I was hopelessly enslaved by a member of the band, but today I find I was mistaken in my feelings, it is the leader who has enslaved me by the beautiful manner in which he gazed at me—or somebody else—while he led Schubert's Serenade in the most impassioned style." In another letter, Frances describes "A Greek God in bronze" who turns out to be the local swimming instructor. "He … is the most wonderful creature. His physique is perfection, simple and pure. I never noticed a man's body before. I was always so actively employed searching for their brains—but his—Mon Dieu! Gott im Himmel! Santa Maria—and things! He wears a dark-blue woven, tight-fitting garment, reaching to the knee and leaving his superb arms and divine antique legs bare. He has a head like, oh, like Augustus Caesar etc., close, crisp hair and a Neapolitan fisherman's close, dark-blue cap on it. And that is not the worst of it, either. The color of him, Julia, the color of him! He is sun-burned all over—the most exquisite pure bronze! I grow wild and have to erase!—and far be it from me to presume to ask him how much it is a lesson."

More important, of course, than one-sided flirtations with bandsmen and swimming instructors, was the two-sided flirtation with Richard Gilder, her "dear R.W.G.". She wrote, again to Julia Schayer:

> When we were at Milton one day, R.W. said to his wife, "See here, Helena, could I take this girl down to Long Beach and keep her all night? Would it be proper and all that sort of thing?" And Helena said, "Certainly it would. You couldn't do it if she was not married, but under the circumstances it is perfectly proper."

A strange remark to make concerning a young woman with a novel in her luggage, which would show "a dangerous tendency" to undermine the institution of marriage.

> I regarded it rather as a joke and forgot about it, but "Lo en beholes!" as Uncle Remus says, when I met him at the train the

creature inquired where my satchel was and to my utter amaze-
ment it turned out that we were really to stay all night—and we
did—and of all the lovely times!

We rambled about on the beach and grubbed in the sand and
then went back to the hotel (only a few yards from the beach) and
dined on the immense piazza, and then went back to the beach
and sat in the sand again and bayed at the moon and talked and
talked and talked, and I sang little songs, and things loomed up
generally as they haven't for a long time, and we sat there until
midnight and then went and had lemonade on the porch, and
he said he was afraid to leave me for fear I would say something
interesting after he was gone and finally we retired, and as all our
baggage consisted of one small pocket-comb, we had to perform
our toilets with it by turns—he throwing it over my transom, and
I returning it under his door.

It is perhaps significant that this episode seems to mark the end
of the close relationship between Gilder and Frances.

Esmeralda was finally finished, in spite of the distractions of
sand and tennis dresses. Daniel Frohman, then a young producer,
agreed to put it on at the Madison Square Theater, New York. It
was one of the newest and best equipped theatres in the country.
The play opened in Newark, New Jersey, in September and had
its first night in New York on 29th October 1881. The critics
were not particularly enthusiastic. One apparently got extremely
wet on the way to the theatre: "The cosy little house was quite
full of the different kinds of our best people, in spite of the
rain that made umbrellas or rubber coverings a necessity to all
who scorn hacks." It was "a charming enjoyable play" but the
thing that pleased the critic most was the chance to see Kate
Denin again. The delicate girl had once been a fixed favourite
in the city but had gone to California twenty-seven years before.
"The thousands upon thousands who applauded her ... have
been slowly but surely contributing to the wealth of such close
corporations as that of Greenwood Cemetery. It is wholesome

for New Yorkers to see Kate Denin again. It gives rise to such cheerful thoughts."

Whether it was because of Kate Denin's presence, the performance of Annie Russell in the title role or Frances' skill (Will Gillette admitted she had done most of the work), *Esmeralda* was a distinct success. It ran for three hundred and fifty nights and made a good deal of money. Two years later it was produced at the St James' Theatre in London under the title *Young Folks' Ways*. *The Times* gave it a great deal of space. "Freshness of scene, character and motive, combined with perfect healthiness of tone ... [are] happily to be found in the new play ... A simple and truthful picture of American life ... as it is lived in the log cabins of North Carolina and amid the oppressive gaiety of Paris, this play with many faults possesses a distinct value as what M. Zola calls a *document humain*, and must be assigned in that respect a higher tank than any recent production of the English stage."

A "Casual Critic", writing anonymously in the *Pall Mall Gazette*, lamented the state to which the theatre had come if this were indeed so: "It is not, we may say at once, a drama with a very sensible life of its own, and that it should be exactly what it is, and yet be, as we may say, where it is, suggests a good many reflections as to the sources at which the English stage, so robustly constituted in so many ways, and yet so sadly athirst, is at present compelled to drink."

We hardly need the confirmation of a letter Henry James wrote the next day—"I have written an article (anonymous—*don't mention it*) for the *Pall Mall Gazette* ..."; this serpentine sentence could have come from only one hand. But fortunately perhaps for their future friendship, Frances remained in ignorance of the authorship of this long review entitled so discouragingly, "A Poor Play Well Acted". James showed some particular perspicacity as to where Frances' future success might lie when he wrote: "It is composed of elements of a touching simplicity, put together with an ingeniousness which would be commendable in a moral tale for the young."

Fortunately again for Frances, the taste of the New York public was less mature and sophisticated than that of Henry James. She came to the end of 1881 with her play playing to full houses at the Madison Square Theater. Moreover her novel, serialized in the *Century*, was being devoured monthly by eager readers. She was tired and she could afford to sit back. It was time she saw more of the boys. They were sorry she spent so much time writing things they could not possibly understand. When she next wrote, it would be something for them.

4

The Universal Favourite
1882–1886

Lionel was now seven and Vivian was five. Frances said, more than once, "The one perfect thing in my life was the child-hood of my boys." It is not a remark any of us would dare to make nowadays. And it seems, at a first glance, to fit in only too neatly with the popular idea that the Burnett boys, like little Lord Fauntleroy himself, must have been an unnatural pair of mollycoddled mother's darlings. Certainly Frances made great demands on them—she had great plans for them. She saw them as temples she was building, clay she was moulding. In 1897 she wrote to Vivian, "I daresay it would surprise you if you knew how I have thought it out and planned it ever since you were born." She had planned that he should be happy, that he should have every opportunity she had not had as a girl, that he should always enjoy the Party.

"They must be happy," she would say to herself. "Their lives must be as bright as I can make them; as far as lives can be perfect, I must make them so. Nothing must be lacking." In his book, Vivian put it like this: "Her pattern was the Fairy Godmother and her guiding principle, love." "Perhaps one's children are like the talents in the parable," she wrote to Vivian after Lionel's death, "and when I show you two boys at the end—whatsoever the End is—some-one will say 'Well done, thou good and faithful servant.'"

The dangers and difficulties inherent in her attitude were obviously enormous, and there was much heartache in store for Frances. But the extraordinary thing is that the boys' childhood does seem to have been most attractively normal. They were not spoilt. Frances' particular mixture of periods of absorption in their characters and activities, alternating with periods when she was completely involved in her own work and pleasures, seems to have worked surprisingly well.

Lionel was the shy, sensitive one; Vivian the outgoing, talkative one. Both were affectionate, generous, courteous, acquisitive. They climbed up to Frances' workroom, her Den at the top of the house in I Street, laden with treasures for the drawer in her desk—"bits of grass or pebble, gorgeous advertising cards, queerly shaped twigs or bits of wood, pictures out of papers" and five-cent toys from the Misses Stutz' emporium on New York Avenue. "Please may I come in?" they said, "I've brought a treasure for you, Dearest."

They took part in the life of the household in a way that would have been unusual in England at that time. There were two servants in the house on I Street—a black couple, Carrie, the cook, and Dan, a man of all work. "They were his friends and they formed together a mutual admiration society," Frances recorded in "How Fauntleroy Occurred", an article written in the 1890s for a women's magazine. We learn much about Vivian's childhood from this piece. The way it is told jars on my tough mid-twentieth-century ears but there is nothing nauseating about Vivian himself. Some credit for this must certainly go to his father. Where Frances, as Fairy Godmother, lavished not only love but possessions on the boys, Swan "believed more in the Spartan method and used often to say, when the boys were asking urgently for something: 'Well, I would not give much for a boy who couldn't make something out of a chunk of wood that would do as well.'"

The stories about Vivian are legion and they are good stories. From the beginning, when he carried grubby handfuls of exhausted violets upstairs to his mother, he seemed determined to be charming. Even in an age which suspects charm, it is difficult not to be charmed. Told off for playing with the fire, he said, "Don't you *know* I'm a Westal Wirgin?" He was interested in everything, the strata of the earth, the nature of a simoon, the interior arrangements of camels. The day before he was three, he was pinching his own arm and, finding it seemed to be built on something solid, he asked his mother about it. She gave him a few simple facts about his anatomy, the nature of bones.

"If I could see under all the fat on your little body," Frances said, "I should find a tiny skeleton."

"If you did," said Vivian, delighted. "If you did, would you give it to me to play with?"

One day, he asked a neighbour if she were "in society". She replied by asking him what "in society" meant, hoping to hear his views. "It's—well—there are a great many carriages, you know and a great many ladies come to see you. And they say, 'How *are* you, Mrs Burnett? So glad to find you at home. Gabble, gabble, gabble, gabble. *Good* morning!' And they go away. That's it." He was not criticizing. In fact, he enjoyed society. He liked handing things round on Tuesday afternoons. He was merely giving an impressionistic picture.

The one thing the boys disliked about society was having to dress up, and Frances did have a weakness for picturesque clothing. The boys had blue jersey suits with red sashes and they also had best suits of black velvet with lace collars. These last may well have been partly inspired by Oscar Wilde's clothes on his visit to them but they were by no means unusual wear for small boys at this period, a year or two before the Fauntleroy cult spread their appeal. In the *Lady* in 1885 (a few months before *Little Lord Fauntleroy* began to appear as a serial in *St Nicholas*) there are illustrations, and descriptions of a style for a "little fellow of seven … tunic and knickerbockers of sapphire-blue velvet and sash of pale pink. Vandyke collar and cuffs, if not of old point lace, should be of Irish guipure." Velvet had been a popular material for boys' suits since the 1840s. Compared with this sapphire-blue and pink, the Burnett boys' black and white seems positively plain. It also seems extremely tough and masculine when compared with the skirts and frills which eleven-year-old Inglis Synnott, E.M. Forster's father's cousin, was wearing in 1848. But the other point of comparison, of course, is with Tom Sawyer—with his bare feet, pants, shirt and straw hat.

Mark Twain admired Frances and it was just at this time that he was dreaming up a scheme for himself, Frances, William Dean Howells and one or two others, each to write a long story based on the same characters and roughly the same situations. Unfortunately it came to nothing. Nor did his scheme that they should hire a private rail-road car, complete with cook, and travel all over the country reading from their works. Frances never did any public storytelling. She preferred the hair-curling sessions by the fire with her boys. Writing about it, she said she knew it sounded incredible, but the boys actually enjoyed having their tangles taken out. The reason was that she told stories while she did it. One of these Hair-Curling Stories was later published as "The Good Wolf"—the wolf being an amiable animal, who brought about all sorts of good things for a small boy, "who never wriggles when his hair is brushed". The best part of this story is the robbers who agree to stop being robbers and be nicer things, such as bakers, hairdressers and pew-openers, and to come back twice a week and tell stories as "The Combined Robbers and Pirates Story-telling Club".

There was a slightly more realistic criminal in another story of this time, "Editha's Burglar", which first appeared in *St Nicholas*. When Mary Mapes Dodge had started the magazine in 1873, it had been with the intention of providing wholesome enter-tainment to offset the didacticism which dogged most writing for children. She encouraged Frances to send things to her, and most of Frances' children's books first appeared in the pages of *St Nicholas*. The heroine of "Editha's Burglar" was a child in Vivian's mould. She was always asking questions. On this particular day, she has happened to ask her father, "What do you think of burglars—as a class?" When she finds a burglar in the house, she asks him please to burgle as quietly as he can so that he doesn't disturb her mamma. How sweet, how charming Editha is.

There is absolutely no doubt that Vivian's charm was genuine and not an invention of his mamma's. There is plenty of independent evidence. One incident happened in the summer of 1882. Frances was not well that summer. She was burdened with feelings of lassitude and spent a great deal of time in a hammock. They gave her affliction the name of neuritis. Was it really just that she did not want to work? There was no need for her to work. Money was coming in. The play was still running in Madison Square; the novel was still running in the *Century*. But it was only illness or the appearance of illness that allowed the pen-driving machine to stop.

"Why should one object to being ill?" Bertha asks, revealingly, in *Through One Administration*. "It is not such a bad idea to be something of an invalid, after all. It ensures one a great many privileges. It is not demanded of invalids that they shall be always brilliant. They are permitted to be pale, and silent, and heavy eyed, and lapses are not treasured up against them … When one is ill, nothing one does or leaves undone is of any special significance. It is like having a holiday."

One day that summer, when they were staying in Massachusetts, the boys were pillow-fighting and romping about while their mother was in bed. They were asked to be quiet and Vivian said, "Oh, we wouldn't disturb Dearest for the world." But a little later "they forgot their good intentions", recorded the witness, "and again became hilarious. Mrs Burnett stepped from her bed and appeared to them in the doorway. 'Now, Dearest', said Vivian, 'if you must spank us, just put your little bare feet right on this,' at the same time stripping a pillow from his bed and spreading it before her. Dearest said that was quite enough. She just kissed them both and went back to bed."

It was this summer too—1882—that Vivian, aged five, pronounced himself a supporter of the movement in favour of female suffrage. "I believe they ought to be allowed to vote if they like, because what should we do if there were no ladies? Nobody would have any mothers or any wives ... And nobody could grow up. When anyone's a baby, you know, he hasn't any teeth and he can't eat bread and things. And if there were no ladies to take care of him when he was very first born, he'd die."

But he could fight as well as charm. Frances sent the boys to the local school, half a block up 13th Street, the Franklin Public School. It was by no means a genteel establishment and the two boys had to learn to stand up for themselves. One day when they came home from school, Lionel said, "Vivvy has had a fight." Questioned, Vivian said, "A boy said to me 'D'you want to fight?' I said to him 'I don't want to fight but I *will* fight.'

'Then I started in and hit him till he hollered." "The boys in my school knock me down and jump on me because they want me to go Democrat," Vivian wrote to his mother at the time of the bitter 1884 election campaign, which returned the first Democratic administration for twenty-three years. "But I am still a strong Republican," he assured her, "Your obedient and humble son and servant, Vivian." The boys might call their mother Dearest and wear black velvet suits when they had company, but they could be tough too.

There were many stories about Frances in the newspapers at this time. Most of them were friendly enough, many of them almost embarrassingly admiring. But not all. An unintelligent, unsigned piece in the New York *Truth* for 8th June 1884 has the sub-heading: "Her Novels and Exposition of Disagreeable Types, The Sameness of Her Characters in All Her Books—'Esmeralda' a Feeble Play." And there was one story, which was repeated over and over again, and which finally roused Frances to deny it. The newspaper had declared that Mrs Burnett posed her boys about the drawing-room, with the purpose of impressing strangers. Frances' denial took this form:

> ... I have, it is true, two little boys. I have also a mantel-piece
> and a rug, but the four objects are not compatible in the manner

described, as the mantel-piece is rather high for the elbows of six and seven, and that even six and seven years of the most careful training have failed to instil into the boys that delicate respect for the truly artistic which would lead them to lie on a rug in one position, however distinctly beautiful, for two seconds unless they were chained and padlocked; and to this last device I have not yet, even in my most artistic maternal agonies, had recourse.

That the little boys have been beautiful has not been my fault nor their misfortune. Their tendency to pose I have sometimes had reason to regret. I have seen them pose in attitudes replete with grace, suspended by their feet from apple trees with the hyacinthine locks sweeping the dust and having somewhat the appearance of an entirely new species of yellow mop. I have seen them pose upon one foot upon the top of an iron-spiked fence; I have seen them pose on adjacent roofs, their purely Greek countenances aglow with rapt contemplation of the thought that at last they had attained an altitude which a mis-step would cause to result in their being dashed into minute fragments.

... A few summers ago, one newspaper announced that Mrs Burnett very sensibly refrained from trammelling her beautiful boys with any unnecessary clothing, and that among her neighbours they were known as the young Arabs. I spent some moments in absorbed reflection upon this paragraph. My beautiful boys and I have but one slight difference of opinion; that is upon the question of what amount of clothing is strictly necessary. My mild arguments have so far usually been refuted by more irresistible ones. Their theory, possibly founded upon their artistic instinct and studious daily contemplation of the antique marbles, is that all clothing is unnecessary, as witness the Apollo Belvedere, and that therefore, the sooner it is left in fragments fluttering in the perfumed zephyrs of the spring upon the fences, trees, tree-boxes, etc., the sooner it is lost in the form of hats, worn into dilapidated disgrace in the shape of shoes, and shorn of its buttons in any guise whatever, the better for all art in its highest and most noble ideals.

… That the little fellows have worn velvet and lace, and being kindly endowed by Nature, have so adorned it as to fill a weak parent with unbridled vanity, before which peacocks might retire, is true, but I object to their being handicapped in their child-hood by stupid, vulgar, unfounded stories, and I advance with due modesty the proposition that my taste for the picturesque has not led me to transform two strong, manly, robust boys into affected, abnormally self-conscious little mountebanks.

None of the most sentimental stuff about the boys was written when they were actually small children. At this stage, as Frances repeatedly said in *Through One Administration*, "Sentiment is out". But the children were a refuge, "the only safe thing". With them she could try to be herself, that self she often felt in danger of losing. She always genuinely loved playing—building houses, playing marbles or "fish pond". It was true that when she played with the children on a wet day "the toys all got nice again". What is less attractive is the way she congratulated herself on this later. Marghanita Laski takes her sternly to task for her "offensive whimsy" and "abominable conceit". She extracts the piece about Frances playing from the unpublished fragment "His Friend", written in 1891. "They had an idea that after all their mother was a sort of little girl. She was little to look at and had curly hair like their own; and she used to sit on the nursery floor …"

"I readily agree," wrote Miss Laski, "that this gives one a touch-ing picture of just such a young, pretty little mother as Little Lord Fauntleroy's 'Dearest'. But, unfortunately, photographs of Mrs Burnett taken at this time show her to have been distinctly matronly in appearance, with one of those tight, forbidding Manchester faces." Poor Frances. She never did like having her photograph taken, but, in fact, the photographs contemporary with the boys' nursery days are pleasant enough. The tight Manchester look is there all right in the handsome photograph taken with Lionel and Vivian in 1888—but is it fair to deduce anything from those long-frozen exposures? Nearly all her interviewers speak of the mobility and animation of her face.

There is, incidentally, an exact parallel to the passage quoted from "His Friend" in *Through One Administration*, emphasizing yet again how closely Frances identified herself with Bertha Amory. But Bertha could never have written "His Friend"; nor could the Frances of the early 1880s. What changed her was the phenomenal success of *Little Lord Fauntleroy*. It changed everything. Some said it even changed relations between America and Britain. It certainly changed lives and attitudes. One historian has put it like this: "For good or ill, other immigrant Britons left traces on America between the Civil and the Spanish American wars," such as Alexander Graham Bell, "but only Mrs Burnett could claim so deeply to have affected the emotional health of so many American boys." Its success, of course, affected Frances even more than her readers. It changed her from being a serious writer, striving to master an art, into a craftswoman who had discovered she had the Midas touch. She had begun something she could not stop. The pen-driving machine was to become a machine for printing money. The more she made, the more she needed. "I always need so much money," she was to write in 1894, and so it always was.

But before we come finally face to face with *Little Lord Fauntleroy*, we should look a little longer at Frances in the early 1880s. She was in her early thirties; she was considered one of the most important writers in America—though this was admittedly not long after the time when Trollope felt able to dismiss the whole of American fiction as "trashy beyond all description". An article in the July 1883 issue of the *Century* called "The Native Element in Fiction" listed Frances as one of those "who hold the front rank today in general estimation", and "had their visible beginnings in the five years following 1870". The others were William Dean Howells, Henry James, George Washington Cable and Constance Fenimore Woolson. The *Century* critic said Frances' ball scene in *Through One Administration* "would draw tears from a piece of Canterbury flint". But he decided that she "sympathizes with people in humble circumstances, not, it would seem, because they are misunderstood or particularly unhappy in their lives, but because their surroundings are not what she herself would like". It was not wholehearted praise but it is something to be included in a short list of the most important writers in the United States. It is something of a responsibility. Had she in fact reached the height of her powers with *Through One Administration*? Was there anywhere to go but down? Or to stop altogether? She wrote very little for three years and she made sure that her next book could not be compared with her last.

One newspaper at this time recorded that Mrs Burnett "lives quietly and pleasantly in Washington. Although professionally literary, she is so domestic that those unacquainted with her writings would not suspect the fact. Her graceful fingers show no trace of ink. She is very simple and unaffected in manner and strikingly bright and original in conversation. Personally she is plump—almost too plump for her short stature. She wears her hair braided behind and frizzed in front to cover what she calls a horrid great forehead, which really is too square and too projecting for beauty. Her nose is good though rather large; her jaw and mouth are firm with pretty teeth and a cordial charming smile. Her eyes are large, intense, expressive. She seems to have no jealousy or envy, to be wholly unconventional and everyway free and large. She gets pleasure from all kinds of occupation and all kinds of people."

The Cincinnati *Enquirer* was more flattering about her looks. It declared she had a slight and supple figure, "with a girlish grace of face and figure … Her eyes are large, brown, soulful … the face, so full of genius, is crowned by a luxurious suit of hair, which fringes in long rings about her intellectual forehead. In colour it is auburn. It is coiled in a loose mass at the back of her superbly poised and classical head. In conversation Mrs Burnett is animated and brilliant. Her language is well chosen and is after the manner of Thomas Carlyle, its resemblance lying in the use of good, strong, short Anglo-Saxon words. She uses her hands in expressing her meaning and very small, shapely hands they are. Her toilets are generally of some neutral tint, black being her favorite color. This she illuminates with bright harmonious tints and about her shoulders there is usually wound a lace or netted silk fichu. Her manners are easy and affable."

It was at about this time that Frances began to be called "Fluffy" by her friends. It seems to have derived from her fluffy fringe (the hair "frizzed in front") and her taste for frills and furbelows and fichus. As Vivian said later, the nickname "was a betrayal of her real character", but it stuck, and Frances must have liked it; she used it herself, often signing her letters with it, and even with variations such as Fluffina.

The *Boston Herald* described the house on I Street. "Her home is tasteful and at once recognizable as the abode of culture—comfortable rather than luxurious. On the third floor is the 'Den' fitted up in answer to her own fancy with heavy hangings and dark, rich walls. In the centre of the room stands a large table, upon which is a handsome antique covering. Here is ample evidence of work—piles of manuscripts, books, letters etc.... In the Den are cosy easy chairs, each with character and history. An open fire, a rack and an old brass tea-kettle indicate agreeable possibilities.

Everywhere there is something suggestive in the way of relic or souvenir. It is a very personal place and each article has to its owner's mind a pleasant association—paintings, drawings, bric-à-brac, flowers, an old piano ... A small circle frequently passes the evening with music and conversation ..."

There is very little recorded of these years 1882, 1883 and 1884. There was apparently very little to record. Frances was unable to write—and so she was ill. Or she was ill and so she was unable to write. They called it a "nervous prostration". Her admired toughness, "the refusal to be overpowered by circumstances", seemed to have deserted her. Each summer she went to Lynn on Massachusetts Bay with the boys. In 1884, when they went back to school, she went to Boston and stayed at the Vendome Hotel, Commonwealth Avenue. She had become interested in mind-healing, of which there was a great deal of talk at the time, particularly in Lynn, where the founder of Christian Science had lived for a number of years. The first Church of Christ Scientist had been established in Boston in 1881. In 1884 Mary Baker Eddy and her husband were living in Columbus Avenue, Boston. People spoke of the extraordinary cures she had made.

Frances knew that there was not much wrong with her physically. There was a great deal about mind-healing which appealed to her. Although she had been brought up in Manchester to attend Anglican services regularly, she had long since given up membership of any church. But she had a strong religious sense and a continuing desire to see some purpose in life. Her Bible was well used and marked in many places with notes and the dates on which particular texts had helped her. Often she wrote out passages. The following passage from St Paul's *Letter to the Philippians* she copied many times: "Be careful for nothing; but with prayer and thanksgiving let your requests be made unto God. And the peace of God, which passeth all understanding, shall keep your minds and hearts through Christ Jesus. Finally, brethren, whatsoever things are true, whatsoever things are honest, whatsoever things are lovely, whatsoever things are of good report, if there be any virtue, think on these things."

It was this peace which passeth all understanding she needed so badly. Christian Science, of course, claimed to be able to give it to her. If only, Christian Science taught, she became convinced of the power of controlling mind, she would be lifted above the chances and changes of this mortal life, and taste of the peace which the world can neither give nor take away. It was an attractive thought. But Frances could not accept that Matter is simply a false impression, that evil and sin, sorrow and illness are unreal in an absolute sense. She had seen too much evidence of their reality. Her illness, she would like to believe, could be overcome by the power of the mind. Thinking only on things that were good and lovely might perhaps just possibly free her from this "nervous prostration" or whatever it was. But Christian Science told her that its theology was essential to its healing. It must be accepted in its entirety or not at all. She never became a Christian Scientist, though, much later, Vivian did.

In 1884 she "took several courses of treatments with a local mind-healer" in Boston. These seemed to be nothing much more complex than an encouragement to her to think that, if she wanted to be well, she would be well. She did not feel able to return to Washington. There are no existing letters from or to Swan at this period, and it is difficult to know just what was going on. But it seems certain that their marriage had already ended in every real sense. Our only clues are from *Through One Administration*. There Bertha decides to stay with Richard for the sake of the children. For the same reason—and of course because divorce was rare and controversial at that time—Frances made no open break for another fourteen years. Frances met the Halls that year and it was largely the attraction of their company which kept her in Boston—this and the more admissible reason of her mind-healing "treatments". Madam Edna Hall, as she was known, was a singing teacher, who had had some success as a concert performer in her younger days. There were three daughters: Marguerite (Daisy), a singer like her mother, Grace (Gigi), who painted and Gertrude (known as Kitty) who was a poet. Kitty was at this time working on her *Verses* which were later to be favourably reviewed in the *Atlantic* by the respected William Dean Howells. Frances was at once attracted to her and the friendship was to last throughout their lives.

When Frances finally returned to Washington in the autumn of 1884—just in time for the festivities to mark the beginning of the Cleveland administration—Kitty Hall came too. Kitty remembered Frances telling Vivian at her knee—in that short interval between breakfast and the time to start for school—the beginning of the story of the little American boy who became an English Lord. "The effect of testing her plot on the imagination of a child indubitably satisfied her. He had heard her tell many stories and so had I; *Die Lust zu fabulieren* was in her inborn and life long; we could have no idea that on this day a classic had been born."

Frances remembered the origins of *Little Lord Fauntleroy* like this:

[Vivian] was such a patriotic young American; he was so engaged in an impending presidential election at the time; his remarks were so well worth hearing! I began, among other fancies about him, to imagine his making them with that frankly glowing face to conservative English people.

"… When a person is a duke," he had said to me once, "what makes him one? What has he done?" His opinion evidently was, that dukedoms were a species of reward for superhuman sweetness of character and brilliant intellectual capacity. I began to imagine the interest that would be awakened in his mind by the contemplation of ducal personages. It amused me to analyze the subject of what his point of view would be likely to be. I knew it would be productive of immense entertainment to his acquaintances … Would he seem "a cheeky little beggar" to less republican minds than his own? I asked myself this curiously. But no, I was sure he would not. He would be so simple. He would expect such splendour of mind and of noble friendliness that the hypothetical duke would like him as Dan and Carrie did, and he would end by saying, "My friend, the Duke of Blankshire," as affectionately as he had said, "My friend, the milkman."

It was only a thread of fancy for a while, but one day I had an idea. "I will write a story about him," I said. "I will put him in a world quite new to him and see what he will do. How shall I bring a small American boy into close relationship with an English nobleman—irascible, conservative, disagreeable? He must live with him, talk to him, show him his small, unconscious, republican mind. He will be more effective if I make him a child who has lived in the simplest possible way. Eureka! Son of younger son, separated from ill-tempered noble father because he has married a poor young American beauty. Young father dead, elder brothers dead, boy comes into title! How it would amaze him and bewilder him! Yes, there it is, and Vivian shall be he—just Vivian with his curls and his eyes, and his friendly, kind, little soul. Little Lord Something-or-other. What a pretty title—Little Lord——Little Lord——, what?" And a day later it was Little Lord Fauntleroy. A story like that is easily written. In part it was being lived before my eyes.

… Almost every day I recorded something he had said or suggested. And how delightful it was to read the manuscript to him and his brother. He used to sit in a large arm-chair holding his knee or with his hands in his pockets. "Do you know," he said to me once, "I like that boy? There's one thing about him, he never forgets about Dearest."

"It is not a portrait; but, certainly, if there had not been Vivian there would not have been Fauntleroy," Kitty Hall heard Frances tell people. Vivian was to suffer from this identification for the rest of his life. It was an albatross round his neck as well as Frances'. It would have destroyed lesser men, but he never lost the characteristics of the charming, helpful boy, who expected the best from everyone. In 1937 the newspaper report of his death had the heading ORIGINAL "FAUNTLEROY" DIES IN BOAT AFTER HELPING RESCUE 4 IN SOUND. "Vivian Burnett, Author's Son who Devoted Life to Escaping 'Sissified' Role, is Stricken at Helm—Manoeuvres Yawl to get 2 Men and 2 Women from Overturned Craft, Then Collapses."

It was an appropriate way for Vivian to die. It was also typically Fauntleroy behaviour, for Cedric Errol, Lord Fauntleroy was, in fact, no sissy. His true character was overlaid by the trappings of the part, by the clothes which he wore, by the hair that curled to his shoulders and by the sweet girl actresses who played the role on the stage. Frances did rhapsodize to excess about Cedric's beauty ("such a handsome, blooming, curly-headed little fellow") and the relationship between mother and son is certainly over-idealized; but this is only a very small part of the book. "Dearest" is in fact a rather minor character. The whole interest lies in the impact of Cedric on his disagreeable grandfather, the Earl of Dorincourt.

Cedric is certainly loving, considerate, tender, but he never deserves the label "odious little prig". He is brave, enterprising, adaptable and unaffected. He is, in fact, a likeable boy. When he hears the news that he is heir to an earldom, having discovered what an earldom is, the young American is appalled. His friend, Mr Hobbs, the grocer on the corner, has always said very severe things about the aristocracy and has confidently expected an English Revolution. "Those they've trod on will rise and blow them sky high. They're a bad lot," he tells Cedric. Naturally Cedric would rather not be an earl. "None of the boys are earls," he tells Dearest. "Can't I *not* be one?"

But there is apparently no getting out of it. Fortunately Cedric expects the best of his own grandfather. And when he arrives in England, he is so pleased to find there is no one actually languishing in the dungeons and that the people take off their hats to his grandfather, that he gets the impression the Earl is, like Mr Hobbs, "a universal favorite". There is nothing unconvincing about the Earl of Dorincourt's reformation under the influence of his small republican grandson. People tend to act in the way that is expected of them, and pride has always been one of the Earl's strongest characteristics. He is proud of Cedric; the rest follows. It is Cedric, of course, who becomes the universal favourite.

The attraction of the book is obvious. Indeed, it fits almost exactly the formula for a bestseller which Claud Cockburn defines rather crudely in his exploration of twentieth-century best sellers: "… to take the reader on a trip to the wide blue yonder, to get one more flight out of an imaginary but ever so noble aristocracy, while indicating one's modern awareness that the old bus might be conking out, these are notable achievements, notably achieved by a whole sales force of authors." The wide blue yonder was in this case not a desert island or a desert kingdom, but the noble acres of the Earl of Dorincourt's estate. The appeal was marvellously double-edged. The reader could have it both ways. He could both enjoy the aristocratic way of life and share Cedric's belief that Mr Hobbs and Dick, the bootblack, were every bit as important as an earl.

It is typical of the best seller, according to Cockburn, that the Sheikh and the Bohemian turn out to be well-born respectable people after all. E. M. Hull's Sheikh (immortalized by Rudolph Valentino) was actually "the son of a tip-top English peer"; Beau Geste, the Foreign Legionary, is Lady Brandon's nephew. W. J. Locke's Beloved Vagabond is, in fact, an old Rugbeian. So too Cedric, the young egalitarian, has the ancient lineage. "Here's to him," Mr Hobbs said, proposing Cedric's health in the small back room at the grocery, "an' may he teach 'em a lesson—earls an' markises an' dooks an' all." Cedric does teach the Earl a lesson, and when the rival claimant turns up, Cedric shows that his own character is undeviating and he will be exactly the same person whether he is an earl himself or a partner in Hobbs' grocery business. The irony, of course, is that whatever happens, he is the Earl's grandson, for all his splendidly American attitudes. The coincidence of Dick, the bootblack, recognizing the rival claimant's mother as his own sister-in-law, is a preposterous one but by then the reader's unbelief has been happily suspended. As Cockburn says, a "rattling good yarn" has incalculable powers of survival. "It can even survive a plot of breath-taking, shamelessly audacious absurdity."

And *Little Lord Fauntleroy* is a splendid yarn. The sentiment we find nauseating ("such a beautiful, innocent little fellow he was, too, with his brave, trustful face") is not really very much in evidence. It would not need cuts of more than a couple of pages of odd sentences here and there to make it perfectly acceptable to today's taste. It is not read now because people who haven't read it think that Cedric is nothing but an over-dressed mother's darling. *The Dictionary of American Biography* said most unfairly, "Chiefly he is made up of a wardrobe and manners." The illustrations, which did the book and Frances so much disservice in the end, were by Reginald Birch. At the end of his life, Birch himself said they had ruined his career; no one ever let him forget them. They were based on a photograph of Vivian taken in Lynn in 1884. It is one thing to wear black velvet in a photographic studio or on Tuesday afternoons, as Vivian did; it is quite another to wear it when riding a pony or watching a bricklayer. The image was wide open to both admiration and ridicule.

At the time the vast majority admired. Frances knew instinctively—and it helped to make the book a bestseller—that the Mr Hobbses of this world are as fascinated by the aristocracy as is everyone else. Mr Hobbs, indeed, that believer in the rights of an English revolution, shut up his New York grocery, opened a shop on the Earl's estate and pored over the Court News every morning in *The Times*. Many people read mainly to substantiate their day-dreams and the Fauntleroy story is the perfect day-dream. Mark Twain's distant cousin, Jesse Madison Leathers of Louisville, was firmly convinced he was the rightful Earl of Durham. Twain said to prove the claim would be as difficult as taking Gibraltar with blank cartridges, but there were plenty of people who had similar dreams. It could happen to my boy, people thought; there was a case in the paper just the other day—an American carpenter found himself suddenly a Scottish nobleman. It could happen. All over America, men, women and children followed Cedric's adventures. The reaction was described like this: "It does not do to say merely that *Little Lord Fauntleroy* was a great success; it caused a public delirium of joy. It had the Cinderella charm and something else. Young and old laughed and thrilled and wept over it together."

It began in the children's magazine, *St Nicholas*, in November 1885—but was it really a children's book? It was certainly written partly for Lionel and Vivian; it has a perfect plot for children and is entirely accessible to them. One of the things that made Frances such a good writer for children was that she was always an extremely natural writer. "It is doubtful," as one critic put it, "that Mrs Burnett ever consciously made a phrase." She wrote "always in the most simple and straight-forward words that she could find", with her eye on the thing she was writing about and not on the way she wrote. But *Little Lord Fauntleroy* appealed even more to adults. Cedric, unlike Sara Crewe and Mary Lennox of her later books, is always seen from the outside, from the adult point of view. And it is adults, of course, who buy children's books. Mothers bought it perhaps for their children but they read it themselves and they loved Cedric. They longed for their own children to be like him.

Louisa M. Alcott, in a glowing review in the *Bookbuyer*, drew attention to the fact that "Grown people, who still love children's books, will enjoy much which escapes the younger reader in the working out of the fierce old earl's regeneration". Miss Alcott considered writing for children "a peculiarly fitting and gracious task for women" and she rejoiced to see "our best and brightest consecrating their talents to this useful and beautiful work". "Nothing could have been more happily conceived," wrote George Parsons Lathrop in the *New York Star*. "The way in which the happy thought has been embodied is nothing less than perfect." The reviews were actually far more sickly than the book.

When it was published in England, the *Pall Mall Gazette* defined its appeal like this: "The grace and tenderness of the sentiment, the childlike natural ways of the small hero, the happy alternation of the quaint, laughable incidents, with touches of real, though unobtrusive pathos, above all the pervading atmosphere of unaffected goodness, combine to form a whole of which the fascination is felt by children of an older growth as much as, if not more than, by juveniles." And the *Manchester Guardian* agreed: "Cedric's simple, truthful, earnest and loving nature is what one would like all children to have, for it was just the same with or without wealth, in the little house in New York or in the great castle."

Among the "grown people", the "children of an older growth" who happily admitted to an admiration for the book, there were some impressive names. Gladstone, the Prime Minister of England, was one. We shall hear more about this later. The poet James Russell Lowell, who had recently been recalled by President Cleveland from his post as American Ambassador in London, was another. The Anglo–American theme was of particular interest to both of them, Lowell wrote to Scribner: "I have just been reading *Little Lord Fauntleroy*. I was very tired and my niece gave it to me, saying, 'Here is something easy to read which I am sure you will enjoy.' I should be glad to have the author know how much pleasure the book gave me. I feel so grateful to her."

Frances had returned to Scribner's fold with this book, in spite of a letter from Swan to Scribner as late as April 1885 which says, "As regards Mrs Burnett's future books, I should hardly feel justified in binding ourselves to a house which allows one of our [crossed out and "her" written above] books to remain out of print for a year. That argues a lack of interest, which is not encouraging for future works." So Swan was still acting as amanuensis and feeling possessive about the books, even though their writer was drifting further and further away from him.

Fortunately for Scribner's, the differences were resolved. They were able to acquire the plates of the two Osgood books and brought them out in their uniform edition that summer. *Little Lord Fauntleroy* was published as a book in October 1886. A year later 43,000 copies were in print. Two years later, influenced by the play, sales soared higher and higher. It became one of the biggest sellers of all time, selling over a million copies in English alone, and being translated into more than a dozen languages. It made Frances at least a hundred thousand dollars in her lifetime. The term "bestseller" is, of course, often used pejoratively—the idea being that more people read bad books than good books. But the sales success of a book often tells us more about the time than about the book itself. Frances had produced a book which fitted perfectly the taste of the time.

Frances had started off as an extreme realist by the standards of the day; now she became identified as a romantic. Marcus Cunliffe sets the book in opposition to Dean Howell's *Indian Summer*. It was "the exotic versus the demotic; the day-dream versus broad daylight; sentimentality versus commonsense". Romanticism was in the ascendant and, with this one book, Frances had stepped into line. It was the age of escapism. In England it was the heyday of Andrew Lang. His influence as a critic was enormous. For him, there were no problems about relative values. As John Gross has put it, "Milton was literature and so was Stanley J. Weyman". There was a craving for escape from life and no aesthetic encouragement to face it. Lang preferred Rider Haggard and Anthony Hope to Hardy and Henry James, Stevenson to Dostoievsky. And thousands, hundreds of thousands on both sides of the Atlantic, agreed with him.

It was in 1886 that Lemuel Bangs, Scribner's agent in England, attempting to introduce a little realism into the list, was told by Charles Scribner to "let up on the nasty books". A list of the best-selling novels in these years is very revealing:

1884   *Heidi*; *Treasure Island*
1885   *A Child's Garden of Verses*; *Huckleberry Finn*
1886   *Little Lord Fauntleroy*; *King Solomon's Mines*; *War and Peace*

Of these titles, all except *War and Peace* would now be considered children's books. At this time there was no rigid demarcation line between adult and children's literature. Publishers did not have special children's departments. There were no children's libraries. Reviews of children's books were not confined to separate supplements; they frequently contained phrases such as, "It will delight all children between the ages of six and sixty" or "Grown-up readers will be as much delighted as the younger ones". Swinburne, writing on Mrs Molesworth in the *Nineteenth Century* in 1893, was to say: "Our own age is more fortunate ... Any chapter of *The Cuckoo Clock* or the enchanting *Adventures of Herr Baby* is worth a shoal of the very best novels dealing with the characters and fortunes of mere adults." Lewis Carroll had had a good deal to do with this. Everyone read *Alice*. Henry James, though depressed by the "beastly bloodiness" of Rider Haggard, admired *Treasure Island* enormously. His copy of *Kidnapped* is heavily annotated. The taste of the general public accorded neatly on the whole with what was considered suitable for children; when *Huckleberry Finn* was serialized in the *Century* (not *St Nicholas*), Gilder deleted, with the author's agreement, all references to nakedness, blasphemy, smells and dead cats.

The increase in public libraries at this period greatly added to the sales. In 1893 there was only one other book that was in more libraries in America than *Little Lord Fauntleroy* (it was in 72% of the libraries but *Ben Hur* was in 83%): it had been a success right from the beginning. "Mrs Burnett's juvenile starts with a tremendous rush," Scribner reported. They had to reprint before publication although the first edition was 10,000.

Frances' success was sweet and easy. There is a portrait of her and an article about her work in the February 1886 number of the *Bookbuyer*. If there was no rigid demarcation between adult and juvenile books for the reader, it was very different for the writer—her early novels had left Mrs Burnett "completely exhausted ... she had entered into the joys and griefs of the men and women she pictured; she had shared their anxieties, suffered and endured all the trials they had passed through; she was possessed by sensations quite beyond her power to govern". But "in writing for children, Mrs Burnett works easily and rapidly". *Little Lord Fauntleroy* she "found it a pleasure to write". It was not surprising that she tried to repeat her success.

The new book was called *Sara Crewe, or, What happened at Miss Minchin's*. It was a story drawing on some of her experiences at the Miss Hadfields', but set in London. There is no evidence, though it seems probable, that Frances had been to London on her three different visits to England in the 1870s. But the reality did not seem to matter as much as it had in the days when she had carefully researched the backgrounds for *That Lass o' Lowrie's* and *Haworth's*. She may well have read Charles Kingsley's *Yeast*, with its picture of the plight of the agricultural poor, but she does not seem to realize that the conditions in Erleboro, the village in *Little Lord Fauntleroy*, could have been due neither to the ignorance and idleness of the workers, nor to the Earl's neglect There is no suggestion in the book of the general national situation, of a country suffering from a series of bad harvests, and disease among animals, culminating in widespread outbreaks of foot and mouth in 1883. They were depression years—but Frances was apparently no longer interested in causes, only in effects.

In Washington, Frances' increased income enabled them to leave I Street, which was going down in the world. She wrote to Kitty Hall in Boston: "We are going into a new house and such a lovely sweet dear of a house—pretty in everything—with charming rooms and hall fireplace (which represents all architectural perfection to me) and shelves over the mantels and inlaid floors and stained glass and all the modern improvements ... The mere thought of it makes me feel better." But the house, 1374 K Street, did not last long. Frances made much of the circumstances in another letter to Kitty:

No, my own Kitty, your Fluffy is not "burned to a crisp"— ... but there are a hundred chances to one that if the fire had broken out in the night while we slept that this might have been the case. We were just beneath it and the whole garret was in roaring flames, and we peacefully reading until a little boy in the street rang our bell and announced to us that we were on fire.

I was in bed—having retired immediately after dinner because I felt very tired. Dr Burnett ran up into the attic—I followed with a pitcher of water, but it was already beyond anything but fire engines and hose. The servants went mad and shrieked alternately, "Oh, my God," and "Oh, my Jesus Christ." I went into my Nasturtium room, climbed on a chair, got my manuscript from the shelf, emptied the closet of my clothes, put them on the back of the first man who appeared who was not a fireman—the flames roared—the skylight fell in with a smash—they would not let me stay long enough to get my shoes—I threw my dear Japanese robe (never be without one) over my night-dress and went downstairs—where distracted men and servants dragged me in my bare feet on to the stone steps and shouted at me to *go*. They clamored so I could not seem to make them comprehend that my innocent little feet were bare and not ready for the street on a cold March evening, even if nightgowns were more popular as promenade costumes than they have appeared to be this winter.

But at last I made myself clear, and a man took me in his arms and carried me across the street to Mrs Nordhoff's; whereupon it was rumored immediately that Mrs Burnett had with much forethought and presence of mind promptly become insensible, and had to be borne, swooning, from the flames.

How fortunate it was that she was wearing "a beautiful, crisp, clean little nightgown with frills of lace standing right straight out nobly in every direction" and blue satin ribbons. Her rescue had "as wildly romantic an air as if [she] had been Clarissa Harlowe". Indeed, Frances said there were accusations in the air that she had engineered the whole excitement and set the house on fire herself, but Kitty would know that she would not have chosen such a dull Washington season. She would rather have arranged it at the Halls' house in Boston, "with a W. B. engagement being played at the Globe". This is the first mention of Wilson Barrett, an English actor who was a friend of the Halls; the newspapers were later to hint of a close relationship between the two of them.

The letter to Kitty was frivolous but the situation was serious. If the K Street house a few months earlier had made her feel better, it now made her feel worse. There were some good moments. The Washington letter in the *New Orleans Times-Democrat* not only said some very nice things about Frances ("She does not look over thirty" when she was actually thirty-six) but recorded that when Mary Anderson, the American actress whose success in London was the basis of Mrs Humphry Ward's novel *Miss Bretherton*, met Tennyson, the great man had asked her to convey to Mrs Burnett his opinion that a certain passage in *Through One Administration* was "the finest piece of English he had ever seen". Unfortunately, to Frances' dismay, Mary Anderson forgot which passage Tennyson was talking about.

In spite of such compliments and the tremendous success of *Fauntleroy*, Frances was not happy. There was a sad and perhaps revealing poem in the August 1886 number of the *Century*. These are three of the twelve stanzas:

> *I laughed at Love!*
> *"The merriest jest of all,"*
> *I said, "a gay, light bounding ball,*
> *Which gathers wit at both its rise and fall*
> *And never flies our grasp beyond recall:"*
> > *I did not know.*

> *"Laughed thou at love?*
> *The day will come for tears,*
> *For pangs and aching longings, heavy fears,*
> *For memories laying waste all coming years,—*
> *Dead hopes, each one a living flame that sears,—*
> > *Then wilt thou know!"*

> *"I mock no more*
> *Great Love, but hear my cry;*
> *Give me the pang, the woe, the bitter sigh,*
> *Hear me, in pity, hear me, lest I die.*
> *Let me bear all, so Love pass me not by,*
> > *Since Love I know!"*

There was another poem written at this time. It appeared in the *Century* in May 1887. "If" is a poem of love that is over, of the barriers of pride and reserve that prevent communication, of how consistently we deceive ourselves, how little we know the results of our behaviour, how little we show of what is in our hearts.

If he had known that when her proud fair face
Turned from him calm and slow
Beneath its cold indifference had place
A passionate, deep woe.

If he had known that when her hand lay still,
Pulseless so near his own,
It was because pain's bitter, bitter chill
Changed her to very stone.

If he had known that she had borne so much
For sake of the sweet past,
That mere despair said, "This cold look and touch
Must be the cruel last."

If he had known her eyes so cold and bright,
Watching the sunset's red,
Held back within their deeps of purple light
A storm of tears unshed.

If he had known the keenly barbed jest
With such hard lightness thrown
Cut through the hot proud heart within her breast
Before it pierced his own.

If she had known that when her calm glance swept
Him as she passed him by
His blood was fire, his pulse madly leapt
Beneath her careless eye.

If she had known that when he touched her hand
And felt it still and cold
There closed round his wrung heart the iron band
Of misery untold.

If she had known that when her laughter rang
    In scorn of sweet past days
His very soul shook with a deadly pang
    Before her light dispraise.

If she had known that when in the wide west
    The sun sank gold and red
He whispered bitterly, "'Tis like the rest;
    The warmth and light have fled."

If she had known the longing and the pain,
    If she had only guessed,
One look—one word—and she perhaps had lain
    Silent upon his breast.

If she had known how oft when their eyes met
    And his so fiercely shone,
But for man's shame and pride they had been wet—
Ah! If she had but known!

The warmth and light had certainly fled; there was no doubt about that. Frances had finished *Sara Crewe* but she was still thinking about London. Perhaps the Party was there. She had money now—plenty of money. "I had nearly six hundred from England a few days ago," she wrote to Kitty, and there was more coming. Why shouldn't she and Kitty take Lionel and Vivian (his hair by now cropped short) to England for Queen Victoria's Jubilee celebrations? It was an irresistible idea, whatever Swan said.

5

The Gratitude of British Authors
1887–1889

In May 1887, Frances, Kitty Hall and the boys—now eleven and twelve—sailed to Southampton on the *SS Ems*. In London, they took lodgings at 23 Weymouth Street, W.1. The city was *en fête*. Flags decorated the streets. Paper banners in windows proclaimed GOD BLESS HER. VICTORIA THE GOOD. THE MOTHER OF HER PEOPLE. The shops were full of marmalade jars inscribed "1837 to 1887. Victoria the Good", and underneath, "Peace and Plenty". But it was only a year since the unemployed had rioted in the centre of London: Henry James, returning from a visit to Robert Louis Stevenson in Bournemouth, had found Piccadilly littered with the glass of smashed shop-fronts. James wrote to his brother of the "immense destitution ... Everyone here is growing poorer—from causes which I fear will continue."

There would have been scenes to remind Frances of Islington Square, Salford, if she had ventured into the backstreets. In later years, she was to see plenty of the sadder side of London life but in 1887 she was happy enough to look only at its party face. Kitty Hall knew London well and had many friends there. Her sister, Daisy, was in London this year too, singing "in oratorio and drawing room concerts". Frances met their close friends, the Lankesters. Ray Lankester was Professor of Anatomy at Oxford and not in London a great deal, but Frances was immediately attracted to his younger brother, Dr Owen Lankester, "a splendid, big man with a boyish pink-and-white round face" and "ever-present good humor". He was to become her "dear, big, immense Owen".

Also this year, Frances met Israel Zangwill, who was to become an even closer friend. Zangwill was, at this time, only twenty-three, fourteen years younger than Frances. He had not yet published *Children of the Ghetto*, which established his reputation. It was many years before he was to become leader of the Zionist movement. They had first started talking when fellow members of a party visiting Madame Tussaud's. It is not surprising to Frances visiting the waxworks. She was a tourist, after all, and she had the boys with her to be entertained and instructed. Moreover, one of her early stories, "Smethurstses", is about a man who owns a waxwork show. Madame Tussaud's was an obvious place for her to spend an afternoon. But what was Zangwill doing there? Whatever the answer, it was certainly the scene of their first meeting and she said he had "rescued" her from her own fright in the Chamber of Horrors.

Both Owen Lankester and Israel Zangwill became regular visitors to the Weymouth Street drawing-room on Tuesday afternoons. Frances had taken the rooms for only three months but she immediately filled them with interesting things—including Liberty hangings and "greenery-yallery Grosvenor Gallery" bits and pieces which displayed her awareness of the aesthetic revival. It was at a soirée at the Grosvenor Gallery that Owen Lankester introduced Frances to Stephen Townesend. The young men had been medical students at Bart's together. Frances did not meet him again that year and she forgot his name, but she remembered him—"the one with the nice eyes and the lovely demeanor".

The sun shone on the Jubilee pageant. Frances would undoubtedly have preferred to have seen the Queen in crown and robes of state, but the glimpse of the formidable old lady in the jewelled bonnet was impressive enough. "The procession itself thrilled her," Vivian recorded, "perhaps more greatly than it did the boys.

It was seen under the most favorable circumstances—from well-placed seats just opposite one of the minor palaces, in front of which played the mounted band of the Royal Horse Guards. Certainly all that was English in her rose up as the members of the Royal Family passed." The boys, being Americans, thought it more appropriate to be cooler. They were staunch republicans, after all—though they probably did not go as far as the eight-year-old E.M. Forster, watching the same procession, who had been rebuked by his great-aunt for saying that he did not like the Queen.

London was full of Americans that summer. Henry James said it was "fast becoming an American city". He had gone to Italy, partly to escape the ones who wanted to hold on to his coat-tails, thirty of them at least. Vivian thought that James and Frances first met this Jubilee summer but it seems unlikely, for James did not return to his rooms in De Vere Gardens until 22nd July, and by then Frances was packing for Suffolk.

She was again unwell. There is a letter to Austin Dobson—the only English writer to appear in the newly revived *Scribner's Magazine*. He had invited the boys to spend an afternoon with his children: he had five daughters and five sons, and Vivian and Lionel had already met Cyril and Bernard—"such sweet gentle little fellows", Frances called them. She wrote, "I wish that I were able to go with them but I am feeling really ill. Yesterday I was obliged to remain in bed all day and send for the doctor. Today I feel very weak and forlorn." Crossing the Atlantic had not improved her health.

But the doctor thought "bracing air" might help. Frances, Kitty and the boys, with a London girl called Millington as maid, stayed at a hotel in Southwold on the Suffolk coast. There was not much to do but gaze at the sea, write letters, and browse in Miss Chicksby's circulating library, "where one could buy toys and drinking-mugs inscribed in gold letters A PRESENT FROM SOUTH-WOLD". When they had read their way through the odd volumes of Miss Braddon, and works by the author of *The Heir of Redcliffe* ("three volumes at a time for sixpence a week"), they moved on to Elm Farm, Wangford. Kitty and Frances walked in the lanes enjoying the wild flowers, talking to the tinker's children, leaning on gates and calling the sheep. "My friend and I used to call upon them by … uttering all sorts of queer little sounds, in the hope of hitting upon the one which would attract their attention … We always managed to bring them huddling together in a woolly mass round the gate, where they stood and stared at us with their unmeaning, clear amber eyes and silly gentle faces uplifted. We used to wonder if we did not look as silly to them as they did to us, but we both agreed it would be very difficult to decide what a sheep was thinking about, or if it was thinking at all."

The boys were happy—rabbiting with the farmer, hay-making, learning Suffolk songs from the young shepherd. They were furious when it was time to leave Suffolk for Italy. "They began their journey in silence, leaning back in their corners of the carriage, their arms folded and tears in their eyes."

Florence was an obvious choice for the winter for several reasons. Kitty Hall had spent much of her childhood there. Her friends, the McNamees, were running a pensione in the villa which had once belonged to Trollope, and they promised Frances could have the very room in which Trollope had written. Then also Frances had heard of a wonderful school, "whose master, a fine old Frenchman, had prepared boys for colleges in England, in France, in Germany and America". They stopped off in Paris on the way and showed Vivian the house where he had been born.

Florence was wonderful. Frances wrote at great length to Owen Lankester in Wimpole Street:

… I walk up and down white marble stairs, surrounded by colonnades with arches and white pillars—I occupy a suite of huge rooms just vacated by an English countess—I have a piazza of my own, big enough for a ballroom, and I lean over massive balustrades of stone to look into a garden full of orange and lemon and magnolia and cypress trees, and oleanders, and roses, and oleafragrante, and fountains, and ancient medallions, and Russian boar hounds, and servitors who say "Buono giorno, Signora," and who are called Lisa and Pasquale and Carlo and Vittorio and Luigi and Assunta, as if they were part of an opera.

And I have on my table a glass full of wild crocuses, gathered in the Cascine, and a brown rosary bought from a brown old woman in the Piazza Santissima Annunciata—a rosary about two yards long and with carved beads as big as potatoes, and it is worth "quattro lire" and was evidently made and blessed for you because it is just your size—for of course you know you never could commit a little sin—you are too, too big, and consequently a little rosary would prove inadequate to any of your occasions …

I can only endeavour to console myself by writing a new book and taking unlimited French and Italian lessons. When I return, I shall be able to say to you in the most fluent manner, "Have you seen the pink umbrella of the baker, or the blue boots of the respectable aunt of the Russian General?" Then you will be so overjoyed that you will dissolve into floods of tears.

Yesterday we went to the Duomo and to Santissima Annunciata. How beautiful—how beautiful that Duomo! I must send you a picture of the new facade. The Piazza Santissima Annunciata is the one in which stands the statue of the Duke Fernando Browning has written of in "The Statue and the Bust". There he sits on a great bronze horse, looking forever at the upper corner window of the Palace, and he is evidently quite capable of many things. I think, my friend, of that bronze face, always, always upturned through all the sunny days and moonlit nights to that window from which the beautiful answering eyes vanished hundreds of years ago. This is romance—this is Italy! They *never* did things like that in Wimpole Street.

The new book was "an English story". It could have been *The Fortunes of Philippa Fairfax*. Mysteriously, although Scribner's made an offer for it that year, it was apparently the only one of Frances' books never to be published in America. It was published by

Warne in England in 1888. My feeling is that this may have been a re-writing of an earlier story, which Frances, still smarting from the accusations, years earlier, of selling chaff after wheat, chose not to publish in America. Poor Philippa Fairfax is the daughter of "an adorable rascal", who is always in debt. In desperation, he despatches her to Scotland to stay with a rich kinswoman and to try to induce the heir, "a handsome charming young fellow" called Wilfred Carnegie, to marry her. The plan works: Philippa and Wilfred fall in love. But then Wilfred discovers Fairfax's plan … In spite of some strong scenes, it is difficult to believe that this was written after *Through One Administration*. The other "English" story of this period was *Miss Defarge or A Woman's Will*, which was published by Warne in 1887, and by Lippincott in America the following year. This, although a brief, uncomplicated story, is far more accomplished.

A new French governess, Térèse, arrives at a dilapidated stately home. Hugh, aged eight, is the other side of Fauntleroy's coin. He wears an "actually ragged suit of black velvet". Everything is moth-eaten, threadbare, dusty, rusty. The children are all unmanageable. They "behave themselves like young savages". The parents' marriage is desperately unhappy. Sir Roderick Dysart is either drunk or absent; his wife, feckless and incompetent. Térèse's acceptance of the challenges is impressive and convincing. She enjoys the subjugation of Hugh: "I am interested. It is like playing a difficult close kind of game." She is in fact a remarkable young woman. Frances was to use her again, and many other threads in the story, in the much longer and more complex book, *The Shuttle*. Elizabeth, the Vicar's daughter, is another excellent piece of characterization—a lazy, amiable, unquestioning girl.

The story seems, surprisingly, to have sunk without trace. Published only a year or so after her famous best seller, it must have been completely over-shadowed by it. It is never mentioned in any accounts of Frances' work. But another book, published soon after by Scribner's on 29th February 1888, was again a great success. *Sara Crewe*, which Frances had finished before leaving

Washington, was just what her public wanted. The child Sara is as charming and admirable a character as Lord Fauntleroy. Like him, she has "wise old-fashioned thoughts" and like him she is a real child, original and individual. Where Cedric was undoubtedly Vivian, Sara was undoubtedly Frances herself. She imagined herself as she would have liked to have behaved, if she had ever been in Sara's position. Sara, the rich indulged pupil at Miss Minchin's seminary, is reduced to an attic and the life of a small drudge, when her father dies apparently bankrupt. What saves Sara from despair is her imagination. "You can make a story out of anything", as Frances knew. When Miss Minchin is cruel to her, Sara, imagining herself a princess, can spare her the executioner's block, knowing the teacher is a poor, stupid old thing, who doesn't know any better. The moral is exactly as in *Little Lord Fauntleroy*: true nobility lies, not in outward trappings, but within oneself.

Sara Crewe was very short and Frances accepted an outright payment of three thousand dollars for it, instead of royalties. Scribner's were sorry to hear Frances had sold "Editha's Burglar", which had appeared in *St Nicholas*, "to Messrs Jordan, Marsh and Co, the dry goods firm of Boston". They were very sorry for any of her books to go elsewhere. Without seeing it, they were prepared to offer three thousand five hundred dollars for the serialization of her next full-length story, plus a 12½% royalty on the book. Both in England and America, dramatized versions of "Editha's Burglar" had recently been staged. The American production at the Lyceum, New York, in October 1887, was chiefly distinguished by the acting of the child Elsie Leslie as Editha. E. H. Sothern, who played the Burglar, wrote to Elsie a few years later: "I still have some affection for the poor old burglar—although you took all the piece away from poor me—no matter how hard I cried nor how well I burgled." "The little piece was very favourably received", too, at the Princess's Theatre in London, in a dramatization by a different writer, though one reviewer objected to "the partial undressing of the child on the stage" for its awkwardness, not its indelicacy.

With the boys settled at school and Kitty staying with an old friend in Rome, Frances took a companion, who had been recommended to her by the McNamees. The young woman was called Luisa (or Lisa) Chiellini and remained with Frances for a number of years, as a sort of secretary and general factotum. They moved from the pensione into an apartment on the Lung'Arno Nuovo, next to the Russian church. Sitting at her window, Frances would see Queen Natalie and the young Prince Alexander of Serbia arrive in their carriage to worship. On Sundays Frances and the boys passed them in the Cascine, the park by the Arno, as the military band played and fashionable Florence promenaded in the sun. Alexander was studying with the same masters as the Burnett boys. Frances followed his fortunes after his return to Serbia, after his father was deposed and the boy became King. It may well have been this glancing contact with Balkan politics which was the first seed of Frances' children's novel *The Lost Prince*.

Frances worked regularly that winter in Florence but she also met a great many people. She saw a good deal of Constance Fenimore Woolson, visiting her at Bellosguardo where Henry James had been staying only a few months before and where Hawthorne, the Brownings, Ouida and James Fenimore Cooper had all lived or visited at various times. Ouida was in Florence still and Frances visited her, but "it was not at all exciting. She did nothing whatever to me." Vernon Lee (Violet Paget) was a different matter. James had called her "the most intelligent person in the place". Maurice Baring went even further. He called her "by far the cleverest person I ever met in my life and the person possessed with the widest range of the rarest culture". She was not happy that winter in Florence and she spent part of it in Rome, but when she was at home in the Via Garibaldi, she received daily between four and seven. She was interested in the author of *That Lass o' Lowrie's*, if not in the author of *Little Lord Fauntleroy*. She had often stayed with the rich and philanthropic Fords at Adel Grange near Leeds, who were much concerned with the conditions of women employed in the mills. Just the year before,

Emily Ford had taken her to visit a night-school, which had been started by the Fords, very like the one started by Paul Grace in Frances' book. "The wealth of her ideas when she develops a theory makes her so elaborate as to be difficult to follow," Lady Ponsonby remarked of Vernon Lee. But her stimulating company was just what Frances needed at this point, when too many of the people she met did little more than coo over Lord Fauntleroy.

His admirers were legion and among them Gladstone, who was visiting Florence that winter. James had recently called him "a dreary incubus", mouthing platitudes. Frances found his words delightful. Would she have found them quite so delightful if they had been spoken by the grocer in Washington? In theory Frances was a passionate egalitarian. It had been her great strength, her concern for the people, the poor. R. H. Stoddard, writing an essay in the *Critic* in 1881, had praised her for "profound sympathy with and intimate knowledge of what English statisticians call the lower classes". And certainly Frances continued to be always interested in ordinary people; but she was becoming more and more often seduced by labels and titles. For Henry James, Wilde might be fatuous and Gladstone dreary; to Frances their glamour and fame made them both inevitably delightful.

The Prime Minister had apparently asked his friend Janet Ross if she knew Mrs Burnett; he wanted to meet her. Accordingly, just as James had been the winter before, Frances was invited to the villa at Castagnolo. James had described Mrs Ross as "an odd mixture of the British female and the dangerous woman—a Bohemian with rules and accounts". Certainly she was a lion-hunter. Frances sat next to Gladstone at lunch. He had strong views about education and asked her what she was doing with her boys. "Don't give them too many modern languages," he said. "They are excellent tools for work but a man needs something more than the things that are merely useful. I hold he should be given the ability to understand and appreciate the old classic wonders which will help him to make his mind beautiful and develop his poetic powers. We are too utilitarian in these days. Let them learn their modern languages but give them the classics too."

Frances described the meeting to Kitty Hall:

I find Prime Ministers agree with me. He is a fascinating old man, and said the most lovely things. Fauntleroy has charmed him—he told me he believed the book would have great effect in bringing about added good feeling between the two nations and making them understand each other. He and Mrs Gladstone and his son and two daughters and the Duchess of Sermoneta went out to the villa—which is seven or eight miles from Florence—in the train, which, finding itself overweighted with the Irish Question and so much Statesmanship, promptly broke down about two miles away from the house, landing the party in the road—at least, placing them there.

I am not fond of trains, and had driven out in a victoria with two horses, and so my carriage went to pick them up—all of them it could carry—the rest came in Mrs Ross' donkey cart. Afterwards I took Mr and Mrs Gladstone home and it was a lovely drive. He was very much agitated because he thought they had taken possession of my carriage—and so was Mrs Gladstone. They were quite insubordinate at first and wanted to sit in the back seat, but I tucked myself into it and coaxed and beguiled them and related suitable anecdotes until they were soothed and resigned, and at the end of the drive he said, "I will no longer feel remorse, Mrs Burnett, I will only blush a little," and, of course, I replied, "Then you will be very wicked—to blush at having given a pleasure." Mrs Gladstone is coming to see me and she asked me to let them know when I arrive in London.

But there is no record of any further meeting. Frances returned to London much earlier than she had expected, and in circumstances which made it difficult to follow up even an acquaintance with the Prime Minister.

Frances joked about the situation but her blood was boiling. She had had an obsequious, flattering letter from a man signing himself E. V. Seebohm, who had made a play from *Little Lord Fauntleroy*. "I sincerely trust," he wrote, "that I have written nothing that could cast a slur on one of the most beautiful stories it has ever been my pleasure to read." His compliments cut no ice with Frances. It had been bad enough when unauthorized plays had been made from *That Lass* and "Editha's Burglar", but *Little Lord Fauntleroy*, her most valuable property, had to be fought for. She wrote to Owen Lankester:

> 50 Lung'Arno Nuovo,
> Florence, 1887

Benevolent Giant:

Do something for me—I am a distracted little person—A thief has quietly dramatized Fauntleroy and I am engaged in fierce battle with him. A large young woman—possibly your size—is to play Cedric. Figuerez vous! Figurativi! (French and Italian ensembles. It is *so* difficult to speak English.)

Accidente! Brutta bestia! Some of that is swearing. I am very proud of it. Madonna Mia! O, Signore!—What I wish you to do is to be present at the first night of that play—if it has not yet been done—and take with you some other intelligent mind and feeling heart and then write to me in your most powerful language.

The brigand, whose name is Seebohm, *knew* he was doing a miserable, dishonest thing, and knew I thought myself protected by the "All rights reserved" on the title-page. He kept his plan most discreetly secret until he was ready and it was too late for me to hurry my play and secure myself—and then he calmly informed me that he had "dramatized my charming book". Then, letters and telegrams and general excitement. Then I think he realized that he was in a rather glaringly ugly position and that public opinion would be against him, and after having told me I couldn't help myself, etc. etc. he finally telegraphed that he would give me half profits if I would sanction.

But I will not sanction any profits if my dear little boy is spoiled. Will you go and see? Take your dear "Mamma"—yes, your dear *Mamma*—in the midst of my agitation I pause to defy you. Oh! yes, and if you can allure the gentleman whom I loved in secret last summer—but whose cherished name I have unfortunately forgotten—the one with the nice eyes and the lovely demeanor—the one who was molto bellino-er than you—you will be able to pick him out by that, because there could not possibly be more than one. His opinion, combined with *yours*—would decide anything for me …

… Now I must dress and go and call on a Duchess, to whom I have owed a call for two weeks. She probably won't let me in when I arrive, though she is a very nice duchess. You know the one I told you about, who may call the King "Cousin".

I want to be a duchess myself. I think it would be nice.

Addio, Illustrissimo Signor

It was a joke, of course. She would never have written like that to Vernon Lee. She would never have spoken like that to the boys. But in one way it was true. How delightful it would be to be a Duchess … But if she couldn't be a Duchess, she could at least, thanks to her books, pay calls on them, not too effusively or enthusiastically ("I have owed a call for two weeks"). And she could write about them too.

But now Frances had to concentrate all her energies on saving Lord Fauntleroy from the pirates. If it meant changing the law, then the law must be changed. In the letter to Dr Lankester, she seems mainly concerned about whether Seebohm has ruined her creation in dramatizing it, whether he has spoiled her "dear little boy". But the more she thought about it, the more she resented his action. Why should he have even half the profits? The difficulty was that Seebohm was technically acting perfectly legally as the law stood at that time. He came to Florence to try to persuade her to let him go ahead, but she had just left on 12th March. He followed her and they met briefly on the railway station at Turin. It was their only meeting. Frances refused to accept any of his suggestions for collaboration and profit sharing. He hurried back to launch his play before Frances had a chance to produce a rival version.

If we are to believe Vivian (who with Lionel was left in Italy in Kitty Hall's care) Frances travelled to England "with her companion Miss Chiellini and a generous supply of manuscript paper, pencils and ink", and started her dramatization on the train. A good proportion of it was apparently done when she arrived in London. She had decided not only to see for herself what Seebohm had written but to follow it up as rapidly as possible with *The Real Little Lord Fauntleroy*.

Seebohm's play was produced at the Prince of Wales Theatre, London on 23rd February 1888. Frances was already in consultation with Kaye and Guedalla, a firm of solicitors recommended by the Lankesters. The case, with Warne, the English publishers, named as plaintiffs, was heard in the Chancery Division of the High Court of Justice on 2 March. Not all the press comment was entirely favourable. The *Era*, the stage paper, said: "If Mrs Burnett thought that *Little Lord Fauntleroy* was worth preserving for the adaptor, why did she not secure it in the legal way? A copyright performance can be easily done for about £30, a mere trifle to a successful lady novelist." Surely, they said, she could not really have believed herself protected by ALL RIGHTS RESERVED on the title-page? "We are not inclined to take a sentimental view of the grievances of adapted novelists, who get an excellent advertisement, by the way, out of the fuss over their sufferings. But we are willing to wax as indignant as their most enthusiastic champion could desire at the existing state of the law … Why do the novelists not all 'pull together', agitate fiercely and get the law altered?" But Seebohm lost any sympathy there might have been for him by claiming that his play was only "suggested" by Mrs Burnett's book, whereas it turned out that plot, characters and dialogue had all been lifted bodily.

The novelists did not "pull together" to get the law altered. Frances—with her solicitors and counsel—did it on her own.

The plaintiffs decided to base their case on an infringement of the Copyright Act of 1842, which forbade the making of copies of copyright material. Seebohm had admitted the existence of four copies of the play, one of which had been deposited at the office of the Lord Chamberlain. The play contained large chunks taken directly from the novel. A previous case (Reade *v.* Conquest) had held that the mere representation on the stage of a play did not infringe the Copyright Act, "but representation was one thing and copying another". Seebohm might have the right, under the law as it stood, to represent the novel on the stage; but he had no right to make copies of any parts of the book.

The case showed the law to be an ass. "It being granted that it was not illegal to dramatize the story of another person, could it be contended that for this purpose the dramatizer could not write a single copy of his play without infringing copyright in the story—but must commit the whole to memory and impart it to the actors by word of mouth?" Defendant's counsel could not believe this was reasonable.

Mr Justice Stirling, in giving judgment, said a lot of the play had been extracted almost verbatim from the book—more than one quarter of the lines in the first act alone. "I think that what has been done and is intended to be done by the defendant constitutes an infringement of the plaintiffs' legal rights no less than if the defendant had published his play. I grant a perpetual injunction to restrain the defendant from multiplying copies of his play. The plaintiffs further insist on an order directing the delivery up of the existing copies of the play ... the costs of the action must be paid by the defendant."

Victory was total. It was not possible for a play to be licensed unless a copy was lodged with the Lord Chamberlain, and unauthorized dramatists would no longer be able to lodge copies with the Lord Chamberlain. Judgment was delivered on 10th May and Frances' own play was ready to open on 14th May at Terry's Theatre.

Wilson Barrett "is doing everything for me," Frances had written to Kitty in Florence, "and reads the play as I write it ...

Yesterday he brought me a mechanical tin cart to play with." Madge Kendal agreed to produce it and an excellent cast was assembled, many of whom were later to become well known. Dearest, for instance, was played by Winifred Emery, the Earl of Dorincourt by Alfred Bishop and Mr Havisham by Brandon Thomas, the author of *Charley's Aunt*. Vera Beringer, who played Cedric, was then nine years old. Years later (she died only in 1971) she recalled:

> I played the part between six and seven hundred times—and with what a wonderful cast ...
>
> Little Lord Fauntleroy was a real person to me. I loved him dearly, and it was a daily joy to go down to the theatre for each performance and "be Cedric", as I used to say.
>
> It was an amazing time for any child—a time of success, of spoiling, of triumph; but somehow it was more connected in my childish mind with Fauntleroy than with myself. I remember so vividly the first performance of all, at Terry's Theatre, when Mrs Burnett sat in a stage box, and in her enthusiasm flung me her immense bouquet of pink roses. Such an exciting thing had of course never happened to me before, and I remember saying, "thank you" in a burst of gratitude, whereupon she replied, "Bless the child, and she did not forget a single word!"

Frances had the pleasure of taking Vera up to the box to meet the Prince of Wales and Princess Alexandra, when they came to see the play. Vera was worried whether she should curtsey or bow to royalty. It would seem odd to curtsey in black velvet knickerbockers. Fortunately the royal pair solved the problem by kissing her. "Mrs Burnett," said Vera, "occupied a rather odd position in my small mind. I looked on her as a kind of relation of Lord Fauntleroy's and consequently I had for her the same sort of affection I had for Cedric himself."

The Times of 15th May was enthusiastic. "*The Real Little Lord Fauntleroy* proved to be in all respects superior to the pirated version, which Mr Seebohm has been restrained from performing. It reflects in a great measure the fresh, delicate, exquisitely pretty sentiment of the book ... the piece is exceptionally well-acted." William Archer in the London *World* of 23rd May agreed that the new Fauntleroy was in every way better than the pseudo-Fauntleroy. "Mrs Burnett shows herself a true poet though her Pegasus may be a rocking-horse." He praised Frances for taking her case to the courts. "Novelists need no longer fear to see their brain-children kidnapped, distorted and sent forth to pick up pence for the kidnapper in the theatrical highways and byways." In celebration of her achievement, Frances appeared as one of the few women in an impressive volume of portrait-photographs called *Men and Women of the Day*. But it was another photograph, taken by Barrauds of Oxford Street on the same occasion, which pleased Frances more. For once she thought the likeness "really excellent", so it gives us a good idea of how she liked to think she looked: intelligent, thoughtful, a little quizzical and severe, not "fluffy" at all.

On 11th July, Lewis Carroll (seeing himself as the Aged, Aged Man) was at Paddington Station to meet Isa Bowman, who was to appear later in the year in the operetta version of *Alice in Wonderland*. That afternoon they saw *Little Lord Fauntleroy* and Carroll commemorated the occasion in a frivolous journal:

> Little Vera Beringer was the Little Lord Fauntleroy. Isa would have liked to play the part but the Manager at the theatre did not allow her, as she did not know the words, which would have made it go off badly. Isa liked the whole play very much: the passionate old Earl and the gentle mother of the little boy and the droll Mr Hobbs and all of them.

The boys, with Kitty Hall, rejoined their Dearest in the house she had taken at Regent's Park West. Frances was working on a short novel, *The Pretty Sister of José*, which she had begun in Florence. It is a mystery why she chose to set a book in Spain, where she had never been, rather than in Italy, where she was writing. It is a conventionally romantic story about a self-willed girl who scorns love, even that of everyone's hero, the dashing bull-fighter, Sebastiano, until the moment when he leaves Madrid and she realizes she has loved him without knowing it. There is a passing nod to progressive thought: "She was a Spanish girl and not so far in advance of her age that the terrible features of the pastime going on before her could obscure its brilliancy and excitement." For the most part, the story is rich in the stage properties of Spain—the fans and guitars, the jasmine, the roses and the grapevines—and poor in any feeling of reality.

It was difficult for Frances to work on something new when everyone was talking about Fauntleroy—not just the success of the play but also the significance of the judgment of the courts. All questions of copyright were in the air. Two years before, Frances had been one of forty-five writers who had contributed open let-ters to the *Century*, demanding international copyright. All classes of literary workmen, they said "still endure the disadvantages of a market drugged with stolen goods". "A right to the control and the protection of the products of one's brain", it seemed to Frances, could not be questioned. In this summer of 1888, the Society of Authors decided to give a dinner "in honour of American men and women of letters now in England", partly to thank them for their efforts on behalf of international copyright. Henry James, who was invited to be one of the guests of honour, took strong exception to the whole affair. He had an aversion to public dinners anyway ("I *can't* come to a thing of speeches," he once wrote to Vernon Lee) but this one seemed to him a particularly ill-judged occasion. He wrote to Edmund Gosse, one of the committee: "To give American authors a dinner when the Copyright Bill is *not* passed—mon cher ami, y-pensez-vous?" It would be torture for him to attend it. "The dearest wish of my heart—it is really what, as a literary man, I live for—is the coming to pass of such relations between the two countries as that the copyright matter shall be but a drop in the deep bucket of their harmony." James Russell Lowell was still in London at this point: James said that Lowell was shy about attending, "not at all wishing to be publicly thanked for having, as yet, achieved nothing at all". However, Lowell turned up and so, of course, did Frances. After all, she *had* achieved something and she was very happy to be thanked for it.

The Times records that the dinner was held at the Criterion Restaurant on 25th July. Mr Bryce, M.P., presided and there were present, among others, Mr J. Russell Lowell, Mrs F. Hodgson Burnett, Mr Wilkie Collins, Mr Jerome K. Jerome, Lord Brabourne, Mr E. Gosse, the Master of the Temple, Mr Rider Haggard and Mr Walter Besant. Lord Tennyson telegraphed warmest greetings to "our American guests". Lowell made a splendid speech in reply to the toast "Literature". It was interspersed with cheers and laughter and Hear Hears. On the subject of International Copyright he said, "I am not so sure that our American publishers were so much more wicked than their English brethren would have been if they had had the chance." He remembered that his old friend and neighbour, Longfellow, had once invited him to eat a game pie with him, "the only honorarium he had ever received from this country for reprinting his works".

Frances was presented with a magnificent diamond bracelet inscribed "To Frances Hodgson Burnett, with the gratitude of British Authors". There was a diamond ring to match and a parchment scroll, illuminated with the names of those who had helped to make the gift. "The under-mentioned Men and Women of Letters desire to express to Mrs Frances Hodgson Burnett their appreciation of the great service they believe she has rendered to British Authors by so strongly attracting public attention to the unsatisfactory condition of Copyright Law in England…" Eighty-four writers associated themselves with the address and the "accompanying Souvenir", including Ralph Abercrombie, Rider Haggard, F. Anstey, George Meredith, Arthur W. Pinero and Oscar Wilde.

"There is no danger of my becoming vain," Frances had written to Gilder in 1877. Eleven years later there was a danger—but not from any recognition at this stage from her admired Henry James. "The incorporated society of authors"—he wrote to R. L. Stevenson, "I belong to it and so do you, I think, but I don't know what it is—gave a dinner the other night to American literati to thank them for praying for international copyright. I carefully forebore to go, thinking the gratulation premature, and I see by this morning's *Times* that the banquetted boon is further off than ever."

After the banquet, Frances took the boys off for a holiday at Joss Farm, St Peter's, on the Isle of Thanet. It was an attractive place—a rambling, ivy-clad cottage and a tousled garden full of lavender and phlox, amid cornfields sloping down to white chalk cliffs above the English Channel. Frances bought blue and white cretonne in the village shop at sixpence a yard and made the sitting-room resplendent. She hung white muslin curtains in "the queer low-roofed dining-room" and put turkey-red cotton on the chairs. She walked in the fields with her arms full of poppies and listened to the skylarks. But not for long. Plans were going ahead for the American production of *Little Lord Fauntleroy*. It was to open in Boston and then move to New York for the winter season. It was time she returned.

Before leaving from Liverpool, Frances visited Manchester as guest of honour at a reception given by the Manchester Arts Club. Both *That Lass o' Lowrie's* and *Little Lord Fauntleroy*, they told her, were "distinguished by a broad humanity". Mrs Burnett "had conferred, by her genius and her various works, honour upon Manchester". *Little Lord Fauntleroy* "had done an immense amount of good in raising the character of human nature throughout the English speaking race". ("Hear, hear.") Frances told them how delighted she was to be in her native city after so many years. Then there followed an impromptu concert. Fortunately, Miss Dawson, of Rhodes, near Middleton, "a vocalist of considerable ability", was present.

Frances reached the United States—after sixteen months away—on board the steamer *City of New York*, with Lionel, Vivian and her secretary, "Signorina Chiellini, a beautiful Florentine", as the papers put it. She found the newspapers full not only of the success of her play, which had opened at the Boston Museum Theater on 10th September, but also of the death of E.V. Seebohm, which seemed to be subsequent to that success. The journal *Spirit of the Times* reported the story like this:

> Last week, when the news of the immense success of the author's version of *Little Lord Fauntleroy* at the Boston Museum reached New York, a young Englishman committed suicide, at the Hoffman House. He had been known as Lawrence Herbert, had talked much about the chances of English dramatists in this country, and had expended all his money. On the London tailor's tab in the pocket of his overcoat was written the name of E. V. Seebohm. It will be remembered that Mr Seebohm dramatized *Little Lord Fauntleroy* in London, and was stopped by an injunction. He then left England for a tour round the world. The identity of the suicide was much discussed by the daily papers. Cablegrams were received describing Mr Seebohm's appearance. Now it is claimed by the *Herald* that a great detective feat has been accomplished in the discovery, that Mr Seebohm was the suicide. A greater detective feat would have been the discovery that the suicide was not Mr Seebohm, but that somebody else had killed himself in Mr Seebohm's coat.

Frances was mobbed by reporters on the docks. "You want me to talk about Mr Seebohm," she said, "and I do not want to talk of him, now that he is supposed to be dead ... From my brief acquaintance, I should not imagine that he was a man to commit suicide. It is much easier for me to believe that he was murdered even than that he should have destroyed himself." It was an unpleasant business; she did not let herself dwell on it.

She despatched the boys to their father in Washington. Lionel was now fourteen and Vivian twelve and they were well able to travel alone. She went herself immediately to the Halls' home in

Boston. She found waiting for her a letter from Elsie Leslie, the child who was playing Fauntleroy, and replied at once, telling her to look out the following night for a little lady in a yellow brocade dress in one of the boxes. She told her about the boys and how they had always called their mother "Dearest". "That was why I made Fauntleroy call his mother so." Elsie Leslie was an extraordinary child; everyone was agreed on that. She had had her seventh birthday only the month before Fauntleroy opened. She was already a veteran actress but was unspoiled and natural to a remarkable degree. Mark Twain wrote *The Prince and the Pauper* for her and embroidered her a slipper (William Gillette made the other one). He used to work on it on trains during his lecture tours "and was in danger of being put off as a raving lunatic".

Frances was delighted with Elsie's performance and with the production: the settings were more lavish than in London. Indeed, everyone was delighted with it. Oliver Wendell Holmes, nearly eighty and much honoured, wrote from his house on Beacon Street: "We had a most delightfully memorable evening, though we were all crying like babies half the time. The tears that will not flow for real grief will sometimes come unbidden at the call of the writer of fiction who knows the human heart, and has access to its hidden fountains. You should be very happy, for what mother ever had such a darling child as your dear little Lord Fauntleroy? And to think that he was not born to die, or to grow out of his beauty and infinite charm, like the poor little creatures of flesh and blood all around us."

A long review in the *Boston Transcript* of 11th September agreed with Holmes. "It is a play for moist eyes, even in its comic parts … A susceptible person will hardly get the tears down out of his throat through the whole piece." The great majority of the first-night audience were watching to see how closely the play followed the book. They had all read it; half of them had read it twice. And they were not disappointed: Elsie Leslie is a "remarkable child … Her acting is thoroughly natural … and her full-faced rosy beauty helps to make her Fauntleroy the more real—a distinct advantage when it is considered that the slightest touch of pallor and fragility would turn this impossible little lord into a pure idealization ... We should say that, unless the development of the fishery troubles should bring the public too much into sympathy with the views of Mr Hobbs and diminish the taste for representations of the British aristocracy, this play will have a long and successful run." In Boston the theatre was always full; Frances received nearly eight hundred dollars a week from it.

The only critical voices were those of some "prominent people" in Boston who complained to the Society for the Prevention of Cruelty to Children that Elsie was "much overworked". T.H. French of Samuel French and Co, who were to put the play on at the Broadway Theatre, wrote to Elsie's mother saying the child must have a week's rest between the Boston run and the New York rehearsals and that, on arrival in New York, she should be "examined by the said society". It was also arranged that Tommy Russell (nephew of Annie Russell, who had played Esmeralda) was to share the part with Elsie. She was to play six times a week and Tommy on Wednesday afternoons and Saturday nights. French was enormously conciliatory to Frances. She wrote to Kitty Hall from the Grand Hotel in New York: "It appears that I am to have all I want—do all I want—rule the earth—for this matter everything is to be subservient to my royal will. 'This' I say 'appears'. '*Just* as you please, Mrs Burnett—*all* that you wish ...' Every actor is to do exactly as I wish. Let us hope it will turn out so.

The first night in New York was on 3rd December 1888 and the success in London and Boston was repeated. It was now that the fashion for Little Lord Fauntleroy suits boomed. All over America, reluctant small boys were forced by their mothers into black velvet suits with lace collars and other outfits based on Cedric's clothes. In Davenport, Iowa, an eight-year-old burned down his father's barn in protest at being dressed as Little Lord Fauntleroy. In Worcester, Massachusetts, a boy traded his suit for some old patched clothes belonging to a gypsy. In New York it was reported that Stephen Crane gave money to two small boys and sent them to have their curls cut off; one mother went into hysterics, the other fainted. When I was in Washington in 1970, an old woman, at the mention of the name Frances Hodgson Burnett, recalled a family story. Her mother had ordered two of the suits for her brother. He hated them so much he stuffed them in the coal cellar. The mother was furious: "Just you wait till your father comes home …" But when the father returned, he took the boy's part. Irving Cobb, in his fictionalized memories of his childhood, published in 1924, gives an exaggeratedly graphic account in a chapter called "Little Short Pantsleroy": "A mania was laying hold on the mothers of the nation. It was a mania for making over their growing sons after the likeness of a beatific image. *Little Lord Fauntleroy* infected thousands of the worthy matrons of America with a catching lunacy, which raged like a sedge fire and left enduring scars upon the seared memories of its chief sufferers—their sons, notably between the ages of seven and eleven." Mrs Custer, the mother in Cobb's book, had imagined that clothes could convert her unsatisfactory son into a Fauntleroy, charming, courteous, thoughtful. "It was the mistake of many another baffled mother."

It was not only in America that the fashion caught on. Compton Mackenzie recalled "that confounded Little Lord Fauntleroy craze, which led to my being given as a party dress the Fauntleroy costume of black velvet and Vandyke collar … the other boys at the dancing class were all in white tops [sailor suits]". Sir Adrian Boult recorded that the fashion was still raging, "when I was first conscious, somewhere, I suppose, about 1894 or '95". In Russia, Elizaveta Fen wished for curly hair like Cedric's and wore a boy's black velvet suit and a black velvet hat with a big feather. "People stared when I rode through the village. This rather embarrassed me, but I enjoyed it all the same."

It was not only Fauntleroy clothes which sold; there were Fauntleroy playing-cards, Fauntleroy writing-paper and toys and models of every sort, wooden, plaster, clockwork and chocolate.

There was even a perfume named after him. In December Scribner reported to Frances the extraordinary continuing demand for the book: "It surpasses all our expectations." All the publishers and theatre managers in America wanted her to write for them. A New York syndicate offered fifteen thousand dollars for a serial. A publisher suggested she went round the world in a yacht "to write letters from strange lands for children". "A certain newspaperman has offered me," Frances wrote to Owen Lankester, "four hundred dollars a month if I will let him come to me one day a week to *talk* over a special department, which is to be devoted to children. I am to do nothing but give my ideas. Would you give a hundred dollars a day merely to talk to me? No, base ingrate, you would not. And, yet, where do you find conversation like mine?"

Not everyone was equally charmed by Frances' conversation. One newspaper said she seemed to be able to talk about nothing but "shopping, dress, her feelings, a recipe for chapped lips and like subjects". A number of reporters, to whom Frances had refused interviews, had their revenge by publishing highly critical articles. Frances was beginning to become very wary of the press. They were always getting things wrong, and the more she refused to see reporters, the more inaccurate were the stories they published. In *Fauntleroy* itself, she gives an amusing account of the different versions in the papers of the affair of the rival claimant. "One paper described ... Cedric as an infant in arms, another as a young man at Oxford." As for the claimant's mother, "sometimes she was a gypsy, sometimes an actress, sometimes a beautiful Spaniard". Mr Hobbs used to read the papers until his head was in a whirl. He never knew what to believe.

Similarly we never know what to believe when we read the descriptions of Frances in the papers of the period. "Like all children of genius, Mrs Frances Hodgson-Burnett is eccentric and, as the altitude of her almost phenomenal successes heightens, the scope of her vagaries widens until her friends liken her to a sort of modern Galatea. She belongs to the steadily increasing society of grass widows and the fact that marriage with her has been a

failure may account for some of her harsh treatment of women."
When Wilson Barrett returned to England after an American
tour, this paper claimed "Mrs Burnett gave herself up to despair
and would not be comforted". But her eccentricity seemed to
consist mainly in the wearing of Kate Greenaway-style dresses
in vivid colours "with mitts of stocking length, her hair frizzed
about her head like a misfit halo".

The *Boston Transcript* kindly suggested she might rest on her
laurels and enjoy, as she obviously did, being lionized by the "cul-
tured circles of Boston". But the *Literary News* (February 1889)
regretted that Frances was leading the life of her own Bertha
Amory. "She now longs more to impress upon the world her
personal magnetism, brilliant conversational talents and fascinating 'woman's way', than to retire from publicity, work hard, study
and acquire fresh, unused material which she might put into a
work that would live after her pretty, reddish-brown hair is white
and all her original and often outré costumes have been gossiped
about, admired, condemned and worn out … All careful readers,
who twenty years ago felt the fresh talent that had come into the
world of fiction and steadily and proudly watched their prophe-
cies of success and good work fulfilled year by year, are saddened
to think that for three years past Mrs Burnett's reputation rests
more upon a shrewd legal battle, a success in frivolous society and
the little details of her habits of life that now so freely float around
in the papers, than upon any one piece of work calling forth her
matured and practised hand. We will not yet give up hope of a
writer who has shown so much imagination and industry. Perhaps
… something will happen to make Mrs Burnett will to write a
book worthy to be placed even ahead of *That Lass o' Lowrie's* …
and *Through One Administration*."

These were stern words and near enough to the bone to give
Frances considerable pause. Was it true that she was talking too
much and not living enough within herself? It was always the
danger for a writer who had seen success. It was to be another
seven years before she published her next full-scale adult novel;

more than ten before she published one which could stand up beside the two books named. She had worked so hard for so many years; now that the need for it was over, with money flowing in from the play and the book of *Fauntleroy*, it was so much easier to amuse herself. She could not stop writing; she could not write seriously. If she had listened, she might have heard the words she had given Bertha Amory sounding a warning:

You find us very flippant and trivial. That is how we strike you!

After I have been out a great deal—I wonder. But I know I could not be serious, if I tried.

I thought I enjoyed living on the surface.

Sometimes I have been so tired of the feverish, restless way we have of continually amusing ourselves, as if we dare not stop.

One must be amused.

She wrote to the boys in Washington to tell them of the success of the New York first night. The people shouted and shouted for her and she went out twice with Elsie and each time the curtains had to be raised twice. "Elsie is a dear child and we are very fond of each other. She has a flat in the house I am in and she comes to see me every day and calls me Dearest." But Frances said that she longed "to be home in quiet Washington—I am tired of noise and rattle".

At some moment between the Boston and New York productions, she had managed to rush down to Washington and buy a house. She spent Christmas in the K Street house, repaired after the fire, where Swan had lived his lone life during the eighteen months of her absence. But early in 1889 they moved—Swan as well—to a twenty-two-roomed house at 1770 Massachusetts

Avenue, "the most beautiful avenue in Washington". On 31st January, Frances wrote to Scribner: "I have been so busy with workmen of all kinds and with the new play I am writing, which is to be produced shortly, that I have not had a moment even to think of the new book."

She had bought dark carved furniture, rich rugs, brocades and tapestries in New York. She was as interested in matching things, in the colour schemes, "as if it were a doll's house". One room was all in a deep "crushed strawberry" colour; her Den was "golden yellow and golden brown and crimson, the nasturtium colours". But she was not to spend much time in it. By February she was away again, for there survives a good letter from twelve-year-old Vivian, dated 9th February 1889:

Dear Mama [not "Dearest", for he was feeling justifiably aggrieved],

I am very glad to have written to you but I am very sorry you will not write to me. This, I think, is the third letter I have written without receiving one from you. Please tell me the reason. Lionel and I are having fine times with Henery Valentine printing cards, a specimen of which I enclose. We are doing a great deal of printing: printing cards, advertisements etc. Henery Valentine is our canvassing agent, he goes to the people's houses and shows them specimens of our work which generally makes them order some cards. One man had found a business card and came to our house and asked for the printers. He was a very good costumer as he gave us an order for two hundred cards, for which we charged him one dollar and twenty-five cents. We have had other costumers, paying costumers to but none payed as much as he. Lionel, in his relations to the *Post*, managed to scrape together a great deal of work. The old press that you gave us Christmas before last is the one we print with. There is one thing that has survived a year under our rough treatment. We have been writing compositions in school all this week. Miss Morgan says that she is surprised at the way the school spells. Mr Powell the school suprintendent, seems to be

very much intrested in our school, especially in the compositions.
Miss Morgan reminded me last night that she had received a letter
from you and that she was going to answer it. This letter is for Liza
and you and I hope she and you will forgive the combination. I
hope you are getting well although I have no means of knowing.
Now I will say goodnight and with many kisses.

V.B.

"I hope you are getting well although I have no means of knowing." It sounds as if Frances had gone back to Boston again, in
search of mind-healing, or to get away from Swan. "When one
is ill, nothing one does or leaves undone is of any special significance." On 6th March, Lisa Chiellini, writing to thank Scribner
for a cheque for $7,276.61 (six months' sales), said that Mrs
Burnett was "seriously ill". It was much easier to be ill and run
away. The huge house on Massachusetts Avenue was a monument
to her worldly success, just as Jem Haworth's had been. *Fauntleroy*
was still running in both London and New York and netting her
one thousand five hundred dollars a week. But the dust-covers
were over the furniture in her splendid new rooms. What use was
a bedroom with pink roses and loops of ribbon without love?

If she had longed for quiet Washington, when she had it she
did not want it. Lionel chose to stay there with his father. But in
the early spring of 1889, Frances returned, with Vivian and Lisa
Chiellini, to London.

Death and the Doctor
1889–1892

In Manchester, the previous autumn, Frances had visited the Hadfields, with whom she had always kept in touch. Two of the daughters, her old teachers but no longer teaching, were running a boarding-house without a great deal of success. Now, with her Fauntleroy money, Frances really could play the Fairy Godmother rôle: she felt blessed by one herself. Now she could wave wands and change people's circumstances. She took a lease of 44 Lexham Gardens, just off the Cromwell Road. It had four stories, plus attics and basement, a pillared portico and a view down the length of a rectangle of grass, bordered by plane trees. She furnished it from Liberty's and handed it over to the Hadfields to run, with Frances herself as their star boarder.

There were others who needed her help. She wrote to Owen Lankester from an address in Oxford Street, Manchester:

> I found my poor little cousins of the "unfortunate family" need-ing my attention very, very much. When I look at their poor little shabby clothes and their poor little shabby house and see how they live and then reflect that I disdain the second best box at the theatre and that my simplest garment must be running over with lace and tied with satin ribbons, I feel as if I was a criminal. They are such good little things—and you know I am such a bad little

thing—and yet, it was I who was given a gift which makes my life a brilliant, successful thing and gives me a thousand friends on every side ... The contrast is too strong and I keep saying to myself, "Why did *you* deserve to be the one blessed by the Fairy Godmother? Why should you have everything and they nothing?"—because I have everything—but one thing. I feel as if I want to devote every moment to them, to change their lives somehow, to sweep away the cobwebs and let in the sunshine and make things more hopeful.

You can't think how poor they are and what a dreary place they live in. I want to find a brighter house for them and I have been walking hours, looking in clean little streets at tiny bay windows, and I have also been buying all sorts of things—none of which you would have lectured and berated me for buying, I am sure.

"I have everything—but one thing." It was impossible to have all three: love, admiration and money. Frances never really made up her mind which she valued most. At this point, she had a great deal of admiration and a great deal of money, but love was elusive. She could win it perhaps with good deeds. But in spite of this feeling that she wanted to devote every moment to the unfortunate family, she did not stay in Manchester for long. She soon installed herself comfortably in Lexham Gardens to enjoy the London season. There were all sorts of attractive invitations— to festivities looked forward to with almost as much eagerness as the long-ago parties in Islington Square. Surely this dinner, this reception, would make her really feel at last that she was at the Party.

There were also rehearsals of her new play *Phyllis* "a domestic drama", which opened at the Globe Theatre on 1st July 1889. It was not a success, this adaptation of her novel *The Fortunes of Philippa Fairfax*. Clement Scott in *The Times* condemned its construction. Even worse, the actors forgot their lines at the first performance and ruined the final act. It was a pity they forgot so many, Scott said, for those they did remember were quite good.

The Spirit of the Times in New York, commenting on the London production, was even more scathing: Mrs Burnett "should let experienced dramatists do this sort of work for her while she writes more stories. It is quite as absurd for her to make her own plays as it would be for her to make her own dresses. They do not fit and what she saves in wages she loses in time."

Frances was hurt. But if she needed admiration and flattery to salve her wounds, there was plenty available. She began seeing a great deal of the young man she had first met at the Grosvenor Gallery two years before—the young man whose nice eyes and lovely demeanour she had recalled in a letter to Owen Lankester. His name was Stephen Townesend and his story was also one well calculated to appeal to the Fairy Godmother in Frances. "You know my forte," she once said to her sister, Edith, "is to believe in people, not when things are going right for them, but when they are going wrong." So it had been when Swan was penniless and obscure; so now it was with Stephen Townesend.

Stephen had been born on 15th October 1859, almost exactly ten years after Frances. He was the youngest son of the Revd George Fyler Townesend, who had been for the past twenty-seven years Rector of St Michael's, Burleigh Street, Strand. His grandfather was a Canon of Durham Cathedral and one of the founders of Durham University: a considerable theological scholar, a polemicist and a poet, whose entry in the *DNB* is a long and impressive one; his own father was an independent minister. All three of them had published sermons and had been learned and serious gentlemen. Townesend sons were expected to take up a profession, and acting was not considered a suitable one. Stephen's interest in the stage seems to have been aroused when he was a boy at St Paul's School, and Irving and Ellen Terry were occasional visitors at the Rectory. It would have been difficult for Stephen to avoid the influence of the theatre. He was surrounded by theatres. He lived a stone's throw from the Queen's (where Irving and Ellen Terry had acted together for the first time), from the Lyceum, the Savoy, from Drury Lane, from the Royal Opera

House, Covent Garden. But the Rector's son could not go on the stage. It was outrageous, unheard of, impossible.

Frances later described the situation like this: "A strong-willed father and a weak-willed mother made him suffer tortures until he at last gave way." Certainly Stephen's father was strong-willed. There is a portrait of him in Stephen's novel *Dr Tuppy*. ("How clever of Stephen," said his mother. "It's just like George!") Canon Tuppy is a "narrow old Tory and rigid churchman", irascible, eccentric, storming around to Bow Street police station to complain of the language of the costermongers and the braying of the donkeys and of the children who rang his doorbell, in spite of the notice DO NOT RING. Mrs Townesend, like Mrs Tuppy, was undoubtedly weak-willed, but she was "the dearest little woman in the world" and only made Stephen suffer because she could not stand up for him to his father.

Stephen finally agreed to become a medical student but nothing could stop him acting. He and Owen Lankester and eight other students founded the Amateur Dramatic Club of St Bartholomew's Hospital. The first performance, "with a row of candles for footlights", was in January 1883. Stephen was the life and soul of the Club—leading actor, producer, performing original sketches at the Nurses' Meetings. In spite of the diversions, he took his M.R.C.S. in 1883, studied physiology at Edinburgh and became a Fellow of the Royal College of Surgeons in 1887. He went to China as a ship's surgeon, and worked briefly at hospitals in London and Birmingham—all the time nourishing his ambition to become a professional actor. His dislike of the profession he had been forced to take up was accentuated by his fierce opposition to vivisection. ("He insists on discussing it. That's why the chaps rag him so and think he's crazy. Of course, he never ought to have gone in for Medicine …") Stephen's feelings were shared by many, including Queen Victoria, Irving and Ouida, but not by his fellow doctors.

In 1888 Stephen wrote the history of the Bart's Dramatic Club, together "with a few hints to Amateurs on the Art of Acting and Stage Management". It included the following passage:

Every character will generally be found to present at least three phases, all of which have to be sketched to the audience in distinct colours. First, there is the side a man presents to society at large—in his daily intercourse with his fellow men, perhaps he is "Such a charming fellow, you know". Then there is the side he reserves for his family and his closest friends, "Such a bear, my dear". Lastly what he really *is*, to himself and to his God. And what this side of a man is generally only God knows.

Stephen Townesend was to Frances in 1889 and to society at large "a charming fellow". As they became closer, over the years, he was to become far worse than a bear. What he was really like, only God knows. Certainly as Frances observed (at times with sympathy, at others with exasperation), "I never saw a human being with such a self-tormenting, nervous temperament. It is dreadful. He never fails in anything he has to learn, but he always goes through the same process of distrust of himself and wretchedness." It was true all his life.

Stephen was twenty-nine that year. He had had one or two professional engagements but the success he had in the Bart's Dramatic Club eluded him when he appeared in Miss Lytton's Company. He was "embittered and broken by discouragement" according to Frances. It was a very different matter to enter a profession at twenty-nine rather than nineteen. His parents had taken ten years away from him. "They were not consciously bad or heartless people. They were only stupid and selfish." Frances, enraptured by Stephen's charm, determined to help him. She knew so many people in the theatre, surely she could get Stephen on the path to achieving his ambitions. As a start, she would employ him as her business manager.

She was so busy with her plans for Stephen and the delights of the season, that again one of her sons had cause to complain that she had not written. Lionel wrote from Washington: "I have not received a letter from you for about three weeks, but I suppose you have a great deal to do ... Yesterday, Monday, July 8, 1889 was the day of the great prize fight between Sullivan and Kilrain for the championship of the world. Sullivan knocked Kilrain out in seventy-two rounds. I suppose you do not care for prize fights but you can tell Vivian about it."

Vivian was spending much of his time watching cricket at Lord's, though he was occasionally prevailed upon to present a bouquet to a duchess, when accompanying Frances to a garden party. He was thirteen now and still worrying, as he had as a small boy, about the state of the world. He came into Frances' room in Lexham Gardens one day and announced "Dearest, I just wanted to tell you I am a Socialist." He had been reading a book called *Looking Backward* by Edward Bellamy. This book, a probing of the evils of capitalism, was high on the bestseller lists of 1888 and one of the few books which disproved the general picture that the public wanted their reading sweet and light. It fired Vivian with enthusiasm for righting wrongs and injustices. Frances rather unkindly suggested that he could start being a good socialist by hanging up his hat, not leaving his cricket bat in the hall or his tennis racquet on the piano. "You see one of the points is that everyone is to do his own work and not leave any of it for the others to do." But she also told him, "If you are a good socialist, you must remember that gifts are only workman's tools," and that we should never feel superior to those who have fewer gifts than we have.

For all Frances' cracker-barrel wisdom, it was difficult for Vivian to hope for a just world when it was only too clear that, in their world, it was a case of to those that have shall be given. That summer the developers of a new estate called Bellagio, somewhere in Surrey—a collection of bungalows built in a carefully preserved woodland area on the shores of a lake—obviously thinking it would be good publicity for their enterprise, named one of the bungalows "Dorincourt", after the castle in *Fauntleroy*, and presented it to Frances.

Vivian returned to Washington with his father, who had called in briefly on his way home from an international medical congress in Berlin. Frances, Lisa Chiellini and Stephen Townesend moved, when the season was over, into the miniature Dorincourt. Frances invited Owen Lankester to stay—"We need you to make our circle complete"—but he couldn't get away. She wrote to him describing their "horse-breaking" activities:

> I am sitting in the rather tremulous condition attendant upon Mr Townesend's being out taking his ride on Gordon. Gordon is a lovely new horse I have bought, who is considered extremely dangerous by prejudiced persons at the stables. Mr Townesend takes him out mildly but firmly every morning and has always returned with his system underanged so far … Notwithstanding what the grooms say, he does not seem to have trouble with the darling brute when he is driving him, and we have been miles and miles.

The gloomy predictions of the grooms were justified one day when Frances, with the chestnut cob harnessed to the red and black, high two-wheeled trap, set out to meet Stephen at the station on his return from a visit to London. Gordon bolted and threw Frances out of the trap and on to her head. Stephen, worried at not having been met, hired a station hack and came by just in time to see her apparently lifeless body being carried into a nearby house. She had "concussion of the brain and was quite stiff and unconscious from Saturday till Tuesday". As she came round, she kept moaning, "Oh dear! Oh dear!" and thought it was because there was something the boys wanted "which their Dearest could not get for them". It was many days before she was considered fit to be moved to Dorincourt from the house where she had been taken, but she was back in Lexham Gardens in September.

Stephen was constantly beside her, and there were nurses from St Bartholomew's as well. She was deeply depressed—terrified that the awful blow had stunned "the vivid, vital part of her brain that made the stories". Long before she was really well, she tried to put it to the test by propping herself up and scribbling—a page or two at a time—the first act of a new play.

Scribner's London agent, Lemuel Bangs, went to see her about a volume of her *St Nicholas* stories, which they hoped to publish. Lemuel Bangs was a character. Every night at the Garrick Club he could be seen with a pint of champagne. Gerald Duckworth was one of those who called him the "Senator". He had large moustaches and a tremendous wardrobe. On his death it was found to contain, among hundreds of other items, 188 ties, 26 lined fancy waistcoats and 14 overcoats. It was not, then, surprising that the first thing he noted on his visit to Frances was her clothes:

> She looked an exceedingly interesting invalid in a rich and harmonious loose costume, bolstered up with comfortable cushions etc. and was very cordial and pleasant during my long call (two hours or so) ... Evidently she has had the benefit of careful attention and has made wonderful progress but is not yet well, by any means. She enjoyed telling me about her illness, her books, especially associations connected with the stories under consideration and it seemed almost cruel to bother her with business, however she appreciated the necessity of it.

She was to receive a 12½% royalty and an advance of one thousand pounds on publication day. There was "no written agreement as she could not sign it, even if it had been necessary". It was strange she could talk for two hours but not sign her name.

The new book, to be called *Little Saint Elizabeth and Other Stories*, was to be uniform with *Fauntleroy* and *Sara Crewe*. "The title story is so good," Scribner wrote to Bangs, "it deserves all the success of the others. Mrs Burnett is a very curious customer. She is always 'on the make' and you were very fortunate to come off so easily. It is necessary to burn much incense at her shrine in order to accomplish anything."

During Frances' illness Stephen had become indispensable. He had certainly been prepared to burn a good deal of incense.

How fortunate he was a doctor. For three months, as she put it, he had carried her "concussed brain in his pocket, day and night". He had hardly left her side. By November, seeing no immediate prospects for him on the professional stage, with his patron temporarily unable to help him, he returned to his old stage at Bart's. At the annual general meeting of the Dramatic Club, he was elected stage manager (their term for producer) and appeared in their next production as Shylock in the fourth act of *The Merchant of Venice*. ("Mr Townesend's interpretation of Shylock was highly artistic.") In January he played the part again and also appeared as Puff in the second act of *The Critic*.

The winter was dark and drear. Bangs reported to Scribner in December that London was so foggy that gas light was necessary throughout the day. Frances, by now well enough to travel, left England. After a stay in the South of France, she moved on to Rome. "I wanted to be quiet, so I went to a hotel which an English Roman told me afterwards was 'the oldest, the most respectable and the dullest in Rome'. But that exactly pleased me and I could not be dull with three interesting people with me and all old Rome around me."

One of the interesting people was certainly Lisa Chiellini. She helped Frances deal with the mountains of letters and manuscripts which had piled up during her illness. There was a charge of plagiarism which had appeared in the *St James' Gazette* a few days before her accident. A Miss Winthrop had accused her of copying her *Wilfred*. Now Frances replied that the only things Fauntleroy and Wilfred had in common was that they were both grandsons of earls, and as Miss Winthrop could see from Debrett there are any number of those. A man in Washington who had seen the item in the *Gazette* asked her to submit the two books to a critical expert for a disinterested judgment. If she were maligned, generous justice ought to be done to her. He enclosed credentials from the Governor of Massachusetts and other notables and said "You can determine what you will pay." There were numerous children's stories submitted for her opinion. To the authors of these she replied invariably, "Children might like it." As she said, "One can say that much of any book intended for children. It is civil and not untruthful." There was a facetious letter from Edmund Gosse, commenting on a photograph of her in a literary magazine which seemed to be directing a glance of "withering scorn" at a paragraph about Gosse: "If you feel like that, let us part … O don't look at me like that, or else you will reduce me to some such scarcely human object as poor Stevenson appears below." There were hundreds of letters.

The most interesting were those from the boys, busy in Washington with electricity and printing. Lionel, now fifteen, wrote that he and Vivian were doing everything by electricity: "I light my gas by electricity. If you and Lisa want to get me anything, I want it electric. Anything that has to do with electricity … Will you get Lisa to get me some books on electricity and send them to me, because I like to do experiments. Papa gave me two books on electricity but I have nearly exhausted them …" Besides putting contraptions on the burners to light the gas by sparks, they had wired the Massachusetts Avenue house with burglar alarms so that after they had set the master-switch in their bedroom, a cat could hardly step on the doormat without waking the neighbourhood with the buzzing of bells.

And they were still interested in printing. It was two years since Frances had given them an old press. Their activities the winter before had brought them a fair number of "paying costumers" in Vivian's phrase. Now they wanted to expand their activities. Certainly they had not been brought up to believe that money grew on trees:

> 1770 Massachusetts Avenue,
> February 26, 1890

Dear Mamma:

I want to tell you about something Vivian and I have set our hearts on. Vivian and I have taken to printing a great deal.

We have been printing, I think, since the first part of Jan. and have made quite a little money, besides the pleasure we got out of it. Of course, we did not have all the type and things we wanted, so we had to buy them. I saw an advertisement in a paper of a man who sold presses and things, and so I sent to him for a price list. In this price list there were some printing outfits. One of these I am going to tell you about. It costs quite a large sum, but Vivian and I think we can make enough money with it to pay for it. This is the outfit:

O.K. Rotary Job Press	$100.00
Furniture	2.00
Hand Roller	0.50
Black and Colored inks	2.00
Twelve fonts of type	24.45
Eleven type cases and cabinet	12.00
Leads, bodkin and tweezers	1.50
Six gauge pins and Screw driver	0.60
Mallet, planer and oil can	0.75
Composing stick	1.00
Can of cleaning preparation	0.30
Lead cutter	2.00
Rules, dashes, borders	2.90
	————
	150.00

I know the price of it startles you, but I have a way to get over it. Vivian says that he will give up his bicycle that you said you were going to get us when we came over, and I am willing to do the same, and I think that will make the amount. I think Papa will pay the express for us, which will be quite a good deal, I think.

If you will do it, will you cable yes, for we, of course, want it very much. We have talked with Papa about it and he said that he thought it was very good, but that it cost such a lot. He said he would get it for us if he could afford it.

I send you a little book I printed on the press that was given me
Christmas before last. I call it "Job Lots", because it is composed
of all kinds of poetry. I put in "There was an old man up a tree",
because I know you always laugh at it. I printed the book all by
myself ...

> Your loving son,
> L. BURNETT,
> Job Printer

Needless to say, Frances cabled the money. Vivian and Lionel had
produced the first few issues of a weekly paper when Lionel fell
ill. In the beginning it was thought to be "la grippe", the name
given to an epidemic raging in Washington that winter of 1890.

The news turned Frances pale. Lionel, as Vivian pointed out in
his book, "was high strung, sensitive and emotional and not able
to protect himself very well from the knocks and disappointments
of the world". He found his school work difficult—he was in the
same grade this year as his bright young brother, Vivian, which
could not have been very good for his morale. He was often ill. He
needed his mother but she was never there. He had not seen her
for a year. Frances was stirred by deep feelings of guilt and love.
Of course, her accident had been to blame, she assured herself. If
it had not been for her accident she would surely have returned
home before this. She wrote from Rome, from the dull Hotel
Minerva, reminding Lionel that Dearest thought all the time of
her boys. "I shall send you a cable every now and then to show
you I am near enough to talk to you."

Lionel was fifteen. She had never come to terms with the
boys growing up. She wrote to him as if he were a child of
Fauntleroy's age—a seven-year-old—sending him photographs
of the Carnival at Nice and the ruins of Pompeii, and boxes of
construzione, to cheer him up.

Lionel responded perfectly: "Don't bother about me, darling
Sweet. What I want you to do is to get well, and not to worry
about me. I also want to see you very much, but don't start until

you feel well." He thought he was getting better but he was not. Specialists were consulted. The verdict was "galloping consumption" with no hope of recovery.

Frances sailed from Rome on Easter Day, 1890. Two days later the play which Frances and Stephen had been working on between drives with the chestnut Gordon the previous summer, had its first performance at Terry's Theatre. It was called *Nixie*, and was an adaptation and elongation of the story "Editha's Burglar". It was "very patiently received" according to the *Era* "and at the end some applause brought Mr Townesend to the footlights to offer his acknowledgments and to promise to cable to Mrs Hodgson Burnett news of the favourable verdict". But most of the success was due to "the remarkably clever performance of the little lady entrusted with the title-part", Nixie, "the most precocious child ever brought into this wicked world ... whose pretty prattle caused many a ripple of laughter". Altogether, however, it was a "crude and unsatisfactory concoction" and did not run for long.

But Frances could not worry about that. She arrived in Washington to find Lionel in bed waiting for her, his "cheeks and hands hot with fever". He was dying; but she would not believe it. Her childhood reading had been full of children who died young and beautifully. In *Haworth's*, she had made Janey say, when questioned about her Sunday reading, "It's a nice book an' theer's lots more like it in th'skoo' library—all about Sunday skoo' scholars as has consumption an' th'loike an' reads the bible to foak an' dees." Now Lionel was dying of consumption. He had never been a Sunday-school scholar. His reading had been a manual of electricity and a compositor's handbook, not the Bible. Where, in those, would he find the strength to meet death gladly? Frances had no conviction that he, like the dying children in *East Lynne*, could be "brought to look with pleasure, rather than fear, upon the unknown journey". She determined he should not know the truth. They would look for a cure. In the long, sad journeyings that followed, Lionel did not know that he would never return to the house in Washington. She wrapped him round in make-believe. She could not say, "Yes, you are very ill. You cannot use your cameras or your engines or your bicycle any more. You must lie still and take medicine and peptonoids all day and night. When you travel to different countries you will have a doctor and a trained nurse always with you and your medicine chest will be in the railway carriage. I shall spend a great deal of money for you but I don't know when you will get well." Instead she said, "We will pretend you are the Prince Imperial."

There were possibilities of treatment in America. They spent a few weeks in Atlantic City, a few more in Philadelphia. His condition did not improve. Frances was recommended to take the boy to a sanatorium in Göbersdorf in the pine forests of South Germany. Vivian and Lisa Chiellini travelled with Frances and Lionel. Stephen Townesend and a nurse from St Bartholomew's joined them at Southampton. From Göbersdorf, early in August, Frances wrote to Scribner, "the condition of my poor boy is so hopeless and sad a one that I have no prospect of any near return to America if I can have the heart and courage to return at all. If my boy lives so long, we shall probably winter in Nice or Cannes." But by 22nd August she was in Marienbad. Stephen wrote from there to Scribner acknowledging a royalty cheque for £1,575. Vivian returned from Marienbad to America ready for the new school term. The others took Lionel to Paris, to see yet another specialist, and because "it was too cold at Marienbad and too hot to go to the South of France".

Frances turned the anguished experiences of these months, as she turned all her experiences, into a story, but one she never finished. She has been taken to task for the vulgarity of admiring herself in her fictional form. In "His Friend", Noel's mother is certainly a marvellous woman. She has the strength to accept without flinching the fact that her son is dying. She can act well enough to disguise the truth from the boy. In front of him "it was as if another creature spoke. Her voice was full of cheer and freshly young; there was not a note of pain in it." Every time she sees a new specialist, she hopes; but when finally there is no hope, what she wants from the doctor is help in killing pain and in keeping from the boy the knowledge that he must die. She pledges herself with the help of scientific aids and iron self-control and love to keep the secret. There is no suggestion in the fragment of the story published by Vivian in his biography that Noel's mother ever failed in her self-imposed task. And Lionel's mother consoled herself in the loss of her son by her success in making his last months free of pain and fear.

It was natural for her to write about it and some comfort to her to feel she had behaved well. It was a way of assuaging the guilt she felt at having been so much away from the boy the year before. There *had* been a special bond between them, hadn't there? She *had* loved him with all her heart, hadn't she? In the story, the boy is fatherless; the mother widowed just before his birth. It is an indication of how alone Frances felt as she faced Lionel's death. The story was not published in her lifetime and it seems unfair to criticize her for something undoubtedly written only to ease her heart.

What is more unsympathetic, more open to criticism, is the way she shared her distress and despair with her younger son. Vivian, at fourteen, was surely unfairly burdened with the letters his mother wrote to him from 16 Rue Christophe Colombe, Paris:

> Lionel is reading and I have crept away from him to see if I can snatch a few minutes to write to my far away boy and tell him I received his letter last night and I never forget him and always love him, however deep my trouble is …
>
> It is very difficult to find anything our poor boy can eat. Mamma racks her brains to invent things and takes her own plate to coax him into eating something from it—but try as we will, he *cannot* eat enough, and during the last two weeks has changed very much.
>
> … You know he always wanted me to be near him, but during the last four or five weeks it has seemed as if he could not bear

me to be away from him a moment. I sleep in the room opening into his and I ask the nurse to call me in the night if he
wants me, and then I go and hold him in my arms and soothe
him until he is quiet, because no one else can comfort him
now.

... He has a mournful little way of calling "Mamma" that would
bring me to him if I were dying on my bed. If I move away from
his side he says, "Oh! *where* are you going? Don't go, Mamma
darling." I think I would never move away at all, but you see I
have to spend so much money that I feel very anxious to be able
to write something.

... My poor dear! It is so sad to see him. Yesterday I read your
letter to him and he did so admire it, but it made him cry. He
said, "He is such a funny boy. I could not write a letter like that."
And then the tears rushed into his eyes and he said, "He is having
such fun! I wish I could help Uncle Gimmie make a Nickel-in-
the-slot machine. Oh, I wish I could get well! I wish I could get
well!"

... Nobody will ever know what Mamma suffers. It is too hard
to bear. I have found out that I really truly cannot get away from
him to write, so I have made the plan of getting up in the morning *very* early, when it is quite dark, and everyone else is asleep. I
have a fire laid overnight in the room where I write and I light it
myself and sit with my feet in Lionel's fur-lined foot warmer and
two dressing gowns over my nightdress and write by candlelight.
I think after a while that I shall get so used to doing it that I shall
not mind. I *must* write. I buy nothing new for myself at all, and I
go nowhere and see no one, but it costs so much to live as I must
keep him. Do not think, my darling, that I do not think about
you and love you when I cannot write. You are always close to
my heart, but I am very unhappy, and I have a trouble that breaks
down my strength ...

Your
Dearest

In spite of the fact that "no one else can comfort him now", she felt she had to go to London on business in October. It was the need to make money, more and more money, which was to propel her for the rest of her life and turn her irrecoverably into the pen-driving machine she had already felt herself to be ten years before. "I must work ... it costs too much to live". The beautiful apartment in Paris, the "good, quiet servants who do all they can", the drugs, the nurse, Stephen—the outlay was immense.

Stephen went to London with her, leaving Lionel in the care of Lisa and the nurse. They were delayed longer than they expected. Stephen wrote explaining: "You will remember the most important of the business matters on which your mother came to London. Well, the man she has to see is not in town, and will not be till early next week. But anyhow it will only be some few days now until Mamma returns. We'll have a real jinks then. Goodbye, Dearie. Your Stephen."

Frances wrote, as usual, as if he were a very small boy: "Every day I am going to add something to the Fairy Box and we will have s'prises all winter." But Lionel was beyond high jinks and surprises. Frances brought him treasures from London; she ransacked the shops and bazaars for things that might entertain him. She had a model engine made with 'the pieces left separate and a little unfinished and brought him tools so that he could put them together by himself while he was in bed". But he had had every wish gratified since he was born—models of vertical and horizontal engines, Remington typewriters, Edison's talking doll, "purchased that he might extract the internal phonograph", dynamos, a Naphtha launch. Nothing could amuse him now. "I don't want anything, darling, only to get well." He had everything but the one thing he wanted.

He died in the Paris apartment on 7th December 1890 and was buried in the cemetery at St Germain. The inscription reads simply: "Lionel, whom the Gods loved". Frances described his death in a letter to her cousin, Emma Daniels, in Manchester:

It will perhaps seem almost incredible to you, as it does to others, when I tell you that he never did find out. He was ill nine months but I never allowed him to know that I was *really* anxious about him. I never let him know that he had consumption or that he was in danger—and when he died he passed away so softly and quickly that I know he wakened in the other world without knowing how he had left this one. I can thank God for that.

… I shall never get over it. I suffered too much. But I kept it up to the last. The day before he died he slept softly all day and said he was quite comfortable, only so sleepy.

… The last words he spoke to me were, "God bless Mammie", when we kissed each other good night. Early in the morning he coughed a little and when the nurse bent over him she saw the end had come. When I spoke to him and kissed him he gave one little sigh and was gone. I have to tell it briefly because I cannot bear to write more.

… His nurse is still with me, and his doctor seems like my brother. I shall never forget them and how they helped my dearest fellow to pass through death itself without fear or pain.

"Death is always sudden, however long one waits," Frances wrote, years later, remembering. She had suffered so much, she would never forget it. She was quite sure of that. Stephen had made himself indispensable, just as he had during her own illness after the accident the year before. Lionel had certainly loved him. Stephen was always gentle and loving with Lionel. But there is a revealing passage in the notebooks Frances kept in the months after Lionel's death, notebooks which record her deeply disturbed mind, her attempts to reassure herself that Lionel could still hear her:

Do you remember how you comforted me with your arms round my neck that day Uncle Stephen was so cross to me? He was always sweet to Boy, though, wasn't he? I forgave him all for that. "Never mind, darling," you said, "*we* are *always* friends. We are two staffs that always stand together."

With the one staff taken away, Frances collapsed: "There is only one place where I want to go and I think I shall reach it—it is where Lionel lies among his flowers at St Germain." But Kitty Hall took her to the Hotel Bellevue at Cannes and on to the Grand Hôtel des Anglais at San Remo, "a great gay hotel with a concierge in gold buttons, and white marble steps". There is a vivid picture of this time in the title story of the collection *Giovanni and the Other*. Lionel is called Leo and Vivian Geoff.

"Sometimes I think Leo seems even more real than Geoff." Frances occupied herself with reading *Revelations*. "If Leo had gone to Africa, I think I should have read about Africa. As it is, I read over and over the parts of those last chapters which tell about the City, the City that has streets of pure gold, like unto clear glass. It always seemed like a beautiful fairy story, until Leo went away. And then I was so hungry for him—it seemed as if I must have something *real* to think of, so I began to read, and imagine … I can't help trying to make it a place that would not seem too dazzling and strange and solemn for a boy to like … I try to remember more about the green pastures and the river of crystal than about the walls of jasper and sapphire, and emerald, and the streets of gold. But somehow I love the gates made of great pearls, and always standing open."

Frances' belief in an after life never wavered. There were those comforting words of Longfellow's:

> *"Dust thou art, to dust returnest"*
> *Was not spoken of the soul.*

She certainly did not imagine the dead as conventional angels with harps and wings, or as spirits lifting tables and throwing things about. She had had some experiences of seances in Washington and had never been very impressed. But she was quite sure Lionel was still Lionel, real, himself, able to look over her shoulder and help her. This feeling she conveyed most strongly in *In The Closed Room*, published in 1904, a work that looks like a children's book

1 Frances Hodgson Burnett

2 Manchester, at the time of Frances' birth

3 Edwin Hodgson's trade advertisement in the Manchester City Trade Directory of 1852

4 Knoxville, Tennessee, in 1865

5 New York Avenue, Washington, D.C., near I Street, in 1880

6 Dr Swan Burnett,
from a miniature

7 Richard Watson Gilder
in 1873

8 Frances with her sons,
Vivian (aged twelve) and
Lionel (aged fourteen)
in 1888

Right: 9 An illustration drawn by Reginald Birch for the first edition of Little Lord Fauntleroy

Below left: 10 Elsie Leslie, the first American Fauntleroy on stage, in the New York production

Below right: 11 Buster Keaton, aged ten, on tour in New England as Fauntleroy

Left: 12 Freddie Bartholomew in the 1936 film

Below: 13 Mary Pickford, aged twenty-seven, in the first film of Little Lord Fauntleroy

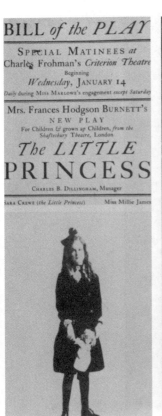

Above left: 14 The first American production of *The Little Princess* in 1903, with Millie James as the Little Princess

Above right: 15 Frances Hodgson Burnett in *Men and Women of the Day*, 1888

Above: 16 Israel Zangwill, after the painting by Solomon J. Solomon

Left: 17 Henry James

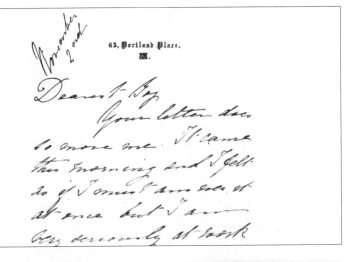

Above: 18 Letter from Frances to Vivian, 2 November 1895

Right: 19 63 Portland Place, London W1.

20 Dr Stephen Townesend

Above: 21 Frances in 1888, her favourite photograph, taken by Barrauds of Oxford Street

Right: 22 Vivian Burnett at Harvard

23 Edith Jordan, Frances' sister

Right: 24 Mary, Colin and Dickon in the Secret Garden, from the first edition illustration by Charles Robinson

Below: 25 Maytham Hall, Rolvenden, Frances' English home from 1898 to 1907

26 Plandome Park, Long Island, built by Frances in 1908

MRS. FRANCES HODGSON BURNETT

JAMES MONTGOMERY FLAGG

1 9 2 1

27 Frances in 1921

but is not. The small girls in the frontispiece playing together with the dolls and the dolls' tea-set are, at the end of the book, both dead. The message is that those we love are never far away when they die. The mother is comforted because the child is not "millions and millions and millions of miles away", as it had seemed to her in her first grief. Frances never wrote of the death of a child in one of her real children's books—though there are plenty of off-stage deaths of parents. Cedric's father is dead; Sara Crewe and Mary Lennox are both orphaned; so are the two little Pilgrims. Colin's mother is dead; so is Marco's, in *The Lost Prince*. There is not a complete set of parents in any of the books. But she never uses the death of a child to bring easy tears in the way, for instance, that her friend Kate Douglas Wiggin had done in *The Birds' Christmas Carol*, published in 1887.

"One night when I was lying awake at Cannes," Frances wrote, "after I had left him in Saint Germain, it came to me suddenly, why, that prayer has been answered." This was the prayer she had prayed when carrying the baby Lionel. "It does not matter what was done to me but he is happy." Her feelings, often so alien to ours many years later, were closely in key with her time. *Why Weepest Thou: A Book for Mourners* (1888) contains verses called "The Lambs Safely Folded" which show exactly the same anguished resignation:

> *I laid him down*
> *In those white shrouded arms, with bitter tears;*
> *For some voice told me that, in after years,*
> *He should know naught of passion, grief or fears,*
> *As I had known.*

The *Queen* of 1880 had maintained that twelve months' strict mourning was the correct period for the death of a child, but by 1889 there was some restlessness about the etiquette of death. An article on "Mourning Clothes and Customs" in *Woman's World* declared that many customs no longer met with general approval. It even suggested the adoption of black armbands but the Victorians, with a Queen who fetched Albert's shaving water every day, and wore black during the forty years of her widowhood, were not ready to discard their mourning clothes. It seems certain that Frances, like the bereaved mother in *In the Closed Room*, wore "garments heavy and rich with crape" and a "long black veil". For many years she used writing paper edged in black—"middle" width, correct for the mourning of parent or child.

In the San Remo hotel the rooms she shared with Kitty Hall were "hung with old brocades and pictures and fans, such as one sees in the shops for antiquities". However short a time she stopped, and she was always stopping briefly and moving on, she made her rooms belong to her: "I see that in each room there is a glow." In San Remo they were "filled with flowers and there were many pictures of a boy, who is dead". "Sometimes one wishes to be quite silent, one cannot speak at all, but sometimes one must go over it all again, one cannot help it," she wrote.

Frances returned to London, to the house in Lexham Gardens, in the spring of 1891. There were things she had to do. Most important was her feeling that a "short life is not wasted if another's is built upon it". There was Stephen's life to be saved from waste, his career to be made. And there were countless unhappy children in London for whom she might do things in Lionel's name. In her story "Giovanni and the Other", Frances wrote of the bereaved mother: "She has a strange wish that he should seem still to live on earth and do things for other boys … Her plans are sensible in spite of her fancies." Frances' own fancies, imagining Lionel at the prow of a boat gliding over sapphire deeps, did not stop her making the most practical plans for doing good in his name.

There were two particular London charities which attracted Frances—one was Invalid Children's Aid and the other the Drury Lane Boys' Club. Before Lionel's death, Frances had taken an interest in St Monica's, a children's nursing home at Brondesbury. In an article published in *Scribner's Magazine* she described London streets swarming with children, ill-fed, ill-clothed, uncared-for. She wrote of the prevalence of spinal and hip diseases among them; of sick children lying on rough boards under dirty sacking in the richest city in the world, of crippled children, fed on dry bread or, if they were lucky, "strange things from the cook-shops with sips of gin or beer", unable to play, unable to move, with nothing to do. Through Invalid Children's Aid, Frances visited some of these children, taking them the sort of trifles she loved herself—"brilliantly artistic wooden dinners on tiny platters with very green vegetables and very juicy wooden rounds of beef", donkeys with panniers and nodding heads, dolls in scarlet bodices with the announcement "My clothes can be taken off", three-penny picture books for children who had never heard of Little Boy Blue, and oranges and spongecakes and penny bunches of flowers. "Everything is new to them but pain and poverty."

Frances visited St Monica's during her brief time in London when Lionel lay dying in Paris. After his death, she took some comfort in arranging a memorial corner in one of the wards. She endowed a bed in Lionel's name and hung his portrait above it. On the Japanese cabinet beside the bed she put books and Lionel's own musical box and other trinkets which might amuse a sick child; at the foot of the bed a palm in a blue pot. She arranged that the bed should always be available to Invalid Children's Aid. At St Monica's she once had the chance of meeting Princess Mary, who had just become engaged to the Duke of Clarence (She later married the Duke of York and became Queen of England.) Frances managed to interest the Princess in Invalid Children's Aid. "It ended by her becoming the Patroness," she wrote to Vivian, "and as she is the only young Princess who is a Patroness of a Society, it is very helpful to them." Frances, more secretly than Daisy Ashford's Mr Salteena, was inclined to be "very fond of royalties", and was delighted with a letter from the Princess, but in fact her support seems rather tardy and unimaginative: "I will do my very best to help this excellent charity, and I hope next November" she wrote in May, "to be able to send a grant of clothing from the Surrey Needlework Guild. Would you kindly let me know whether books and toys would be acceptable?" Frances' own visits to St Monica's continued for many years.

She had first become interested in the Drury Lane Boys' Club in 1889. Watching a pantomime, she was conscious of real ogres in the gas-lit streets outside the theatre. Inside there were children in Eton jackets and gauzy white frocks enjoying the ogres of fairyland. Outside were "the ogres of Hard Life, of Poverty, of Misfortune, of Lack of Opportunity, Ignorance, Hopelessness, Hunger and Disease". The ragged children darted among the carts and horses' heads, begging for pennies as the "powdered footmen descend to open the carriage doors for pretty women". These were children like Anne, the beggar child in *Sara Crewe*, and the Rat's friends Frances was later to write about in *The Lost Prince*. She was curious about them and sad for them. "Even the best seeds wither if planted in unfavourable earth."

The Boys' Club was started by a boy called Andrew Buckingham in his own cellar; his mother sold her mangle to make room for them, somewhere where they would not be forever told to "move on". It outgrew the cellar and moved into the Parish Room in Russell Court; they served forty dinners three times a week. Before her accident, Frances had occasionally gone along to help the Rector's daughter, Stephen Townesend's sister; she had cut up food for the youngest boys. By 1891 they needed to expand. Frances interceded successfully with the owner of a building in Kemble Street. She decided to give the Club a comfortable reading room in part of the building, in Lionel's name. The nucleus of the library was to be the books Lionel had been fond of, but she also got book lists from two boys she knew. And Harold Warne helped, providing many of his own publications. Frances chose the linoleum and the fittings, including the "glacier window decoration" which would still give light but cut out the dreary view. She was not over-optimistic about the reading room. She knew many of the boys would "prefer the gymnasiums and the cricket and the fife and drum band", but she wanted them to have the chance to enjoy Jules Verne and Harrison Ainsworth, and there were many who would.

Frances opened the reading room on 27th February 1892 in the presence of the MP for the district. He was the son of W. H.

Smith, "the speaker of the House of Commons and the King of the book trade of the railway station bookstalls throughout the land". Frances shook hands with all the seventy-five boys. She gave each of them a copy of a letter she had written: "Whether a man's world is at the West End or at the East, in Drury Lane or Grosvenor Square, Nature gives him a capital of his own"—heart, brain, two hands—"I think I put the heart first." She asked the boys to make the very best of themselves and do all they could to make the best of others. Then there was an entertainment: the fifes and drums played and the boys sang, "Wot cher ... Knocked 'em in the Old Kent Road". At the end, Frances went down to her brougham in the dark street, clutching her bouquet of violets and lilies of the valley, thinking of the crowds of lively poor boys and of the one rich one, dead.

These were the things she did for Lionel. For Stephen, during the mourning months of 1891, she concentrated on a play, *The Showman's Daughter*. It had been begun in moments snatched from Lionel's bedside, in Göbersdorf, Marienbad and Paris. In the May of 1891, Stephen took part in a nurses' entertainment at Bart's. He recited "My Brother Henry" and took part in *The Curio*, "an unfinished tragedy in one act". At the Annual General Meeting of the Amateur Dramatic Club in October that year, it was proposed, "in view of the great services rendered", that Mr Stephen Townesend should be "elected Vice-president with a perpetual vote on the Committee". The proposal was carried unanimously. But it was success on the professional stage Stephen longed for, and Frances was determined to give him that.

She decided to produce the new play herself, as the only chance of giving Stephen a good part. "Until you produce a play," she wrote to Kitty Hall in November, "you can never know what it means." Stephen was not being easy. She wrote to Vivian in Washington: "Of course Uncle Stephen takes care of my business and is very particular about things of that sort, but as for the rest, I feel as if I was the one who had to take care of him. He is so delicate and nervous and irritable, poor boy. But I have to remember when he seems to be unreasonable, that he was never anything but *perfect* to Lionel, and that he was his comfort and strength and beloved to the last minute." Vivian wanted Frances to come home. He wrote low-spirited letters which depressed Frances terribly. "I *cannot* bear it if he gets ill." She had not seen him for over a year. But she could not abandon *The Showman's Daughter*.

Stephen had originally declined the part of the showman, Joe Hurst. He longed for his chance, but when it came to the point he had no confidence in himself. It was too important a part for his first—but he agreed to understudy the rôle. Perhaps he would play it in America. However, the first actor engaged to play Hurst was a complete failure and Frances managed to persuade Stephen that he could do it. She wrote to Kitty Hall:

… He *is* a genius, I do believe. He really quite thrills me sometimes in the pathetic parts. I decided that he *must* do it in London, and finally convinced him that if I was willing to risk a thousand pounds on his success, he ought to believe in himself. We are having another week out of town so that he and the others can work into their parts.

But you may guess what I am going through with that poor, overstrung boy. He is excited and worried by everything. We are going to keep the thing as quiet as possible—I mean the fact that Hurst is not to be played by a London star—because there is much jealousy and spite among professionals, and, of course, the actors will all hate him before he does the part, and be ready to poison him when he has succeeded. But you can imagine how many chance speeches from outsiders crush him, or rankle.

Oh, how I pray the poor fellow may have a triumph. I shall feel I have not lived for nothing if I can help that one poor life into the sun. If I had done no other one thing in my life but help Lionel to die as he did, I should feel as if I ought to be grateful to God for letting me live to do it—but if I can help Stephen to *live*, that will be another beautiful thing to have done.

The play was to open at the Winter Gardens, Southport, in December 1891, the same theatre where Henry James' first play *The American* had had its first performance eleven months before. Frances had proposed to see James' play in Manchester before it opened its London run that September, but she had been gently but firmly discouraged by James in the earliest of his surviving letters to her.

> "Your plan of going to Manchester," he wrote, "is so wonderfully gracious that I shrink from administering the least little *douche* of cold water, and yet, I rather quake, too, at the responsibility of encouraging your friendly presence; the whole being, as yet, on so provincial a basis.

It was even possible that the Manchester performances would have to be postponed—two of the actors had influenza. Moreover he told her, unaware he spoke of her birthplace, "Manchester is far and hideous … the journey is long and fatiguing; the play is only *provisionally* cast". If she did come, he would feel "honoured and exalted and truly *tested*". But there was too much cold water in the letter. She did not go, and concentrated on her own production.

James was finding the theatre a strait-jacket: "What can you do with a character, with an idea, with a feeling between dinner and the suburban trains?" He was "overcome by the vulgarity, the brutality, the baseness of the condition of the English-speaking theatre today". But there were the possibilities of fame and fortune, and the game itself had some entertainment and allure. The dramatist's work did not end once the play was written. Speeches had to be re-written; James found himself showing the actors how certain bits were to be played. It was part of the life of the world, not the study.

While *The American*, after mixed notices, played to poorish houses at the renovated Opera Comique Theatre in the Strand, Frances was rehearsing *The Showman's Daughter* at the Royalty.

"Everything *seems* to be going well but of course a play is an anxious thing." She had a proscenium box arranged with a chair and writing-table, writing materials and candles; she could make notes during rehearsals and speak alone afterwards to any member of the company. The provincial run began at Worcester. It opened at Southport on 14th December. "The actors were quite excited and delighted. But I am not as courageous and full of belief as I used to be and I shall only feel confidence if the box office receipts in London are large enough," Frances wrote to Vivian. "I do hope it will be a success in London. It has been such work and anxiety to me. I had a special reason for taking all the trouble." The special reason was of course Stephen. It was Stephen whose life was to be transformed by his success in the play. But he was an unrewarding protégé, moody and irritable. Frances wrote, "I have more work and responsibility than I ever had before and I have no one to brace me up. Uncle Stephen simply drags me down and takes all the life out of me."

Vivian too, on the other side of the Atlantic, was a worry to her. She mourned and longed for not only Lionel but the child Vivian—"the two little fellows with picture faces and golden love locks whose going has left me forever a sadder woman". Adolescence was worrying, not charming. She once joked that boys should be buried at fifteen and dug up again at twenty. Was Vivian, so far away, going to turn into an acceptable young man, a gentleman in fact? If only he liked riding. "I wish you cared for riding but I know you don't … It seems as if a gentleman ought to ride well, as well as dance well and speak well. I want you to ride, to dance, to fence and to shoot." Shooting was obviously part of the gentlemanly way of life—but when it came to the point at Fryston Hall in 1895, she was to write to Vivian, "I don't think I care to see the pheasants shot". French was another essential. "Dear, I hope you are not allowing your French to slip away … Est-ce que tu connais quelque un a Washington qui tu pouvais parler Français meme un petit peu?" It was obviously important his French should be better than hers.

Frances was comforted to think that soon Vivian might be old enough to understand all her business affairs. If only she could be sure he would turn out the way she wanted … In Southport, her chief consolation was a boy called Cecil Crossland, the son of Lady Somebody (her writing is often difficult). Frances hired a bicycle for him and he was "wild with joy". He reminded her of Lionel. As for the play, she was sick and tired of it. "There are such anxieties connected with actors and actresses", particularly when one of them is the author-producer's protégé.

Was Stephen anything more at this time than protégé and busi-ness manager? It seems likely, though there is little evidence to prove it. After their first meeting in 1886, five years before, Frances had joked to Owen Lankester that she had loved Stephen in secret all summer. It was the sort of joke she would probably not have made if it had been really true. Years later, at the stormiest, most bitter period of their long relationship, Stephen claimed that Frances had begun to "make love" to him at their first meeting, but at that time the phrase meant no more than flirt. From the earliest days in Tennessee, Frances had always been a flirt. She loved to attract men; she loved the titillation and the provocation. Stephen claimed he had kissed her only two weeks after their first meeting. This was said in insult and in anger, and, if it had been true, Frances would surely have remembered his name when writing to Owen Lankester from Florence: she did not. It is highly unlikely that there was any physical relationship between them until the idyllic weeks in the miniature Dorincourt, just before Frances' accident. Through the period of Frances' own illness and that of Lionel, Stephen's medical training made it perfectly proper for him to enjoy a close relationship which would otherwise have been a subject of scandal.

Now they were in a new professional relationship. Stephen was not only Frances' business manager but her star actor. The jealousy and spite Frances had written of to Kitty were a daily nightmare. But at least Frances' faith in Stephen was justified. He did well in his part. When *The Showman's Daughter* opened at the Royalty Theatre,

London on 6th January 1892, "Will Dennis" (the name Stephen had taken) was praised. "The Showman finds a very congenial representative in Mr Dennis," wrote *The Times* critic. As for the play, it was a variation of the story Frances had told in *Louisiana*. The Showman—the proprietor of a travelling waxworks show—has a daughter whom he had educated as a lady. But can the daughter of a waxworks' showman be a lady? "It must be confessed that the talk as to what constitutes a true gentleman or a true lady is a little tiresome … but the authoress has aimed at enlisting the sympathies of the public and this … she may succeed in doing."

Frances was not given the chance to succeed. A week after the play opened the Duke of Clarence died. He was "darling Eddy", the eldest son of the Prince of Wales, the most popular young man in the Royal Family; it was six weeks before his wedding to the young princess Frances had met at St Monica's. England was plunged into mourning. Nobody went to the theatre. *The Showman's Daughter* closed with a considerable deficit, and Stephen had one more circumstance to justify him in his frequent declaration that he was "always unlucky". On 15th March, knowing it was time she saw Vivian and glad perhaps to escape temporarily from Stephen's problems, Frances returned to Washington.

She was, though she did not know it, obeying Henry James's advice. On 7th January, the day after the opening of *The Showman's Daughter*, he had written of Frances to his friend Mrs Hugh Bell: "She is a fatally deluded little woman, and I'm afraid cunning hands are plucking her of her downy plumage. I wish she would gather up her few remaining feathers while yet there is time and flutter them westward, where she has, after all, a husband and a child." She would not have either much longer. Vivian was nearly sixteen, hardly a child, and Swan had for many years been her husband in name only and would soon not even be that.

Henry James's unease about Stephen Townesend's "cunning hands" would prove well founded, but Frances's infatuation survived her absence from England. Townesend's power over her remained immense.

The Life of the World
1892–1895

Frances was "spending the Spring very quietly in Washington", according to an interview she gave a New York paper on 16th April. There is nothing to suggest that Lionel's death had done anything to heal the breach between his parents. Swan Burnett is hardly mentioned in any of the surviving letters of the fourteen months Frances was now to spend in America—though he was still concerning himself with her business affairs. On 26th April E. L. Burlingame, Frances' editor at Scribner's, wrote that Mr Doubleday "hands me a letter he has received from Dr Burnett" about *The One I Knew the Best of All*, Frances' story of her own childhood. This was originally supposed to be a brief sketch to be added to her collection published in England as *Children I have Known*, which later appeared in America under the title *Giovanni and the Other*. Dr Burnett wrote that he had Frances' consent to offer it to *Scribner's Magazine* and mentions an offer "made for it by a syndicate", obviously in an attempt to get Scribner's to improve their terms. Burlingame was surprised, as he had understood it was for children.

Frances replied that her memories had turned out rather differently than she had expected. "It is only mature and thinking people who will get the real flavor of the humor and pathos of it … It is most interesting to me as I write it, because I find I remember the juvenile mental attitudes so clearly … It belongs to the grown-ups—especially those who are interested in children as a sort of phsycological [sic] study … I wonder if it will be as interesting to people who do not regard children as a serious study. I am not sure it belongs in any magazine." But it did eventually appear in *Scribner's* between January and June, 1893, and then, as a small volume, later in the year. The illustrations were by Reginald Birch, as they were for so many of her books. For this one, he was paid a thousand dollars—forty dollars a drawing, and some of them very small. Scribner's paid Frances three thousand seven hundred and fifty dollars in advance of royalties. Frances preferred that to the flat five thousand dollars which McClure had offered.

I have quoted from *The One I Knew the Best of All* a great deal in my first chapter. It was in a letter to Burlingame this year that Frances mentioned she would not include "the only really sentimental episode" of her life, when she was nine years old and in love with a man of thirty. Was the implication that this was the only time she ever really, without qualifications and reservations, loved any man? Frances had used the possibilities of passion and unswerving devotion in such a relationship in her early story, "Kathleen Mavourneen". It seems likely that Frances felt that no love she had had later came near the excitement and wholeheartedness of that early adoration. In another letter, in May, she told Burlingame that she was working on the chapter called "The Party". She paraphrased for him, as she rarely did in letters, the passage about the child, in the middle of polkas and muslin frocks and sashes and bonbons and lights, saying restlessly, "Is *this* the Party? Is it the Party? Somehow it doesn't seem to be the Party—as one says—all through life, all through it."

There were no parties in 1892. She sat in her writing room in the large house she had bought three years before and in which she had spent so little time, and remembered her early days. She wrote long letters to Burlingame. She told him she had become so carried away by her own childhood that she was working harder than was wise: "three days ago, having written steadily from nine o'clock in the morning until six at night with only about fifteen minutes for lunch, I rather went to pieces ... I must go to the sea."

It was not only hard work that was getting her down. She had spent a great deal of time and emotional energy on the case of Frances Courtenay Baylor. It is worth going into this story in some detail, for it is typical of a number of such incidents throughout Frances' life. She meant so well. She wanted to be so kind; but she was a hopeless judge of people and she was not a very good judge of other people's work. In this case, she had not even read Miss Baylor's novel *Claudia*—but Miss Baylor was an old friend who had written other books Frances had liked. When she heard that Lippincott had offered only a paltry sum for the new novel, Frances was indignant. She knew Miss Baylor badly needed money. "It is such a burning shame," she wrote to Burlingame, "that she should be the prey of people like the Lippincotts."

Poor Miss Baylor, so gentle, so timid, so sad, had, it seemed to Frances, fallen among thieves. Frances suggested Miss Baylor should send her manuscript to Scribner's, to "a firm of gentlemen" So Miss Baylor refused Lippincott's offer, which was as surprising to them "as if a bowl of milk had drawn a sword", as Frances put it to Burlingame, rather spoiling the effect by adding "which I consider rather a neat figure of speech" Frances was sure that if Lippincott "get her again she will always be in bondage and the one thing left to me in life is to try to free people from bondage". Miss Baylor sent *Claudia* to Scribner's. But Scribner's did not like it. They could not publish it.

Frances was distraught. "I was so sure—so *sure* I was going to be able to help her, I was positively thanking God in advance for letting me have the chance to do it. But I don't know about God—who does? It seems to me sometimes as if He—or She—or It—or They—whatever it is—were only made furious at me for these poor little struggles to help those who need helping so much. It is not only that it always comes back upon me in the form of trouble or anxious responsibilities—but it seems to hurt the ones I am trying to care for. It would have been so much better for this sad little lady if I had never tried to help her ... Shall I ever learn? No, never–never–never. Tomorrow I shall do something quite new and brilliant in its inspirational idiocy." She asked Burlingame to write a letter to her which she could show to Miss Baylor, which would soften the blow—saying that "Miss Baylor has not been at her best when she wrote the book, because you know her best is very good indeed and this work does not do justice.... And *please* be so kind, kind, kind as your heart can be—and please try to encourage her for the future ... If you could just give [her] the feeling that this failure is only *pour le moment* ... I believe it is just encouragement—a little good luck—that she wants ..."

Burlingame wrote the required letter and Frances sent Miss Baylor the cheque she had been counting on. If the way to hell is paved with good intentions, Francis said she had decorated streets "in the most intricate patterns". She never learned from her mistakes; over and over again some well-meant interference led to trouble, worst of all twenty-five years later when she found herself sued for fifty thousand dollars.

In 1892 there were other irritations. The English reviews of *Children I Have Known*, a collection of short pieces, were pleasant enough on the whole, but the *Athenaeum* urged Frances to pay more attention to her style. "The warmest admirers of *That Lass o' Lowrie's* cannot but earnestly hope that Mrs Burnett will be on her guard against tendencies dangerously akin to gush and verbal redundancy, which have been too observable in all the most recent successors of that fine work. Over-great fertility is always demoralizing. How little first-rate work is done by even first-rate novelists." Frances was surely reminded of the strictures of the *Literary News* in February 1889. Another three years had gone by and still she had written nothing worthy to stand with *That Lass o' Lowrie's* and *Through One Administration*.

Frances was plagued by reporters, curious about what she was up to, about her unconventional marriage, about the possibility of another *Fauntleroy*. Mostly she was not communicative, but occasionally she was charmed into talking and regretted it afterwards. "I am ever so stupid sometimes when I am talking to a person who seems nice-minded and honorable ... But I have such a horror of the American Newspaper creature that I am afraid of him after he has gone, howsoever respectable he has appeared." If journalists were anathema, publishers were a different matter. This was the happiest period of Frances' relations with Scribner's, even though to her surprise she suddenly realized that they were only paying her a royalty of 12½%, whereas Warne in London paid fifteen. She decided she was not businesslike, but it seemed extraordinary that such a thing could have escaped her attention. "I admit being perfectly ridiculous in such matters and only saved from ruin by the fact that I record everything in black and white and keep it in a dispatch box." She hoped they would alter her terms for *The One I Knew the Best of All*—but at least they were gentlemen. Some day she would write a beautiful article about publishing, and parents would say of their sons: "If he is Clever enough and Noble enough—and sufficiently akin to Seraphs I will make him a Publisher."

"I have had publishers in various countries", Frances wrote—American, English, French, German, Italian, Swedish, Polish—but the publisher whose publications she was most interested in was the one who presented the story of the Drury Lane Boys' Club, seventy-eight small pages in pale blue covers with hardly a lead or a misprint in the whole book. The printing was done in the basement of the Massachusetts Avenue house on the press of the *Moon*, the weekly paper. The publisher was of course Vivian. Frances had written the account for him to use. When *Scribner's Magazine* used it with Vivian's permission, they printed a notice to the effect that it could be obtained in the form of a small book. They bought from Vivian eight hundred copies of his publication at eighteen cents a copy. Frances was thrilled about the whole thing. He talked of "galley proofs" like a professional, she said.

In an article written at about this time, with Stephen's experiences uppermost in her mind, Frances encouraged parents to let their children follow their own inclinations. If her son wants to be a butcher, Frances wrote, "I shall endeavor to help him secure a butcher's shop in the best possible business situation and to try to invest his legs of mutton with an air of picturesque distinction." But it would be much nicer if he were to become a publisher, or a musician.

Washington was becoming unbearably hot. It was time they got to the sea. They found Marshall Cottage at Swampscott, Massachusetts, not far from Lynn, where they had spent earlier summers. Vivian, aged sixteen, wrote to his father in Washington as Frances finished off *The One I Knew the Best of All*.

> Swampscott, Mass.
>
> July 9th '92
>
> Dear Daddy:—
>
> Since you absolutely refuse to write to me after I have written to you once I suppose I must needs write again. No more news than there was at first hardly. I have been doing absolutely nothing. I take pictures, walk on the sands and come back and take pictures again. At present that is all there is to do. I don't know intimately one girl or boy of my age in the place, yet somehow or other I am not having such a miserable time. I have taken some quite good pictures, for me, and I would enclose some of them but I have no paper to print them on. We have resurrected a guitar of Mama's and Kitty, who is here now, is teaching me how to play. An old banjo has also been brought to light which, counting *my* banjo, makes three string instruments in the house. Kitty plays the Guitar and I the banjo and Kitty sings and it is real pretty. We did it last night on the veranda and the effect was quite nice. I tried singing a little too and Kitty says she thinks I am going to have a nice voice … I am having a little row boat built for "me and the rest".

It is going to be very pretty and we are going to call it "Cherie".
I will probably bring it down to Washington to use on the river.
My stock of information has about run dry so, dear old Daddy, I
will close this letter by hoping you are not too lonely.

Lovingly,

Vivian

With her autobiography on its way to Burlingame, Frances started
turning over various ideas. She felt "in a working mood" but
was not quite sure what to do next. *In Connection with the De
Willoughby Claim* was still waiting to be finished but she wanted
to do something new. "I wonder if the Regency—or one of the
earlier Georges would be attractive. Do you think so?" she asked
Burlingame. "Or is the past out of fashion?" She was being businesslike. "If I did these things would the Magazine want them and
what would it pay me by the thousand words … I cannot afford to
waste time." She was fascinated by the fact that the Regent who
wore stays and curled his hair had once been a beautiful ardent
boy. "If the people will not *live* for me as really as if they walked
down Piccadilly today I shall throw them aside," she ended the
letter reassuringly, though she would hardly have done so if the
past was in fashion and Scribner's offered a vast sum per thousand
words. Frances' interest in this period eventually went into a play,
The First Gentleman of Europe.

Giovanni and the Other, the collection of short stories about
children which had already appeared in England, was published
in America that winter. The *Dial* was harsh: "To us it seems an
unworthy successor of the book which made her famous. The
titular story is far too melancholy to be healthful for the young.
The grief in it—that of a mother for the death of her son—is so
far from being restrained that it is sentimental and morbid in the
extreme." But fifteen thousand copies had been ordered before
publication. It sold briskly. All her books were selling briskly.
Dolly had recently been re-issued in England. F.C. Burnand
wrote a lyrical letter about it: "It is the most perfect book—most

charming, most natural—but I have no words at hand to convey my admiration of it. You will read what I shall say in *Punch*." He hoped it would sell a hundred thousand in various languages all over the world. "Pardon my enthusiasm—it masters me and breaks out once 'in a blue moon'."

Early in 1893 Frances was reunited with her sister Edith, the audience and solace of her childhood. They had not seen each other for many years. Edith's first husband, Pleasant Fahnestock, the Knoxville carpenter, had died of smallpox many years before, soon after they had gone to California on the trail, it seems, of gold. It was probably from Edith's letters that Frances had got the detail for Octavia's background in *A Fair Barbarian*. Edith had been left a widow with two very small sons, Archer and Ernest, the younger boy scarred for life by the smallpox which had killed his father. Years later Edith had married again, to a man called Frank Jordan, and the child of this marriage, a small girl, had recently died at the age of six. Edith had had more than her share of unhappiness. Frances urged her to come East for a holiday and then proposed that they should travel to England together. Frances would show Edith the country she had not seen since leaving Liverpool twenty-eight years before.

Just before sailing Frances wrote to Scribner, asking him to send some of her books, which had been requested for exhibition in the Women's Department of the World's Fair in Chicago. "I have grown so tired of Woman with a capital W, though I suppose it is rankest heresy to say so. I don't want to be a Woman at all—I have begun to feel that I want to be something like this—'woman'. Nevertheless if everybody is sending books, I must send mine."

Frances must, at the same point, have gone to the Chicago Fair herself, for her *Two Little Pilgrims' Progress* could surely not have been written otherwise. The Fair was an extraordinary phenomenon, with streets thronged with characters straight out of the Arabian Nights, 'hootchy kootchy' dancers, a cyclorama of the Swiss Alps, a full-size knight in armour on a full-size horse, both made out of dried Californian prunes, a Ferris Wheel, a

Lapland village, a collection of nasty-tempered ostriches and a Chinese theatre. There was something for everyone—a City Beautiful with Rose Gardens and minarets and fountains. Julia Ward Howe thought the Cairo Dancers indecent, but thirty years later Theodore Dreiser was still breathless, remembering "this vast and harmonious collection of perfectly constructed and snowy buildings ... this fairy land". Frances had been commissioned to write the story, originally as part of a *World's Fair Book*, and although Eugene Field, the instigator of the scheme, had written "you could not be dull or unfelicitous, even though you tried to be", this was by far the weakest of her full-length children's books, a fairy-story without real savour, a box of chocolates with no hard centres.

Edith and Frances sailed in May 1893. Soon after their departure, Swan wrote to Charles Scribner for their address: "Did Mrs Burnett leave her London Banker's address with you? She left it with us but it has been misplaced."

Frances was glad to get away from America again. The old restlessness, the old feeling that the Party was going on somewhere else, was strong in her. She could never stay in one place for long. This was her thirteenth Atlantic crossing. In the next twenty years, she crossed it twenty more times. This may seem unremarkable nowadays with businessmen flying back and forth constantly, with television personalities commuting, with the journey time counted in hours. When Frances travelled, it was still an event. Messengers hurried up the gangways "leaving baskets and boxes of fruit and flowers with cards and notes attached", farewell offerings to be placed in staterooms. Passengers lay for days on deck in steamer chairs, looking at the dark water, listening to the throb of engines, drinking beef tea and reading novels. Others walked "their customary quota of carefully-measured miles the day". The voyage made a decent interval, a pause for thought, between the two ways of life. "One seems to need them both," Frances said. Now she wanted a home in England. It was not enough to have a banker's address. She needed to belong.

The house she eventually chose—after summer months reading Pepys at The Glade, Long Ditton Hill, just across the river from Hampton Court—was 63 Portland Place, London W.1. Frances rented it from the autumn of 1893 until 1898, when she found Maytham Hall in Kent, which was to be the English house which meant most to her. The Portland Place house, though it combined the utmost respectability with an interesting atmosphere, was a continual worry. It was large and demanding. It was a giant with an open maw "whose only diet is coin of the realm". "I always need so much money in spite of the most muscular effort," Frances wrote in May 1894, relieved to receive from Scribner's a royalty cheque for $2,181.30. At the end of August there was another $2,394.30, royalties on *The One I Knew the Best of All*. But it was a considerable task to run a house like 63 Portland Place, not on inherited money, not on income from investments or the toil of other hands, but on the earnings of one pen. The fuel bills alone were enormous. "I have fires everywhere, of course," she wrote in February 1895, "but the ceilings are so lofty and passages so endless that to go from the library to the drawing-room or a bedroom is like going on a voyage to the open Polar Sea. I always rather expect to encounter icebergs with bears on them in my blue bathroom." There were servants to be paid, and carriages to be kept up—a landau and a new Victoria ("delightfully cushioned and springy"). There were horses. There was entertaining. And there was Stephen, who made himself more and more indispensable throughout these years.

The Portland Place house was the inspiration for Frances' next major novel, which was intended to show the world she had not become just a scribbler of charming stories for children. Another volume of these was published in 1894. In England it was called *The Captain's Youngest*—a good title, as Warne said, because the English "are so fond of soldiers". In America it was called *Piccino and Other Child Stories*. The *Dial*, though conceding that "Mrs Burnett's graceful style makes everything from her pen agreeable reading", took her to task for the picture of domestic misery in the story "The Captain's Youngest", "which no child should be able to understand; its termination is entirely too tragic". *The Two Little Pilgrims' Progress*, on the other hand, was criticized, justly, for exactly the opposite reason. The two small pilgrims "meet no difficulties whatever. They have no fear. They never get lost or confused, and find only courtesy and kindness." We don't know Frances' reactions to these reviews. She never comments on them in her letters; she *said* she never read her critics. Scribner kept telling her the books were "going splendidly" in spite of the *Dial*. But it was nearly ten years before she wrote another book for children.

The new book was to be a new departure. Underneath the high-ceilinged rooms, the fine Adam interior of 63 Portland Place, there is a large basement area with long underground passages leading out to the Mews behind. *A Lady of Quality* apparently had its beginning "in a dark back chamber, revealed at the end of one of the corridors by the chance scratching of a match". "What a place to hide the body of a man you had accidentally killed," Frances remarked to the group of guests that she had taken on the excursion as part of the evening's entertainment.

The body was that of Sir John Oxon, killed with a riding whip by the heroine, Clorinda Wildairs, the Lady of Quality herself. The time was the early eighteenth century, and Frances thought she was telling the story "exactly in the style of Richard Steele". "I find I can imitate it so easily and the story is so exciting." Frances was thrilled with her creation. Clorinda "is a magnificent creature who rides over laws as she leaps fences. Perhaps Scribner's would turn pale at the sight of her—but to her last word she will be read and fought over and discussed." "A brilliant London critic tells me it is the book of my life and the opening of a new career," she wrote to Charles Scribner in New York.

It might be the opening of a new career but Frances suddenly realized that Clorinda was not at all a new departure. She wrote to Israel Zangwill that Joan Lowrie had been "a Clorinda in disguise ... so were Rachel Ffrench and Christian Murdoch in *Haworth's*. So was Bertha Amory, who laughed and wore tinkling ornaments and symphonies in red when she was passing through the gates of hell—so was little Sara Crewe when she starved in her garret and was a princess disdaining speech. Oh, she is not a new departure. She represents what I have cared for most all my life—from the time I was eight years old." It was something to do with the invincibility of the human spirit, the refusal of women to be mild and submissive, the acceptance of all experience, courage born of adversity. There was certainly no sign that she wanted to write Woman in a small typeface.

Edward Burlingame, in London on business seeing Barrie and Meredith and Henry James, was also being told that Frances was sure she had written her greatest work, that she had run the proprieties and conventions very close and challenged Scribner's to make a suitable offer. Burlingame, while taking her protestations with a pinch of salt, wrote to Scribner: "I can see decided possibilities that she may have done a strong thing and still greater ones that she may have done a popular one." He agreed to read immediately the eighty thousand words already written. On 9th May 1895 he wrote to Scribner: "The arrangement was that I was to read it and talk with her about it on Friday night when she had invited us to dinner … I gave weight in my reading to every circumstance in the book's favor … but I could only come to one conclusion—that she had undertaken something quite out of the line of all her best powers and had done a tawdry and artificial thing, in which the attempt at an archaic style had effectually wiped out the kind of thing generally liked in her writing, and the desire for sensation and aggressive dealing with big elemental violences had wiped out the sentiment. And I can't see that she has put anything of equal attraction in their place … I know what experience there is on the side of these widely-read people's instinctively knowing an audience better than we do"—but he thought the book "downright dull".

"Naturally I had a hard time of it at the dinner. I knew and felt the importance of our getting the book anyhow. Zangwill, who was at the dinner [he was undoubtedly 'the brilliant London critic', Frances had quoted to Scribner and very likely other people], had been telling her 'George Eliot couldn't touch it' etc. etc. I spare you my difficulties. I can be quite still at times and I don't think I said anything to pain her; but of course I don't flatter myself that I succeeded in concealing from a shrewd woman that my personal enthusiasm was not at that pitch. I confused myself, in a long talk with her later, to discussion of details in the story and to showing her the importance of our having the book and arranging for it at once ..." The final arrangement was a $5,000 advance on a 20% royalty, but it was not concluded until November. There were attempts to persuade Frances to bowdlerize Clorinda's speech. "I have drawn my pen through the most violently improper but not through the others," Frances wrote to Scribner when she was correcting the proofs. "The child swore and she swore as disreputable grooms and stable boys had taught her to. In her first encounter with Sir Geoffrey I might have made her exclaim 'Now you really quite annoy me' but it did not occur to me as being characteristic." The actual words the six-year-old girl uses are: "Damn thee! I'll tear thy eyes out! I'll cut thy liver from thee! Damn thy soul to hell!"

It was certainly a great change from Fauntleroy. "A stronger contrast could not be imagined than that which exists between the exasperating little prig ... and the superb creature of violent passions." But in spite of the superb creature, the *Dial* reviewer was "forced to pronounce the performance crude and the method coarse. The author's conception of her heroine is certainly bold and the work has a vitality so abounding as to atone in part for its lack of subtlety." It was as if Frances had been deliberately setting out to refute Henry James' charge that most of the stuff that was reaching him from America seemed to have been written "by eunuchs and sempstresses". And, in spite of Burlingame's reactions, which are easy to share, it was eventually to sell extremely well both in England and America.

But much more than the writing and negotiation over *A Lady of Quality* was going on in 1895. It is the most highly documented of all the years of Frances' life. If not at the peak of her writing powers, as she herself imagined, she was certainly at a high point as far as the life of the world went, and the letters and papers which survive reflect her crammed engagement diary, her rich contacts with a widening circle of London society.

She had had a terrible shock in the summer of 1894 when her sister Edith's second visit to England had been cut short by news that Vivian was very ill. "Five years ago I went home at a day's notice from Rome ... there is a resemblance in the two voyages that makes me shudder," she wrote to Zangwill hurriedly before leaving. Vivian had typhoid and was at the point of death as Frances crossed the Atlantic. But he made a marvellous recovery. By the November he was well enough to start his freshman year at Harvard, and Frances returned to Portland Place, taking Archer Fahnestock, Edith's elder son, with her. 1895 was to be a good year. In February Swan left her house in Massachusetts Avenue and moved into one of his own in Farragut Square. Something had been resolved. Edith and her husband Frank Jordan took over Massachusetts Avenue. Frances felt she could go there whenever she wished and have things the way she wanted. But for the moment she was happier in London. Stephen was at his most helpful and charming, she was pleased with what she was writing, and the only worries were money ones, a constant concern that she could earn enough to support the comfortable and elaborate way of life she had chosen.

Archie Fahnestock was twenty-two and good company. He could look very nice in a dress suit and was "sufficiently quiet in manner not to be out of place" on even the grandest occasions. Henry James "continued to take the liveliest interest" in him, as he wrote in a postscript to a letter in May. Frances saw a lot of James that year. He, like Israel Zangwill, seemed happy to spend a fair amount of time in her company and even to listen to her reading aloud:"I want to hear the rest of the female highwayman," he wrote. His letters are full of what he himself called the "mere twaddle of graciousness", and certainly many of them consist of elaborate reasons why he had to refuse an invitation: "I haven't a pin-hole until after the 1st of June", "I have French celebrities on my hands", "I only want you to know that if, on the 25th, I don't encumber your staircase, it will be because I'm a hermit in a hermitage". But when he did come to Portland Place, and he came many times, he liked it to be at a time when he would find Frances without other visitors. On Wednesdays she was at home. If he came on a Wednesday it would not be until 6 "because at that hour you may be less hedged about and encompassed than at 4 or 5". But he preferred to come on Friday. "The kind of entertainment I like best is weak and lovely lukewarm tea administered toward 6 o'clock or so by the hand of genius—administered, of course, in Portland Place." "I will come to nothing that anybody else does. It must be *all* for me." He said he saw too little of her. He wrote from Playden in Sussex, in an "ovine, bovine, asinine retreat to which weeks ago—discouraged of knocking again and again at your inexorable door where caretakers were monosyllabic, I betook myself—in my misanthropy". On another occasion, he wrote to her with equal hyperbole: "See with what success I arrange just to catch you … I feel so the prince of manoeuverers—and the prince of spellers to be able to say so," signing himself *Machiavelli H. James.*

Frances had been saddened at the reception of James' play *Guy Domville*. "I cannot understand why the audience should have behaved so badly at its first night," she wrote to Vivian at Harvard, just after she had seen it. On the first night there had been pandemonium—fifteen minutes of boos and hisses. She had heard that "the insulting uproar was something awful. Henry James stood before the curtain looking like a man who had steeled himself to *anything—everything.* The play certainly ends most unconvincingly and feebly—but it was charming in the first act … [It] is of the period of my *Lady of Quality* … I never saw anything on the stage so pretty and so real as that apple-tree against the window. I cannot tell you how it breaks my heart to think of Henry James as the victim of what happened at this first night.

It is too tragic to contemplate. Oh! *Why* had it to be so! I rebel against it. He is a man who is so a gentleman and fine and kind in every instinct. And he cares so much about the drama ... I cannot see why—having such good in it—this play was not better ... I am afraid he will be too shocked and outraged and hurt to try again." Frances' fears were justified. James said the failure had been "the most horrible experience of my life". He never risked it again. The "poor little play" was taken off after thirty-one performances, to be replaced, to James' particular indignation, by *The Importance of Being Earnest*. "The title is rather clever," Frances wrote in her weekly letter to Vivian, "as it appears that 'Earnest' is not an adjective but a young man. If Oscar Wilde were not such a blaguer, he would fill me with delight." She had "boldly" driven to the St James' box office to get tickets for the first night but they were all sold out. "I am particularly fond of first nights in London. They are rather like theatrical parties and one learns to know all the people. I wanted to see this one but Oscar Wilde is a party-giving man and knows so many people that he would be sure to have to send seats to half the world besides providing for the critics."

It was the period of elaborate realism on the stage. If *Guy Domville*'s apple-tree was pretty, Burne-Jones' scenery for *King Arthur* was spectacular. Ellen Terry, as Guinevere, and the ladies of her court "had a Mayday festival in the forest—and all the trees and bushes were loaded with white may and the troop of lovely ladies came winding down a sloping shaded path with branches of may in their hands. It was exquisite. One expected to hear the birds burst into singing on every side ... After all, what Irving does in these days is more or less a kind of poetic, highly cultivated and literary pantomime ... there are people who scold at Irving a good deal but ... for my part I should not sigh particularly for the days of *The Bells* and *The Lyons Mail* and *The Corsican Brothers*."

The very day Frances went to *King Arthur* she had lunched at Lady Dorothy Nevill's. Sir Edwin Arnold was there and Bret Harte, George Boughton R.A. and his vivacious wife, and Forbes

Robertson, the actor who played Sir Lancelot—"He is a very attractive fellow with a curiously cleancut, ascetic sort of face—an excellent actor but I do not think at all the type for Lancelot."

Frances saw him again in March in Pinero's *The Notorious Mrs Ebbsmith*. She took a party to the first night. "It gave me a feeling that Pinero had been filled with a vaulting ambition to do something, but has not been in the least clear as to what he aimed at ... It is ... no more dramatic than a pair of galoshes ... It is a thing which seems to casually place before one half a dozen extremely wearisome problems and then say amiably, 'There, my friends. Just go in and settle it your own way. I'm not prejudiced. Lord, no, I never even attempt to settle such things—but I have no doubt it's healthy exercise for you' ... We had to get out of our carriage yards away from the entrance and walk through the rain to get in in time—there were so many carriages in line." Part of its success was undoubtedly due to Mrs Patrick Campbell. Frances had previously disliked her, but this Pinero play almost persuaded her to join the devotees. "The woman can convey herself so."

"The supper was very nice afterwards. Everybody was a person with a point of view—Gosse and Zangwill are so delightfully clever and the Hepworth Dixons are stimulating creatures and Mrs Gosse charming."They had "consommé in cups, lobster mayonnaise, cold fowls, tongue in aspic, foie gras in aspic, cold game pie, amontillado jelly, creme Bavoureuse, Anthony eggs, beautiful strange little cakes—lemon cheese cakes—bonbons, salted almonds, olives farcis, sherry, Burgundy, champagne and brilliant conversation".

The party broke up at about two but Zangwill remained until half past three. Zangwill was one of the party, too, on a less interesting occasion, the first night of Sardow's *Delia Harding*. "It was too imbecile," nothing but a twopenny melodrama. "My leg is the only sensible part of my body," Zangwill said halfway through, "it has gone to sleep."

Israel Zangwill was a remarkable man and if we are tempted to think, on other evidence, that Frances had become worldly, materialistic, enthralled by her own success, it is her developing friendship with Zangwill that makes us think again and realize that she still had that hunger in herself to be more serious which she had always had. There is no doubt whatsoever that Zangwill was extremely fond of Frances and spent many hours talking with her. By 1895 he was much better known than when they had first met in the Chamber of Horrors in 1887. He had published his two novels, *Children of the Ghetto* and *Ghetto Tragedies*, and he had a regular column in the *Pall Mall Gazette* under the title "Without Prejudice". He had been born in London; his father was a Russian Jew. He combined a passionate concern for the Zionist cause with a marvellous sense of humour, a lightness of touch which rarely failed him, even when his anger was aroused.

He was a realist, upsetting many Zionists by his firm belief that "*any* land in which Israel should find his soul would be a Holy Land". He always regarded the Arabs as brother Semites and saw that if the Jewish State was to be established in Palestine, Jews and Arabs would have to have equal national status in "a Semitic Switzerland". He eventually succeeded Herzl to the leadership of the Zionist movement and was president of the Jewish Territorial Organization at the time of the Balfour Declaration. But this was all in the future. What is extremely relevant to Frances is his attitude to money. At a dinner in 1892 he quoted one of his own verses, "as no one else is likely to". It aimed to shake his fellow Jews out of a state where

> *it seems*
>
> *Ideals, aspirations now are "dreams",*
> *Fine clothes and furniture are all in all—*
> *The carriage and the operatic stall.*

He would hardly have given so much time and affection to Frances if she had been as materialistic as her detractors suggest. If she loved money (and of course she did), one reason was that it enabled her to provide dinner and operatic stalls for such as

Zangwill. "Money is made for spending and the good things in life are made to be bought by it," she wrote in *Two Little Pilgrims' Progress*, published this year. She knew what it was like to be without it. But it did not mean that she did not have ideals and aspirations. Zangwill was not a man to waste time in idle gossip. "Cultivate those who can teach you," he quoted at a dinner for Joseph Jacob. "I hope the awakened interest of our community in literature will help to undermine further the tottering supremacy of money."

The earliest letter I have seen from Frances to Zangwill describes how she rushed down to Hatchard's on publication day to buy Zangwill's new book. "Has it come in yet?" the assistant asked a passing youth. "Just," was the reply. Frances gave a sigh of relief, "Oh," she said, "I shall be so *glad* to have it." She told Zangwill she "handed out a golden sovereign with the air of being quite ready to pay twice that and more". It was enough to disarm any author. Zangwill found nothing too much trouble where Frances was concerned. He listened to her reading her work in progress—because it spurred her on. "Can you find an evening soon when you can come in to dinner as you did last week?" She read to him often in Portland Place and sometimes in his study in Oxford Road, Kilburn.

In 1894 Zangwill had applied himself to summer-house-hunting for her, suggesting a cottage at Farnham ("35/- per week—a homely place, of course") or one at Aldeburgh ("an ugly darling of a seaside townlet unknown to Aunt Sally"). He took her on an expedition to "the wilds of Haslemere", Tennyson country. "'It takes so much time to earn one's living, that one has no time to *live*,' he said the day we came to Haslemere." It is a feeling most of us know now and one Frances had certainly known, though many of the people she met did not. It was a bond between them.

Reading his books, as well as talking to him, she felt this bond. Referring to one of his stories, she wrote to him: "I am learning … that there are thousands of people who cannot understand any of the things that are like the *meaning* of that story; who cannot understand *anything*. And one may beat one's brains out against the dead wall of them and die raving mad, if one will let oneself and hence those vivacious spirits the which you envy me. But you see far and much—and great things, I think—and one should give oneself a half-holiday and let off a few modest crackers when an understanding strays across one's paths." He called her "Clorinda" and lent her books. She gave him neckties and he wore them—"one at a time".

Sometimes when she came home she would find him on the cushions of her big soft Chesterfield settee looking pale and exhausted. She would ply him with coffee and cigarettes and engage him in "undisturbing but interesting phsycological [sic] conversation". Frances never could spell that word, though it greatly attracted her. "My house is a nice one. It is a sort of tired brain hospital where patients can move from one pile of cushions to another and there is nothing irritating in the atmosphere," she wrote to Vivian. She found the cigarettes relaxing herself. She had been smoking for years, in spite of some raised eyebrows. It helped her "neuritis"; she was sure of it. So did Zangwill's admiration.

This was the closest of her friendships at this period. And what of Stephen? Zangwill never mentions him. He was obviously not living at Portland Place. In the autumn of 1893 he had appeared with Cyril Maude and Winifred Emery at the Comedy Theatre in a play called *Sowing the Wind* and he had spent some time on tour, but fortunately for Frances he was available in April 1895 when she badly needed his services.

"What do you suppose I am involved in now?" she wrote to Vivian. "Another Fauntleroy fight. Two men in Paris ... have made a play of the story and it has been put on by Bertin of Comédie Parisienne with a success that seems enormous. The Paris papers are full of it and into the fray I have had to plunge once more ... Stephen has been able to take the matter in hand and see lawyers and authorities for me and will go over to Paris on Monday to have an interview with the pirates." The maddening thing was that Elizabeth Marbury had had her expenses paid but had tried in vain to place the play on the Continent years before. Now Frances had joined the Society of Authors and their solicitor offered advice. So did Brandon Thomas, who had played Mr Havisham in Frances' own play; he had had all sorts of experiences with *Charley's Aunt*, which was being performed everywhere. "But for Edmund Gosse I might never have heard of the French *Fauntleroy*," Frances said. He had greeted her: "Dear Mrs Burnett, do let me congratulate you on your enormous success in Paris." Frances wrote to Vivian, "I can only hope fervently that this will end in money." She had just paid one of her visits to St Monica's, the nursing home for crippled children: "How I wish that I were a very rich woman that I might help it as I should like to! ... It is so grievously needed."

Owen Lankester was one of the consultant doctors at St Monica's. His sister Fay was involved in the National Health Society in Berners Street, and it happened this year that the Duchess of Albany, a daughter-in-law of the Queen, was attending a course of lectures there and regularly took tea in Miss Lankester's sitting-room. "Last week she expressed a desire to meet me," Frances wrote to Vivian, "so Fay invited me and I went and made my little curtsey to the dear woman and drank tea with her ... I am always so sorry for Royalties. They are always stupid—poor dears—and as it is etiquette that one must wait until they speak—and as they can rarely think of anything to say and look as if they were frantically casting about in their minds for a lucid observation, they are frequently quite touching. H.R.H. is a nice plump German person with an amiable face and an accent. She has two children and is devoted to them. I could have made her talk quite fluently if I had not been aware that etiquette demanded that I should wait until she made some opening for agreeable conversation. *I* could have begun but she did not know how and so we were not absorbingly interesting."

If Frances, again like Mr Salteena, was not quite "the real thing", she had by now been so well rubbed up in "Socierty ways" that one would hardly notice it. She could talk to a duchess without a tremor, although always aware that it would make a good story, that "high life" was something people liked to read about, though it was even more important in literature than in life to disguise any snobbish leanings one might have. People like to read about marquesses, but mainly to be assured that, under the delightful trappings of their rank, marquesses are but men.

For the most part, however, Frances mixed, not with the aristocracy, but with writers and artists and theatre people. Some of them she met through her new friends Ella and Marion Hepworth Dixon, already mentioned as guests at the party for the Pinero first night. They were the daughters of William Hepworth Dixon, a Manchester-born editor of the *Athenaeum*, a well-known biographer and friend of many writers. Their mother was an ardent suffragette and admirer of Ibsen. Ella, who was to become one of Frances' closest friends, had been educated in Germany and had herself published a novel the year before. It was called starkly *The Story of a Modern Woman* and created a considerable stir: T. P. O'Connor had devoted the whole front page of his *Weekly News* to it. Ella was herself the editor of a monthly magazine, the *Englishwoman*, and she moved with an independence Frances naturally admired. The admiration was mutual. After Frances' death, Ella wrote of her modesty, humour and lack of egotism, of her generosity, loyalty and gentle manners, and her ability to tell a good story against herself, "a rare trait in a woman". But she was still inclined to be impressed by the people she was meeting. She would never have talked of the "little dapper grocer, Gosse", as Virginia Woolf did.

"My tablet is full of engagements," she wrote happily to Vivian. Here is a selection for a part of May 1895:

May 8:   Edward Burlingame and Zangwill at a dinner party
          in Portland Place.
May 10:   Dinner with the Edmund Gosses. Rider Haggard and
          the Crackanthorpes and Alma-Tademas among the
          guests.

May 12: Lunch at the Boughtons at West House. Dinner at Lawrence Sterne's bachelor apartment at Park Side.

May 13: To the Alma-Tademas' wonderful house. Heard music and saw pictures.

May 14: Amateur theatricals and Beatrice Herford monologues at the Crackanthorpes.

May 15: Elinor Calhoun, the actress, to lunch. At home in Portland Place.

May 16: Dinner at Lady Lindsay's.

May 17: Ought to have gone to a tea at the Poulteney Bigelows but mistook the date.

May 18: Calls.

May 19: Lunch with the Countess of Kintire. She has been away from London for a few years, Lord Kintire having been something important and official either in India or Australia. I blush to say I cannot say which.

May 20: Tea with Zangwill.

Hubert Crackanthorpe, whose name appears twice in that fortnight's engagements, is perhaps now familiar only from William Plomer's lines about "The Widow of Bayswater", who

> *Talked scansion with Bridges and scandal with Wilde,*
> *To Drinkwater drank and at Crackanthorpe smiled.*

He was one of the *Yellow Book* writers. His *Wreckage*, a volume of short stories published in 1892, had established his reputation as the best prose-writer of the group. He was an attractive young man, gentle and chivalrous. When he drowned himself in the Seine in 1896, his friends were stunned. "He seemed the happiest of fortunate youth," wrote Richard Le Gallienne. Frances had sent "the new *Yellow Book*" to Vivian in February, 1895. She thought it "affected and pretentious beyond description. The Squeaking Boys cry 'damn' louder than ever and there is a picture of Mr George Moore which looks like an extremely decayed lemon."

But "a little poem by Richard Le Gallienne touched me. Oh very much. I know what it means and I have begun to cast about in my mind as to who shall help me to meet him." She did not have to look very far for Le Gallienne had once been a sort of literary secretary to her old friend Wilson Barrett, the actor who had "done everything" for her when she was working on the Fauntleroy play. "Dear Princess," he wrote to her from the Lyric, "will you come to see my play tonight? If so, I will save a box for you." Introductions were easy. The names were all becoming faces. She met Aubrey Beardsley at Walter Besant's.

Vivian admired Beardsley. He thought him "superlatively gro-tesque". He envied Frances her London life. Life at Harvard was not all roses. He was enjoying his music and he did quite well in his first exams but there was a girl from Vassar who had become rather a drag: "I gradually let her understand … that I could not attend to all her wishes, appease all her cross fits, keep cheering her up and still at the same time attend to my lessons here and do myself justice." And the reporters were on to him: "I'm being persecuted again … On Sunday there appeared in the *Journal* a whole column on me … If that kind of thing happens often it will queer me for any of the societies." Ernest Fahnestock, his cousin, was worrying him by being ill and ashamed of his shabby room. And the situation in Washington was even more worrying. He could "never feel anything but a stranger" when he went to the house on Massachusetts Avenue now his father had left.

Frances wanted him to come to England for the summer—she was taking a house called Broomfields, not far from Hindhead—but her expenses were so heavy, and her income so uncertain, she was pleased to hear from Daisy Hall that return tickets on the American Hamburg line were twenty per cent off, and she hoped Vivian would take advantage of the reduction. "If the Chicago thing [*Two Little Pilgrims' Progress*] is successful and the French play brings in an income and Clorinda is well paid for, I shall be in splendid condi-tion—but I know I am unduly timid where money is concerned and, until these things are settled, I am wretched. Archie and Stephen laugh at me." She was "almost driven to a frenzy" by the American income tax. "I am a poor wretch panting under the effort merely to live—and they want to charge me two per cent for it."

However, there were others far worse off than she was. The poor Poulteney Bigelows had had to give notice to all their servants and let their lovely house on the Chelsea Embankment. She had dined there the very day they had heard they were "ruined"—with "Du Maurier's daughter, just like his women in Punch", and F. Anstey, of *Vice Versa*, who had once parodied "Editha's Burglar" with devastating effect.

Then there were poor Lady Anne Sherson and her inseparable companion. Frances invited them to Portland Place for Holy Week so they could enjoy "an orgy of church services" in London. She gave them "big charming rooms and easy chairs and books and nice dinners" and lent them her carriage to take them to their services. "I am afraid they will be spoiled for the cottage at Sutton and twopenny buses."

Worst of all, there was a mysterious character Frances called the Duke, in whom she had apparently invested no less than twenty-three thousand dollars. "I received the saddest possible letter from the Duke," she confided to Vivian. "He has been dangerously ill from anxiety and suspense. He has lost everything—has had to give up his house, his business, all his property and has gone to live with his wife and daughters in three rooms. He cannot possibly pay the interest and God knows where the capital is. He says I shall be paid either during his life or at his death, but though I know he hopes it is true, I do not see any reason to believe that it is. It is terribly hard on me. I thought I could depend on that interest for your college expenses … It does seem a hideously cruel thing to lose twenty-three thousand dollars when one has worked so hard for it, and needs it so terribly and yet I am so sorry for that man that it overwhelms me. Surely you must have heard something of his misfortunes …"

There is a vivid picture of the summer at Broomfields in Stephen Townesend's novel, *A Thoroughbred Mongrel*. Frances appears thinly disguised as Mrs Flufton Bennett, cooing over a tiny dog which has been sent to her. It is supposed to be a chihuahua from Mexico but turns out to be "an impudent fraud", a mongrel from Seven Dials stunted by the consumption of gin. Vivian, Archie and Zangwill, Owen Lankester, Constance Fletcher and Eleanor Calhoun all appear. Archie has a taste for practical joking. His inclination is to "drown the little beast and send her the corpse by parcel post; it would serve her right for fooling over the darned thing so much". Zangwill, as Singwell, has some good lines, as he always had in real life: "On a dog, a flea feels he has a house of his own—on a man, he has only apartments—at any moment he may have notice to quit." Stephen's own personality comes over most strongly in a harsh, vivid description of a medical demonstration using a live rabbit. The mocking light tone of the rest of the book is transformed by his anger and it doesn't need the footnote which tells us that the incident "is founded on a scene witnessed in the Physiological Class of Edinburgh University, 1882".

The summer at Broomfields was not entirely carefree, quite apart from any canine complications, though Zangwill wrote a warm letter after one of his visits: "You gave me a very good time at Broomfields and Miss Fletcher was an unexpected treat. But I mustn't make invidious distinctions, for everybody was charming to me ... May you all have fine weather and cigarettes and peppermints ad lib. May the play continue to evolve and the collaborators to be friends."

The play was *The First Gentleman of Europe*, which Frances was trying to write with Constance Fletcher; she was known as George Fleming and had recently had a success with her *Mrs Lessingham*, starring Mrs Patrick Campbell. The reference to cigarettes and peppermints was not a casual conjunction. Frances always interspersed puffs on her cigarette with bites on a peppermint. Certainly there was no sign of her neuritis during the summer of 1895. "I want to tell you, Vivie, how curiously well I am. Suddenly it seems as if I had passed out of the heavy cloud of dreary tiredness which has closed about me for so long."

But she was not sanguine about the play. There were three good acts "but the construction of the fourth does not seem to me safe ... Constance is not a person I can argue with when she is in one of her grandiloquently cocksure moods. It is really 'not good enough'. I do not think I shall ever allow anyone to collaborate with me again ... I have not had any quarrel but it is because I was determined there should be none and I am very good at *not* speaking." The play was eventually produced by Daniel Frohman at the Lyceum in New York but did not run for long.

Frances returned to Portland Place "to find scarcely anything in the bank—the rent due, the taxes sent in and divers innumerable small bills". "I should have been in despair," she wrote to Vivian, "if it had not been for Stephen. I did not know he could be so nice. The touch of real anxiety seemed to bring out a new creature in him. He has managed for me, arranged things and seen people and persistently cheered me up and insisted that we could get through the time of difficulty and that once through it should be easier than ever."

While the time was difficult, Frances made bold attempts at economy. "I have taken the housekeeping into my own hands," she wrote to Vivian, "think of your Mammy going to the kitchen every morning ordering dinners and, what is more, going out and buying them her very self. I allow *no* bills. I buy everything myself and pay for it on the spot and the result is absolutely amazing. What I paid eleven or twelve pounds for before I paid *five* for last week." She said she felt too poor to talk about Shakespeare, though Irving's *Romeo and Juliet* was filling the Lyceum every night.

But by December, as Stephen had predicted, things were easier than ever. There was a large cheque from Scribner's—the advance for *The Lady of Quality* and her royalties on the books in print. There was also a £500 advance on a 22½% royalty for the same book's English publication by Warne. There was good money from the French *Fauntleroy* coming in and a telegram from Berlin to say that the *Little Lord* had opened there "amidst storms of universal public enthusiasm". Stephen had arranged all this. He must certainly have a good part in the new play—"You know I really invented the play because it is of his favourite acting period"—but he did not care for either the Prince or Carteret. He chose Lord Carisbrooke. It would make matters easier to arrange with actor-managers who must have the best rôles for themselves.

Frances had now taken up again the book she had first started in 1880—*In Connection with the De Willoughby Claim.* "It is very interesting to pick up a half-written book, not touched for nearly fifteen years, and find it absolutely worth finishing ... It covers a larger canvas than anything else I have done." She read the first chapter to Zangwill and he said: "You have touched that big man so clearly that even now I could go and write a book about him myself." "I care for his opinion," she said to Vivian. His was the only opinion she cared for, at least of the people she knew intimately. This was almost equal to saying she had no particular respect for Stephen's opinion of her work. He was useful, a valuable business manager. He was friendly. He and Archie gave her violets and lilies of the valley on her birthday. But that he had been, or would be again, something much more there is no hint.

To judge from her letters, she seems to have seen a great deal more of Israel Zangwill than of Stephen at this time. On 30th November 1895, Zangwill wrote to her, "I see that you are to be the guest of the Vagabonds on the 9th. I presume you will be making a speech. This is indeed the new woman. Kind regards from the old man." It was nearly twenty years since the jokes about the "coming woman". The phrase "the new woman" was on everyone's lips in 1895. It was not always a compliment. *Punch* filled in a spare inch with the lines:

> *New men, new manners*
> *New women, no manners.*

It would still be unusual enough for a woman to be asked to speak as guest of honour at a dinner given by a men's club.

Frances was also invited to Mrs Humphry Ward's on 9th December ("quite a small party. Mr and Mrs Du Maurier and a few other friends") but the Vagabonds' invitation was a challenge. It was in fact Frances' first public speech. She had got away with murmuring a few words on earlier occasions, such as the Society of Authors' Dinner and the opening of the Boys' Club Reading Room. She had, she said, always hoped to be spared three things— hanging, drowning and being obliged to make a speech. "I am torn between two emotions—one is the hope that I shall be able to make you hear me; the other the fear that it might be better for me and for you, if I could not." After such pleasant nothings and some more solemn stuff, suitably modest, about her work, Frances sat down to what the *Queen* called "prolonged cheering". After years of refusing to speak in public, she had addressed four hundred people in the most difficult banqueting hall in London and had the success of her life. "To do a thing you *can* do—such as write a book—what is that? But to do a thing you can't do, and find yourself called a brilliant thing, is really worthwhile." Zangwill sat at her right: when she had finished speaking, he took her hands in both his and said, "It was perfect. It couldn't have been better." Everyone agreed. Jerome K. Jerome said, "I would give a great deal to be able to make such a speech as that."

A week later she set off for Yorkshire in high spirits. She was going to stay with the Earl of Crewe, whom she had first met the year before when he had been Lord Houghton, Lord Lieutenant of Ireland. He had spoken, as his father's son, at the unveiling of the Keats memorial in Hampstead Parish Church. That had been an occasion. There had been lunch first at Walter Besant's. Gosse was there and Du Maurier, Theodore Watts-Dunton, Sydney Colvin and Aubrey Beardsley. The Gosse children hung laurels on the bust when it was unveiled. Looking at it, Zangwill said: "The irony of it! Just as they did to him then they would do to another today, who had his genius."

Frances had thought Lord Houghton "a charming, modest and lovable young giant". He was created Earl of Crewe in 1895 and endeared himself to Frances by taking "special pride in claiming Sara Crewe as a relation". "Henry James visited him at Dublin Castle last season," Frances told Vivian. James had apparently not told her, as he had told his brother William, that he had found the visit "unmitigated hell … a very chill and second-rate house party". James might have had the same opinion about the party at Fryston Hall but Frances was ecstatic. Crewe was not only "the most beautiful Earl in England", there was something touching about him. His wife had died after only seven years of marriage, leaving him with three small daughters. Moreover he was a poet. She wrote from Fryston while "Mrs T.P. O'Connor and Bret Harte are walking and the great T.P. is doubtless at work upon a thundering leader." Mark Twain had long ago decided that Bret Harte was "a liar, a thief, a swindler, a sot, a sponge, a coward". At Fryston his ill temper had to be calmed with lemon tea, but he did not upset Frances. She enjoyed everything: Lady Celia, one of the twins, tearing up the avenue on her horse "like a little witch", the Romneys and the Reynoldses, the rare books—a Spenser which had belonged to Charles I, a book containing some manuscript poems of Rochester's. Her hostess was Florence Henniker, Lord Crewe's sister and Thomas Hardy's "rare, fair woman". At dinner, Lord Crewe was entertaining rather than touching, quoting Dr Johnson and Carlyle as well as duchesses. He recalled a verse he once heard Tennyson quote as the finest poem of its kind:

> *Mrs Boem wrote a poem*
> *In praise of Tynemouth air;*
> *Mr Boem read the poem*
> *And built a cottage there.*

Edith Sichel was also at Fryston that week. Her "great fat book" *Catherine de Medici and the French Reformation* was later to be one of the first books Virginia Woolf reviewed for the *Times Literary Supplement*. Her description of Frances, written with no thought of publication, is of special value, for it is one of the very few objective descriptions we have of her. Most of the time we have to deduce everything from letters to her and from her and from newspaper reports which aimed at entertaining their readers rather than conveying an exact impression: Edith Sichel does not seem to have read Max Beerbohm's "Defence of Cosmetics" in the first number of the *Yellow Book*, but she certainly had no axes to grind. This is what she wrote:

> I have spent most of my day in trying to fathom Mrs Hodgson Burnett. I think she is very interesting, and I have grown to like her through her vulgarities of manner, her dyed hair, rouge, blacking and endless stories of Liberty hangings and hotels. I can mention them comfortably, because she has not got a vulgar soul and I am sure her heart is large. At first, it was impossible to fit her on to any of her books except *Little Lord Fauntleroy*, but now I understand how she wrote her beautiful stories. She has the power of intense suffering and intense admiration, both conferring distinction of soul.

Vulgarity of manner and distinction of soul: it is a strange mixture. With her manner, was Frances trying to shock the bourgeoisie? Certainly she shared with many writers of the nineties a determination to escape from outworn conventions. I cannot understand the "endless stories about Liberty hangings and hotels": Frances had hardly been inside a hotel since the sad months after Lionel's death five years before, and that was not a time she would willingly recall.

It is relevant to look at a passage in the book she was working on; surely she was thinking of herself.

> I once knew a woman; she was the kind of woman people envy, and whose life seems brilliant and full. It was brilliant and full of the things most people want, but the things she wanted were not for her, and there was a black wound in her soul. She had a child who had come near to healing her, and suddenly he

was torn out of her being by death. She said afterwards that she knew she had been mad for months after it happened, though no one suspected her. In the years that followed she dared not allow herself to speak or think of that time of death. "I must not let myself—I must not … One thought or word of it drags me back and plunges me deep into the old awful woe … It is as if it had happened yesterday."

Perhaps Frances had wanted to assure Miss Sichel that she was not a fearsome new woman. The Liberty hangings might have been a gesture of cosy domesticity. How little we know what people will remember, or how differently we will appear to different people.

To Frances, the Earl of Crewe was everything that an earl should be, although he had only been made one apparently because no one else wanted to go to Ireland. "He is exquisite and lovable and perfect-natured and of finer clay than the rest of the world." She was not alone in her high opinion of him; four years later he was to marry, at the age of forty-one, the eighteen-year-old daughter of the Earl of Rosebery, at Westminster Abbey in the presence of the Prince of Wales. He was to become Lord President of the Council, Lord Privy Seal, Secretary of State for India. But to Henry James, he was "quite pathetic and desolate and impossible. He means well but he doesn't matter." If only we knew what James *really* thought of Frances.

Certainly he seems to have had a soft spot for her. A few weeks after the visit to Fryston, on 2nd February 1896, James was writing to his friend Edmund Gosse about the pallbearers at Lord Leighton's funeral. As for his own funeral, he added, "When *I* am borne it must be by you & Norris & Arthur B. and Mrs Burnett: with the P. of W. well back." To us it seems a motley crowd, but Frances would have been well pleased to have been named with Edmund Gosse, W. E. Norris, Arthur Benson and a shadowy Prince of Wales. And soon Henry James would address her himself as "noblest of neighbours and most heavenly of women".

Affairs Theatrical
1896–1899

Frances' life continued to seem "brilliant and full … full of the things most people want". The coin of the realm needed to fill the maw of the Portland Place house—and of that other house in Washington—flowed freely. She was even able in January to contemplate having her portrait painted for the Academy. Zangwill recommended Solomon J. Solomon, A.R.A., but his fee was two hundred pounds for three-quarter length. If she rarely liked photographs—only that one by Barraud had ever been known to please her—might not the portrait turn out to be unflattering too? It would be hard to pay two hundred pounds to be hung on the line looking like a "drunken Irish cook". The idea was abandoned.

She was entertaining and being entertained as much as usual. Mrs Humphry Ward was not well, but she liked Frances to come and chat. She loved *Louisiana* and proposed to give Frances *Bessie Costrell* in exchange. She was at the height of her fame. *Robert Elsmere* had sold over seventy thousand copies in England alone. Though hampered by writer's cramp (her letters to Frances are in her daughter's hand) she was as prolific as Frances herself. She was much concerned with the position of women (she had been the first secretary of Somerville College) and she was deeply involved in all sorts of social work, including the education of physically handicapped children. The large number of crippled children in

Frances' later books (Ughtred in *The Shuttle*, Tom Hibblethwaite in *T. Tembarom*, the Rat in *The Lost Prince* and *The Little Hunchback Zia*, quite apart from that self-induced cripple Colin) was surely influenced by something more than memories of Swan's lameness or a recipe for instant pathos. Frances' cousin's son, Willie Daniels, may have contributed; but they undoubtedly owed something to her talks with Mrs Ward and her continued interest in the Invalid Children's Aid Association. Mrs Ward's attitude to Christianity also influenced Frances. Her belief that it would be revitalized by discarding its ritualistic elements and concentrating on its social mission was one of the seeds of *The Dawn of a Tomorrow*. Just as Zangwill's friendship suggests a side of Frances it would have been easy to ignore, so does that of Mary Ward.

There were other friendships in these years which were rewarding. Bernard Berenson was extravagantly grateful for grapes and peaches, when she had heard from Zangwill that he was not well: "Let me know when I may come to see you. I was listening with big eyes to the fascinating things you were telling me when we were interrupted the other afternoon. I want them continued and I want to know you better. You scarcely can be the first person who has been kind to me but you are the first person whose kindness has come home to me so closely." "Be kind," Eliza Hodgson had told her so long ago. In another letter Berenson wrote, "I have not forgotten your kindness and never shall." It was not just of grapes and peaches he spoke.

Hamilton Aïdé enjoyed her company too. He was a poet and novelist, but what is remembered is his friendships. At his memorial service James was to muse on "the immense number of persons one had always known him to know". It was at his home in Ascot this year that Frances met Lord Ronald Gower, sculptor, writer and uncle of dukes, who was to become one of the closest friends of her later years. "I went to Ascot on a visit to Hamilton Aïdé," Lord Ronald wrote in his diary. "Mrs Hodgson Burnett came for the day, an interested and interesting lady, with pretty golden hair and a pleasant, sunny face and expression."

When .the pressures of the social round became too intense, Frances escaped to Paris to finish *In Connection with the De Willoughby Claim*. It was a big book, one hundred and thirty thousand words in the end. She was naturally indolent, she surprisingly told Vivian when he had decided at Harvard that he was himself lazy: "You inherit that from me … I have reasoned it out long ago that by nature I am lazy. I believe if I allowed myself I should be always dreaming and never doing anything. But being forced either to work or to own none of the graces and beauties of life I have will-power enough to compel myself to do things." Back in England, Frances put aside the De Willoughby book yet again, to concentrate on the play *A Lady of Quality*. Frances and Stephen—and Archie—took a cottage at Medmenham, near Marlow on the Thames. The hedges were white with may and the house a mass of purple wistaria. The nightingales sang all night in the trees; but Frances could enjoy nothing. Like Vivian, she wrote, she mistrusted plays "but with every Manager in New York cabling for Clorinda, I could not directly refuse to write it". It was not an easy book to adapt. The third act was particularly troublesome. Frances and Stephen toiled over it together—"walking, talking, discussing, constructing and reconstructing". She appears to have forgotten she had vowed the previous summer never to collaborate with anyone again. "It ended last week," she wrote to Vivian, "in something so like delirium for us both that I made up my mind we must stop entirely for several days. I have written and rewritten until I feel as if I had done the act fifty times. It has fixed itself so in my brain that I dream about it … As a Japanese play, continued through a week, it would be delightful …"

Frances was "worn out with all the load of responsibilities and work". She was in the mood to sell all she owned and retire to a cottage in the country. "The book is having a great sale however and one must have courage." She returned to London in July to be fêted by the Authors' Club, "at the first public dinner which we have ever given to a lady writer". Frances was a public speaker again. She laughed at staid ladies who had criticized her *Lady of Quality.* "Why, I think she is just dreadful," an American had told her. "She uses such bad language ... I think she was real unprincipled to kill that man." "What?" said Frances, "you think it unprincipled to kill a man! I have been gathering the impression lately that societies were to be formed to make that kind of thing a sort of religious observance." And then more seriously: "I can only say that I meant by it exactly what I meant by Fauntleroy and many other things, that after all good is stronger than evil and that love is greater than hate ..."

She enjoyed the occasion but she was not well. Vivian recorded that, during that exceptionally warm and dry summer of 1896, she had "a heart weakness that brought her very close to death's door". She was not able to do more than dream. Zangwill wrote to her, as she convalesced in the country: "Mind you keep your brain quiet; you think too much ... London is depressing just now and the TO LET over 63 Portland Place does not add to its attractions for yours glumly, I. Zangwill."

Frances was well enough by November to sail for New York on the *Campania* with Archie. She delivered the bulk of the *De Willoughby* book—still not quite finished—into Burlingame's hands, and he was relieved to be able to be much more enthusiastic about it than he had been over *A Lady of Quality.* It was one of the best things she had done: "There is something particularly attractive about the way it is told on large lines, and with a vigor that seems to me uncommon. The construction is very successful; at all events, it held a hardened old reader like myself."

Frances spent Christmas in Washington with Vivian and her sister Edith's family, who were still living in the house on Massachusetts Avenue. But the main reason for her visit to America was *The First Gentleman of Europe.* Daniel Frohman had agreed to produce it and it was to open at the Lyceum Theater, New York, on 25th January 1897. She wrote to Burlingame on 23rd December, "As soon as all this play business is disposed of, I shall take my *De Willoughby Claim* up again, but just now I am so involved in affairs theatrical that I am not sure I shall emerge alive." It may be that Frances had to put up some money for the play or perhaps it was to help finance Ernest, Edith's younger son, an inventor always in need of money to further some idea which one day, surely, would prove to be just what the world needed. Whatever it was for, on 29th December Frances was writing urgently to Charles Scribner asking him to act as a guarantor for a loan from her bank. The letter is interesting for the light it casts on her relationship with Swan.

> While waiting the arrival of my English returns, I find I have unexpected need of a thousand dollars. The totally stupid law of the District of Columbia is that I cannot borrow this upon my real estate without applying to Dr Burnett for his signature to the note. As he has never had any connection whatever with anything I own and has conducted himself in such a manner that I should not think of approaching him, this is entirely out of the question.

Frances sent for Stephen to join her in New York to help with the play. He was given the official rôle of stage director but was not to have a part. He had been very obliging about it, although Frances had chosen the period especially for him. "He does not want even Carisbrooke if it makes any difficulty for us in the matter." Frances suddenly, in one letter to Vivian, starts referring to him as "Mr Townesend", as if to emphasize that their relationship in New York must appear to be wholly a formal business one. Frances was completely involved in the production. The following letter gives a good idea what this meant, a formidable undertaking for someone who had so recently been seriously ill:

Jan 8   14 West 23rd St

I have been sitting at rehearsal from half past ten till nearly four. I have just returned home, had a little food and am trying to rest before I give up the evening to rehearsing in private the young man who is to play Carteret [Edward J. Morgan] and who now seems hopelessly impossible. But for him I think the play might be excellently acted. Mr Townesend has been working at the thing like a slave for a week so that it might not seem too desperate when I went to my first rehearsal. *If we had not come it would not have had a ghost of a chance.* It makes me shudder to think of it. If it is acted properly it will be a *success* and charming. We shall have to work and work and work. I have gone over Lady Sark's part with her here and must do it again. On Sunday morning I take Daphne. It is no light work I can tell you. It is as exciting as having to play the parts oneself. I am just now in despair about Carteret. We shall have to *hammer* him into his part—and alas! I am afraid he cannot be hammered. His figure *is* so bad—his delivery so awful. Pray for your Mammy and burn candles for her. I cannot write more. It is a wonder I am not killed. Edith and Mr Townesend are so frightened for me all the time—but I am behaving wonderfully. This morning Edith took brandy with her in her bag but I had not *time* to touch it. Still I have not had any faintness today. I enclose you a cheque for $200. *Where* is the music? I am afraid it will be too late. Frohman wants to produce the play on the 18th. I tell him he cannot possibly. It will not be perfect enough. I shall be working like a maniac until it is all over.

… Your frantic but loving Mammy

Frances had suggested in November that Vivian should "compose some music to be done between the acts. If the play went well and all the music played was yours Vivian Burnett's career would be begun." But Vivian, perhaps reluctant to advance himself tied to his mother's apron strings, had been dilatory in getting down to it. And did he have sufficient talent to become a professional musician? He was not at all sure.

He did write the music, but it arrived too late to be used:

Your music came but rather too late. Frohman had expected to produce on the 18th and had got his own music man to write an air. It is not half so pretty as yours—but it is more within the range of the ordinary voices. I think it frightfully commonplace but there was no time to change. Together I believe Stephen and I have saved the play and made it a success. How we have worked—how we have had to *manage* all sorts of things (this in confidence) I will tell you later. I believe it is going to be a brilliant and charming little play and a *success*. Even Stephen said last night he was very hopeful. I will send for you if I feel I can afford it. I want you here ... Stephen works, arranges, manages in a way which sets his price above rubies ...

The reviews were not enthusiastic: "The thoughtful brightness of dialogue that characterized the earlier of Mrs Burnett's works is marked by a very well-disguised absence in *The First Gentleman of Europe*." "A dialogue between the sentimental and the lachry-mose, balanced on a solid log of fine dramatic construction." "It is interesting, pretty throughout—tender and touching. A woman's play with the line of passion that occurs now and then of an entirely unconvincing character."

While it was still running, plans were going ahead for the production of *A Lady of Quality*. Julia Arthur, who had been "taking Ellen Terry parts during her illness—Irving will speak for her fitness", was "wild for Clorinda", so were her friends and backers who were willing to do *anything* to give her her chance. They took Wallach's Theatre, New York, and spent twenty-five thousand dollars on re-arrangement and decoration for the open-ing. Stephen cabled a friend he trusted, asking him to see her in *Cymbeline* in London, and the reply came: BEAUTY INTELLIGENCE POWER. So Frances was not prepared for the intense disappoint-ment she felt when she first saw Miss Arthur's Clorinda. "When one writes for the stage one is a bird flying with wings bound by limitations of time, of space and of the powers of actors," she told an interviewer from the *Sunday World*. "It is immensely exhilarat-ing and immensely depressing."

It was a relief that summer to put the theatre out of her mind and concentrate on a new book—the only drawback being that Scribner's were anxious it should be published to coincide with the production of the play, for it was to be, not a sequel, but a complement to *A Lady of Quality*. It was called *His Grace of Osmonde* and, as the sub-title put it, it was "the portion of the history of that Nobleman's Life" which was "omitted in the relation of his Lady's story". The most remarkable thing about it was that it was finished on 4 October and published on 13th November, in both England and America. Such was her confidence in Scribner's speed that Frances wrote on 18th October wanting to put in some new passages in Chapter 28: "Is there time to get these in the English edition without delaying date of publication?" There was not, but the whole timetable is still incredible to anyone familiar with publishing today.

Frances had worked "like a galley slave"; they had been "the hardest pushed months" of her life. But there was no time for dreaming or relaxation. There was trouble over the play. Vivian had read reports in the newspapers: "They are all lies", Frances told him. "The trouble was not between Miss Arthur and myself ... It was a matter of these amateur greenhorns having the impertinence to refuse to allow me to talk over the conception of the parts with the actors alone ... I could not be driven mad by discussions with vulgar incapables ... Miss Arthur has not—I regret to say—got the right conception. This quotation will illustrate all. In the Rose Garden scene, instead of standing drawn to her full height, she huddles down on a seat and sulks and nags and shakes her shoulders. Instead of crying at last 'Go! Back to your kennel—cur!' she says 'Go back to your kennel you cur.' [That] is a woman of the gutter having a row—the other a creature of race and fire and flame and magnificent defiance and disdain ..."

The play opened at Detroit Opera House in the first week of October. On the 7th, Stephen, who was playing the Earl of Dunstanwolde, sent Frances a telegram: SORRY TO SEND BAD NEWS STOP THEATRE BURNED TO GROUND STOP EVERYTHING LOST BUT I BELIEVE ALL OUR STUFF INSURED. Frances replied: SPLENDID ADVERTISEMENT STOP IF ALL INSURED MEANS ONLY DELAY NOT LOSS ... CLORINDA WILDAIRS IS NOT BURNED AND WILL RISE LIKE A PHOENIX

FROM THE ASHES STOP COURAGE COMRADES ALL.

On the 14th, Frances wrote to Burlingame: "All the really beautiful and valuable scenery and costumes [were] utterly destroyed … The company I believe returns to New York tonight. If they have the pluck to dash out into the fray, get more costumes and scenery, rehearse their parts every day until they get a perfect thing and keep their opening night in New York in the teeth of grinning Fates, the curtain ought to go up in a roar of sympathy and applause."

Miss Arthur was a mule, Frances wrote to Vivian on the 27th, and she was not very pleased when Scribner's brought out a new "Julia Arthur" edition of the novel: "I trust the appallingly depraved looking person who is depicted on the cover will not be supposed to be a representation either of A Lady of Quality or of Frances Hodgson Burnett. It really does Miss Arthur cruel injustice." She might not be able to act Clorinda but she was not hideous. And she liked the drinking song that Frances herself had composed. "The refrain of the chorus suddenly appeared in my head as I was walking down Sixteenth Street. I ran into the MacFarlanes and picked it out on the piano and wrote it down in *letters* … If you require a collaborateur on your new opera," she wrote to Vivian, "you know now where to find one."

Vivian came up for the first night on 1st November but it seemed in the excitement of things they scarcely met. One of the newspapers described Frances in her black evening dress, manipulating a black fan of feathers while "a bunch of mauve orchids reposed on the railing of the box". The applause was generous and there was no doubt it was going to be a financial success—but Frances thought it was dreadful: "If the woman had the brain to understand it, the play would be a different thing." She thought the actor who played Osmonde was terrible too. The whole evening dragged. One of the reviewers said rudely: "Whatever you took away would improve it"—but Frances was sure "it was not the play which was long but the acting and the scene setting". Stephen emerged with some credit.

Most people liked his performance and one reviewer paid a "special word of compliment to Mrs Burnett's collaborator, Mr Stephen Townesend, for the unobtrusive dignity and quick grace with which he played a part slight but difficult".

If Frances had thought before that money and success were synonymous, now she knew it was not so. There *was* money and she was grateful enough for that. As usual, the more she had, the more she seemed to need. "You shall go through your last year at College as a gentleman," she assured Vivian, but hoped his father would pay for his new winter outfit. The theatre was packed but there was a real feeling of failure. There was criticism from all sides. What was particularly galling for Frances was that Julia Arthur was praised and the play was damned. "Miss Arthur, being a clever woman, infused more meaning into the part than she could possibly have found in it." She is "a beautiful, gifted woman with a voice like an aeolian harp" but the play was full of "pomposity, inanity and artificiality". Was it meant to "assert a wicked woman's right to be as freely bad as a wicked man"?

The *Boston Herald* invited Frances to reply, particularly to suggestions that she dealt "with topics that are not savory". "There are only about half a dozen emotions in the world (quite sufficient for discomfort one finds them)," Frances wrote. "Remove from the drama the man or woman who has fallen upon catastrophe, through love or hate or fear—who has broken a law of society or the State—and there remains little but material for comic opera. There is a thing I have rebelled fiercely against for many years. It is the doom which the mere surroundings the human creature is born into may pronounce upon him … Mere circumstances of life may close about a man or woman like the awful iron shroud and crush out will, hopes, gifts … I would cry out to the victims 'Courage! Fight! Fight!'" She was an advocate of one moral standard for both sexes, for tolerance and justice. "Let him who is without guilt cast the first stone." The play may have been full of the "most naïve and weather beaten theatrical tricks imaginable" but its message was a brave one.

Frances was tired, but there was *De Willoughby* to finish and plans for an English production of the play. Stephen had already handed his part over to an American actor, and at the end of January Frances and Edith followed him back to England. Did Edith have anything in common with adoring, plain Anne Wildairs, Clorinda's sister in *A Lady of Quality*? It is tempting to think the character may have been based on her. At this period, more and more she was at Frances' side. "The world knew Mistress Anne but as a dull, plain gentlewoman, whom her more brilliant and fortunate sister gave gracious protection to, and none missed her when she was absent, or observed her greatly when she appeared upon the scene." This seems to have been the case with Edith, too. That perceptive child, Pamela Maude, daughter of Winifred Emery who had played Dearest, wrote of Edith that she "was kind and wispy; everything about her was grey—her hair, her eyes and her clothes".

Soon after their arrival in England, Frances and Edith went up to Manchester. They had had a worrying letter from their cousin, Emma Daniels, who had been widowed and left with the small boy Willie who suffered from "hip disease". They were living, with Emma's two unmarried sisters, in very poor circumstances—"letting three rooms of their tiny house to young men who pay them only six shillings a week ... Out of that they had to pay twelve shillings a week for rent." Their furniture and carpets were in the last stages of decay. It was a world "where one farthing counts and where no one expects or dreams of any hope of pleasure or comfort". They were in even worse straits than they had been nine years before when Frances had done a good deal to help them. It was obvious that they needed more than temporary palliatives. She determined this time to improve their circumstances permanently in the way that she had done for her old teachers, the Hadfields.

It was a situation ideally suited to Frances' favourite rôle of Fairy Godmother. She set up her cousins in a much better lodging-house. "I went and found a pretty, new, fresh little house, with more and better rooms, for more and better lodgers," she wrote to Kitty Hall. "I took it and paid the rent and gas and taxes in advance for a year; then I furnished it all from top to bottom. I made it pretty, actually pretty. Fancy even fifteen-shillings-a-week young men having rooms which are fresh and comfortable and furnished and wall-papered in harmonious color ... I upholstered beds and painted a room and bedstead and hung curtains ..." Even more practically, Frances interested a manufacturer in the scheme and encouraged him to provide the lodging house with tenants—"young men who can pay decent prices". Five-year-old Willie, the lame boy, became Frances' special concern. She kept in touch with him for the rest of her life.

It was this year, 1898, that Frances broke finally with the past. She started divorce proceedings against Swan Burnett on the grounds of desertion and failure to support, grounds which would have been impossible under English law at that time. And she established a new kind of future for herself in renting a country house, Maytham Hall at Rolvenden in Kent, which was to be the background of many of the rôles that remained to be played and many of the books that remained to be written.

Divorce was, of course, by no means commonplace at this date, but there is no evidence to suggest that Frances felt the sort of guilt Edith Wharton was to feel fifteen years later, believing that the price of divorce must be suffering, that a heavy price must be paid for freedom. Frances was not seeking release from an intolerable marriage but merely rationalizing an existing situation. "For a number of years," Frances wrote to Vivian at Harvard on 28th February, "many of my friends have expressed themselves strongly on this subject and finally I have decided that they are right ... to be neither married nor unmarried is a difficult position ... I have purposely avoided making my appeal upon any grounds which would involve scandal. I have put it merely upon the ground of 'Desertion', which Dr Burnett himself made quite simple by leaving my house of his own will. I have always thought he did this with intention. This matter will be arranged privately and with dignity and it is better for both that it should be done." But it was of course impossible to keep it out of the papers. A typical story was in the *New York Herald* on 20th March, the day on which Frances' lawyer instituted divorce proceedings in the Supreme Court of the District of Columbia:

The circumstances which led up to and caused the action to be taken cover a considerable period of years ... Intimate friends of both Dr and Mrs Burnett had known for a long time of their strained relations, and they only remained as husband and wife for the sake of their child and until he should become of age and able to care for himself. All during the time that he was in the High School in this city there was domestic discord. Husband and wife were rarely if ever seen together, and conducted themselves toward one another only as acquaintances. While Mrs Burnett never posed as a new woman, yet she entertained very advanced ideas as to the rights of women and the duties of a wife, which in no way accorded with those of her husband, and hence what was at first only a difference of opinion grew to be the cause of their final separation.

Mrs Burnett is a woman of pleasing appearance and much personal magnetism, while her husband is of less than ordinary stature and is a cripple. It is said, too, that, while a man of some means, an oculist enjoying a large practice and a writer on scientific subjects, he nevertheless grew jealous of his wife's reputation which exceeded his, as did also her fortune from her books.

While their son was preparing to go to college and Mrs Burnett was on her way home from Europe, two years ago last fall, Dr Burnett moved from their residence in Massachusetts Avenue, and took a house in Farragut Square. This, it is charged, is the desertion charged in the suit for divorce. Friends, knowing that their differences could never be reconciled, have frequently advised that a divorce be secured.

It is the understanding that the proceedings instituted are with the mutual consent of Dr Burnett and Mrs Burnett and looked upon as a business matter. Dr Burnett will not discuss the case, but his friends say that he will not file a cross bill or take any steps to prevent Mrs Burnett from securing the decree. She is at present in England, having sailed from New York about ten days ago, in company with a lady friend.

The *Herald* was six weeks out in the date of Frances' sailing from New York and its summing up of the situation may have been equally inaccurate. But worse was to follow. The *New York Telegraph* of 25th May carried these lengthy headlines: MRS BUR-NETT TO MARRY HER STAGE MANAGER. WEDDING OF AUTHORESS AND HER CO-WORKER IN A LADY OF QUALITY NEAR AT HAND. TOWNSEND A MINISTER'S SON. IS 35 AND HIS BRIDE TO BE IS 45 AND BOTH ARE WEDDED TO ART.

All the troubles over the production of *A Lady of Quality* were dragged up, with the suggestion that Stephen was the cause of the friction.

Mrs Burnett threatened to do all kinds of things unless her director was permitted to have his little say, and she even declared that she would go to law if necessary in order to uphold him in his position ... It was at Mrs Burnett's own suggestion that Mr Townsend came to America. While here it was noticed that the couple were constantly in each other's society and that Mr Townsend paid the authoress rather more attention than normally falls to the lot of a woman of her age and one who is allegedly wedded to her art. The bride that is to be is 45 years old and she is exactly ten years the senior of her future life companion.

The news of the coming wedding will without doubt be in the nature of a surprise to persons who know the couple. Mrs Burnett has before now placed herself on record as stating that matrimony was a distinct hindrance to the votary of art. Mr Townsend, too, never gave any indications of yearning for the wedded life. He, too, adores art with a capital A.

Mr Townsend's family is said to have some swell connections on the other side of the water. Personally he is a reserved young man who purposely or unknowingly impresses those who meet him casually with a sense of his keen regard for himself.

Three weeks later, the *New York Telegraph* carried a photograph of Frances with a small denial: "Despite rumours of remarriage, Mrs Burnett declares she will not again commit matrimony." She did not, of course, correct the ages mentioned by the *Telegraph*. She was indeed ten years older than Stephen, but she was now forty-eight. It was twelve years since she had first been attracted by his nice eyes.

It was as well Frances had her new country house to take her mind off her American reputation, which had not been helped by a revival at the Castle Theater of *Esmeralda*. Seventeen years before, it had held the stage an entire year at the old Madison Square Theater. Now it was seen to be "over-sentimental" and "color-less" and only welcome as an antidote to current "mechanical sensationalism". Frances' brain was in "a gruesomely overstrained condition". It badly needed a diversion. The first mention of Maytham Hall was in the same letter to Vivian that told him about the divorce proceedings. She wrote from Portland Place: "I think I am going to take a place called Maytham Hall, Rolvenden. It is a charming place with a nicely timbered park and a beautiful old walled kitchen garden. The house is excellent—panelled square hall, library, billiard room, morning room, smoking room, drawing room and dining rooms, seventeen or eighteen bedrooms, stables, two entrance lodges to the park and a square tower on the roof, from which we can see the English Channel."

"People's houses are always like them," Frances had once written. How splendid to be like Maytham: hospitable, welcoming, rich, important. Its external façade might be somewhat commonplace and modern—the old house had been partly destroyed by fire in 1893—but the brick walls of the gardens, leaning and lichen-covered, evidently belonged to the period of the original Hall, begun in 1721, and so did many of the outbuildings, the bakeries, piggeries, dairy, stables and so on. Immense trees, broad-flagged walks, a croquet lawn and talk of underground smugglers' passages amply compensated for the mock Tudor timbering on the three gables.

There is no doubt that Frances saw Maytham as much more than a pleasant house. It was to be an ideal base for *giving*, for being the sort of person she wanted to be, Fairy Godmother, admired writer. She relished the idea of the rôle that went with the house—Lady of the Manor, distributor of charity, cynosure of all eyes. Sitting and writing in the Rose Garden she would make from that walled kitchen garden, she would be not a mere pen-driving machine, but a much more romantic sort of writer, inspired and surrounded by roses, not bills to be paid.

English village life was deeply attractive to Frances. Later she was to write in *The Shuttle* of the allure of "a manor house reigning over an old English village and over villagers in possible smock frocks ..." She thought that "the most ordinary little anecdotes in which vicarages, game keepers and dowagers figured" were bound to be exciting. For years she had had "a vague unexpressed yearning" for "sweet green lanes, broad acres rich with centuries of nourishment and care; grey church towers, red roofs and village children playing before cottage doors". "I believe I shall *love* this life," she wrote to Vivian.

"We are only ten miles from the sea and the roads are perfect for bicycling." It was less than ten miles from Rye, where Henry James was now installing himself at Lamb House. "We are neighbours and can borrow cabbages from each other," Frances declared with a lack of practicality. James had taken to the bicycle in 1896 and it was one of the attractions of Rye that it was "somewhere I can, without disaster, bicycle". Ellen Terry was only two or three miles away at Small Hythe, and Kipling could sometimes be encountered "trundling his bicycle up a difficult hill". The rent for Maytham was half that for the Portland Place house and Frances decided that she could "work so much better in the country. It is under two hours from town so one can have Saturday to Monday house parties and can also run up to London for either business or pleasure when it is necessary."

Bicyling was all the rage but there was little bicycling that summer. "Edith and I drive every afternoon in the Victoria ... The bicycling is superb but ... we are too tired in the afternoon after carrying the Rolvenden workmen about in our arms all morning ... There are two or three people in the village who have *always* done the work for the Hall—there has been no competition so there is no need for them to learn how to move or think. And they are so *sweet* and so well-meaning and so simply amiably dawdling. One able-bodied young man stands on a step-ladder to put up a hook or a pole and an old man gravely holds the ladder. It takes two of them to do anything—and Edith and I believe that they go away and play marbles together. We lose them so often. It took two of them a whole day to put down a plain bedroom carpet."

From an immediate practical point of view, this was frustrating, but Frances felt she was getting to know the real pace and atmosphere of "rustic English life". "I believe I shall come upon hoards of 'material'." Like her own character Olivia Ferrol, she had long ago "fallen a victim to that dreadful habit of looking at everything in the light of material". As material, Maytham was splendid. She could never—the Manchester-born half-American that she was—experience English country life as a real insider, but she was going to have a very good try. "There is a nice old square-towered church at Rolvenden with a Maytham pew for the gentry at the Hall and a Maytham pew for the servants. I am going to Church. I *may* teach in Sunday School (though I am not sure there is one) and I know I shall have school 'treats' in the Park. When I drive through the village, people touch their hats and I know almost everyone is related to me by baker-age or brewer-age or blacksmith-age. Just you give me time to make them adore me."

Frances was aware of the temptations of the situation. She makes Sir Nigel in *The Shuttle* sneer, "I suppose it gratifies your vanity to play the Lady Bountiful." Was it only her vanity that she was gratifying? Was it not more that desire she had always had to be needed, wanted, loved? Frances knew that love breeds love, that charity without love is useless. She had drawn a graphic picture more than ten years earlier in *A Woman's Will* of loveless charity—Barbara Dysart distributing largesse, but making notes to take Forbes to task about his idleness, and to "read portions of Job to Mrs Feggs the next time she complains of her rheumatism". "And yet Forbes gets drunk and Mrs Feggs *will* complain about rheumatism. And they hate her into the bargain. And I am sure there is no reason why they shouldn't," comments Térèse, "I should." *A Woman's Will* is really a sketch for *The Shuttle*, the book that was later to use so much of the Maytham material. It was Maytham that enabled Frances to expand and enrich the attractive sketch.

Frances enjoyed her first Christmas as Lady of the Manor. She was already really at home at Maytham. "When I enter its gates, I feel as if I had belonged here always!" She involved herself in everything. "I am a Clothing Club and a Mothers' Union and several other most respectable things," she wrote to Edith. She went visiting from cottage to cottage with "the little Vicaress", Mrs Percival-Smith. "I took bundles of baby-clothes and little frocks and petticoats and found out names and all the rest. It was so nice." She filled stockings with marbles and dolls for the village children and took part with enthusiasm in the annual dinner given by the "gentry" to the "old villagers" at the Bull Inn. "The great entertainment is to sing songs with choruses ... Every year each man sings the same song. Old Johnny Hook with the nutcracker nose and chin and the white smock—he's almost a hundred years old and each year he sings, 'The Mistletoe Bough, Ah, the Mistletoe Bou-ou-ough ...' And then we all join in. You never saw your sister shine as she does when joining in choruses. I just sang and sang as loud as ever I could. It was a lovely party!"

Was this happiness? It seemed very much like it. The people of Rolvenden were apparently prepared to accept Frances as the Lady of the Manor, and her washerwoman, Mrs Burgess, admired the quantities of lace on her chemises. *Little Lord Fauntleroy* helped, of course. She was not regarded as a divorced novelist, an outsider, but as the author of a much-loved book. Everyone who could read had read *Little Lord Fauntleroy* and those who couldn't took her at her face value, friendly, generous, sympathetic. Like Rosalie, in *The Shuttle*, "her sympathies were easily awakened and her purse was well filled and readily opened ... Newly born infants or newly buried ones, old women with 'bad legs' and old men who needed comforts, equally touched her heart."

In a letter to a close friend of this period, Rosamund Campbell, Frances wrote more than twenty years later: "It goes to my heart to be told that Rolvenden remembers me kindly. I loved the place so. Maytham was *home* to me." In 1971, sixty-four years after Frances had left Rolvenden, I found it was still true. She was remembered and stories were told of her imaginative kindness in the village those long years before. Jenny Jenner remembered how she and her sister Hetty were given dolls dressed in velvet and how Frances would stop her carriage as she drove through the village (the two coachmen in top hats) and let the children ride the length of the village street. Alice Freeborn, the vicar's daughter, also remembered toys at Christmas time (dolls in sailor suits) and a Christmas party in the school for all the village children. And old Mrs Judge, whose sister-in-law, Emily, worked at Maytham, remembered Frances visiting her when she was unable to earn money hop-picking because she had a new-born baby. She said she looked like Marie Lloyd in her large hat and feathers. Frances gave her port and left a gold sovereign in the baby's fist. Mrs Judge's situation had not eased a great deal in seventy years. She was still living with one cold tap and an earth closet down the garden, but, like Mrs Welden in *The Shuttle*, "she made no complaints". The other person who remembered Frances was Harry Millum. His father worked at the Hall for many years as a gardener and Harry went there as a stable lad in 1898, just at the time Frances took over the house. He was twelve and earned half a crown a week. "The calm here is good for me," she wrote to Vivian at the end of her first summer. "I hope to go back to first principles and merely *live* without thinking—heretofore I have thought without living." An important part of the new life was the garden. Frances had always loved gardens but she had never, until now, been a gardener. She spent a great deal of the autumn deep in the study of Kelway's Seed and Plant Catalogue. Everyone was enlisted in the cause of her new enthusiasm.

David Murray, A.R.A., fresh from a visit to Maytham, discussed her need of roses with Sir James Blyth. He had roses, grown out of doors in December, fit to decorate his table when he dined the Duke of Cambridge, and he and his brother were happy to despatch three hundred roses (of a French variety called Laurette Messimy) to be collected from Ashford station. The Blyth brothers were "delightfully reminiscent of the pleasure they had often derived from passages" in Frances' books and were eager to thank her with roses.

The Rose Garden at Maytham became extremely important to Frances, for it served as an outdoor workroom. Whenever it was fine enough, she would go there in her white dress and large hat, and write. The gardeners knew not to disturb her. "It was as if she had something inside her she just had to get out," Harry Millum said, looking back seventy years. In the Rose Garden, Frances wrote most of *The Shuttle* and *The Methods of Lady Walderhurst*, she turned *Sara Crewe* into *A Little Princess* and she finished *The Dawn of a Tomorrow*. And it was here in the Rose Garden that she felt the first ideas for *The Secret Garden*, as she made friends with a robin which would come to take crumbs from her hand "the instant I opened the little door in the leaf-covered garden wall". Robins are "almost as friendly as dogs if you know how to get on with them". Frances was thrilled to find that she did. When she arrived at Maytham, the Rose Garden was an old orchard reverted to wilderness, full of ancient apple trees, with pears, peaches and plums clinging to the walls. "It was entered by a low, arched gateway in the wall, closed by a wooden door. The ground underneath the twisted, leaning old apple tree was cleared of all its weeds and thorns and sown with grass" (Frances watched the "thin little green beard of grass" anxiously) "and then at every available place, roses were planted to climb up the ancient trunks and over the walls." There Frances had her table and chair, her tuffet and rug, and a large Japanese umbrella, flowery with bamboo ribs, for shade if it were needed.

Harry Millum does not seem to think the gardeners at Maytham appreciated Frances' actual gardening, but her letters record her transplanting seedlings and pruning; and *The Secret Garden* shows that her knowledge of gardening was practical and not merely a matter of waving her hand at her gardeners and saying "Let that be an Herbaceous Border!" Indeed in her last book of all, *In the Garden*, published after her death, she wrote:

> I should always have preferred to have been at least two strong men in one and to have done all the work with my own hands. I love it all. I love to dig. I love to kneel down on the grass at the edge of a flower bed and pull out the weeds fiercely and throw them into a heap by my side. I love to fight with those who can spring up again almost in a night and taunt me. I tear them up by the roots again and again, and when at last after many days, perhaps, it seems as if I had beaten them for a time at least, I go away feeling like an army with banners.

Anyone who can so elevate and enjoy the tedious job of weeding is surely a true gardener. Her hatred of ragweed and pussley was intense ("I prefer not to speak of pussley"); and so was her love of old-fashioned flowers, such as petunias and zinnias and marigolds.

One of the happiest memories of her life, she wrote at the end of it, was "of a softly rainy spring in Kent when I spent nearly three weeks kneeling on a small rubber mat on the grass edge of a heavenly old herbaceous border bed, which a big young gardener was trenching and remaking, while I followed him and tucked softly into the rich sweet damp mold the plants which were to bloom in loveliness for me in the summer. The rain was not constant. It only softly drizzled in a sort of mist on my red frieze garden cloak and hood … Day after day, I knelt on the grass edge and tucked my plants into the dark rich mellow English earth."

But Frances did not, of course, spend all her time writing and gardening. The life of the world went on. There were many visitors. "The charmingest Americans shall all be invited to Maytham," she told Vivian. Annie Russell was one who came. She had starred in that earlier, vastly more successful production of *Esmeralda*. Now she had been playing *She* and stayed at Maytham for a week before sailing home. But the American Frances wanted most was elusive. Dear Henry James at Rye was so near and yet so unattainable. His letters protest how much he regrets how little he sees her, but perhaps they protest too much. Was it that "mere twaddle of graciousness" again?

Just before leaving Portland Place, Frances had bought a set of James' books and had sent them round to De Vere Gardens to be autographed. He returned them with this note:

> 34 De Vere Gardens, W.,
> June 16, 1898

Dear Mrs Burnett

And yet I *lingered*—I never leave your presence and precinct on wings or by leaps—I was leaden-footed and most reluctant. And now I'm glad of anything—even anything so dreary as my own books—that may renew our communion.

I am divided between joy at the thought of so many copies sold—my publishers' statement is usually *one* on alternate years— and anguish for your having added that thumping, pecuniary excrescence to the treasure you are lavishing at Maytham.

But I will charge you nothing for the signs-manual. There, don't take them to Maytham (unless you are really otherwise homeless); they will require an extra van. However, if you do, I will speed over and scatter broadcast that I am

> Yours most respectfully,
> Henry James

But when they were both in Kent (that cabbage-borrowing distance apart) James did not do much speeding over. They did not see as much of each other as they had in London. There was a good deal of discussion on paper about meeting but very little actual contact. James was busy, weighed down by work or visitors or heavy colds. The following extravagantly phrased letter is undated:

> Lamb House, Rye,
> Wednesday.

Noblest of Neighbours and Most Heavenly of Women!—

Your gorgeous, glorious gift shook Lamb House to its foundations an hour or two ago—but that agitated structure, with the light of purpose rapidly kindling in its eye, recuperates even as I write, with a sense of the futility, under the circumstances of a mere, economical swoon. We may swoon *again*—it is more than likely (if you *can* swoon from excess of—everything!)—but we avail ourselves of this lucid interval absolutely to *fawn* upon you with the force of our gratitude.

It's too magnificent—we don't deserve the quarter (another peach, please—yes it *is* the 7th—and *one* more fig—it *is* I can't deny it—the 19th!) Well, I envy you the power to make a poor, decent body so happy—and, still more, so proud. The decent body has a pair of *other* decent bodies coming to him for the week's end, from town, and—my eye! *won't* he swagger over his intimate friend, the Princess of Maytham, for whom these trophies and treasures are as mere lumps of sugar or grains of salt.

For once in my life I shall be as I have always yearned and fondly dreamed: I shall say, "Tomkins, hand the fruits." And Tomkins, who has a red nose and is universally hideous, will look for the occasion like the celebrated picture of Utica's daughter, with the groaning, golden salver furnishing in the air.

It has its crushing side—but I shall have sufficiently rebounded, even from *that* week's work, (under the grape cure) to ride over to you again and pour forth at your feet the unalterable

sentiments of yours, dear Mrs Burnett, more and more gratefully
and constantly,

Henry James

Did James really relish the gift so much? He was not usually
short of fruit at Lamb House. In 1901 he wrote to Miss Muir
Mackenzie that his figs were "unprecedently numerous". If the
letter was written that year, it would have been a case of coals to
Newcastle. And, in any year, James rather resented a munificence
which cast him in the rôle of comparatively unsuccessful writer.
It was going to be hard when Edith Wharton bought a car with
the proceeds of her last novel when, with the proceeds of his, he
had merely been able to buy "a small go-kart or hand barrow on
which my guests' luggage is wheeled from the station" and with
the proceeds of the next he might just about be able to paint it:"It
needs a coat of paint." James was very conscious of the grandeur of
life at Maytham compared with that at Lamb House. She was the
mountain, he the molehill, at least in terms of books sold. In 1899,
preparing to buy Lamb House, he wrote to his brother William:

> My whole being cries out aloud for something that I can call
> my own—and when I look round me at the splendour of so many
> of the "literary" fry, my confrères (M. Crawford's, P. Bourget's,
> Humphry Ward's, Hodgson Burnett's, W. D. Howellses etc.) and I
> feel that I may strike the world as still, at fifty-six with my long
> labour and my genius, reckless, presumptuous and unwarranted in
> curling up (for more assured peaceful production) in a poor little
> $10,000 shelter—once for all and for all time—*then* I do feel the
> bitterness of humiliation, the iron enters into my soul, and (I blush
> to confess it,) I *weep*! But enough, enough, enough!

He was desperately writing *The Awkward Age* (it was already being
serialized in *Harper's*, before it was finished, in the way that some
of Frances' books were) when Alice Skinner, the parlour-maid,
rebuffed Frances. She would always turn people away from the

door when he was working for "when interrupted during his work, he would shout". Frances wrote to give him the invitation she had tried to give verbally. This is his reply:

> Lamb House, Rye.
> November 11.

Dear Illustrious and Gracious Neighbour:

Your letter has the fullest charm of kindness and wit, and I am in a poor frame to acknowledge it worthily, being half blind with a sickish cold—which is agreeably developing, however, so that if I wait for it to leave me clean and alert, I shall risk seeming to you a laggard in courtesy.

Take it from me then, in staggering accents and with profuse pocket-handkerchiefs, that I am touched greatly by your horribly frustrated little glimpse of my really amiable and almost interesting little old house. Yes—it has a meaning—but you couldn't read out a word or two of that.

If I had only known you were coming I would have pulled myself so straight! I shall insist on knowing it very soon. I stay here till (toward) Xmas—perhaps even through it, on to Jan 1st, the latter, in fact, most probably, if I see my way on Jan. 1st, as I desire to go abroad till April.

I am finishing, for dear life, a book—and the day after it is done shall wheel straight over to ask you for luncheon, when I will arrange and settle everything—anent, I mean, the *other* visit.

I will come with pleasure for some Sunday. I much desire a long, fraternizing talk with you, and as full a comparing of notes as a molehill can compare with a mountain. I've the faintest recollection of your view, your woody gardens, garden produce or wild park scenery. I hope you are taking root half as firmly as I. I'll pull up mine for a minute just to *show* you. But I require just at this moment more of a tucking-in treatment. I am yours in a passion of appreciation and sneezes.

> Henry James

P.S. I hope to finish about the 25th.

When Frances finally suggested two dates for his coming, after *The Awkward Age* was finished, it was not work but hospitality that prevented his accepting: "Alas, dearest lady, I too continue overwhelmed with people ... This Sunday and the following one are—it breaks my heart to say—*impossible* by reason of the very phenomenon, here too, that rages at Maytham—viz: some friends from London who arrive on the 2 Saturdays and whom I can't abandon."

Four pages of profuse apology (ending "Yours, dear Mrs Burnett, through it all, ever Henry James") rather softened the blow of not having the pleasure of his company. One visit to Lamb House that is recorded by Ella Hepworth Dixon does not seem to have been a complete success. "Having invited Mrs Hodgson Burnett and the whole of her house-party to luncheon at Lamb House, he began the affair handsomely enough, talking to all his guests, playing the perfect host. Suddenly, in the middle, he got up from his place, walked out without any apology, and could be seen, by his amazed guests, pacing the green garden in a brown study." Such behaviour was allowable in a writer, and it certainly did not diminish Frances' desire for his company. That she felt James was more than just an illustrious neighbour, a lion to grace a dinner table, is proved by a reference in one of Frances' letters in 1900 which we shall come to soon.

One of the most appreciative of the guests who did come to Maytham in the summer of 1899 was David Murray, who had brought the Blyth roses to the Rose Garden. In a thank you letter on 13th June, he called his weekend "one of the most completely happy visits I ever had to a country house". He took back to town with him a "merry-leaf". Frances had a fancy (nauseatingly whimsical or attractive according to one's temperament) that one of the trees in the Park at Maytham—a five-trunked tree—had magical properties. Frances decided its leaves would be as effective as those that the Christmas cuckoo brought from the tree at the World's End. "A merry leaf in one's pocket will make everyone happy and everything go well," she wrote in her introduction to an edition of *Granny's Wonderful Chair*. "If you carry one you cannot help being adorable and you cannot help doing your work well"—the two things that really mattered to Frances. David Murray endeared himself by declaring that the leaf worked for him. "I fancy I benefit by its charm for I am happy enough for any lord and did a good day's work." He had also been a useful escort for Stephen's dog Hett, taking her up to London in the train with him. "At Charing X he was duly claimed by Mr Townesend (looking more sunburnt even than I), some considerable demonstration took place between them and we all separated."

For some reason, Stephen had not been at Maytham that week-end, though he was there constantly, coming and going between Maytham and his rooms at Crown Office Row with complete respectability in his rôle as Frances' "business manager". There was plenty of business to take care of. The London production of *A Lady of Quality* was not well received when it opened at the Comedy Theatre in February with Eleanor Calhoun as Clorinda, though personal friends, such as Grete Moscheles, were able to be enthusiastic. Both she and her husband, Felix, had liked it "even better than the book. It held us spell-bound," Grete wrote, "and I pity everybody who has not seen it." The play was also revived in Boston but again got a fairly rough handling from the reviewers, one of whom complained that such "a dire conglomeration of theatrical horrors and crudities" should be inflicted "upon a defenceless public". There was a cheap American edition of *A Lady of Quality* (one hundred thousand copies). When Stephen saw Harold Warne, he was told English sales were already forty thousand of *A Lady of Quality* and twenty-nine thousand of *Osmonde*. There were lengthy negotiations with Scribner's over *In Connection with the De Willoughby Claim*, which was finally finished this autumn, nineteen years after it had been begun. Scribner's eventually agreed to a 25% royalty, the rate Frances was already getting from Warne's. They were understandably reluctant about it. Charles Scribner wrote to Stephen that "25% does not leave the publisher a suitable margin to manufacture, advertise and sell the book but I am most unwilling to lose an author so identified with our house. I do not wish Mrs Burnett to run any risk of sacrifice in bringing the book to us. We will therefore pay the 25% royalty."

The book was sent off to the printers before it was finally finished and was published only seven weeks after the last word was written.

Frances was by then in New York, irritated to find that the reporters who descended on her on the wharf were more interested in her life than in her writing. What were her plans? "One seems to need them both—America for mental stimulus and England for picturesqueness and rest," Frances had written before leaving England. But what she most looked forward to was visiting Vivian in Denver, Colorado, where he was busy proving himself no lace-collared mother's boy but a tough go-anywhere reporter.

Vivian had finished at Harvard in 1898 with "Honorable Mention" in four studies out of five. ("Tell me just how grand Honorable Mention is," Frances wrote to him, "I feel as if it were very important.") He had got himself a job on the *Denver Republican*. "I wish I had a million to give you. I believe you would found a great newspaper with it." However, she consoled herself, Vivian had qualities worth more than a million: courage, kindness and a capacity for hard work. Frances had written to Edith: "Imagine his going fifteen miles at night in an unheated car, the thermometer 20 degrees below zero, then plowing his way on foot through six miles of deep snow …" It was rather sad that this effort was merely to report "a race-club supper-party"—but he had been asked to do it and he had done it. "I never was so proud of anything in my life," Frances said. Vivian was doing a bit of everything—the courts, the hotels and railways, "even a bit of art and music criticism". On slow Sunday nights, he was allowed to take a turn at the Assistant City Editor's desk.

It was a great blow when her doctor told Frances she should not go to Denver. "I am told with my weak heart I cannot *live* in that high altitude." Her heart had been behaving reasonably well for some time and she took a great deal of dissuading. Fortunately, Vivian was able to come to Washington for Christmas. There were things Frances had to tell him which could not be said in letters. The end of the century found Frances, as she explained mysteriously in a letter to Kitty Hall, "wound up in the web of having tried to help one person and borne the consequences, and in rejoicingly beginning to help another, which, in this case, will of course turn out *quite* differently. They always are quite different—when one begins, and it would be so impossible not to stretch out a hand. But we are what we are, and the kind of thing it is the law of one's nature to do one does in the face of the condign punishments which are inevitably inflicted as the reward of what we think are good deeds."

Frances' good deed in putting out a helping hand to Stephen ("the poor boy", "so delicate and nervous and irritable", who thought he was "always unlucky") was now to reap this inevitable punishment. In February she left Washington and sailed to Genoa. There she was met by Stephen Townesend and married him.

9

The Amazing Marriage
1900–1907

The American newspaper reactions were predictable. The *New York Journal and Advertiser*, for instance, had enormous headlines right across the page: LOVE'S AFTERNOON IN THE LIFE OF LITTLE LORD FAUNTLEROY'S MAMMA. THE AMAZING MARRIAGE OF MRS HODGSON BURNETT, AMERICA'S GREAT WOMAN NOVELIST, TO HER PRIVATE SECRETARY, YOUNG ENOUGH TO BE HER SON.

The exaggerations and inaccuracies were not confined to the difference in their ages. The reporter drew a vivid picture of the child Frances in a ragged, homespun dress—"visitors to Cornwall called her 'The little Girl of the Mines' ..."

Journalists, with little knowledge of the facts, were free to write their own romances. There is something that fascinates the public imagination about women marrying men a great deal younger. Henry James had once written to his mother: "Old women are marrying young men, by the way, all over the place. If you hear next that Mrs Kemble or Mrs Proctor or Mrs Duncan Stewart is to marry me, you may know we have simply conformed to the fashion." At this time, James was thirty-seven and the women were all over seventy.

The sub-editor used the word AMAZING lightly. It was not, on the surface, in fact amazing for a rich and ageing writer—Frances had just celebrated her fiftieth birthday—to want to secure the permanent attention of a handsome, vigorous man in the prime of life (Stephen was forty) whose services as secretary, agent and business manager she relied on. To the world, it would seem likely that she loved him or at any rate needed him.

It seemed less likely that he loved her. Frances had never been a beauty, and now she was stout, rouged and unhealthy. It was said that she wore a wig. Certainly her hair colour owed more to henna than to nature. By her very kindness, her encouragement, her giving him chances to shine, she had confirmed his own belief that he could not stand on his own feet as an actor. The newspapers liked the performances he gave under Frances' aegis but managers did not come running for his services. Everything he did—his antivivisection speeches, his writing, his acting—he agonized over. He needed Frances. "All his psychological problems held her as their centre," as Frances wrote of one of her characters in *De Willoughby* at this time. "An appreciation by an old friend" which appeared after his death in the *Animals' Guardian* referred to "his highly strung nervous system and too sensitive temperament", his "tortuous questioning". "Everything that upset or wounded hurt him to the quick." With unusual frankness in an obituary, the writer said that Stephen had "the delicate hypersensitiveness of a highly strung woman".

In the most Freudian of errors, Frances, in a letter to Edith written on the honeymoon, refers to a muddle on arrival in Genoa as "the wild agitation of losing my new born bride". The rest of that letter is an amusing description of the horrors of honeymooning in a wet Italian spring. "When I remember that I would not go to Cornwall because I was afraid it might rain—and reflect upon this week spent as it were shut up in Noah's Ark—the Mediterranean roaring at us just below our balcony and the poor beautiful red and white camellias beaten and shattered to pieces—all their petals scattering the ground—I can scarcely avoid a rueful grin." This was Pegli. Arenzano was a little better. At least the sun shone. But it was cold. She sat with her fur coat buttoned up to her throat, her feet on a cushion and two hot water bottles. "It is not gay." This was an understatement. Two months later she decided there was no point in dissembling to Edith. Stephen was an impossible husband. He "scarcely seems sane half the time ... He is like some spiteful hysterical woman. He will work up scenes. He will not let things alone." Had marriage changed their long relationship to such an extent that they could no longer live tolerantly together? Or had the relationship always had these extremely black periods? There is plenty of evidence of tensions and unhappiness between them in the past. Frances always admired Stephen's nice eyes but they had only very briefly distracted her from the knowledge of his feet of clay. She had no illusions about him. Why then did she marry him? My reluctant conclusion is that he had literally blackmailed her into it and that the reason he did so was her money. He needed her financial support and her patronage, but he was sick of being an underdog. As her husband, he would have rights.

There were plenty of people at the time who believed Stephen had married Frances for her money. His family told me that, to deny the allegation completely, Stephen actually insisted on paying his own board and lodging at Maytham. There is no evidence of this. My justification for the word "blackmail" comes from Frances herself. In May 1900, she wrote to Edith:

> He talks about my "duties as a wife" as if I had married him of my own accord—as if I had not been forced and blackguarded and blackmailed into it. It is my duty to end my acquaintance with all such people as he suspects of not admiring him ... It is my duty to make my property over to him—to live alone at Maytham except when he wishes to bring down a hospital man or so—he is to be provided with money enough to keep his chambers and spend as much time there as he likes. It is my duty to work very hard and above all to *love* him very much and insist on his writing plays with me. If I had married him because I loved him and believed he loved me what hades I should have passed through.

"His chambers" refers to his set of rooms at 5 Crown Office Row, Inner Temple, which he kept for many years. Frances stayed there several times in 1900. "He gives me the little blue and white bedroom and sleeps on the lounge in the sitting room."

"If I had married him because I loved him …" She certainly did not love him now. Had she married him to save her reputation? Were there revelations about their relationship in the early 1890s with which Stephen had threatened to ruin her? He certainly had some sort of hold over her. "But for the fact that he could not injure me quite as much unmarried as married I should never have got the divorce. His most infamous threat, you know, used to be that he would get Dr Burnett to join him in hounding me down." But how had she been so stupid as to believe marriage would end her problems? She apparently thought "that when this marriage was a fixed fact, he would feel so secure that [she] would at least have peace". But it was not so. It was "a grotesquely hideous position". She loathed marriage. How had she found herself "shackled" to two husbands, she who could write of a robin, "Never since I was born have I loved anything as I have loved you—except my two babies"? Birds did not demand money or work up scenes or sulk. When things were desperate indoors, Frances retreated to the Rose Garden. The new roses were superb.

She put a great deal of her own experience into describing the unhappy marriage in *The Shuttle*, the major novel she began this summer in the Rose Garden, though it was not often fine enough to work outdoors. Henry James wrote of "a brave August of fires and floods and storms and overcoats", following "a torrid but not wholly a horrid July". But the weather was, of course, the least of Frances' problems. *The Shuttle* is the story of an Anglo-American marriage. It was very much a story of the time. In 1909, it was to be estimated that more than five hundred American women had married titled foreigners and some two hundred and twenty million dollars had gone with them to Europe. The most publicized, the most commercial perhaps, of all these marriages was that of the reluctant Consuelo Vanderbilt in November 1895 to the ninth Duke of Marlborough. It was no coincidence that the American heiress in Frances' novel was called Rosalie Vanderpoel. Frances was "not in the least anti-international marriage", as she wrote to her old friend, Richard Gilder, who was interested in serializing the new book in the *Century*. She was only against "a certain order of particularly gross, bad bargain".

She had undoubtedly sealed a bad bargain herself. Although she was not a young American heiress and Stephen was no aristocrat with a crumbling stately home, there are, as so often, parallels between real life and this new fiction. In England, she wrote in *The Shuttle*, "women's fortunes, as well as themselves, belonged to their husbands, and a man who was master in his own house could make his wife do as he chose". Stephen, like Sir Nigel Anstruthers, obviously had no intention of playing "the part of an American husband, who was plainly a creature in whom no authority rested itself … [Anstruthers] had seen women trained to give in to anything rather than be bullied in public, to accede in the end to any demand rather than endure the shame of a certain kind of scene made before servants, and a certain kind of insolence used to relatives and guests". Nigel Anstruthers is described as "a liar and a bully and a coward". In a letter to Edith, Frances wrote of Stephen, "When a man shows himself a blackguard, a liar and a bullying coward, one does not forget."

The accusations, insults, sulks and sneers were intolerable. The demands and scenes were shocking. Stephen taunted her with her past. She had seduced him from the beginning: "He said I began to make love to him when first we met …" Even allowing that in current usage, "make love" meant no more than "flirt", it was the sort of accusation that it would have been impossible for Frances to have borne being made in public, as Stephen seems to have threatened in order to make her comply to some fresh financial demand. For months, Frances longed for death and prayed for it every morning: "Oh, God, if I have ever done a good deed in my life, kill me before the day is over." At times, it seemed it must all be a dream, "one of those nightmare things", she described in *The Shuttle*, "in which you suddenly find yourself married to someone you cannot bear and you don't know how it happened, because you yourself have had nothing to do with the matter". She wrote to Vivian, "Understand that when I say your father never assumed a single responsibility of manhood, I know another who has assumed even fewer and has done more evil."

There was talk in the village, of course. Harry Millum, the gardener's boy, said that they reckoned the master just came down for his money and then was off on his cob, back to the station and London. He thought more of his horse than his wife, they said. "In a place where naught much happens, people get into the way o' springin' on a bit o' news and shakin' and worryin' it, like terrier does a rat. It's nature."

But Frances tried to keep up appearances. There were a few hours of pleasure, times when the happiness Maytham had seemed to hold returned. It was a joy on 19th May to celebrate the relief of Mafeking—not just because she was glad for Mafeking and brave Colonel Baden-Powell but because she had been feeling "that only the devils win on this black earth". She wrote to Edith:

We clambered up onto the tower and Stephen showed me how to run up the flag myself. I ran it up and it flew in the breeze, the church bells were ringing as loud as the ringers could make them, the under-gardeners were in the kennel yard and they saw me run up the flag and threw up their hats and cheered and we cheered back in a frenzy of joy. Then I sent Stephen chasing up to the Church to give the ringers a sovereign and tell them to drink Colonel Baden-Powell's health. Then we ordered out the phaeton and drove up to the village because I thought we might get up a children's treat in the park and call out the band—But there was not time to arrange it for that afternoon as the children and the band people were too far scattered to be collected in a short time. But we drove to the little shops and I bought red, white and blue ribbon and made big collars and bows for all the four dogs—and

I bought the only flags I could rout out and a whole card full of badges of the British lion holding a Union Jack and then I stopped the phaeton opposite Miss Jessup's and got out and pinned the badges on every child in sight. You may imagine how they came running up and I gave out the flags for them to put on their cottages. Then I went to see two poor cottagers I had just heard of and gave them money and ordered in beef for them. One of them was such a poor wretched old woman—she had a fall in the winter—poor old thing she looked almost senseless with suffering and could only cry and gibber at me—as she seems to have lost her voice. But I cheered her up a little, I think, for she clung hold of my hand with her poor old cold bony claw and gibbered out "Ah come again—come again." I can tell you I am going again. I told her the good news and I was so glowing with it that I seemed to waken her up. I think any intense, warm feeling communicates itself to suffering people chilled with woe.

Frances had the sense to let such suffering put her own troubles in perspective. Rolvenden seemed full of the dead and dying that year—old Mrs Weybourne, speaking of Frances on her deathbed; "dear little old Miss Wells", dying of cancer in her white, white little room. After all, Frances did have her writing, and visitors were some protection. "People are coming to stay tomorrow. I shall keep visitors in the house," she ended one letter to Edith. And there was always the possibility of escape. "Sometime you and I may have to live in California together." She would not let Stephen cut her off from her family and friends as he seemed, in his darkest moods, to want to do. "I told him," Frances wrote to Edith, "I would not let him cut people off from me—I said I would call on a few of my men friends— ... Kenneth [Campbell], Henry James etc. to talk the situation over with him—that the matter must be decided. He was mad with fury but I think he saw I meant what I said ... He threatened that he would drive me from Maytham ..." The inclusion of Henry James' name is interesting. Obviously Frances felt she knew him intimately, to ask such a thing of him. Equally obviously she did not really know him. James, who later could not bear to have his old friend, Violet Hunt, to stay when she was involved in the Ford Madox Hueffer divorce suit, for fear of having to hear about her "private affairs", would certainly not have been the man to help bring Stephen to his senses.

The situation was, of course, making Frances feel ill—and it did not help that she knew she must not be ill, that she *had* to write, to earn the money she seemed to need in ever-increasing quantities. She wrote to Vivian the following February: "I am trying to lay aside a capital which can be relied on to bring me a thousand pounds a year"—but it was so much easier to spend than to save. In September 1900, she was "bowled over by an attack of heart failure". It stopped her writing for several weeks. It was just as well the *Century* had not begun to serialize *The Shuttle* before she had finished it. "If I had tried to do the thing, I should now," she wrote to Richard Gilder, "have been decently interred in some unpleasant cemetery and my readers would have been rending their garments, because they could *never* know how it worked itself out … I will send you some more presently. Yesterday I left Bettina [Rosalie Vanderpoel's sister] in the train on her way to pay a visit to Stornham … I am waiting breathlessly for tomorrow when she will reach Stornham and I shall discover what she finds there and how she finds it. I don't know this morning—except in that nebulous way …"

When she was ill, and unhappier than ever, she received a letter written by Vivian from his father's house in Washington. On the envelope, she wrote "A dear dear letter written to me at my darkest hour". "Dearest," Vivian wrote, using the old childhood name, "Don't ever think that for a moment in the troubles you are having my heart has ever left you." He raged that she had felt it necessary "to take the gall, the bitter lees". To what things her idealism had led her. "If you need me to help you or shield you, I am at your call." But he felt cut off and separated from her. "Because [Stephen] is the head of your house, and because he has shown himself my enemy more than once, it would be both a task and a risk for me to sleep under the same roof with him and you. So it is that I find myself ... thrust into my father's arms by you."Vivian wrote that he had attempted not to take sides in the quarrel between his parents and he still will not let his father talk about his mother, but he feels he has lost his mother. His father had been ill, but was making a complete recovery. "If the Fates had robbed me of him too, it would have been too much for me to bear ... You must think of me, dearest, as wishing always to give you as much help and comfort in this unhappy time as it is in my power to."

Frances was quick to assure him that her new marriage made no difference to their relationship. "Above all things you are to remember that you come *before all else on earth* to me. I do not care twopence for the rest. You are my child. I have never had a husband, God knows ... These last years have been awful things for me. Could you have believed that I could ever *hate* a creature and wish him ill? What I have to struggle with now are these surging waves of awful hate which sweep over me in my own despite. They are not like me."

Frances could not stand the thought of a winter at Maytham, cut off, shut up with Stephen. In November she rented 48 Charles Street, off Berkeley Square, a house belonging to Lord Burghclere. It was a delightful house and it helped a great deal. "I never dreamed it could be possible to like another person's house as I like this."The walls were covered in old prints; there were superb pieces of antique furniture. "I can construct Lady Winifred and her husband from their books, their pictures and their perfect taste."The great dining-room was particularly superb, with panelled walls of carved white wood, family portraits and gold chairs, covered with crimson brocade."It is really too huge and imposing to sit in over one's meals so we have taken the morning room for our daily bread ..."

Things were much better at Charles Street. For one thing, Edith had arrived from Washington."The comfort and pleasure of having her with me are more than I can describe." And Stephen was behaving "quite amiably and nicely". His self-esteem had been helped by the very favourable reviews of the book pretending to be by his dog Hett. *A Thoroughbred Mongrel* was sub-titled "the tale of a dog, told by a dog, to lovers of dogs". England being a nation of dog-lovers, it had "*excellent* notices", according to Frances, and sold extremely well. It remained in print for many years, the eighth edition being published in 1913, the year before Stephen's death. The dog became so celebrated that she herself was given an obituary in the *Animals' Guardian*, which later appeared as an addendum to the book.

Stephen was in more demand as a lecturer for the Anti-Vivisection Society. "If he continues to be sane and perseveres in his intention to get work of one kind or another—perhaps I may grow quieter in mind," Frances wrote to Vivian. The anti-vivisection work brought some pleasant contacts. The American Countess of Portsmouth was a kindred spirit. She wrote to invite them to stay and said, "What would the world be without children, animals and flowers?" She was at the time "much absorbed in the starting of our Anti-Vivisection Hospital".

In December 1900, Frances sounds almost her old self. She was back into the pattern of her life at Portland Place: "I am devoting my mornings to my book (*The Shuttle*) and the rest of the day to the keeping in working order the wonderful complicated machinery of life … In each hour of my life I have quite 120 things to do." She was seeing a great many people. The dining-room was perfect for dinner parties. ("Society is charming if your arrange it your own way," she decided, "not if you are obliged to let it rush you about.") One of her guests was T.P. O'Connor, the Irish Member of Parliament, whom she had first met at Lord Crewe's. She discussed Vivian's career with him. "If he wants to come here, I could get him in with the Harmsworths directly," O'Connor said. "Though the amiable things even the most genuine and influential persons say may be safely discounted—because even influence has circumstance to deal with," Frances wrote to Vivian, she wanted him to take the idea seriously. "You have international education and international qualities and they have international enterprise. This is the hour of international things." But she did not wish him to come to England to make his career just to please her. "Perhaps America promises and attracts you more."

It was nearly Christmas and she was enjoying choosing unusual presents for the servants at Maytham. "I am giving my second gardener music. I discovered the simple bucolic creature played vaguely at the violin. I guess that new music must be a yearning and impossible on under-gardener's wages ..." After Christmas, the entire household in Charles Street went down with influenza. "Still I have done an amazing amount of work in the days I have not been propped up by pillows." Sometimes she wrote even in bed; she produced an article, a rare thing for her, for newspaper syndication. It was about Queen Victoria: "The Queen fell ill—all the world seemed to pause ... and I was so full of that one woman." She died on 22nd January. Frances, like the vast major-ity of Victoria's subjects, had never known a time when she was not on the throne. She watched the funeral procession, perhaps a little consoled by the fact that she had been paid forty pounds for work that had taken her two mornings; she immediately sent a hundred dollars to Vivian to buy himself a new dress suit and some "fine linen".

Frances had put aside *The Shuttle*, which was becoming a very big book and would not be finished for many months, in order to supply something to the *Century*, which had already advertised a new Frances Hodgson Burnett story. She wrote *The Making of a Marchioness* in less than two weeks. In England it appeared in the *Cornhill*. This brief book has claims to be the best novel Frances wrote. "The little American tale-tellers (I mean the two or three women) become impossible to me the moment they lengthen," Henry James wrote to W. D. Howells early in 1902. And many people would agree with him and find impossibly long-winded and drawn-out such books as *Through One Administration*,

In Connection with the De Willoughby Claim and *The Shuttle*, and the later *T. Tembarom* and *The Head of the House of Coombe*. They all run to more than four hundred pages of close print.

The Making of a Marchioness, even when printed with its sequel, is a much more digestible length. Marghanita Laski wrote an attractive introduction to a re-issue of the book (1967). She calls *The Shuttle* "poor man's James", a reasonable comment, and goes on to quote Frances' own description of the shorter book:

> This is such a dear thing, I can't tell you how I enjoyed writing it. It is a study of a type and in an atmosphere I know so well. It is called *The Making of a Marchioness* and it is a picture of a nice, simple, sweet prosaic soul who arrives at a good fortune almost comic because it is in a sense so incongruous. Its heroine is a sort of Cinderella—a solid, kind, unselfish creature—with big feet instead of little ones. Her name is Emily Fox-Seton and I absolutely love her—as you will … The cleverness of the thing (I know it is clever) lies in the studies of character and the way in which the most wildly romantic situation is made compatible with perfectly everyday and unromantic people and things.

Marghanita Laski comments:

> She is right. The book *is* "a dear thing". But apart from its charm and deft storytelling, it is, far more than Mrs Hodgson Burnett could have realised, a cruel revelation of the nature of Edwardian high society.
>
> She knew, of course, as an American, that this society had faults. Their castigation and often correction by nobler transatlantic cousins was her most usual theme. What she could not have known was how very nasty it would, half a century later, appear.
>
> This is … the best novel Mrs Hodgson Burnett wrote, and good at the level she intended, that of the fairy story diluted with unromantic realism. But it is, in today's light, a more interesting novel than she could have known it would become, for she could

never have supposed its realism to be as harsh as we now perceive it to be.

It is a measure of the real joy Frances had in writing, in storytelling, that she could find such happiness in producing this book, even at this particularly unhappy period of her life. Her gifts made it possible for her to escape for hours on end from the intolerable pressures of real life. Stephen seemed no longer quite so intent on tormenting her, but things were difficult enough. At times, he seemed to have forgotten his summer behaviour. "Why can't you trust me? Why can't you love me?" he would ask, again and again. And Frances could only gaze at him, amazed, and wish she could forget. She found it best to speak to him as little as possible. But it was not easy to live with him. She wondered how long she could go on with this grotesque marriage. She felt powerless in the face of what George Eliot had called "the dreadful vitality of deeds". What she had *done* lived and acted apart from her will. She could not rewrite her own story, erasing without trace the passages she did not like.

At least Stephen was still dealing with disagreeable business matters. On 5th March 1901, he broke the news to Scribner's "that Mrs Townesend has decided (entirely on her own initiative) to place the production [of *The Making of a Marchioness*] in the hands of a New York firm, which has agreed to give it a greater advertising push than it would pay an established firm to accord it". Scribner was horrified. He knew it was too late to have *The Making of a Marchioness* but he was determined *The Shuttle* "should not go from us". Had they not sold more than one hundred thousand copies of *The De Willoughby Claim*? Stokes could make no similar boast. There was a royalty cheque for five thousand three hundred and seventy dollars due in June. How could she complain? On his next visit to London, Scribner rushed down to Maytham to see Frances. It was an embarrassing visit. He had lost the larger book as well. "After hearing my fate I fear that I must have been a very dull guest." It was a blow to be repeated later by the desertion of Edith Wharton, who was to leave her old publisher on being offered a bigger advance by D. Appleton and Co. Fortunately for Scribner he had at last secured Henry James, whom he had long wanted to publish.

Frances and Stephen had returned to Maytham at the end of March with a new acquisition, a pianola, to distract them. Frances wrote pages to Vivian about this pianola, as if to convince her musical son that it was neither an extravagance nor merely a mechanical contraption. "Lord Borthwick—who has a musical passion"—was apparently as impressed as she was when they first heard it at the house of Mr Ashton-Jonson, who wrote on Wagner. "It is really wonderful—not entirely mechanical. Though anyone can make it strike the notes, one must *practise* and know and love the music before one can make it express itself." Paderewski had two. "He uses them as a means of enjoying music too abstruse for concert-room taste and so difficult as to require too much practise to allow of his giving the time to it."

Stephen spent a great deal of time that spring playing on the pianola in the billiard room. Pamela Maude, who stayed at Maytham in April and May of that year with her sister, has vivid memories of them both. "We felt a queer sort of sympathy for Mr Townesend—his silences and his pianola playing. He seemed so alone. He always seemed to be alone. I can't remember them ever speaking to each other." As for Frances, the children were rather disappointed that she was "stout, stocky and dressed in white". She took to her bed with "headaches" and wore a red wig and was not at all like Fauntleroy's Dearest, but she did see "things in the same way as ourselves".

Pamela Maude was not quite eight at the time but I trust her memory completely. Nearly everything she records in her short memoir of the visit in her book *Worlds Away* is confirmed by Frances' own letters of the period to which Pamela did not have access when she wrote. "Never shall I forget—and never will they," Frances wrote to Vivian, "a day we spent in the ruins of Bodiam Castle." And they never did. Frances knew how to make a day memorable for children. She told them stories of life in ancient castles, of knights and ladies and palmers and minstrels: "We were twelfth-century ladies all day … the day was a perfect thing and I can imagine what a picture it will always remain in those children's minds. Every day was perfect for them in one way or another." It was an extraordinary spring, that was to go on into an extraordinary summer. As James put it, "4 or 5 months from April of almost merciless fine weather—a rainlessness absolute and without precedent".

The brilliant days gave endless time for exploring and acting, gathering primroses, listening to stories and playing with a pet lamb. The primroses were later to appear in Frances' story *The Spring Cleaning*, in which Queen Crosspatch and her Green Workers set to with hot-water bottles, delvers and tuggers to make sure the primroses are not late for a young London flower girl to sell on Primrose Day. The pet lamb nuzzled and butted its tight-curled head into the sides of the Maude children just as Dickon's lamb nuzzles Colin in *The Secret Garden*. Its bleat reminded the children—Margery was then twelve—of Gerald Lawrence, one of their favourite actors. Lawrence had recently appeared in the unsuccessful English production of *A Lady of Quality*. He was a close friend of Stephen's and it was to him, when he died in May 1914, that Stephen entrusted the letters he had received from Frances. "Make such use of them," he was to say in his will, "as may be in any way helpful in the defence of my character and reputation." But these letters seem to be lost and none of his, apart from those to Scribner's, appear to have survived. There is no evidence for the defence of Stephen.

Pamela and Margery Maude were the daughters of Cyril Maude and Winifred Emery, the actors. Winifred had played Dearest in *Little Lord Fauntleroy* and Stephen had appeared with them in *Sowing the Wind* at the Comedy Theatre in 1893. There was some question that Cyril Maude might put on a dramatized version of *The Making of a Marchioness*. It seemed to Frances, working on her plan to "keep visitors in the house", an excellent idea to have the children to stay. Stephen would never make scenes in front of children. Inviting the small girls originally as protection, Frances came to revel in their visit. They were "two of the most lovable and wonderful children I ever knew". They had imaginations just like hers. They had a perfect passion for acting and gave "wonderful little performances in the billiard room every evening". The highlight was when Pamela took the part of Little Lord Fauntleroy. She described this and other delights of the holiday in a letter to her parents:

Darling Dad & Mum

Yesterday I dressed up as Little Lord Fauntleroy. Mrs Townesend said she would like to see us play it. So I was Cedric and after Mrs Townesend said I was the best little Lord Fauntleroy she had had & she wished I could play it in London, was not that nice!!!

It was the real suit that Mrs Townesend's little boy had (Vivian) it was brown velvet with lace cufs & collers & a yellow silk sach with my hair loose.

Yesterday we went into a wood called The Primrose World & dug up primroses & I got four scractches & Margery got 3 or 2 … To day we went to Bodiam Castle & it was great fun. We had lounchen out of doors we had cutlets & peas & carrots then for pudding orange jelly, then after pudding, we had little cakes. Mrs Townesend when comming back she told us fairy stories all the way back. They were lovely.

Your loving Pam

Seventy years later, reading Marghanita Laski's brief study of Mrs Burnett, Pamela Maude was moved to protest that she was not conceited, she was not offensively whimsical: "When we stepped into the Fairy Tree and she read us *Sara Crewe*, she seemed to be completely forgetful of *herself* … What Marghanita Laski has not brought out—how could she, not having known her?—was her complete stepping into another world, the world of her imagination, which she was able to make real to others. She was not 'bogus', not vulgar." Children do detect insincerity, they are generally suspicious of adults who try to endear themselves by behaving as children. But they recognize kindred spirits—"She saw things in the same way as ourselves." It is obvious from the books that she did, indeed, that the child's eye view was natural to her. But it is pleasant to know that she could share things not only with her readers but with children face to face. It was perhaps this reading aloud of *Sara Crewe* which made Frances see how she could dramatize it.

Frances was at this time working on a sequel to *The Making of a Marchioness*, which Smith and Elder, its English publisher, wanted in order to make the book a reasonable size. There was also *The Shuttle* to finish, but Frances did not begrudge any of the time she spent with the children, even when they, not she, were the centre of the stage. When they had gone, the book was finished. "As in the first story, wildly romantic things happened to unromantic persons, in the second wildly melodramatic things will happen to undramatic persons. I think it is all right. It is to be called *The Methods of Lady Walderhurst*." It is "all right" but not much more. Emily Fox-Seton, so admirable in the first book, becomes merely irritating in her Patient Grizelda rôle in this one.

Vivian was as ever in Frances' mind. She worried about him, constantly and wished they were living their lives together. She worried that he was working too hard ("a man who is counted of value in a newspaper office is obliged to do three men's work"), that he was not getting enough sleep, that he should see more of Europe, that he needed a new piano and new summer clothes and that he was beginning to go bald. For this last anxiety, she recommended "one part of ordinary blistering fluid to ten of Petrole-Hahn". Most of her other anxieties would be stilled if he could take a holiday in Europe: "I will give it to you of course and it might be useful to you as well as ornamental."

Vivian was in Paris in July and Frances longed for him to come to Maytham. She was filling the house with guests and the plan was succeeding. On 22nd July she was awhirl with preparations for a cricket-match and house-party the following week. "It will be the greatest fun. We shall have about twenty-five people staying in the house—a band—and tea on the field and all our county neighbours looking on ... Lord Maitland (who is playing in our eleven) can only come on Saturday morning as he is to be hung over with medals by the King on Friday. So you see you will be in time for the match if you get in by 11.39 when he does. I should not ask you to come if I did not know you would find all will go well. This of course will be an excellent time to arrive—in the midst of a big house party and I want you very much." But none of Frances' persuasions ("You have never enjoyed yourself in your life as you will if you come now ... You and Lord Maitland will have so much to say to each other of photography"), nor anything else, could make Vivian be his "stepfather's guest". Frances said he must not talk like that: "You have no stepfather in the ordinary sense. Stephen is only Stephen to you and so long as he is perfectly nice the best thing you can do for me is to act as if nothing had really changed."

And, amazingly, Stephen *was* being "perfectly nice". He fell in with Frances' plans for the cricket-party with enthusiasm and "worked like a Trojan to make people comfortable". Everything went smoothly, even the problem of giving "nine or ten men baths enough after cricket and tennis and Bumble Puppy". There were forty people in the house, counting the servants. It was more complicated than producing a play. Was *this* the Party she had been waiting for all her life? If only Vivian had come ... If only, every time she looked at Stephen's face, she did not see, in spite of its temporary calm, the ugly passions and demands and sneers ... At least, her guests seemed to be happy: "Everyone went away—as people always leave Maytham—longing to be asked to come again."

She and Edith left Maytham themselves after the party and met Vivian in London. Later the three of them travelled to Holland and Belgium together. And in December, they sailed on the *Minnehaha* to America. "At no period of her life," Vivian recorded, had Frances "been in so nervous a condition. The task of keeping the surface of things at Maytham smooth while struggling with the temperament of Stephen had brought her to the last frayed edge of her endurance." She took refuge at the Riverside Sanatorium at Fishkill-on-Hudson. She was as usual feeling short of money and was glad to have an advance from Scribner's on the royalty cheque of $1,951.21, not really due until June. The story was put out for the papers that she was forced to rest as a result of overwork. "She is suffering from the effects of too constant application to literary work and is being treated for neuritis." "My suffering," Frances was reported to have said, "makes it impossible for me to work hard at present. I am glad of the chance to rest but I deplore the cause."

The real cause, Stephen, crossed the Atlantic and went to see her at the Sanatorium in April; and there she found the courage, apparently, to tell him he could say what he liked about her, she was not going to live with him again. Did she in fact buy him off? Did she agree to let him have her English royalties in spite of the Married Woman's Property Act of 1882? It seems likely. But at least he made a real attempt to find work. On the front page of the stage paper the *Era* of 20th December 1902, among the columns and columns of actors and actresses making known their availability, there appears an advertisement put in by Stephen:

Mr Will Dennis
Address Stephen Townesend
5 Crown Office Row
Inner Temple.

By this time, of course, Frances was much recovered. Everything was settled. She knew where she was. Dr Whilinell's treatment had been excellent and a summer of working quietly in a cottage at East Hampton on Long Island had completed the cure. It cheered her to know from letters how much she was missed at Rolvenden. "If I heard you were at Maytham Hall," wrote someone called

Mary Snood, "I would come *directly* for the happiness of seeing you once more." It also cheered her when her new play, so speedily written that summer, opened on 20th December 1902, at the Shaftesbury Theatre, London, under the management of Seymour Hicks, with Beatrice Terry as Sara Crewe. It was at first called in England *A Little Unfairy Princess*. Franklin Fyles wrote in the *Mail & Express* of 15th January 1903, just before it transferred to Terry's theatre: "Mrs Burnett has attempted to duplicate the success of her *Little Lord Fauntleroy* and in my opinion she has done it."

The New York production (without "Un-fairy" in the title) opened at almost the same time. She and Vivian were living that winter in a house on West 87th Street. It was convenient for Vivian, who was now working for a book-publishing firm connected with *McClure's Magazine*. It was also convenient for Frances to help rehearse the new play. It opened at the Criterion Theater, New York on 14th January 1903. Millie James played Sara: "Dainty, winsome and lovable," said the papers. "She drew from the part funds of pathos and gladness." Clara, one of the schoolgirl bullies, was played by Pauline Chase, who was later to be Barrie's favourite Peter Pan. The production drew a great deal of admiration: "Such minor faults as exist are a thousand times over-balanced by the beauties of the piece." For critics, in those days, were not afraid to say "we are all children—all of us. And we are ready to feel once more the keen delights and exquisite griefs of the days that are gone." They were prepared to admit their pleasure that *A Little Princess* "took from their nostrils the reek of the problem play and the stench of the French farce". Strong men found themselves with lumps in their throats; women and children wept. It was indeed the success of *Fauntleroy* all over again. "Sara Crewe, like the famous boy, appeals to old and young alike," wrote one critic, and Millie James' clothes drew attention to the parallel. At the first performance, Frances smiled and bowed. "I just want to say that I thank you all, my dear children, for coming to the party." This was the Party certainly, and it was not over in a single evening but went on and on.

Facing the house on West 87th Street, there were some boarded-up houses, the basements occupied by caretaker families. Frances sometimes saw a child playing by herself on the side-walk in front of the house opposite. This child became Judith and her strange story, *In the Closed Room*, has already been referred to at the time of Lionel's death. It was published by McClure's as a very pretty illustrated "gift book" for Christmas 1904. The *Dial* called it "a story of spiritual and mystical significance, of true literary value". It shows how much Frances was still obsessed by Lionel's death fourteen years earlier.

Not long before, worrying about Vivian's health, she had written to him, "You shall not be killed as Lionel was. I will not have it—*I will not have it*." Lionel was gone from this world but she never felt he was very far away. She could never put him out of her mind. Writing a letter of sympathy to an old friend, Emma Anderson, Frances once put her feelings like this:

> They have not gone away from you—those who loved you every hour of their lives. They are close to you—they are a guard around you—they are talking to you—listening to you—taking care of you as you took care of them ... When Lionel went away, I know my soul was saved by things he surely said to me when I could bear no more ... I am not thinking of your dearests as conventional angels with flapping wings or as spiritualistic creatures, lifting tables and throwing cushions about—I am thinking of them as real—real—as themselves.

Years later, Frances was to use her conviction about an after-life most vividly in *The White People*, with its haunting account of an encounter on a train journey. The girl Ysobel notices a mother in mourning enter her railway carriage. Clutching at her skirts and clamouring for attention, but totally ignored, is a pale child. Ysobel is distressed that the mother weeping for the dead ignores the living. It is only much later she realizes that the pale child at the mother's side was in fact the dead one, and only she could see it.

There is another passage in this book which was "a real thing. It was a wonderful dream—No, I cannot believe it was a dream—which I myself passed through and which ... made the greatest difference in my life and in my feelings about those we can no longer see with human eyes." This passage is Ysobel's experience "out on the hillside". It was nothing less than a glimpse of heaven. "The difficulty is that there are no earthly words to tell it." Frances' experiences appealed particularly to those, and there were many, who questioned conventional religion but disliked the trappings of psychical research, the automatic writing, the spirit photography, the atmosphere of seances, the necessity for mediums.

In the summer of 1903, Frances returned to East Hampton, renting a cottage called Dune Crest. It was there *In the Closed Room* was written: ten thousand words in four days, which brought in a thousand dollars for the magazine rights alone. Then Frances turned back once again to *The Shuttle*. She had begun it in the summer of 1900 and it was not finally finished until the autumn of 1906. This book was a real labour to her; the pen-driving machine refused to function in its usual smooth professional way. The material (that "fresh, unused material" she had been urged to acquire as long ago as 1889 by the *Literary News*) was intractable. The struggles continued right to the end. "I have been thinking of nothing but the book," she wrote to Kitty Hall in August 1906, "which has not been rushing headlong as sanguine Vivian thinks. It has definitely hung back because it knows it *ought* to be finished by September. It simply holds on to each obstacle it is dragged past and screams and kicks up its heels and tries to dig its toes into the ground at the same time. That is difficult, of course, but it is devil enough to accomplish it. For one thing, you see, it knows it can't have as much room as it wants, because it has to be serialized, and if I gave it all the room it wanted, the *Century* would be brimming over. But, grinding my teeth, I push it along, holding on to its collar and kicking it on the shin at intervals. What I say is—between me teeth—'You won't, eh? Well, we'll see which of us two is the master.' That isn't joy, you know. If the serialization could have been kept from it I dare say it would have given in long ago. But I just let my tongue slip in its presence one day—it always *is* present, you know, and it has behaved like the D—— ever since. Stories are that there 'eadstrong."

Frances was able to joke about it but part of the problem, back in 1903, was that so much of the material was too near the knuckle; Sir Nigel Anstruthers was Stephen writ large, distorted, exaggerated, but still Stephen, and as Frances described Rosalie's sufferings (so different from her own, as Rosalie was so different, but so imaginable), her pen faltered. She was glad of any excuse to put *The Shuttle* down and turn to other things. On these other things, that summer of 1903, the pen-driving machine was working with incredible efficiency. There were all sorts of proposals. E.L. Burlingame of Scribner's had an attractive suggestion. He wanted Frances to produce a new longer version of *Sara Crewe*, which Scribner's had originally published in 1888, incorporating the new material she had used in the play *A Little Princess*. Naturally he wanted it quickly. The play was still running and Christmas sales would be splendid. His letter arrived to find Frances already committed to two dramatizations. Charles Frohman was interested in producing a play of the 1889 Spanish novelette *The Pretty Sister of José*, as a vehicle for his star Maude Adams. And an actor, Robert Hilliard, was keen to appear as De Willoughby. Frances' letters to Burlingame written from East Hampton in July give a good idea of her impressive mental energy even when she was not well.

I have been obliged to spend much time lying down on account of being possessed of a devil which a distinguished physician has now pronounced to be not neuritis but osteoperinestitch. Do not quail. I did not. But for this polysyllabic trifle I am in glowing health—but the trifle itself was by the Inquisition invented, I think … To make a new book for the winter trade, you must know in advance *when* you can get it. I am just beginning a new play and another comes after that. Sometimes things finish themselves like a whirlwind for me but one cannot be sure of two plays doing themselves in a month. If I were not in such an extraordinary mood about work, I could not think of touching anything after the work of the summer, but I think I might do this.

She asked when was the last possible date they wanted the book and was told the middle of September if it were to be on sale for Christmas. On 30th July she agreed to a two-thousand-dollar advance on a royalty of 12% for a book of sixty thousand words.

But it was too much to expect. The book, fortunately (for it must surely be a much better book for not having been rushed), was postponed. Frances could concentrate on the plays. She could also find time to remember her friends at Rolvenden. There are letters of August 1903 from John Stedman and Mary Snood in Rolvenden which give a very good idea of how far she had succeeded in making herself loved ("Just you give me time to make them adore me," she had written to Vivian in 1898). John Stedman wrote to thank her for the cheque for Mrs Almond "to pay up her rent and one pound over to get herself a few comforts … She is most grateful to you for your kindness, does not know how to express her gratitude, says she never had such a kind friend as you have been to her, poor woman. She has been very sadly for some little time … She gave me the enclosed fern frond and asked me if I would send it on to you. She hopes to be spared to see you again and we all hope to have the great pleasure of welcoming you back again to Maytham, it has not been the same place since you left." Everything was going wrong in Rolvenden: "The Hay and Corn both very much spoilt. Apples, Pears and Plums quite a failure."

Mary Snood wrote, "You would like to hear the people exclaim when I talk about you coming home. 'Do you think she really will come back to us?' and when I answer I do indeed, it is sure to be, 'Oh! I hope I may live to see her.'"

Perhaps next summer she would return. In the meantime for the winter she rented "a modest little house" at 105 Madison Avenue, New York, to finish off her plays and be on hand for their productions. An interviewer, disguised as Mlle Manhattan, visited her from the *Sunday Telegraph* and was admitted by "a solemn and literary-looking butler". She noted the grand piano and the bookcases full of Ruskin, Balzac, Addison, Gibbon, the Lake Poets. "All look equally well thumbed," wrote Mlle Manhattan, but they may well have been somebody else's thumbs, for the bookshelves of rented houses are often full. Frances received the interviewer in a pretty bed-chamber. Senator Depew had apparently once described her as "a woman with a man's intellect" but the journalist found her totally feminine, "a warmly womanly creature". She had, she said, "a wonderfully interesting face with deep eyes of that rare shade of dark violet blue which grows black and hazel and azure with the shifting emotions of the mind behind them". A rare shade indeed.

Maude Adams, the star of the new play, *The Pretty Sister of José*, was equally fascinating. She was known to be an "elusive ascetic". She had recently returned from a trip abroad which had included a visit to the Holy Land, crossing the desert by camel, living in a tent for several weeks near the pyramids, a sojourn in a French nunnery, and a stay in London with J.M. Barrie. She had not appeared in a theatre for nineteen months and she was, according to the *New York Telegraph*, "by far and away the most popular female star on the American stage today". When Frances' play opened at Wieting Opera House, Syracuse, on 15th October 1903 two thousand people gave it "a rapturous and uproarious welcome". Some critics even went so far as to say it was "the most artistic of Mrs Burnett's works". Only one realized the "utter absence of anything approaching Spanish atmosphere and temperament".

The first night in New York was at the Empire Theater on 10th November. "It was one of those nights that are not soon forgotten," wrote the *New York World*. "For an hour before the curtain went up, Broadway was packed with teams and pedestrians and it was necessary to employ a special force of policemen to keep the carriages in line and the cars moving."

On 25th January 1904, *That Man and I*, the play derived from *In Connection with the De Willoughby Claim*, opened at the Savoy Theater, New York. It was her third New York production within a year. Frances was not happy about it. There was not much about the reception of *That Man and I* to make her happy. "The play is dreary," one paper said, "the acting drearier still." "It is fascinating to write plays but bitterly disappointing to see them acted," she told a reporter from the *New York Herald*, who had dubbed her "The Lightning Playwright". She admitted she *had* written *That Man and I* in two weeks, "always in the morning, I rest in the afternoon and talk to my friends in the evening". She said that the most important thing "we can do is try to be happy and make others happy". She did not seem bitter or disappointed. She smiled at him. "When she smiles," the reporter commented, "it is the best natured, pleasantest face in the world. You feel sure she is your friend." "Do you dictate?" he asked. "Never. I could not possibly do it. There is a typewriter in the house on which my manuscript is copied but I write it all out myself."

A few days before she had at last found time to write a long generous letter to her friend, Kate Douglas Wiggin, praising *Rebecca of Sunnybrook Farm*. "The normal spirit and good cheer of her are adorable." It's interesting to notice that the Rebecca books, like *Fauntleroy* and *Sara Crewe* and later *The Secret Garden*, were read as much by adults as by children—Mark Twain wrote praising *Rebecca*, and so did Jack London from his headquarters with the Japanese Army in Manchuria—and this was also true, of course, of *The Wind in the Willows* and *Winnie-the-Pooh*. It seems that children's literature, that great twentieth-century growth area of publishing, in erecting its own complex structure, its separate children's book editors and librarians and review journals, has cut itself off from the possibility of being read and enjoyed "by young and old alike" as these books were. It is sad, because many people who have rejected the modern novel could find much enjoyment in the descendants of *The Secret Garden* and *The Wind in the Willows*, in books like *Tom's Midnight Garden* by Philippa Pearce and *The Mouse and his Child* by Russell Hoban.

One of the people behind *That Man and I* was an Englishman called R.A. Stanley. Frances found herself promising to collaborate with him in order to make up for money he had apparently lost on the English production of *A Little Princess*. She went to Asheville, North Carolina, to work with him. She had some extraordinary idea, reminiscent of the old *Lady of Quality*, that Maude Adams might be induced to play "a mysterious highwayman attired in white", who would turn out to be a sort of female Robin Hood. In March 1904 this play, *Judy O'Hara*, was finished, though it seems never to have been produced. Frohman turned it down, perhaps, Frances persuaded herself, merely because "he did not want Miss Adams to do a thing with a brogue".

This same month that the play was finished, Swan Burnett took as his second wife an old family friend, Margaret Brady. Frances left New York and travelled in Italy, still with the Stanleys: Florence, Venice, Milan, Como. She thought it "the most adorable country in the world". In June she was back at Maytham Hall and the welcome she had from Rolvenden must have come up to her happiest hopes. As the carriage bringing her from the station drove by, people stood at their gates to see her. "Nice old Mr Stedman had worked a motto in leaves on a sort of banner scroll, 'Welcome home to Maytham', which was hung over the hall door. He had also sent up a beautiful decorated cake with WELCOME on it." She felt she had really come home.

It was a marvellous summer. The Rose Garden was "full of leaping cascades of roses". The only problem was to remember which of the two footmen was Philip and which was William. "When one thinks one is speaking to Willip, he turns out to be Philliam." Maytham was not spoilt by memories: "all the past tragedy has melted into nothingness … It has been so perfect to return after an absence and find more roses and more friends to welcome me." Friends and acquaintances came all through the summer. After the activity of the previous months (she had also finished the dramatization of *The Making of the Marchioness* and called it *Glenpeffer*), it was delightful to bask in the sun with congenial company. The Hepworth Dixon sisters were there a great deal of the time, and Rosamund and Kenneth Campbell, and so were her own sister Edith and her husband, Frank Jordan. Other people came and went. One of them was Ellen Terry, who drove over from Small Hythe. She saw the grassy slope between the terrace, where they were walking, and the lawn. "What a lovely place to roll down!" she said, and immediately did so. In her brown gown and brown cloak, she resembled a long brown German cigar.

Ella Hepworth Dixon brought William Heinemann down ("complete with one of those curious new-fangled high-power motor-cars") and it was as a direct result of this visit, which developed into friendship, that Heinemann later published a number of Frances' novels, including *The Secret Garden*. Another guest, Poulteney Bigelow, recalled Frances' conversation at this time as "a cascade of intellectual scintillation … One feature of her talking impressed me in particular—never did I hear her speak unkindly of rival writers—of unfair critics—even of publishers!" "Not a cloud has crossed my summer," Frances wrote to Kitty Hall, "or a single thing happened to disturb it. Never was I so glad of anything as I am that I came to Maytham just at this particular time."

The only hint of a cloud is in a letter written this September to Frances by the wife of the Vicar, as she and her family prepared to leave Rolvenden: "Circumstances have kept the Hall and Vicarage apart, but the memory of the first old days lingers. I sometimes think perhaps I might have been a truer friend than I was. We may meet again some day, but my husband and I send you our earnest wishes for your future, both in this life and in the life to come."

They had accepted Frances in 1898, divorced though she was, but they could not accept her remarriage, nor her new state as a woman separated from her second husband. There must have been others who felt as they did. But there were plenty who didn't. "Eight or ten people came in to tea and we have been very gay," she wrote to Vivian.

It was one of the happiest summers of her life, though Vivian was not there and though she was beginning to worry about money again. "I shall be very poor soon if I do not complete that 'brilliant work' or place some plays." *The Shuttle*, unfinished, still weighed on her mind. She could not look at it yet, not at Maytham anyway. And neither *Judy O'Hara* nor *Glenpeffer* had found producers. But at least she was in the right mood to write *A Little Princess*. On 22nd September, she reported to Vivian, she was writing two thousand words a morning "with lightning rapidity … The story tells itself so well and with such nice things in it that it will reach the new race of children like a new big fat book." She planned a preface to explain that *A Little Princess* is like the bits in a letter you didn't remember to tell. "I should not like the book to be published under the false pretence of being entirely new … This place is so good for work. Nothing is like the Rose Garden. I have been writing there for some time and I could almost weep because the air is just a little autumny and hints that I cannot write amongst roses much longer. But the golden days go on and on as I never saw them in England before. Never never was such a summer——" Not since 1901, anyway.

There were pleasant distractions. Kenneth Campbell's valet was an astrologer and also a motor cyclist. He and Kenneth spent long hours on the coach-house floor soaked in petrol. After the hours of hard labour, the machines "are pronounced absolutely perfect—absolutely—and they start to go to Tunbridge Wells or Eastbourne and break down at the Lodge gates". Frances' horoscope told her "that the most brilliant work of [her] life was now to be done". It was a nice thought.

On 4th November 1904 Frances sent Scribner's the final chapters of *A Little Princess*. "I wish I was a child and had not read it or seen the play." She knew the joy in store for such children. But it would not be out in time for Christmas. New methods were coming in: "In the case of children's books," Charles Scribner wrote, "the machinery of publication has become very elaborate and the booksellers place their orders long in advance. The travellers go out with their sample copies in July." Scribner had another attempt at persuading Frances to admit that he was as "enterprising" as any of the younger publishers. He hoped she would be disposed to consider them "when making arrangements for any new work".

Scribner did get Frances' next book, *The Dawn of a Tomorrow*, but it was the last he published, although she was to write seventeen more in the last twenty years of her life. The new book seems to have had its origin in a dense fog, which held her ship at Liverpool in December that year. She began it in New York during the four months she was in America. She was much entertained during this period but did not always make a good impression. At the Underwood Johnsons—he was later to be American Ambassador in Rome—she met the Findlater sisters, popular Scottish writers, middle-aged spinsters, at this time on a visit to the States. Mary Findlater took an instant dislike to Frances and described her in her diary as "a short, grossly fat woman, with an evil eye, dyed hair dressed low and tied with ribbons, a dirty crushed white gown, very décolletée". Miss Findlater was inclined to suffer, according to her biographer, from "black moods and destructive criticism and disgust", and Frances was not the only one similarly described. A singer, Miss Kitty Cheatham, was "dressed in soiled white net" with "a huge head of yellow hair". One feels that it must have been their talents and their life styles, not just their hairstyles and their clothes, that Miss Findlater objected to.

Fortunately Frances had no idea what had gone into Miss Findlater's diary. She would have been horrified at the reference to her dress. "Mrs Burnett is noted for her charming gowns," said a newspaper columnist, praising "the pale blue panne velvet affair" she wore to the Lyceum one night. And Vivian called dressing up her "indoor sport". She loved clothes, particularly "clinging, trailing chiffon things with *miles* of lace on them". Her nickname, Fluffy, was still in use: it had little to do with her character and much to do with her taste in clothes.

There was nothing frivolous about her attitude to work. Now she was working enthusiastically on *The Dawn of a Tomorrow*, encouraged by E.L. Burlingame's reception of the first part. We know how anxious Scribner's were to keep Frances on their list and it would be interesting to have Burlingame's frank comments to Charles Scribner. To Frances, he wrote on 1st May 1905: "It continues to seem to me one of the most interesting of all you have undertaken." She was on the Atlantic by then. On 10th July the book was finished at Maytham and she despatched it with this letter to Burlingame:

I send you the story. It has not written itself rapidly because it has written itself strangely in spite of me and I have argued with myself saying continually "No. I can't say what I think of that. The time is not ripe enough." But it had to be done in this way and no other. If it does not suit your particular purpose do not mind telling me so—not in the least. Out of all the propositions and argument of the New Thought the things said in this story are what I *believe*—not what I have been able perfectly to relate to, but what I believe. Harold Warne came down to Maytham a few days ago and my experience with him with regard to this manuscript was a great surprise to me ... I did not think he could possibly care about it. You see, I have not known him intimately and I imagined he was the kind of purely business man, who would start back at the mere idea of a thing so unlike all that is conventional ... Singularly enough a mere chance brought the topic forward and, more singular still, I saw he was extraordinarily interested. He almost lost his lunch and his train in his eagerness. He went away with the manuscript in his valise and plans for having designed and sent to me a model for the book he hoped to make of it ... He said "it seems to me, Mrs Burnett, that you have come upon one of your great subjects—like *Fauntleroy*." I wonder. I know the subject is great—I have no doubt of that—I only wonder how the public will *see* it.

She felt it was part of "the new wave which is swelling upon the century's shore." Even the English bishops ("whom one thought no new thing could move") and stubborn medical men were being infected by it, this knowledge of the new power of the mind. In Vienna, Freud was soon to celebrate his fiftieth birthday and his findings and those of other psychologists were at last becoming more generally accepted.

Frances said that if there was "the remotest chance of *The Dawn of a Tomorrow* becoming to be the ordinary 'religious story', I should be inclined to cast it to the flames. It is something wholly different." Actually, of course, Frances never cast anything into the flames; everything had found a market since she was a girl of eighteen. But using this image suggests how strongly she wanted to avoid being labelled as a conventional religious writer. In fact there is nothing particularly shocking about the book. The *Bookman* reviewer was able to describe it as "a simple, old-fashioned miracle play set forth in modern London". It is a story of redemption found by a rich man among beggars, thieves and prostitutes through the faith of a child called Glad.

Sir Oliver Holt had known no happiness in life: "Success brought greater wealth every day without stirring a pulse of pleasure, even in triumph." He goes out in the fog to buy a pistol to kill himself and finds himself saved from his own despair by doing things for others. The religion is a belief in Goodness, "knowing no doctrine, knowing no church", in an acceptance that the possibility of the kingdom of heaven is within ourselves. The book is not as trite as this makes it sound. The atmosphere of the fog-bound London of a hundred years ago is excellent—"the halos about the street lamps, the flares of torches stuck up over coster barrows". It is full of vivid circumstantial details. Frances knew these London courts from her visiting for the Invalid Children's Aid Association. Glad's cheerful Cockney optimism is convincing.

The following January, Frances, back in New York, wrote to Scribner: "The story is, I find, making an extraordinary impression. People call me up on the telephone to talk about it and the notes I receive, and the things said by people, are not in the usual vein. There is an intensity in the feeling about it. A person who is passing through trouble came to me and said 'You saved my life the other day ...' and a tired school teacher said 'it made me pluck up heart again—it actually did.'" Frances was annoyed that Scribner did not take advantage of the interest aroused by the magazine publication of the story and follow it immediately with the book. It may have been this failure which caused Frances finally, after nearly thirty years and twenty-two Scribner books, to break her connection with the firm. "I am afraid what might have been an unusual interest has frittered away," she said sadly.

A few days later there was news that stirred painful memories. Swan Burnett was dead. Vivian had gone down to Washington and Frances wrote to him to assure him that she was "only feeling the tenderest things for the one who has got free. He has got free. He sees now the reasons for all the mistakes we made and sees they are not such great things after all. I keep thinking of him as he was when he was a boy, years younger than you ... if souls do meet each other, who would meet him first but Lionel."

In the summer, Frances was back at Maytham, wrestling with the final stages of the reluctant *Shuttle*. She was worried too by rare news from her youngest sister, Edwina, in California. She had suffered in the great San Francisco earthquake: "The windmill I gave her, her stable and her buggy have all been smashed and she had heard no news of Francis, his wife and baby ... My contributions to San Francisco will have to be made to my own relations ... I shall have to renew things. It breaks one's heart to think of them."

Frances' mood was not improved by a copy of *Munsey's Magazine* which arrived with an illustrated article on the literary women of the day. She wrote to Vivian protesting: "Never have I seen anything as monstrous as the thing Munsey drew from your

picture of me—and I have seen monstrous things in my time …
Your photograph was not flattering but the 'drawing' is that of an
elderly, battered and drunken Irish cook with a bottle nose and
deep cuts in her cheeks. It is a thing so coarse and revolting that
it is bad business. I have not a doubt that it has absolutely injured
me, and lowered my market value by thousands a year …"

As for *The Shuttle*, it was causing endless problems. It was not
finished, yet it was too long, hopelessly long for serialization.
Richard Gilder would have to use his blue pencil: "The fact
that one can restore everything in the book after the serializing
makes it possible to gaze on blue pencils with calmness. Still, I
am afraid it won't cut well—I mean *largely* enough to make it
practicable. The leisurely manner of it is the result of the *need*
of atmosphere in such a book." Serialization finally started in
the *Century* for November 1906, before Frances had completely
finished the book. But at last it *was* finished and she went off on
holiday in Europe. She was slightly worried by a clause in her
contract with Stokes, who were to publish *The Shuttle*. Apparently
they laid claim to her next book. and she had never had such a
clause in a contract before. She had written rather surprisingly
to Vivian a few months earlier, when the subject first came up:
"I have not the remotest idea of a new book in my mind and I
could not be bound and perpetually bothered about it. I should
never have an idea. I wish I *could* deliver novels like coals—dump
them down before publishing houses and watch them shovelled
into the cellar." Usually she boasted that she could write a story
about anything, about a fly on the ceiling if necessary, that her
mind was full of stories. And the idea of being a sort of literary
coalman was nothing but the old pen-driving machine again, and
surely equally distasteful to her in a normal mood.

That winter, anyway, she resolved to write nothing. She went
off to Montreux with a party of friends, including Lord Ronald
Gower, whom she had known now for ten years, Frank Hird, his
adopted son, and Josephine Browne. Miss Browne was a splendid
character who became a close friend during these years. Frances

was full of admiration: "She has white hair and is rather—not very—stout, but she has lived on the edge of Dartmoor all her life, when she was not travelling the world over, and she is as strong and full of life and energy as if she were eighteen. She is *never* tired. She climbs mountains as if she were the funicular and comes back smiling and glowing to lunch and says 'Now what shall we do this afternoon?'

In February 1907, Frances was back at Maytham. It was her last visit. Her lease was running out and the owner was selling the estate. She recorded this final visit in a brief, sentimental book called *My Robin*, written in 1912 after someone had asked her if she had "owned the original of the robin" in *The Secret Garden*.

"There had been snow even in Kent and the park and garden were white. I threw on my red frieze garden cloak and went down the flagged terrace and the Long Walk through the walled gardens to the beloved place," the Rose Garden. And her robin came. She could not bring herself to say goodbye to him. "We have been too near to each other—nearer than human beings are. 'I love you and love you and love you—little soul.' Then I went out of the Rose Garden. I shall never go into it again."

There were other goodbyes to be made; it was a sad time. When, on her death, a tablet made by Tiffanys in New York, decorated with ivy leaves and books, was put up in the church at Rolvenden, it justly carried the text "Careful to maintain good works. Titus 3, 8". In *Who's Who* for 1905, Frances had given her recreation immodestly as "Improving the lot of children." In Rolvenden, she had improved the lot of many people, particularly the old and dying. They wept to see her go. Her servants, eight of them, signed a letter dated 21st March 1907. They could not believe she would not come back.

Dear Madame,
    We one and all are taking the liberty to wish you health wealth and every happiness and a very Pleasant Voyage. We all hope to have the Pleasure of Serving you again at dear Old Maytham.

Will you do us the favour to accept this Small Present, From your
Faithfull Servants …

In 1905, possibly to avoid Stephen's claims on her property and
income, Frances took out naturalization papers and became an
American. From this time on, though she was to continue regular
visits to England until the war, she never had an English home.
Back in America, she began to look for a permanent home for
her last years—a beautiful home and a garden that would be
entirely hers.

10

Was That the Party?
1908–1924

In the spring of 1908 Frances bought a large plot of land at Plandome, Long Island. The site, with views over Manhasset Bay, was splendid. The plan was for a white Italianate villa, red-roofed, with a colonnade and balconies and a balustraded terrace. Vivian, now working on a new publication called the *Children's Magazine*, was left to keep an eye on things while Frances set off on *SS Zeeland* to take a "cure" at Doctor Lampe's sanatorium in Frankfurt. She was not at all well—bouts of neuritis, "osteoperinestitch" or whatever it was, continued to plague her. Her digestion was terrible; she existed much of the time on a diet of buttermilk and toast.

But the voyage was delightful; "we go about in white muslin blouses and without hats". And she was happy in the thought of the house at Plandome and of Vivian's future. Whatever happened to her, she was now sure he would be financially secure. (*The Shuttle* was being enormously successful and entirely paid for the new house. Royalties on the first three months' sale of the American edition alone were thirty-eight thousand dollars.) But if only Vivian would marry … She had always hoped he would enjoy the love of wife and children. He was now thirty-two. Had she, with her unhappy marriages and her worldly success, made his life more difficult for him? Surely not. His career did not exactly glitter, but he was a dear, dear boy. She had never suggested that he was a disappointment to her. "You never say or think again," she wrote on board ship, "the thing you said that morning in the train—about always working under the weight of my disbelief. If I thought of words as I once did, that would have meant black discouragement to me. Just look back and *think*."

It *was* difficult being the son of a famous mother; there was no doubt about that. All his life the Little Lord Fauntleroy label remained round his neck. Now there were other minor but irritating difficulties. Moffat and Yard, the publishers of the *Children's Magazine*, wanted to take advantage of Vivian's relationship with the famous writer. Frances had agreed to let them publish "The Good Wolf", one of the hair-curling stories she had told to Vivian as a child, and she was working on a sequel for them, to be called "Barty Crusoe and his Man Saturday" ("I wonder what will happen in it—what queer fantastic things. I think there will be a tribe of Pygmies and perhaps Hidden Treasure"). But she felt there was a "commercial impertinence" in them wanting to title their annual *Burnett's Children's Year Book*. It is "cheapening and undignified and even vulgar—besides the fact that 'Burnett's' certainly does not suggest *me* but might mean Burnett's Extracts or Cocoa ... I am beginning to learn that this desire to *always* do what other people want is too silly ... One gains in return neither respect nor affection."

In Frankfurt, Frances took "electric baths" and enjoyed tea under the blossoming linden trees with Lady Alma-Tadema and Daisy Hall. Later she stayed with Josephine Browne at Tavistock in Devon, but she returned to New York in time for the rehearsals of her new play—the dramatization of *The Dawn of a Tomorrow*, which she had written at Sands Point on Long Island during the land-hunting summer of 1907.

The play opened at the Lyceum Theater on 28th January 1909 starring Eleanor Robson. The *New York World* critic considered it a "theatrical tribute to the New thought—the cults of the Faith Cure, Mind Cure, Rest Cure or the theology of Mrs Eddy ..."

He wrote of the play's transparent artificiality but said "it has many attractive elements. It is wholesome in every meaning of that trite term. It is restful and uplifting. Most important of all, it is entertaining." Frances found herself having to deny Mrs Eddy: MRS BURNETT NOT A CHRISTIAN SCIENTIST was a *Chicago Post* headline. As for the charge of artificiality, in an interview in February she defended the realism of her view of the world. "The most misused word in the language is 'realism'. It has come to stand solely for all that is hideous, sordid and repulsive in life. One would think, to judge from the way in which this word is bandied about, that no real things were beautiful or good ... A rose, a spring day, the sun, kindness, tolerance, nobility, unselfishness—these are as real as poverty and sin and hopelessness." In any case, there was plenty of fog and poverty in the play; why should it be considered "artificial" just because it ended happily?

The Dawn of a Tomorrow was a success in the theatre but stopped abruptly when Eleanor Robson abandoned it to marry August Belmont. Frances wrote ruefully to the Hepworth Dixons in England: "Far be it from me, however, to suggest that any girl should not marry a nice millionaire. I 'ave not a 'eart of stone, even though my play is stopped at the height of its career and I lose a couple of hundred pounds a week."

Meanwhile on Long Island things were not proceeding as rapidly as she hoped at the building site. It seemed that the New World could produce workmen of a temperament remarkably similar to the slow men of Rolvenden who had spent a day laying a bedroom carpet. On 29th June 1909, Frances wrote to the Hepworth Dixons:

> There is a Stairmaker hammering away about four feet from me. He is one of the occult problems I find myself trying with sweet patience to solve. It is certainly three months—or four—since Vivian first began to search the dictionary for language sufficiently powerful to employ with a view to inducing them to "get a move on". But nothing has transpired. (He is now whistling sweetly

some gem from a popular opera.) He comes and spends four
or five happy, peaceful hours with us, cheering us by his bright
presence and then, having put in one balustrade, I think he goes
abroad for a few weeks. He returns, refreshed, and after a joyous
day spent with another balustrade, takes to his yacht again. I think
he must go in a yacht.

… When you come to spend the summer with me in the far off
years when the work is completed, you will say the place is lovely
and you will like the house and the terrace and the big piazzas
and the view—but let no one speak to me again of the pleasure
of building one's own house …

This *will* end—and after it is over the lovely Manhasset Bay
will still lie smiling at the foot of the lawn and we shall go in
the scented evenings down the wide stone steps (which are now
being built) down the rose bank to the little curving beach and
get into the pretty boat—which I can see from my window as I
write—lying like a white dove on the water—and we shall float
about, tinkling guitars and things, or merely being quiet, and we
shall be sure to say, "How lovely! How adorable!" But in the
meantime, let each man, woman and child who loves me at all
understand that I do not write because I cannot.

… We came in on May 25th in the mad hope that by doing so we
might push the workmen out—but we had not counted with the
Stairmaker—the Terrace layers—the Painters, and the Builders of
the garage. I could have endured these better if I had not simply
revelled in neuritis.

Frances found herself forced to mutter through clenched teeth
one of her own lines from *The Dawn of a Tomorrow*: "Things ain't
never as bad as wot yer *think* they are." Why, as Glad had remarked,
she "might 'ave broke [her] back or be in jail for knifin' someone".
Even neuritis and an unfinished house and a garden full of builders' rubble were mere trifles if she practised what she preached.

It was this spring of 1909, amidst the excitement of planning the
garden at Plandome ("superintending the tucking in of plants and

bulbs, making lawns, deciding on the direction of paths, the moving in and planting of hundreds of trees and shrubs", as Vivian put it), that Frances began her most loved book, *The Secret Garden*. This title leaps to the lips of great numbers of people between the ages of seventy and seven when asked to name the favourite book of their childhood. Marghanita Laski, as I quoted earlier, calls it "the most satisfying children's book I know". Philip Larkin has praised it; so has everyone who has ever written on the history of children's literature. It has been filmed and televised. It has never been out of print and it is read and enjoyed as a Puffin by children today, not as a "classic" urged on them by their elders, but as a living story of as much concern to them as any written more recently.

Its impact when it was first published in 1911, by Stokes in America and by Heinemann in England, does not seem to have been exceptional. The American Library Association booklist called it "a 'new thought' story, over-sentimental and dealing almost wholly with abnormal people", while realizing that it would "appeal to many women and young girls". Most of the other critics were more appreciative ("wholesome reading", "will charm everyone", "a quiet, beautiful tale of literary craftsmanship") but it is hardly mentioned in the numerous entries on Frances in encyclopaedias and other reference books. It was not mentioned in her obituary in *The Times*. But on many people, old and young, it certainly made an immediate impression. One of them, Celia, Lady Scarbrough, had a "secret garden", its door hidden by a thorn tree, laid out in 1912 and 1913 at Sandbeck in Yorkshire to commemorate her fondness for the book; her great-nephew, who became Lord Scarbrough, was always called Dickon.

Vivian believed that the book "grew out of a regretful feeling" when Frances heard (mistakenly as it happened) that the new owners of Maytham had turned the Rose Garden into a market garden, with rows and rows of cabbages and turnips, and lettuces under glass cloches. But, as Philippa Pearce has pointed out, "the last thing *The Secret Garden* can have grown out of is a regretful feeling". She first drew my attention to that earlier garden near

Islington Square, Salford, which Frances knew in her childhood, with "the little green door in the high wall which surrounded the garden". This was the cindery desert where the weeds were transformed, by the child's imagination, into a carpet of flowers.

Seeds of *The Secret Garden* had undoubtedly been growing in Frances' mind for nearly fifty years. It may have been at about the same time Frances saw the Salford garden that she read *Jane Eyre* for the first time. Mary's arrival at Misselthwaite is too reminiscent of Jane's arrival at Thornfield to be coincidental. Both girls were plain young orphans who were starting a new life in a mysterious manor house on the Yorkshire moors, a house where the master was abroad most of the time and the place run by servants. There is also the parallel between Mrs Rochester's tragic laugh and Colin's curious cry, both puzzling the listener beyond the closed door.

Maytham had provided the lamb, the rose garden and the robin. The Brontës (Mary "hated the wind and its wuthering") and Frances' visit to Lord Crewe's house in 1895 had provided the Yorkshire setting. Frances' interest in the New Thought, as they called the new realization of the power of the mind, had provided the plot. But the most original thing about the book was that its heroine and one of its heroes were both thoroughly unattractive children. The first sentence makes it compulsive reading: "When Mary Lennox was sent to Misselthwaite Manor to live with her uncle, everybody said she was the most disagreeable-looking child ever seen." And Colin, of course, is a hysterical hypochondriac. It is the entirely convincing transformation of these two unhappy children that gives the story its tremendous appeal, even to children who do not find the natural world particularly attractive.

It was a long time since the heroines and heroes of a children's book had had to be as flat and perfect as creatures in a medieval morality play. Fifty years before, Charlotte M. Yonge had broken that pattern but it was still very unusual for them to be actively disagreeable. They might have their small faults, they might be careless and untidy, but they always had merry eyes. Mary and Colin did not have merry eyes.

The treatment of Mary is quite astonishingly accurate to our own much greater understanding of child behaviour. Other Victorian writers had made deprived children behave quite inappropriately, but Frances' instinct has since been confirmed by child psychologists. A child denied love does behave as Mary behaved. But *The Secret Garden* is far more than a parable or a demonstration of child behaviour. With Frances, as always, the story comes first and she was far too good a writer to spoil it with propaganda. Only at the beginning of chapter twenty-seven does she lapse into sententiousness, with explicit explanations of her symbolism and a bald definition of what the rest of the book conveys so subtly and brilliantly: "To let a sad thought or a bad one get into your mind is as dangerous as letting a scarlet fever germ get into your body." "Whatsoever things are honest, just, pure, lovely and of good report—think on these things" has been part of our collective wisdom for a very long time but it has seldom been put into more delightful form.

The Secret Garden is a book of the new century. Far from encouraging the attitudes instilled in Frances as a child ("Speak when you're spoken to, come when you're called ..."), it suggested children should be self-reliant and have faith in themselves, that they should listen not to their elders and betters, but to their own hearts and consciences. Penelope Lively once said that you could learn the elements of pruning roses from *The Secret Garden*, and another large part of the attraction of the book is its exactly accurate descriptions of real gardening. Frances was always good at detail. She knew children liked it. It is not enough to mention they have tea, she once said, you must specify the muffins. It is the detail of things that makes them interesting. To Colin, the moor is bare and dreary. To Dickon, who knows its every detail, the moor is alive with activity and interest. Frances never lost her appetite for quiddities.

The Secret Garden was first called *Mistress Mary*, surely a title which would have hindered rather than helped. In April 1910, when it had been taken for serialization by *The American Magazine*

("This is the first instance I have ever known of a child's story being published in an adult's magazine," Frances wrote), she was still calling it *Mistress Mary*: there is no record of how it came to have the familiar title.

Frances finished the book before leaving for London and the rehearsals of the English production of *The Dawn of a Tomorrow*. She was thrilled with the cast. Gertrude Elliot "has a depth and comprehension and strength Miss Robson lacked". Ellen Terry came to watch a rehearsal. "Never was there such an everlasting enchantress as that woman. She is such a *real* and vivid thing … She says I must write a play for her if I do it when she is ninety. It is to be full of lovely young things but the Ninety lady is to help them by pulling strings …"

Frances was feeling extraordinarily well for a change. An osteopath called Dr Horn had been helpful. "Has the motor gone to the re-makers?" she wrote to Vivian. "I shall be furious if it is not quite ready and beautiful when I return." The gardens should be beautiful too. If they were not, the gardener, Mr Jaenicke, "is a double dyed villain". The tone was light but with an overbearing note in it which was to become more and more common as she aged. "I expect everything to be radiant and, if I continue to be well, I expect to be radiant myself. I am surer and surer every day of the benefits of osteopathy." She had celebrated her sixtieth birthday by feeling better than she had for years.

Once before, a Royal death—that of the young Duke of Clarence in 1892—had emptied the theatre for one of Frances' plays. Now King Edward VII, his father, died a few days before the London opening of *The Dawn of a Tomorrow*. The success of the pre-London week at Liverpool had been tremendous. "Gertrude Elliot said 'they eat it' and Henry Ainley said, when the news of the King's death came, 'Well, *nothing* can spoil the play.'" Frances would not go to the first night at the Garrick on Friday, 13th May. She spent the following weekend at Lord Ronald Gower's place, Hammerfield. "When I arrived here yesterday, Frank Hird met me with congratulations. He had read Walkley's criticism and said he was, of course, very grudging but that he was obliged to admit that it was a big success ... If audiences like the thing so much that they hush down applause because they cannot bear to lose a single word—the critics may say what they like."

The papers were full of funeral procession routes, pictures of queens and princesses in crêpe, details of memorial services and the requirements of national mourning. Few were in play-going mood and the theatres were so empty there was not really much danger of those who were there missing a word. "The managers however are not disturbed because this was inevitable and they believe reaction will set in next week."

Hammerfield was beautiful with primroses and cuckoo calls. Francis Shackleton, brother of the Polar explorer, then at the height of his fame, was there. He had a house in Park Lane and asked Frances to go there with Lord Ronald and Frank Hird and Josephine Browne to watch the funeral procession. "Lord Ronald is not very well," Frances wrote, "and is, I am sure, depressed by the King's death—not, I think, that he cared particularly for him but after all they were boys together ... It recalls those days when he was very beautiful and young and surrounded by ducal and regal splendours—when his mother, the Duchess of Sutherland, was Mistress of the Robes and the Queen's most intimate friend."

The following Tuesday, Frances watched the procession which moved the King's body to Westminster for the lying-in-state. She stood at one of the windows of the Sutherlands' town place, Stafford House. She found it sad and impressive "watching the slow-moving kings and queens and nobles and troops and listening to the boom of the Dead March from a window of a house where the dead man had played as a child—and standing by a man who had been a child with him. King George walked behind the gun carriage on which the coffin lay covered with a gorgeous pall and with the Crown and other splendors on top. A little prince walked on either side of him." At Lord Ronald's side, Frances felt a participant, not an outsider.

On Friday they watched the funeral procession itself from the Shackleton house in Park Lane. Frances was delighted with herself. "I am a new creature. Thank God! Thank God!" She was up at five, waited and waited for the procession, watched it standing and yet felt strong enough after lunch to write long letters to Vivian and to Euphemia Macfarlane (her life-long friend from early days in Washington). "It is wonderful not to be tired and in pain every hour … It was all so magnificent and dramatic—the thousands of soldiers lining the route for miles—with reversed arms and bowed heads—the gun carriage with its stately solemn burden—the dead king's splendid charger led behind him—the kings and queens and emperors following slowly—slowly—and the myriad silent people looking on." The crowd was dressed entirely in black. "There has not been a touch of color to be seen in the streets since the day of the death. Every shop window is filled with black things and every shop has had to work night and day to provide mourning. Edith and I are in black from head to foot and shall be until we leave for America. Fortunately I had a black chiffon evening dress but we had to provide entire new outfits. We shall be obliged to wear them on the Continent as there are so many English people travelling that it would not be good taste to wear colors."

Frances and Edith were leaving for the Continent on Monday to join Lord Ronald, Frank Hird and Josephine Browne at Lake Garda. Frances felt she "must have some Alps". The first part of the holiday was delightful. They visited Cortina and drove "to Toblach through the Ampezzo Tal again—stopping midway to rest the horses while we lunched on the grass amongst flowers on a hillside". They visited Innsbruck and Zirl, Zaufelt and Mittenwald. "We all feel we have seen all the beauty of the world … Tiny babies of two or three say 'Grüss Gott' to you as you pass. Everybody says it."

But then the weather changed and they were detained at Linderhof, near Oberammergau, by torrential rain which was said to have swept away part of the road, though there was a suspicion that the coachman who reported it was in the pay of the hotel owners. Frances rather enjoyed the rumours and reports and the comings and goings of half-drowned travellers. "Yesterday was really exciting," she wrote to Vivian. She made him feel they might be cut off for weeks, marooned, running out of supplies. But the delays were minimal. She often exaggerated to make a good story.

In July, Frances was back at Plandome, working on a new book. This had been inspired by the success of the character G. Selden in *The Shuttle*—the irrepressible typewriter salesman from New York. Frances apparently had the details of that way of life from Archie Fahnestock, Edith's son, who had tried to sell typewriters for a time. "Unsurpassed paper feed, practical ribbon mechanism, perfect and permanent alignment ... A baby in a perambulator could learn to tick off orders for its bottle." G. Selden's sales talk comes over with great conviction. But it was the character, not his particular circumstances, that Frances decided to use for the hero of her next book, as long and leisurely a one as *The Shuttle*. She gave him a new name and a new job, whose details she again learned from the restless, unsuccessful Archie, now working as a society reporter at ten dollars a week.

T. Tembarom shares with G. Selden the cheerful slang and "picturesque national characteristics" of the young uneducated New Yorker, trying to exist on a paltry wage and optimistic that before long he will earn more. In *The Shuttle*, Selden endears himself to the rich and the aristocratic whom he happens to find himself among after a bicycle accident on the edge of Stornham Park. It occurred to Frances to write an adult version of *Fauntleroy* with a Selden-like character as her hero. Tembarom (a contraction of Temple Barholm), orphaned and penniless in New York at the age of ten, has raised himself by his own hard work and character from selling newspapers to the comparatively respectable heights of a reporter on the *Sunday Earth* with a "hall bedroom" in a third-rate boarding-house. This is his position when he hears the news that he has inherited an English estate with an income of three hundred and fifty thousand dollars a year. The plot is full of preposterous coincidences but Tembarom's character is very likeable and his behaviour in his temporary situation completely convincing. There is an excellent scene when his valet tries to do things for him which Tembarom has never heard of a man not doing for himself. Tembarom finds himself at a loss to know what to do in his vast country home. There's a limit to the number of times you can read a joke in *Punch*. He asks his solicitor for suggestions.

> "If you could ride or shoot, you could amuse yourself in the country."
>
> "I can ride in a streetcar when we've got five cents. That's as far as I've gone in riding—and what in thunder could I shoot?"
>
> "Game," replied Mr Palford, with chill inward disgust. "Pheasants, partridges, woodcock, grouse——"

Tembarom thinks he would be more likely to shoot his own head off first. "He did not know that there were men who had gained distinction, popularity and fame by doing nothing in particular and hitting things animate and inanimate with magnificent precision of aim." Tembarom knows very little indeed about the ways of the landed gentry and he has absolutely no respect for convention. The story, although far too long, is never dull. It had an excellent press. The *Boston Transcript* was typical: "It is an old-fashioned tale that is sometimes romantic, sometimes realistic, sometimes plausible, sometimes incredible but always enjoyable."

Frances enjoyed writing it and was irritated by constant interruptions. This was one of the troubles about Plandome. It was far too near New York. She was plagued by reporters, not all of them as cheerful and charming as Tembarom. Often she refused interviews. When she did agree to give them, her views were likely to be distorted and "written up" in a way which made her irritated. Pictures were even worse. In *T. Tembarom* she writes feelingly of "baffled struggles to keep abominable woodcuts from being published in sensational journalistic sheets". Frances found her views being requested on every imaginable subject. In 1908 she was even asked about "The Thaw case"—the case of the famous architect, Stanford White, murdered on the roof of one of his own buildings. "It seems unbelievable," Frances wrote to Burlingame. "I saw that the young interviewer detested the impertinence but had been forced to come at the point of the sword." It is interesting that on this occasion the girl reporter, a Miss Morgan, was able to interest Frances so much in a poem she had written that Frances sent it to Burlingame for possible publication.

She was asked for her views on marriage: "Women today are freer than ever before from the awful necessity of acquiring the first man in sight." She was asked about women smoking. "Cigarettes are personal and every woman must decide if she wants to smoke," she said mildly. She had begun herself many years before because she felt it helped her facial neuralgia. Her views on hell and the devil were more controversial. A syndicated article by Magda Frances West carried headlines all over the States: "THERE IS NO DEVIL" ASSERTS MRS FRANCES HODGSON BURNETT was carried by the *Kansas City Post*, for instance, in letters half an inch high. "I practise a doctrine of elimination on that which will not make me happy. I stopped believing in hell very early. I can remember the first time I ever said 'There is no such place,' still half-thinking that there might be. I said it to console someone else and I was rather terrified ... Forget the devil and keep your pink lamps lighted. That's a little by-word among my friends. A pink lamp always makes everything look lovely."Years before, Sara Crewe had found "a bright lamp with a rosy shade" when her cold attic was transformed by Ram Dass. It had always been a symbol to Frances of warmth and comfort. But pink lamps, like rose-coloured spectacles, only give an illusion of warmth and beauty.There are some things they cannot transform. It is difficult to believe that someone who had written *The Secret Garden* so recently, who had looked at Mary Lennox in the cold winter light and helped her to blossom and flourish, could possibly have said the sort of things Frances is reported to have said. "I never read about ugly things that I cannot help. I never think about them," she is supposed to have said to a *New York Evening World* reporter, as she sat in her rose and blue drawing-room at Plandome, with potted begonias drooping in the heat from the sizzling steampipes. "That is why I never read newspapers. They terrify me. Gory details, crimes, murders, I don't believe it does anyone any good to read about them." Fifty years before, the tales she was writing were "full of murders and fighting". Now apparently she said the reading of such stories was dangerous to the mind. The *New York Telegraph* praised her views in a leader that November. Her assertion that "the personal devil is the only devil … is a believable doctrine and it would work for greater kindliness in the individual's treatment of his fellow men".

Frances never rejected her own early work. It would be interesting to know just what she thought of *That Lass o' Lowrie's* in these later years. Probably she saw herself as a social reformer, as one who had drawn attention to unacceptable conditions. For this, she was saying in 1910, was the one justification for the knowledge of evil. "Of course, if there were anything that my knowing about could help or avert, it would be my duty to know of it."

But it would obviously be much better if she spent less time talking to reporters and fuming at the reports and more time writing. The New York winter was impossible and there was more building work to be done at Plandome. She must get away. In March 1911, she at last went to Bermuda with *T. Tembarom* in her luggage and stayed at the Princess Hotel. She liked the place a great deal. The climate was perfect for a winter refuge. She found a snow-white bungalow called Clifton Heights, with a garden sloping down to the waters of Bailey's Bay, and rented it immediately. The atmosphere was congenial; Mark Twain had loved it and been there year after year. So had William Dean Howells.

Vivian wrote rare but encouraging letters about progress at Plandome. He had been planting seeds, reading all the directions on the packets very carefully. The bulbs were doing very well, "all about the place I saw little green points protruding". Best of all, the contractors had agreed to have all the building work done before Frances' return. "Don't stay too long," Vivian wrote, "we will have a greenhouse and cold frames in rows filled with mysteriously promising little green things for you when you get here. That ought to excite you."

Frances returned to Plandome for the summer of 1911, full of excitement that she now had secured summer and winter homes, and, even more important, summer and winter gardens. But a happy summer was interrupted. Frank Jordan, Edith's husband, was killed in a motor accident. Edith and Frank had been part of Frances' household on and off for many years. She had been fond of Frank, worrying about him in 1900, even at the height of her own problems with Stephen. Frank had then been having business troubles. Someone called Balser had let him down. She thought him unspeakable "to play with an honest industrious man's prospects in such a manner. Poor Frank, poor Frank!" she had written to Edith. "I cannot endure the thought of the thing." She offered to lend Frank money "*without interest*, and if the money is to be lost, I would much rather lose it in trying to help Frank than in trying to help anyone else."

Now, in 1911, poor Frank was dead. Frances took Edith off to Bermuda as soon as she could. Clifton Heights was ready for them. Frances had bought furniture from the previous tenant, a Captain Joyner, who had been ordered back to Dover and was going in tears of rage. Frances went into his drawing-room and said "Oh! how pretty. May I have all of this?" And into the dining-room and said, "I should like all this. It is so exactly what I want." The sloping garden had a lily field with oleanders on one side and on the other a banana-field. There were palms and cedars and in the lower part of the garden—shielded by a white coral wall—Frances had planted six hundred and seventy-two roses. "They will bloom," she wrote to Ella Hepworth Dixon, "when New York is seventy degrees below zero and London is black with fog or slopped with mud and rain. And on all this island there is not a motor or a train, or a smoking, rattling thing. And the Governor, Sir Walter Kitchener—Lord Kitchener's brother—is a dear who takes you to see his princely chickens in palatial coops taken care of by the army when it is not busy playing soldiers."

Back at Plandome the following summer, she had still not finished *T. Tembarom*, though it was due to begin serialization in the *Century* in January 1913. She abandoned it temporarily for the less demanding task of dramatizing *Racketty Packetty House*. The story was one of four short books for small children Frances had written between 1906 and 1908, a series purporting to be told by Queen Crosspatch. *The Spring Cleaning* has already been mentioned. *The Cozy Lion* was another of this group, which still has some appeal, but, as Frances said, it is essential that "the grown-up person who reads this story aloud to children *must* know how to roar". The lion wished to be good and go into society and the problem was to change his temper and his diet and persuade him to live on breakfast foods and things.

All these stories have some moments of nauseating whimsy to our more astringent modern taste, but, in the light of the tone of the period, it is a wonder they are not more flawed. The advertisements that appeared alongside them in *St Nicholas* suggest contemporary attitudes to children and the language considered most suitable for them. "I just really might as well 'fess up," says a child in a Pond's advertisement. Necco wafers are described as "the kiddies' Feast of Fairy Food". "Have you a little 'Fairy' in your home?" parents are asked. "Your healthy, husky boy, or pretty playful girl will enjoy Fairy Soap." "Healthy Kiddies" will also be "comfy" in Ford and Allen's Tailored Washsuits and in Oblong Rubber Button Hose Supporters. Older children will enjoy "bully good sport" with an Ansco Folding Buster Brown Camera.

Racketty Packetty House is said to owe its inspiration to the de Kay family, whom Frances had come to know in the summers of 1902 and 1903 at East Hampton. Helena Gilder, Richard's wife, had been a de Kay and all the de Kays and Gilders used to congregate at the resort in the summers before the First World War. Ormonde de Kay, the seventh of the eight children, was a particular favourite with Frances. On one occasion she knew he wanted a brightly painted cast-iron ferryboat he had seen in the window of Schwartz's big toyshop on 23rd Street, New York. She bought it for him and hid it in a cupboard. When he next visited her, she waved her lorgnette around as if it were a wand, declared herself his Fairy Godmother and said she would conjure up his heart's desire. The small boy duly named the ferryboat, and Frances, with more talk of her magic powers, waved her lorgnette and opened the cupboard. Ormonde was so convinced by the magic that he ignored the boat and claimed the lorgnette:"I want the thing that gets the things," he said.

His sister Marion remembered Frances reading *The Secret Garden* aloud to them in 1909. She read extremely well, with a Yorkshire accent in the right parts which was entirely convincing to these young Americans. Her own books never failed to move her. Edith would smile and say if you saw Fluffy laughing or crying over a book, it would most probably be one of her own. Marion said Frances was the first woman she ever saw smoking a cigarette and Ormonde remembered being sent out to buy cream peppermints, which she was still nibbling between puffs at her Turkish cigarettes. They were supposed to clear the windpipe. Another sister, Phyllis, remembered Frances "as a very odd and fascinating creature … When I was growing up before 1914 she was *so* kind to me … I remember at East Hampton … she lent me *What Maisie Knew* and one of Gissing's most dreary books—Also *Delina Delaney* and *Irene Iddesleigh*." The last two are by Amanda Ros, once called "the world's worst novelist". It is an odd list of books and gives more evidence perhaps than we otherwise have of Frances' uncertain literary taste.

The relationship between the de Kays and the dolls in *Racketty Packetty House* is presumably that they both "got fun out of everything. You never saw a family have such fun. They could make up stories and pretend things and invent games out of nothing … They were so fond of each other and so good-natured and always in such spirits that everyone who knew them was fond of them." The dolls were also shabby and poor and contented with their lot. The Castle dolls, on the other hand, in their smart Tidy Castle, are grand and haughty and scornful. Lord Hubert reads the newspaper with a high-bred air and Lord Rupert glances aristocratically at his love-letters from ladies of title. Eventually the dolls from *Racketty Packetty House* nurse the dolls of Tidy Castle through scarlet fever, and their characters improve and they promise never to scorn anyone again. The *New York World* called it "a convincing argument against snobbery". The magazine *Theatre* said it was "a very good lesson for the limousine children who scorn those of pedestrian parents".

It was obviously just the thing to open the new Children's Theater on the top of the Century Theater on Monday afternoon, 23rd December 1912. The Children's Theater could seat eight hundred children; the chairs were small, the usherettes were dressed as Little Red Riding Hoods and the booking office was like a gate-keeper's lodge. Each of the boxes came from a different fairy story. At the first performance, Frances was in Jack the Giant Killer's box with Vivian, who had written the music for the play, Edith, her son Ernest, and Mrs Underwood Johnson. The programme was unbearably whimsical: "Madame Sarasco Brignole taught the little Green Workers their dancey steps. C. Alexander Ramsey made the cute little costumes." But the play was far more robust; indeed one of the critics had cause to complain of Peter Piper's vulgarity. He was not quite the sort of boy one would want one's own son to be. He boasted too much; he was too pleased with himself. The critic preferred "well-mannered respectful children as the heroes and heroines of our children's books for they, after all, are the most influential examples in our lives". The children anyway loved Peter and the play. After the first performance, Frances gave a party for the actors. GOOD FAIRY CALLS ON CHILD PLAYERS: MRS BURNETT IS SANTA CLAUS said the newspapers, providing excellent publicity for the play. There were presents and ice cream for everybody.

In February, Frances was in Bermuda again, sending urgent instructions to Vivian about the Plandome garden. "I want Watts to border *all* the herbaceous beds with white Phlox Drummondii and to sow that entire curve by the rhododendron and azalea bed with nasturtium seed. Nasturtiums thrive on poor soil ... Get me some seedlings of Arititos Grandis for the empty spaces—also lobelia, ageratum and white candytuft for bordering the fountain. Be sure to have that fringed and starred annual phlox sown thick round the beds of the Sunk Garden. Now I want these things done. I don't want to come back and find they were forgotten ... The new roses I got for my Secret Garden here are doing beautifully ..."

She had been ill and *T. Tembarom* was still not finished, though the early chapters were already appearing in the *Century*, and Hodder and Stoughton had bought the English book rights. Vivian spent two weeks with Frances and Edith in Bermuda in March. In April Frances returned to Plandome. She hardly had time to notice if the candytuft was in the right position before she was planning a European holiday with two of the Hall sisters. The book was finished. She was feeling very tired and at Plandome everything seemed to press on her. Scribner wrote proposing a new uniform edition of the early novels ("Unfortunately we have not had the pleasure of publishing for you your most recent books"), but Frances was not very interested. "I have left everything behind. Other people must settle things," she wrote from Austria. She was enjoying for the first time the delights of motoring through Europe. "If I were strong enough, I should motor from morning until night." She had had ptomaine poisoning on the steamer to Trieste and it took her a good while to recover fully. But nothing could for long diminish her pleasure in being in Europe. One of her happiest afternoons was spent in "a defense tower" on the walls of Rothenburg. She had asked about the delightful small house and, hearing it belonged to a Mancunian artist called Arthur Wasse, she determined "to see the pictures of a man who had the sense to make a house of that place and live in it". What she thought of the pictures is not recorded but she loved the house and the view and the "cosy, homely Manchester dear" they belonged to.

Frances stayed for nine months on the Continent, until the end of April 1914, perhaps aware that she was seeing Europe for the last time and that, in any case, it would never be the same again. "To live in the best suite of rooms in the best hotels in any part of Europe is strict economy in comparison to living at Plandome Park, Long Island," she wrote to Ella Hepworth Dixon. "And as one can spend an occasional morning at home and lightly earn one's living as one goes—with the aid of a pen and ink and a few cheap sheets of paper—one need not accuse oneself of extravagance."

It was marvellous to be free, to go where one pleased, not to be running a household, instructing servants, deciding on meals, not to be bombarded with requests of one sort and another. During recent years many of the requests had been for permission to film her books. The "Vitagraph" organization was one of the first but "Mr Edwards of Samuel French's agency, which deals with the business of the play 'on the road' advises against my selling the rights. I already know that the motion pictures are said to greatly influence the theatres and, as *Fauntleroy* is continually played still, I feel sure Mr Edwards is right." This was in 1911. The following year, she was less sure, and beginning to be persuaded by the Kinemacolor firm, "which is rich and respectable and whose process is by far the most interesting". There was no doubt that "the Moving Picture rights are becoming an important consideration and are likely to represent definite income in the future".

Her final conversion to the cinema is said to have come during these months on the Continent. "One day in Berechtsgarten, she strayed into what in that part of the world is called a 'Kino', where peasant girls and men in their picturesque costumes were drinking beer at little tables set on a sanded floor, while moving pictures were being shown. In a land so far away, in both distance and manners and customs, she saw stories of American life appreciated and applauded by people who could not have understood a word of English. Mrs Burnett was so struck by the universality of the appeal of the moving picture that, from that time forward, she became an ardent student of the cinema, keenly interested in both the entertainment and the audience." In October 1913, Kinemacolor cabled: GUARANTEE $8,000 MINIMUM FOR FIRST TWO YEARS. The first two films were to be *The Dawn of a Tomorrow* and *Esmeralda*. By the time she returned to America, negotiations were concluded for four more films (*Fauntleroy*, *A Lady of Quality*, *A Little Princess* and *The Pretty Sister of José*) and Frances was considering tackling "an original story for the cinematograph".

But her immediate concern was a new book. *The Lost Prince* is said to have had its origin in a brief talk with Eleanor Calhoun, the actress who had played Clorinda in England. She was now the Princess Hreblianovich Lazarovich and some remarks she made about the history of Serbia had given Frances ideas. An incident in Vienna in October 1913 meant a great deal to her and related itself both to *The Lost Prince* and to *The White People*, which she wrote the following year. Kitty and Gigi Hall had gone to one of the Viennese art galleries alone. Frances had rested in the hotel. "I am not yet strong enough to stand on my feet twenty-four hours of the day, so I cannot go with them always," she wrote to Ella Hepworth Dixon. When they returned, one of them brought a photograph over to Frances and laid it on the desk in her hotel room.

"When I looked at it," Frances wrote to Edith, "I cried out in spite of myself. It was a photograph of a portrait by Van Dyck—the portrait of a boy about fifteen—a young Prince Ruprecht von der Pfaltz of Bavaria and he was so like Lionel that it brought one's heart into one's mouth. The head, the eyebrows, the shape of the face, the eyes were Lionel's very own. It gave me strange things to think of when I found myself looking at my own boy's face in a picture painted three hundred years ago!

What did Prince Ruprecht do? I must find out. Did he come back? And what for?"

It was not just a lack of strength which had kept Frances away from the art gallery that afternoon. More and more, she did not like cities. "Vienna *is* beautiful and splendid, with majestic spaces, and the galleries are full of wonders—but I don't *love* cities—I *don't love* them—I want my mountains every hour ... I have been wild with the unspeakable beauty of this world—and cities seem—not enough." She dutifully went to the Hofburg and the Imperial Palace. She saw the Crown Jewels and the Relics ("a *tooth* of John the Baptist, a bone of St Anne, a piece of the Manger"). "The jewels of Marie Antoinette and of her mother Maria Teresa were more magnificent than any I have ever seen"; but her letters to Edith described not them but her own new clothes.

One from Paris had described a pile of new purchases in the Boulevard des Capucines, including the lacy, chiffony things she had always favoured. In Vienna she went to an excellent tailor. "I know how interested a frivolous and fashionable Edith will be ... I must not buy Viennese clothes and not describe them to my sister." She had had two "perfect costumes" made. One was "of a sort of brownish mole trimmed with sable". With it she wore "a huge muff of gathered cloth and sable bands, and a velvet toque of the same shade", and a long coat of the same cloth, lined with black musquash. As an alternative to the sable muff and velvet hat, there was "a large musquash muff and a soft musquash hat, which you jam down on your head and turn up as you please. The other suit is of the most exquisite black broadcloth which is like soft satin. With it I wear a black velvet hat with an insane feather sticking upright and the big black baby lamb muff and stole ... I was also obliged—as I am by way of going to operas every few nights—to buy a warm evening cloak. It is such a beautiful thing—soft black velvet lined with white satin and with collar and cuffs of ermine and covered with the most unique embroidery of softly shaded silver beads ..." Edith might think her extravagant but at least they were "very much less expensive than they would have been in New York". Knowing her weakness, she was perpetually defending herself against the charge of extravagance.

All of Edith's family were closely involved in Frances' affairs. In this same letter, she wrote, "Ask Archie to send my English bank book to be made up." Archie was now married. Frances had given him and his bride Annie an extremely large cheque to help them buy a house, on the understanding, she thought, that there would always be a room in it for Edith—when Frances was away, and after her death. From Bermuda in February 1913, she had written to Vivian: "As to Archie and Annie, I can hear their screams of rapture traversing the Gulf Stream every hour."

Screams of rapture were perhaps not appropriate to a house shared with a mother-in-law. There were quarrels and problems. Edith took refuge at Plandome. Frances was furious. "But for *you*—absolutely but for you," she wrote to Edith, "the house never would have been there." She wrote to Edith from Munich telling her to go to Bermuda and she would join her there. The affair, which should have remained a private family quarrel, eventually became a public scandal and distressed and humiliated Frances.

On 17th May 1914, Stephen Townesend died. Among his more likeable characteristics had been his intense love for animals. His obituary in *The Animals' Guardian* spoke of two of his last acts: "The one was the tremendous philippic … last November against the sermon of the Archbishop of York in unveiling a stained glass window to the memory of a fox-hunting gentleman, in which His Grace extolled hunting as a diversion. The other incident was a fox-hunt in the neighbourhood of his country retreat at Colney Heath, St Albans. A much-harried fox took refuge in the grounds surrounding his house, and he at once, although he had been in bed some weeks, crept down into the garden in his dressing-gown and told the men and women there assembled on horse-back what he thought of them." This was the actor's finest hour, but his "desperate step" may well have hastened his death. His death certificate, certified by their old friend, Owen Lankester, shows

Stephen died, at fifty-four, of pneumonia and exhaustion. There is no record of Frances' reaction to the news.

And fortunately, in May 1914, there were more pleasant family matters to distract her. LORD FAUNTLEROY GREETS MOTHER recorded the *New York Telegraph* when Frances reached New York aboard the *Minnewaska* from London. It had been her final, her thirty-third Atlantic crossing. How different her life would have been if she had suffered from sea-sickness. As it was, by the end, she had divided her time almost exactly between her two countries. And at last it looked as if Lord Fauntleroy, aged thirty-eight, was to have a new rôle. By July, when Frances and Edith returned from Bermuda, Vivian was engaged to Constance Buel, aged twenty-one. "Now about Constance," Frances wrote to Kitty and Gigi Hall, "she is one of the two daughters of the first wife of Mr Buel, who has just retired from the *Century* magazine ... She is a pet ... a little slim wisp of a child ... quiet and calm and with a sweetly concealed backbone of much strength ... She plainly enjoys herself every minute. She has years and years less than Vivian, but he always was twenty-one and now he is more so than ever. He does *so* love her. And he is so happy." Constance was beautiful and musical, swam like a fish, ran a motor and danced like a fairy. She shared Vivian's love of sailing too. "All Saturday afternoon she and Vivian worked together on *Delight*, preparing the sails etc. and all Sunday morning they sailed on the sound and came back sunburned to the bone."

Frances was genuinely delighted at Vivian's good fortune. "I was wondering what I could do to keep him from growing tired and sad!" Vivian had found his own solution, his own happiness. Frances was determined to be an ideal mother-in-law, but of course she could not help wanting to organize their lives for them. She had so much money and they had so little. They were married in November and the following January she sent them off, in the very first boat to go through the Panama Canal, "on a long and joyous journey to San Francisco, Honolulu, Japan, China and various enchanted islands". Vivian had been contemplating asking his firm for a month's holiday. Frances insisted he should be away for four months. "I sent him away to play with the map and choose the places he has always most wanted to go to." No one could resist that sort of generosity but it obviously carried with it return obligations and responsibilities.

Frances was meanwhile coming to the end of *The Lost Prince*. She had written about it regularly to Fayal Clarke, editor of *St Nicholas*, an extremely emotional man, who was inclined to address Frances as "Friend of our Very Souls", to rhapsodize about her inspiration and hail her as "so wonderful a manifestation of the divine soul-of-things". He encouraged in her the tendency she always had, more at some times than others, to think she was a mere channel rather than a creator, that it was not she who was writing but some power outside herself. At this time Edith and Frances used to have periods of silence in which they tried to find guidance from something—they would not call it God—beyond themselves. During these silences (Frances wrote to Fayal Clarke) splendid thoughts would come from the outside.

Frances read *The Lost Prince* aloud to Edith as she wrote it. "When I read the last chapter to Edith this morning [the last chapter she had written, that is, not the final one of the book] she said it lifted her out of the world and made her blood race through her veins ... I am glad, because when she begins to utter little cries when I am reading to her, all is well. It has always been so, since she was a child." Edith was the perfect audience, as enthralled and grateful as any writer could wish. Frances' only fear about the new book was that it might be too long and would be impossible to cut. "How *could* one cut pages out of the story of a boy—a boy who is a Prince but does not know he is one, though he has always the noble image of a Prince before him, making his way through Europe in the guise of a stalwart little tramp, but secretly carrying a sign and a message to stray men in crowded streets, at palace gates, in forests and on mountainsides, he himself ignorant of all but that he must obey and pass on in silence." The story is too patriotic ("the sword in my hand—for

Samaria") for contemporary taste, and there are ideas of inborn nobility and gentlemanly behaviour which have dated, but once again Frances showed her power as a storyteller. The reader is compelled to turn the page as a delicate hand tightens its grasp on Marco's shoulder in the crowded foyer at the Opera in Munich.

When the book was published in October 1915, following serialization in *St Nicholas*, everybody liked it, although the more sophisticated critics took care to cover themselves by realizing that it could be dismissed as "superficial, sentimental, conventional and other such things". The *New York Times*, for instance, suggested cynics might jeer, but believed it to be "a story for young people of all ages from ten to a hundred, a story fresh and gracious as spring time, full of those high and clean and simple ideals which have never lost, and probably never will lose, their power over the imaginations and sympathies of men".

The war was by this time of course occupying a great deal of everyone's attention. On 4th October 1915 Frances wrote to Josephine Browne in Devon: "For the last two or three days we have been lifting up our heads a little because of the advance of the Allies. And yet, one's heart breaks at the thought of what an advance means to so many who are only the toys of a monstrous cruelty and egotism. I won't go on. The mere writing of it leads to such horror." Frances' own war-work took various forms. She collected books for the Royal Engineers' library in Bermuda. "The battered and ancient volumes on the shelves of the Recreation Room almost make me weep and I am getting together all I can," she wrote to Scribner. "Half the men went to the front long ago and the regimental notepaper is bordered in black." She entertained soldiers and sailors and wrote dozens of letters to them and to her friends in England. When the war was over, Rosamund Campbell wrote to say how much they had meant to her: "I just thank you again and again, dearest, for your wonderful letters during these last awful years."

Her own books were helping too. In 1895, in one of her rare public speeches, Frances had said: "The happiest thing in the world is to feel that, after all, one's work was worthy of the doing." She had never really doubted it but it was always good to be reassured. Of all the fan mail she received in her long writing life, two notes gave her particular pleasure. One had been stencilled in 1889 by a small girl in the Perkins Institute for the Blind, Boston—Helen Keller. ("I do love Lord Fauntleroy because he was so kind to Mr Hobbs and Dick and the poor old woman and Bridget.") The second was a postcard which came in 1917:

> Am just writing this P.C. in a spare minute to thank you for writing *T. Tembarom*. It was lent to me when I had gone sick, and was, in addition, most completely fed up with life in general.
>
> It was a splendid tonic, your novel—it is a real bucker, and braced me up tophole. I should like to receive three such books every week ... I hope it has done dozens of gloomy beggars as much good as it did me.
>
> Thank you again for it. May you write many more such.
>
> One of the Mesopot. Expeditionary Force, Baghdad.

"Cheering up gloomy beggars": that was certainly a part of her life's intention. Not everyone wanted to be cheered up, of course. She lent E. L. Burlingame some "Edinburgh and London Lectures" but he sent them back with the comment, "I am afraid I am a hardened old questioner, not easily turned into an optimist or persuaded that his woes can be taken cheerfully." *The Dawn of a Tomorrow* was doing its bit by sending out its cheering message on the cinema screen. Mary Pickford, at the height of her fame, was "irresistible as the waif in the London slums, wearing a most attractive and delightful costume of rags and tatters ... Everybody knows *The Dawn of a Tomorrow*. One goes merely to see Miss Pickford as Glad. And, often as the story has been told, it is absorbing." Another paper called it "this sublime drama of human suffering and sacrifice that has brought to so many weary souls a new inspiration to bear the trials of today in the expectancy of tomorrow's dawn." Mary Pickford also appeared in *Esmeralda*, "one of the most exceptionally clever films of the season".

But how was it that someone who proclaimed herself "a disciple of happiness", who was on record as saying "we never discuss painful things—that is our religion, our philosophy", whose life-long motivation was "Be kind", how was it that Frances could find herself in court sued for fifty thousand dollars' damages for libel? The papers enjoyed the case enormously and gave great space to it. The author of *Little Lord Fauntleroy*, they said, "had lost none of her descriptive ability when she wrote the letter" on which the suit was based. Middle-aged reporters who, as children, had been "forced by their mothers to wear detestable velvet knickerbockers and broad lace collars" seemed to welcome the chance to get their revenge on Frances. She had said, more than once, "Eliminate anything that makes you unhappy; concentrate on happy things." But she could not ignore the law.

The facts were these. On 21st February 1915 Frances had written a letter to Mrs Emma Prall Knorr, the sister of Archie Fahnestock's wife, Annie. Frances had certainly been very foolish, and indeed malicious. Angry at Annie's treatment of her mother-in-law (Annie had accused Edith of "making mischief" between her and Archie), Frances had called Annie "a liar, slanderer, ill-bred meddler, a shrew and a brawler of doubtful character and antecedents, and subject to brainstorms". Emma and Annie were outraged. They produced a Washington doctor who testified that Annie did not suffer from brainstorms or hysteria. They said Annie had been "held up to scorn, scandal and disgrace". But the letter was of course a private letter and if they had not chosen to take it to court there would have been no question of public scandal and disgrace. It is impossible not to guess that the sisters saw the letter as an excellent opportunity to get money out of an extremely rich old woman. As a result of their action, not hers, everything was washed in public. The court was told that when Archie Fahnestock married Annie Prall, he was earning only ten dollars a week as a reporter for the society column of a New

York newspaper. Annie was a woman of thirty-five when they married. Archie had been reluctant, as he had known he did not earn enough to support a wife.

In her defence, Frances said that she had virtually been the support of her nephew and his wife ever since their marriage. She it was who paid when Annie had to go into a sanatorium. She gave them a cheque for five thousand dollars towards their home. As to the letter, "it was a private communication to a close friend and in no way concerned the public". One newspaper commented, "She probably could pay a judgment for fifty thousand dollars without feeling it, but she says she 'doesn't intend to', if she can help it, when the person seeking it is a member of the family to whom she already has been a benefactor."

The court case dragged on. Can a letter written to a friend and not intended for the eyes of the public be a libel? One judge at least did not think so. The New York *Telegraph* of 17th October 1917 carried the headline LORD FAUNTLEROY AUTHOR WINS SUIT. Mr Justice Brown in the Supreme Court threw the case out. As the letter was written as a private communication, it did not result in any damage to the plaintiff. It was revealed in court that Annie was now living with her sister and Archie with Frances. But it was not all over. Frances wrote to Josephine Browne: "The appalling case came off about a month ago and was dismissed from the court by the Judge … You can imagine our relief—*but*—if you please—they have taken it to another Court;'made an appeal', it is called, and it will be submitted to yet another Judge—not by trial but by giving to him for inspection copies of all the evidence. If he sustains the decision of the first Judge, I think that is the end, but if he reverses his decision, they can bring the whole thing into court again. It is too horrible. After just a few weeks of relief and peace to have that Monster start to life again is almost more than one can endure …"

The result of the appeal was worse than she could possibly have imagined. On 18th March 1918, the New York *American* carried the headlines "COURT LASHES MRS BURNETT. Author of Little

Lord Fauntleroy censured for 'Malice' in her 'virulent letter'. The
Appellate Division of the Supreme Court decided Mrs Burnett
would have to stand trial a second time for writing a defamatory
letter. She had "butted into" a family controversy without cause
and deliberately defamed Mrs Fahnestock. Mrs Burnett could not
claim privilege, as her letter was not written in reply to any letter
directed to herself. The court said that the malice which pervaded
the letter was manifest in almost every paragraph.

Although at the second trial the original decision of the
Supreme Court was upheld, it was a black time. Frances' image
of herself was shattered. She had to admit that she could be spiteful, petty, cruel. For many years she had tried to believe that she
was better than most other people—braver, sweeter, kinder, more
generous. She had become accustomed to admiration and gratitude. Now she had to face other things. If she had herself been
malicious, she now received malice. If she had been cruel, she was
now treated cruelly. Journalists who had been refused interviews
responded with this sort of thing: "She is devoted to osteopathy,
the *beau monde* and solid food with relishes on the side." Toast and
buttermilk would apparently not have sounded equally insulting.
"She recounts interminable and anaesthetic reminiscences. She is
insufferably rude because rudeness seems the prerogative of her
majesty … She crowns her venerable head with the coiffure of
a Titian of twenty and arrays her body in sky blue, plumes and
wampum." "She would extract personal flattery from the reports
of the weather bureau." "Her mesmerized sycophants proclaim
her pot-boilers to be masterpieces." "In the universe of eiderdown
she is high priestess of the omnipotent cult of the second rate."
"She inhabits a saccharine dream-world of her own."

With more accuracy, one man wrote: "She has shattered all the
mirrors which might betray her to herself." No one over seventy
likes mirrors. It is too late to change one's style; the brave face
has too many lines. But it was true she had not valued mirrors
for many years. She had often given not true reflections but
had invented mirages: many of her books were written, as they

were read, to substantiate day-dreams. She had tried, earnestly and genuinely, to be the perfect mother, friend, sister, neighbour, writer, the beloved public figure. She had set the scene on so many occasions: mostly the other actors had played the bit parts she had written for them, receiving gratefully, falling into line. (Though Swan had not, of course, neither had Stephen and neither had Annie Prall Fahnestock.) "It is the most wondrous thing in life to be born a giver," Frances had written in her introduction to the work of Kate Douglas Wiggin. She had sung the praises of tolerance. She had been "the Happifier", the Fairy Godmother. It was fine while other people did as she wanted, receiving gratefully without question, adoring in return.

Fortunately Vivian and Constance (Constance sometimes perhaps with difficulty) were still playing perfectly the parts assigned to them. In 1916, and again in 1918, they had presented Frances with grand-daughters and a new and delightful rôle. After the first child, Verity, was born, Frances wrote to Elizabeth Jordan, editor of *Harper's Magazine*, for whom she was completing *The White People*: "Great Heaven! I have not yet told you that I have a grand-daughter—which seems to have been born by magic—so quietly and beautifully it appeared—and so wonderfully radiant is its lovely little mother. I have now the relationship of Fairy Grandmother. The Fairy Godmother will pale by comparison. I wish you could see the Lilliputian white wicker wardrobe I have lined through every drawer and shelf with softly orris-scented pale blue flowered silk." She took great delight in buying for her grand-daughters all the beautiful things she had not been able to afford when her own boys were babies.

Edith also continued to play her rôle perfectly. She needed all Frances' love and attention at this time and was grateful for it. She too, of course, had suffered greatly through the libel case and, in 1918 in the midst of it, Ernest, her beloved younger son, had died of pneumonia. Ernest had been an inventor, the inspiration of a number of characters in Frances' books—including Joseph Hutchinson, Ann's father in *T. Tembarom*. Like Mr Hutchinson,

Ernest had suffered "periodical fits of infuriated discouragement" but Frances had always believed in him. "I don't want you to be anxious," she had written to him. "You need never be anxious so long as I can take care of you. I shall always try to see that you can have your mind free for the work you are doing." For years he was unsuccessful but before he died he was able to hand his aunt a substantial dividend on her investment in one of his inventions.

The shock and sadness of Ernest's death made Frances put aside the book she was writing—a new big book which was eventually to appear in two volumes as *The Head of the House of Coombe* and *Robin*, her last substantial work. It was finally finished in 1920, began serialization that year, and the two volumes were published in 1922. They had the worst press of any Frances had written. Her day was over; her powers declining. One critic called *Robin* "the apotheosis of Burnettian slush". The *Times Literary Supplement* wrote: "Lush sentiments flow from her pen with a sweetness that suggests syrup rather than plain ink … This is a pity, because once upon a time Mrs Burnett could write differently." She could indeed; if she had died at thirty-five, before she had written *Little Lord Fauntleroy*, she might well have had a reputation comparable with Mrs Gaskell's. Certainly there were those, even as late as 1910, who thought of her as "an author for whom not merely the reading public, eager for amusement, but lovers of true literature, harbour the kindliest feelings". But by 1922 the sort of readers who had admired *That Lass o' Lowrie's* all those years before were now reading Virginia Woolf. *Jacob's Room* was reviewed at length in the same issue of the *Times Literary Supplement* which briefly dismissed *Robin*.

But Frances still had her faithful readers even among the critics. The *Boston Transcript* admitted she had written better stories, "but Mrs Burnett not in her best mood is far better than the average storyteller of the day". And the *New York Times* went so far as to pick out one section and say "Mrs Burnett has done nothing better".

Frances once said how much her readers meant to her, how much she valued meeting "friends" all over the world—people who had read and loved her work. "That," she said, "is the most that life has given me. It began so early in my life that I can form no idea at all of what life would be like without it. And if, by any human possibility, it should ever come about that I should lose this, I am quite sure that I would not want to go on living." She never did lose this assurance, whatever some critics might say, that people were waiting eagerly for the next words she would write, for the next issue of the monthly magazine. She had not lost her power to tell stories and there were many readers for whom that was enough.

From a biographical point of view, there is much of interest. *The Head of the House of Coombe* has the most dramatic of all the changes from riches to poverty which occur again and again in her books. Feather, a silly, feckless girl, is left widowed, destitute with a small baby. It is surely no coincidence that her nickname, "Feather", recalls Frances' own "Fluffy". She is like a caricature of all the basest characteristics Frances feared, of all the tendencies in herself that frightened her, of things she herself had been accused of by the newspapers. She is pleasure-loving, frivolous, extravagant. She has no taste or feeling. There is a marvellously observed scene when the child Robin is brought down to her mother's drawing-room to be shown off.

Throughout this first volume, there is a strong sense of an old order breaking up. "The note of today is: 'Since it has never been done, it will surely be done soon.' ... So many people lived in glass-houses that the habit of throwing stones had fallen out of fashion as an exercise ... A mad dog is loose among us and we sit and smile." A few can hear "The sound of clashing arms and the thudding of marching feet." Robin, fearful, ignored, is an outsider in the heedless, extravagant world her mother inhabits. "Oh! what worlds away from her the party had been." When eventually she is invited to her first dance and meets again Donal, the boy she had known as a child, it is on the night of the assassination at Sarajevo.

The second volume, *Robin*, is set in London during the war. Frances' material was second-hand. The flaws and limitations in the book are numerous but her romancing did not extend to war. She sees the horror, not any nobility or glamour. She sees slain soldiers in "awful heaps". She considers how a boy's eyes would look when killing a man. When foolish Feather, unchanged, unsubdued by war, rushes out with her new lover to see the Zeppelins, all that is left of her is her hand, with a ring and a purple scarf. In her treatment of the sexual relationship between Donal and Robin, Frances was hopelessly hindered by the conventions of the time. She wanted to be daring and outspoken, but she could not quite bring herself to be. She wanted to be realistic but her heart was not really in it.

She was getting tired; she was getting old. She had had her seventieth birthday in 1919. There were still some good times. Constance and Verity visited her in Bermuda in the spring of 1920, leaving the baby, Dorinda, in the care of a "treasure". Frances and Verity fed the red birds together beneath the oleander trees. But her back ached "devilishly". She tried not to complain, but in December 1920, she wrote to Vivian:

… I will—for a reason—frankly tell you now, that for years the greatest part of my strength has been given to a certain game of bluff on more occasions than you have ever guessed. The bluff was to convince the world that I was not an unrelieved Bore who was *always* ill—in one way or another. Sometimes—quite often—I can quite "carry it off"—but not always. The trouble is that sometimes I am absolutely *prevented* from doing things I ought to do—or must do. No one should know at all if the thing did not make explanations necessary. That is why I go into this revolting detail now. I must ask you to do things.

… Oh! I do want to be *let alone* by pain. I do—I do. I am so tired all over my body, Vivvie, that it almost breaks my spirit. If I am allowed to gnaw my dog biscuit in peace, perhaps that will pass away.

It is so quiet here—and so sweet and so like early June. Roses are everywhere. But just now I am so tired. Perhaps I shall bound up again and be quite well—but this is to explain why you must be very faithful to your Mammy and attend to her business.

From this time on, Vivian took care of her business affairs. It was a great comfort to her that she had "tucked away" a fortune and that, when she was dead, Vivian and his family would always be "comfortable and free". But she was determined not to give in to pain and illness and old age. She refused to resign herself to lace caps and folded hands and talk of tombstones. "People meeting her for the first time always marvelled, even in her very last years, at her appearance of vigor," Vivian wrote. She still liked to look forward and not back. Charles Scribner, trying to the end to get another book out of her, suggested she wrote her reminiscences, but the very idea made her "start back violently and turn pale". "I have reminiscences enough," she wrote on 23rd July 1921, "but I cannot see myself writing them." She could hardly admit that she had really, after all, missed the Party, that it had gone on in other rooms, that she had worn the white dresses and heard the music but had only glimpsed the rapture through half-closed doors. "My life has been a heavy burden to me—a burden of work and uncertainty and the responsibility of high ideals, ..." she had once written to Vivian.

Now, at last, there was no anxiety, no uncertainty. She looked forward with hope. She still believed absolutely in some sort of life after death. Even on earth, there was hope. "When you have a garden, you have a future," she wrote in one of her last articles. Early in 1921, she was taken seriously ill while spending the winter in Bermuda. It was feared that she might die but Edith's loving care eventually prevailed. Vivian was sent for and she wrote in a shaky hand, "Please bring Gillet's Fern Catalogue. There are places here too shady for anything but ferns." She was thinking of the Plandome garden too. She sent lists of seeds she wanted, including large supplies of mignonette. "I want to have the scent of it all over the garden." She suggested the gardener could throw it wherever there was a bare place between flowers. She hated bare places.

The story-telling part of her brain still had not stopped working. "When I seemed to be actually dying, there suddenly passed through my brain a new book … and a few days ago there came another—quite clear. They are both comedy things—which came out of the new world. They might be 1930 or something like it … Here are the titles, which I wrote down, but you must keep them dead secret," she told Vivian, "except to Constance: No. 1. The Industrious Apprentice. No. 2. A Transfusion of Blood." But they were never written—and she did not live to see the new world of 1930.

The last years were as happy as they could be in the face of constant pain. She spent the summers at Plandome and the winters in New York hotels. She did not want to die in Bermuda or travel so far from Vivian again, though there were times when she longed for England. "Tell me about all the nice places near enough to you which one might possibly rent for a summer, if one were well and courageous enough. Let us make fairy stories," she wrote to Rosamund Campbell early in 1923. "Sometimes they come true." America was wonderful but it was "roaring and banging and rattling and shrieking and crowding itself with disorder and making a god of speed". Everyone seemed to be wanting to crowd into New York and battle for more money and more speed—building madly and tearing down more madly still. Only under the oak tree in the rose garden on Long Island was there peace.

She derived much pleasure from her grandchildren. A year or two before, she had written to Elizabeth Jordan:

> … Vivian and Constance came in to our mid-day dinner and in the afternoon Vivian brought the children up in the car and they rushed in out of the rain, dancing and shrieking with joy because Nanda was going to play with them. I am Nanda, you know, and I am considered desperately fascinating. You see, *le bon Dieu* so made me that I can "be" any number of persons at a moment's notice.
>
> I am "Mrs Desmond". Verity is my daughter, Lily Desmond, and Dorin is Mrs Clarence, our neighbor, who lives in Archie's

room and goes to market in the bathroom. Mrs Desmond's cook has left her, but Lily cooks perfectly, and we telephone to Mrs Clarence to come to tea and have magnificent collations on the top of a box turned upside down, covered with scraps of silk and set with dolls' tea things.

A great deal of telephoning is done and the "market man" constantly makes excuses and hasn't got what we want. My arm chair is a car and gets out of order, and the garage man can't mend it because he is "so busy". Once he was painting his house. The animated telephonings of these two small things—one four—the other three—form a *resumé* of the difficulties of modern house-keeping. They are always without cooks and cannot get things done.

Verity is growing prettier and prettier. She has a flower petal face, and a halo of curling corn silk hair, and dimples, and roguish eyes—*and* darkening lashes—*and* a quaint, elfish, little sideways smile. Dorin is tiny and fantastic and elfin, but not pretty yet.

My den is a nursery. The closet in the corner contains ... a family of dolls of assorted sizes—half of them dressed in brilliant blue, half in brilliant scarlet. I invented and dressed them. They are the Poppies and the Larkspurs. There is Mr Poppy, in scarlet velvet knickerbockers and silk hat and coat. Mrs Poppy and a little sister Poppy and little brother Poppy. Mrs Larkspur and an equal set of Larkspurs. They make quite showy parties sitting in the wicker chairs round the tea table. And Mrs Desmond and Lily are most superior in their manners.

Frances genuinely liked children. There is no question about that. She would never, as Beatrix Potter once did, have turned children out of her hay-field. In the house at Plandome she kept a Jacobean cupboard she had bought when she was living at Maytham. She had a vertical wooden wall placed down the middle—you can still see the grooves—so that when children opened the doors it was not an ordinary cupboard but a doll's house with four rooms: drawing-room, nursery bedroom, dining-room and kitchen. They were full of the sort of miniature things which had not been available when Frances was a child. There was a writing desk, with a telephone on it, a wringer, a vacuum cleaner, hot-house fruits made of plaster of Paris and a shower that really worked, if you poured water into a thing at the top—and dolls, of course, of every description, bought in Tenterden, Amsterdam, Cortina or New York, over the years.

In her last illness, one of the de Kay family brought her young daughter to see the old lady. Even now she was not finished with her fantasy. She told the child the things Sara Crewe had once said: "What I believe about dolls is that they can do things they will not let us know about. If you stay in the room [my doll] will just sit there and stare, but if you go out, she will begin to read, perhaps, or go and look out of the window." And such was her magic still that the child, a stolid, sensible girl not given to believing in fairies, for a moment felt her reason totter. For a moment, she felt it must be so, as Frances had said—that behind the wooden doors of the Jacobean toy cupboard, the dolls were indeed at work and play, busy in their separate existence and that it was only when she opened the doors that they would freeze into immobility again.

In her last illness, Frances sat propped up in bed, writing *In the Garden* on blue-lined manuscript paper—but the pen-driving machine was wearing out. From her window, she could see beds of lingering roses, gorgeous clusters of dahlias and chrysanthemums, and beyond the flower beds the bay and the boats and the sunset. Someone said that the flowers that autumn "blossomed with unusual luxuriance for her passing", the sort of pretty thought that would have pleased her. She died on 29th October 1924 in her home at Plandome, four weeks before her seventy-fifth birthday. She was buried at God's Acre, Roslyn, Long Island.

Frances' last public appearance had been at the opening performance of Mary Pickford's version of *Little Lord Fauntleroy*. After her death, a gossip writer wrote in the *Bookman*: "We saw her only once, in a box at the opening of Mary Pickford's production of

the famous story. She sat quietly, an imposing detached figure …"
But there had been a muddle. Miss Pickford did not know she
was there, and in a speech at the end expressed her regret that Mrs
Burnett had not been able to come. Afterwards she wrote:

> I am sure there must have been many things in the picture
> that were not quite pleasing to you—certain liberties—and many
> omissions, but from the kind tone of your letter, I am sure that
> you have made allowances for us, knowing that it is not always
> easy to take a classic like *Little Lord Fauntleroy* and place it on the
> cold, silver screen and retain the spirit and charm of the book.
> Fauntleroy cost more effort, time and money to produce than any
> other film of my experience. So you see, dear Mrs Burnett, that we
> did try to do justice to your very beautiful story. I regret exceed-
> ingly I missed the pleasure of being presented to you the opening
> night. I have appeared in four of your stories on the screen …

The Fauntleroy film was certainly an extraordinary techni-
cal achievement. Mary Pickford appeared both as Cedric and
his mother, and the quality of Charles Rosher's photography is
impressive. One shot of Fauntleroy kissing his mother on the
cheek lasts about three seconds on the screen and took sixteen
hours of continuous work to achieve. This shot, and all the others
involving two Marys in the same frame, was accomplished within
the camera. The dividing line is completely imperceptible. The
double exposure work is extraordinarily fine. But who, least of
all Frances, could bear to see a plumpish twenty-seven-year-old
woman playing the beautiful small boy? Mary Pickford had spent
several hundred thousand dollars on the film; she had tried to
make it the big picture of her career. It was shown in about
eight thousand theatres in the United States and Canada and in
many more all over the world. There was some discussion about
a special edition of the book being produced to be sold when the
film was being shown. But it came to nothing, perhaps because
Frances could not bear to have Mary Pickford's photographs as

Cedric illustrating it. Film and television versions of the children's books are so frequently seen that it is a rare child who does not recognise the title *The Secret Garden*, even when the writer's name is unfamiliar.

The most lavish film of all was probably the 1939 version of *A Little Princess*, which starred Shirley Temple as Sara Crewe. The *New Yorker* critic suffered from the delusion that "the adaptors have been faithful to the old kindergarten classic", though he admits that "Mr Zanuck's heart is in the right place and he won't let Shirley's father stay dead or poor too long". Richard Greene played a riding master, though one can hardly imagine a riding master at Miss Minchin's. And Cesar Romero was coached in Hindustani for his part as Ram Dass. But the most surprising touch was "the intervention of the aged Queen Victoria". "Twelve thousand battled to watch Shirley's Film Premier," reported the *New Yorker*, and called the film one of Hollywood's finest achievements. Certainly Frances would have been interested to have been there that night to see the reception by the new world of a confection far more sentimental than its Victorian original.

It was fitting that Frances' last public appearance should have been at the film of *Little Lord Fauntleroy*, for it was Fauntleroy who had made her a public figure. His name was more famous than hers. The small velvet-clothed figure had embedded itself in the national conscience. He had hung round her neck as well as Vivian's. On the centenary of her birth, *Life* magazine carried a long article not on Frances but on Little Lord Fauntleroy, illustrated with photographs of boys large and small, known (such as Buster Keaton) and unknown, all of them wearing velvet suits and lace collars. There was a danger that people would forget she had written anything else.

The Times obituary writer praised her work in bringing about finally the 1911 Copyright Act, but recorded that it was "chiefly, almost solely, by this idyll of child life [*Little Lord Fauntleroy*] that Mrs Hodgson Burnett's name is known to the multitude of readers and theatre-goers. The story has a quality all its own. In her other books and plays, Mrs Burnett was less successfully Dickensian, sentimental, naïve. *Little Lord Fauntleroy* had for millions of readers and theatre-goers the compelling attraction of the laughter that is akin to tears."

The Times readers rushed to mention their own favourites. A Mr A. L. N. Russell of London, W.11, wrote: "The obituary notice of Mrs Burnett might convey the impression that except for *Lord Fauntleroy* (which belongs to a past age) there is no more work of hers worthy of mention. But there are fairly recent books which are read and re-read by many with the greatest enthusiasm. I have found no novel that I can lend with a greater assurance of giving pleasure than *T. Tembarom*, and *The Secret Garden* is one of the most delightful children's books (and one of the best sermons) ever written …"

"Giving pleasure"—the phrase would have delighted Frances. "With the best that I have in me," she had said to Vivian, "I have tried to write more happiness into the world." She had seldom failed to give pleasure with her writing. In life, of course, it was different. Things did not always turn out the way she wanted them to. People cannot be manipulated like characters in a story. Over and over again she had tried to make dreams come true, her own and other people's. As one of her contemporaries put it: "Beauty, romance, imagination—they possessed her all three, but reality shook her cruelly."

A committee placed a memorial to Frances in a part of Central Park, New York, near Mount Sinai Hospital. Statues of a boy and girl—perhaps a romantic epitome of the spirit of children's literature—stand in a garden, but it is not a secret garden; and few children who play there notice the inscription or listen to stories as the committee hoped they would.

Notes

All the letters from Frances Hodgson Burnett, Swan Burnett and Stephen Townesend to her publishers come from the Scribner archives at Princeton, as do all the letters to Frances from her publishers. Most of the other letters used come from her family.

Foreword, p.9 John Rowe Townsend's *Written for Children* was most recently revised in 1994 (Bodley Head).

CHAPTER 1: PREPARING FOR THE PARTY 1849–1865

p. 15   Engels, *The Condition of the Working-Class in England in 1844* (1845). Engels lived in Manchester from 1842 to 1870.

p. 15   Engels, *op. cit.*

p. 19   F.H.B., *The One I Knew The Best of All* quoted passim in this chapter.

p. 22   Revd R. Parkinson, *On the Present Condition of the Labouring Poor in Manchester* (1841).

p. 25   G.F. Watts (1817–1904), English painter and sculptor.

p. 26   Answer to question put to Frances on the contributors' page of an issue of *St Nicholas*, quoted in Constance Buel Burnett, *Happily Ever After* (1969).

p. 29   F.H.B.'s introduction to *Granny's Wonderful Chair* by Frances Browne was published in 1904 by McLure Philips. In it, F.H.B. recalls that she was given the book "when I was five or six years old and went to a tiny school which was kept by two daughters of an old clergyman". But, in fact, the book was not published until Christmas, 1856 (dated 1857), when she was seven and had already moved to Islington Square.

p. 32   Mrs Alexander, "All things bright and beautiful", in *Hymns for Little Children* (1848).

p. 32   Henry Colman, *European Life and Manners* (1845).

p. 34   F.H.B., "Surly Tim", a short story, first published in *Scribner's Monthly* in 1872.

p. 35   Harriet Beecher Stowe, *Uncle Tom's Cabin* (1852).

p. 36   Sarah Hadfield, quoted by Henry Hadfield in his unpublished paper, "Personal and Family Reminiscences of a Manchester Authoress", read to the Manchester Literary Club in 1882.

p. 38   Edith Jordan: "My Sister", *Good Housekeeping* (U.S., 1925).

p. 43   The Diary of John Ward of Clitheroe, 1860–1864 (*Transactions of the Historical Society of Lancashire and Cheshire*, 1953).

CHAPTER 2: MY OBJECT IS REMUNERATION 1865–1873

p. 46   Robert Chambers (1802–71) wrote about his experiences in North America in Chambers' *Edinburgh Journal*, 10th June 1854.

p. 46   Information from Thomas B. Alexander, *Political Reconstruction in Tennessee* (1950).

p. 47   W.Y.C. Humes to O.P. Temple, Temple Papers, University of Tennessee Library, Knoxville.

p. 50   Caroline Matilda Stansbury Kirkland, *A New Home in the Clearings*. This was in the 1830s, but apparently the flood of spittle from the practice of chewing tobacco hardly ebbed until the turn of the century.

p. 50   Vivian Burnett, *The Romantick Lady* (1927).

p. 52   Edith Jordan, *op. cit.*

p. 52   F.H.B., *The One I Knew The Best Of All*, again referred to passim in this chapter.

p. 53   Ada Campbell Larew, article in unidentifiable newspaper, 1925.

p. 54   Ola Elizabeth Winslow, "Books for the Lady Reader" in a symposium *Romanticism in America* (1940).

p. 55   Sarah Josepha Hale is best remembered as the author of "Mary had a little lamb", in her *Poems for our Children* (1830).

p 58   Edith Jordan, *op. cit.*

p. 61   Claud Cockburn, *Bestseller* (1972).

p. 62   Edward Dicey, *A Selection of his Writings* (1972).

p. 65   Daisy Ashford was only nine when she wrote *The Young Visiters*, that marvellous version of late Victorian high society.

p. 66   Charles Scribner, born 1821, the founder of the publishing company, died this same year, 1871, but there have continued to be Charles Scribners until today. The Charles Frances dealt with was born in 1854 and died, after she did, in 1930. He ran the firm with his brothers, John Blair (1850–79) and Arthur Hawley (1859–1932).

p. 66   The editor of *Scribner's Monthly* was Dr Josiah Gilbert Holland (1819–81). His *Timothy Titcomb*, a book of fictional letters, giving advice to the young, was a bestseller.

p. 67   Richard Watson Gilder (1844–1909), assistant editor, was from 1881 to
his death editor of the *Century* magazine. He was a well-known poet
in his day, his books including a cycle of love sonnets, *The New Day*
(1875). He married Helena de Kay in 1874.

p. 72   George MacDonald (1824–1905) is now best remembered for his
children's books, *At the Back of the North Wind* (1871), etc. Henry
Hadfield records the fact that Frances met him on her honeymoon
but, according to his son, "Our last days in New York were spent at Dr
J.G. Holland's house" before leaving in May 1873, after a very successful lecture tour. At this time MacDonald established a lifelong friendship with Gilder, "whose romantic outlook and innocence, so like my
father's, gave him the poetic vision and raciness of humour, that were
the secret of his critical acumen and philanthropic labours".

p. 72   W.H. Auden, Introduction to *The Visionary Novels of George MacDonald*
(1954).

p. 72   Francis Bret Harte (1836–1902), poet and humourist, author of such
stories as "The Luck of Roaring Camp". Frances met him many times
throughout her life but never knew him well.

CHAPTER 3: CHESTNUTS OFF A HIGHER BOUGH 1874–1881

p. 73   Birdie's story is told in *Giovanni and the Other* (U.S.) and *Children I
Have Known* (England).

p. 73   "Behind the White Brick" was eventually published in *St Nicholas* in
1881.

p. 75   James Kay (later Sir James Kay-Shuttleworth): *The Moral and Physical
Condition of the Working Classes Employed in the Cotton Manufacture in
Manchester* (1832).

p. 75   Edith Jordan, *op. cit.*

p. 79   I have copied this poem from a manuscript and do not know if it was
ever published.

p. 82   Nathaniel Hawthorne's *The Blithedale Romance* had been published in
1852.

p. 89   Mrs Emma Southworth (1819–99) lived in Washington. A uniform edition of her novels in forty-two volumes was issued in 1877. She wrote
more than sixty books altogether, with such titles as *The Fatal Marriage*
and *The Maiden Widow.*

pp. 93–4   Mrs Daniel Chester French: *Memories of a Sculptor's Wife* (1928).

p. 94   The parodies of *That Lass o' Lowrie's* appeared in six issues of *Punch*
from 13th October 1877 to 17th November 1877.

p. 98   Mary Mapes Dodge (1831–1905) had published her best-selling children's book *Hans Brinker or The Silver Skates* in 1865. In 1873 she was
appointed editor of the new *St Nicholas* magazine and remained editor
for thirty-two years, until her death.

p. 98   Vivian Burnett, *op. cit.*

p. 98   Ralph Waldo Emerson, philosopher, essayist and poet, was nearly
          seventy-six when Frances called on him. He did not die until 1882
          but already, in his own phrase, his wits had begun to fail. It is doubtful
          whether Frances got much out of the visit. A visitor the following year
          recorded, "He would hardly give an answer in conversation, but smiled
          and turned away his head as if another person had been addressed."

p. 98   John Boyle O'Reilly (1844–90), Irish revolutionary, journalist and poet.
          Banished to Australia, he escaped to America in 1869 and settled there.

p. 99   Frances had visited North Carolina in September 1878: "We rode a
          hundred and fifty miles on horseback over mountain roads ... I didn't
          enjoy it but I was interested."

p. 105   Jay Leyda, *The Years and Hours of Emily Dickinson* (1960). The *Amherst
          Student* of 8th May 1880 recorded that "the novelist Mrs Burnett, Mr
          Bowles and Mr Griffin of the Springfield Republican were in town
          last Wednesday".

p. 107   The description of Wilde comes from Vivian Burnett; presumably he
          was remembering Frances' own description. It tallies with one given
          by Mrs Daniel Chester French (*op. cit.*). Her aunt was present when
          Frances entertained Wilde.

p. 107   Ernest Samuels, *Henry Adams—The Middle Years* (1965).

p. 107   Mrs E.N. Chapin, *American Court Gossip* (1887), reported that Frances
          was "sneered at behind her back" for her *Through One Administration*.

p. 108   Justin Kaplan, *Mr Clemens and Mark Twain* (1966).

p. 108   Kenneth Andrews, *Nook Farm* (1950) is a study of the complex com-
          munity.

p. 108   William Gillette (1855–1937), successful playwright. In Quinn's
          Literature of the American People he is given more space than Frances.

p. 108   James Garfield (1831–81), teacher and Head of Hiram College, Ohio,
          became a major-general in the Civil War. Elected in 1880, he was inau-
          gurated as President of the United States on 4th March 1881, shot on
          2nd July and died on 19th September.

p. 108   Nye and Morpurgo, *The Growth of the United States* (1955).

p. 108   The I Street houses must have been renumbered as the plaque is a few
          doors below the present 1215. It was fixed at the time of the Freddie
          Bartholomew film (1936).

p. 110   E.L. Burlingame (1848–1922) was later editor of *Scribner's Magazine*,
          1887–1914. He had a good deal to do with Frances over the years. This
          story about Guiteau comes from Roger Burlingame, *Of Making Many
          Books* (1946).

p. 110   Ernest Samuels, *op. cit.*

p. 112   *Two on a Tower* was first published in the *Atlantic Monthly* from May to
          December 1882. It seems likely that Frances met Hardy at some point.
          They had many friends in common, including Gosse and the Alma-
          Tademas. Hardy was also interested in the anti-vivisectionist cause with
          which Frances became involved through her second husband. On 11th

June 1896 Hardy entertained "a great American authoress to tea". It could have been Frances. In April 1899, he commented in a letter on the success of "Mrs Burnett's Woman of Quality".

p. 113　　Arthur Hobson Quinn, *American Fiction* (1936).

p. 116　　In Vivian Burnett's *The Romantick Lady*, Gilder is not mentioned again for nearly twenty years.

p. 117　　*The Times*, 22nd October 1883.

p. 117　　A reference in the *Athenaeum*, 27th October 1883, definitely stated that the criticism was by Henry James. George Alexander and Madge Kendal were both involved in this production. Alexander was later to produce *Guy Domville*, James' play and Mrs Kendal, Frances' *Little Lord Fauntleroy*.

p. 118　　In 1881 Roswell Smith had paid Charles Scribner two hundred thousand dollars for his share in *Scribner's Monthly* so he could start a new magazine, the *Century*, and publishing house with Holland and Gilder. Scribner promised that five years would elapse before he began a rival publication. In December 1886, he founded *Scribner's Magazine*. Frances was published in all three periodicals.

CHAPTER 4: THE UNIVERSAL FAVOURITE 1882–1886

p. 120　　"How Fauntleroy Occurred" was later included in Frances' collection, *Piccino* (U.S.) and *The Captain's Youngest* (England).

p. 122　　see E.M. Forster, *Marianne Thornton* (1956).

p. 126　　Marghanita Laski, *Mrs Ewing, Mrs Molesworth and Mrs Hodgson Burnett* (1950).

p. 127　　J.C. Furnas, *The Americans* (1970).

p. 127　　Anthony Trollope, *The New Zealander* (first published 1972).

p. 127　　The *Century* critic was James H. Morse.

p. 128　　*Cincinatti Enquirer*, 23rd December 1881.

p. 131　　Gertrude Hall translated Rostand and Verlaine. Her *Verses* were published by William Heinemann in London in 1890 as well as in the States. Her recollections were in an introduction to an edition of *Little Lord Fauntleroy* fifty years after its first publication.

p. 132　　"How Fauntleroy Occurred."

p. 134　　F.J. Harvey Darton, *Children's Books in England* (1932). "Nine editions were published in as many months, and the odious little prig in the lace collar is not dead yet."

p. 136　　Claud Cockburn, *op. cit.*

p. 138　　William McHaig, "The Young Heart", *Good Housekeeping* (U.S., 1918).

p. 139　　Marcus Cunliffe, *The Literature of the United States* (1954).

p. 139　　John Gross, *The Rise and Fall of the Man of Letters* (1969).

p. 139　　Lemuel Bangs had succeeded Charles Welford on his death in 1885.

p. 139　　James D. Hart, *The Popular Book*, a history of America's literary taste (1961).

p. 139   Frank Luther Mott, *Golden Multitudes*, the story of bestsellers in the
           United States (1947).

p. 140   Justin Kaplan, *op. cit.*

p. 144   There are three more stanzas in the same vein.

CHAPTER 5: THE GRATITUDE OF BRITISH AUTHORS 1887–1889

p. 147   Israel Zangwill (1864–1926), novelist, playwright, critic. He did not
           marry until 1903. In 1904, he succeeded Herzl to the leadership of the
           Zionist movement.

p. 148   Henry Austin Dobson (1840–1921), prolific poet and literary critic.

p. 148   Information about this holiday is from "The Tinker's Tom," included in
           Giovanni and the Other (U.S.) and *Children I Have Known* (England).

p. 151   *A Woman's Will* appeared in America only in a collection edited by
           John Habberton (author of *Helen's Babies*) and this would account for
           the lack of attention paid to it there.

p. 152   Review in the *Era*, 5 November 1887.

p. 153   "Vernon Lee", Violet Paget (1856—1935), essayist and novelist.

p. 162   The *Century*, April 1886.

p. 163   Vivian Burnett records the presentation being made at the Queen's
           Hall on 14th July but this occasion is not recorded in *The Times*.
           The scroll, reproduced in the *Bookman* in September 1911, is actu-
           ally dated October 1888, so the presentation may have been in the
           autumn at another public dinner of which I can find no record. On
           17th May 1890, Henry James recorded the rejection at Washington of
           the International Copyright Bill. "It seems as if this time we had said,
           loudly, that whereas we had freely admitted before that we in fact steal,
           we now seize the opportunity to declare that we *like* to steal." The Bill
           was finally passed in 1891.

p. 164   Information from an article in the *Bookman*, April 1927, by John
           Nicholas Beffel.

p. 168   Irving Cobb, *Goin' on Fourteen* (1924).

p. 168   Compton Mackenzie, *My Life and Times*, Octave 1 (1963).

p. 168   Elisaveta Fen, "The Year I was Nine", *Allsorts* 5 (1972).

p. 173   "It was a big house and a handsome one. It was one of the expressions
           of the man's success, and his pride was involved in it. He spent money
           on it lavishly, and, having completed it, went to live a desolate life
           among its grandeurs." Frances Hodgson Burnett, *Haworth's*.

CHAPTER 6: DEATH AND THE DOCTOR 1889–1892

p. 174   The house at 44 Lexham Gardens is still standing.

p. 177   Stephen Townesend, *Dr Tuppy*, 1912.

p. 177   Stephen Townesend, *A Short Account of the Amateur Dramatic Club of St*

Bartholomew's Hospital from 1883–1899 (1899).

p. 179   From "The Boy who became a Socialist" in *Children I Have Known, op. cit.* Edward Bellamy believed in the nationalization of railways, coal, telephone and telegraph services, light, heat and transport.

p. 187   Marghanita Laski, *op. cit.*: "When Mrs Burnett translates her son's death into fiction and remembers to put down not only the doctor's admiration for the 'intense elemental force' in the mother, but even to give her 'a thin, flexible-looking hand', we must feel that Mrs Burnett has erred a long way that side vulgarity."

p. 206   F.H.B.: *In Connection With the De Willoughby Claim.* "A short life is not…"

p. 207   Mr Salteena is the anti-hero of Daisy Ashford's *The Young Visiters.*

p. 212   F.H.B., preface to *The One I Knew The Best of All.*

p. 214   *The Times*, 7th January 1892.

p. 214   As if to emphasize that Stephen's new career was her creation, Frances gave him the name of her Washington lawyer.

CHAPTER 7: THE LIFE OF THE WORLD 1892–1895

p. 215   Frank Doubleday was then working on *Scribner's Magazine.*

p. 218   The *Athenaeum*, 16th April 1892.

p. 220   F.H.B., essay contributed to *Before He Is Twenty; five perplexing phases of the boy question considered* (1894).

p. 221   Sir Francis Cowley Burnand (1836–1917) contributed to *Punch* from 1863 and edited it from 1880–1906. He wrote to Frances on 11th December 1892.

p. 223   Richards and Elliott, *Julia Ward Howe* (1915).

p. 223   Theodore Dreiser, *A Book About Myself* (1923).

p. 223   Eugene Field (1850–1895), poet and humourist.

p. 223   Quotations from F.H.B., *The Shuttle.*

p. 225   Undated letter (1895?) from Zangwill to Frances: "*I* shall be extremely interested, though you never read criticism—to see how the other critics take it."

p. 225   Thirty years ago these brick passages and vaults under 63 Portland Place remained as they were in 1895 and were chilling enough even in electric light. I was shown over and under the house through the kindness of the Institute of Cost and Management Accountants, who occupied the premises.

p. 225   There was considerable interest in Steele at this period. Frances knew Austin Dobson, whose *Richard Steele* had been published in 1886.

p. 230   F.H.B.'s programme of *King Arthur* records that Arthur Sullivan composed the music and Bram Stoker was the "acting manager".

p. 231   Edmund Gosse was born in the same year as Frances, 1849. By the time he met her he had recovered from the great setback to his career, Churton Collins' attack on his Clark Lectures, *From Shakespeare to Pope.*

He had not yet written his one enduring book, *Father and Son* (1907). He lived until 1928. Somerset Maugham described him as the most amusing talker he had ever met, but he could also be snobbish, malicious and touchy.

p. 234   Winifred Emery had married Cyril Maude in 1888, the year in which she played Dearest in *The Real Little Lord Fauntleroy*. She was one of the most popular actresses of her generation. For years the Maudes appeared together at the Haymarket Theatre.

p. 235   *The Young Visiters.*

p. 236   Woolf on Gosse: diary, 30 October 1926 (Berg).

p. 236   Sir Henry Rider Haggard (1856–1925), author of a number of popular novels, including *King Solomon's Mines* and *She*.

p. 236   Sir Laurence Alma-Tadema (1836–1912), painter, born in Friesland. Edmund Gosse was his brother-in-law.

p.237   Eleanor Calhoun, American actress. Frances saw her first with Mrs Patrick Campbell in *The Notorious Mrs Ebbsmith* in 1895. She appeared as Clorinda in the English production of *A Lady of Quality*. See p. 332.

p. 237   Poulteney Bigelow's father had been American Minister in Berlin and he had been a boyhood playmate of the Kaiser.

p. 238   Sir Walter Besant (1836–1901), novelist, essayist, and one of the founders of the Society of Authors, was at this time working on an immense survey of London.

p. 238   Aubrey Beardsley (1872–98) had done his illustrations for Wilde's *Salome* in 1893 and had become the art editor of *The Yellow Book* in 1894.

p. 239   "F. Anstey", Thomas Anstey Guthrie (1856–1934), regular contributor to *Punch*. His novel *Vice Versa*, a lesson to fathers, had been re-issued with additions in 1894.

p. 239   Stephen Townesend, *A Thoroughbred Mongrel* (1900).

p. 241   F.H.B. forgot this resolution and collaborated later with Stephen Townesend again. Perhaps she did not forget and did it under duress. (See letter on p. 278).

p. 241   Daniel Frohman (1851–1940) managed the Fifth Avenue and Madison Square Theaters, New York, from 1879 to 1885 and the Lyceum from 1885. He had produced *Esmeralda* in 1881. His brother, Charles (1860–1915), who presented several of F.H.B.'s plays, died in the *Lusitania*, apparently with the words, "Why fear death? It is the most beautiful adventure of life."

p. 243   George Du Maurier (1834–96) cartoonist on the staff of *Punch* from 1864, and author of the bestseller *Trilby* (1894).

p. 243   Mary Augusta Ward (1851–1920) was one of the most outstanding women of the time, see page 247.

p. 243   Jerome K. Jerome (1859–1927), humourist, remembered for his *Three Men in a Boat* (1889).

p. 243   The Earl of Crewe (1858–1945) was the son of Richard Monkton

Milnes, the first biographer and champion of John Keats.

p. 243   Theodore Watts-Dunton (1832–1914) is best remembered for his friendship with Swinburne, who lived in his house in Putney from 1879 until his death, in 1909.

p. 243   Sir Sidney Colvin (1845–1927) was at this time Keeper of Prints and Drawings at the British Museum. He had written a life of Keats and edited his letters in 1887.

p. 244   Letter from the Earl of Crewe, 8th February 1896.

p. 244   Crewe's first wife had died aged thirty in 1887.

p. 244   T.P. O'Connor (1848–1929), Irish politician and newspaper editor. He had sat as Member of Parliament for the Scotland division of Liverpool since 1885. His wife was an American. Ella Hepworth Dixon said she "possessed the longest eye lashes I have ever seen, save those of Mr Max Beerbohm".

p. 244   Florence Henniker was Thomas Hardy's friend for thirty years. She was "the one rare, fair woman" of his poem "Wessex Heights" (1896).

p. 245   From Edith Sichel: *Letters, Verses and other Writings*, printed privately (1918).

pp. 245–6   F.H.B.: *In Connection with the De Willoughby Claim*.

CHAPTER 8: AFFAIRS THEATRICAL 1896–1899

p. 247   Solomon J. Solomon (1860–1927) had painted Zangwill's portrait (reproduced in this book); it had been hung at the Academy the previous year.

p. 247   The Barraud photograph is the one reproduced in the Plate section.

p. 248   Bernard Berenson (1865–1959) later became a leading authority on Italian Renaissance art.

p. 248   Charles Hamilton Aïdé (1826–1906).

p. 248   Lord Ronald Leveson Gower (1845–1916), son of the Duke of Sutherland, was sculptor of the Shakespeare Memorial at Stratford-on-Avon, a trustee of Shakespeare's Birthplace and of the National Portrait Gallery. Biographer of Gainsborough, Romney, Michaelangelo, Joan of Arc, etc.

p. 249   In 1892, Sir Edwin Arnold had first roused an interest in the Japanese drama. His "Japonica" first appeared in *Scribner's Magazine*. His version of a Noh play, *Adzuma*, or *The Japanese Wife*, was published in 1893. F.H.B. had met him (p. 155).

p. 255   Euphemia (Effie) Macfarlane was a friend of Frances from Washington in the 1870s until the end of her life. She and Gertrude (Kitty) Hall were the only two friends named when Frances drafted her will in 1915.

p. 256   The *Boston Evening Transcript*.

p. 257   Pamela Maude, *Worlds Away* (1964).

p. 258   Edith Wharton (1862–1937), the novelist, shared many friends with

Frances but I can find no record of them meeting.

p. 261 Quotation from F.H.B., *Two Little Pilgrims' Progress*.

p. 262 Ellen Terry (1847–1928), the leading actress of the day, Frances met on a number of occasions, both in London and in Kent.

p. 262 Rudyard Kipling (1865–1936), poet and novelist, was then at the height of his fame. Scribner's was in the middle of bringing out the complete "Outward Bound" edition of his works. He was at Rottingdean this summer. His later home, Bateman's, was only twelve miles from Maytham.

p. 263 Olivia Ferrol in *Louisiana*.

p. 264 Harry Percival-Smith was Vicar of Rolvenden from 1896 to 1904.

p. 266 Sir David Murray (1849–1933) became an R.A. in 1905 and was President of the Royal Institute of Painters in Water Colour in 1917.

p. 266 Laurette Messimy roses were considered by "Elizabeth", Countess von Arnim, "the loveliest things" in her German garden, "each flower an exquisite loose cluster of coral-pink petals, paling at the base to a yellow-white". The book was published this year, 1898.

p. 266 The quotation is from a letter from David Murray to Frances.

p. 266 F.H.B., *My Robin*.

p. 266 The juxtaposition of "the door into the rose-garden" and the encouraging bird at the beginning of T.S. Eliot's *Burnt Norton* suggests that *The Secret Garden* may have been somewhere in the back of his mind.

p. 266 Description from Vivian Burnett, *op. cit.*

p. 267 F.H.B., *In the Garden*.

p. 270 Letter from Henry James to William James and much other information *passim* from Leon Edel, *The Life of Henry James*, 4 vols (1953, 1962, 1963, 1969).

p. 271 Letter now in the Houghton Library at Harvard.

p. 273 Felix Moscheles (1833–1917), godson of Mendelssohn, friend of Browning, painter and writer.

p. 273 *In Connection with the De Willoughby Claim* eventually sold over 100,000 copies.

p. 274 Information from Records of the Class of 1898, Harvard University.

p. 275 I am not absolutely convinced they were married in Genoa, though the newspaper reports of the time recorded they were. They were certainly married secretly. The letter to Edith quoted on p. 277 suggests they were already married when Frances reached Genoa. Frances' reference to her "newborn bride" [*sic*] reminds me that B.C. Hodgson, a nephew of Frances, described his aunt in 1949 as "a forceful person, a *masculine*, matter-of-fact person, always entertaining" (my italics).

CHAPTER 9: THE AMAZING MARRIAGE 1900–1907

p. 277 The old friend was Sidney Trist, a legatee in Stephen's will.

p. 279 F.H.B., *My Robin*.

p. 279   Information from Hesketh Pearson, *The Pilgrim Daughters* (1961).

p. 281   "In a place where ...", F.H.B.; *T. Tembarom*.

p. 282   Dr Kenneth Campbell, Rosamund's husband, was originally a friend of Stephen's.

pp. 282-3   Information from Leon Edel, *op. cit.*

p. 285   The Harmsworths, at this time, owned the *Daily Mail* and *Evening News*.

p. 286   Anthony Blond included *The Making of a Marchioness* in his Doughty Library 1966, and both that and the sequel are now available as Persephone Books.

p. 288   George Eliot, *Romola*.

p. 289   James' first book for Scribner's, *The Sacred Fount*, appeared this year, 1901. Edith Wharton left Scribner's in 1912.

p. 289   Ignace Jan Paderewski (1860–1941), the Polish pianist, was at the height of his fame.

pp. 289-92   Information from Pamela Maude, *op. cit.*, and her unpublished letters to the author.

p. 290   Henry James writing from Rye, 10th August 1901.

p. 290   Gerald Lawrence (1873–1957) appeared on the London stage for the first time in 1898. The children had seen him with Tree in *Twelfth Night*.

p. 291   Pamela Maude (the Hon. Mrs Fraser), letter to the author, 27th July 1971.

p. 291   Marghanita Laski, *op. cit.*

p. 294   The amount Stephen left at his death suggests this. He left more than eight thousand pounds plus a substantial annuity which did not expire until 1948. At the time of his death, he had not received anything from his father's estate as his mother was still alive.

p. 295   The *Era* critic, however, thought it too "sad and cynical". Like Dr Herbert MacLeod, writing in the correspondence columns, he preferred children to be protected from realities. "Let all things be for our darlings as sweet and beautiful as we can make them." There had been a copyright performance of the play at the Avenue Theatre, 18th September 1902.

p. 296   Letter to Emma Anderson, 12th December 1902.

p. 300   *Sunday Telegraph*, New York, 15th November 1903.

p. 301   Kate Douglas Wiggin (1856–1923), best-selling author. Her *Birds' Christmas Carol* sold seven hundred and fifty thousand copies in English alone. F.H.B. wrote an introduction to the Quillcote edition of her books. She was "always a devoted friend and admirer of my sister's" wrote Nora Archibald Smith. On 29th January 1897, Kate Douglas Wiggin had given a "déjeuner" in honour of Frances at her home on West Eleventh Street, New York.

p. 303   Poulteney Bigelow, then living nearby.

p. 303   Letter from Marion Percival-Smith, September 1904.

p. 305   Eileen Mackenzie, *The Findlater Sisters* (1964).

CHAPTER 10: WAS THAT THE PARTY? 1907–1924

p. 313   "Vivian was a disappointment to her, inevitably." Marion de Kay Rous, who had known them both, in conversation with me, 1970.

p. 313   *New York World*, 31st January 1909.

p. 314   "The most misused word ...", *Philadelphia Times*, 14th February 1909.

p. 316   Philippa Pearce, "The Writer's View of Childhood", lecture to Library Association conference, Scarborough, 13th September 1960.

p. 317   I am indebted here to Joan Bodger's account of a literary pilgrimage to England: *How the Heather Looks* (1965).

p. 318   *Philippians* 4.8.

p. 318   Penelope Lively, letter to the author.

p. 318   The *American Magazine* (formerly Frank Leslie's *Popular Monthly*) had been bought in 1906 by McClure's former partner, Tom Phillips, and a group of leading contributors to *McClure's Magazine*, who had become dissatisfied with McClure's policies.

p. 319   A.B. Walkley (1855–1926), dramatic critic of *The Times* from 1900 till his death.

p. 325   Interview with Nixola Greeley-Smith, *New York Evening World*, 26th November 1910.

p. 325   *New York Telegraph*, 13th November 1910.

p. 328   The ferryboat story was told to me by both Marion de Kay Rous and Ormonde de Kay himself.

p. 328   Letter to Valerie Bradshaw from Phyllis de Kay Wheelock.

pp. 331–2   *Vanity Fair*, June 1914.

p. 334   Written by Sidney Trist.

p. 336   Letters from W. Fayal Clarke, 10th March and 24th January 1914. On a visit to Frances on 3rd March 1915, Mr and Mrs Clarke were two of the witnesses to her will.

p. 337   E.E. Hale in the *Dial*, 25th November 1915.

p. 338   Helen Keller (1880–1968). Deaf, dumb and blind, her story was first told in *St Nicholas*. Mark Twain said she and Napoleon were "the two most interesting characters of the nineteenth century".

p. 338   *Kansas City Times*, 22nd October 1917.

p. 339   I am grateful to Gretchen Gerzina's 2004 biography for telling me the rest of Archie's story. In 1896, FHB had written: "He is made of that material which finally becomes a multi-millionaire in Chicago or New York." After Ernest's death, Archie took over the Fahnestock Electric Company and made a great success of it.

p. 341   From the *Bookman*, 22nd October 1922, and other unidentifiable cuttings.

p. 343   H.W. Boynton, in the *Independent*, 2nd September 1922.

p.343   *The Times Literary Supplement*, 26th October 1922.

p. 343   *Daily Telegraph*, 14th May 1910.

Notes

p. 343   E.F. Edgett in the *Boston Transcript*, 21st February 1922.

p. 343   L.M. Field in the *New York Times*, 23rd July 1922.

p. 348   Memory recalled in B.B.C. TV programme on Beatrix Potter: "…and they weren't doing a bit of harm."

p. 348   F.H.B., "My Toy Cupboard", *Ladies' Home Journal*, April 1915.

p. 349   F.H.B., *A Little Princess*, chapter 2.

p. 349   The child was Marni Hodgkin, once children's books editor at Macmillan, London.

p. 349   The "In The Garden" articles were commissioned for the *Country Gentleman* and published in book form after Frances' death. My copy, given to me by Pamela Maude, is inscribed: "My beloved sister's last word to the world—Sincerely yours, Edith M. Jordan, Plandome Park."

p. 349   The United Artists film was directed by Alfred E. Green and Jack Pickford in 1921.

p. 349   Hamilton Williamson, the *Bookman*.

p. 351   New Yorker, 11th March 1939.

p. 351   *The Times*, 5th November 1924.

p. 352   Ella Hepworth Dixon recorded that she was thanked for her subscription to the memorial in these terms: "We are very gratified at receiving a contribution from a foreigner." It was a shock to her as she had always thought Frances was "very English". The South garden, in which the memorial stands in a waterlily pool, was restored in the 1980s. It is to the left of the wrought iron gates on Fifth Avenue near 104th Street.

Dates and Places

1849	24th November: Frances born at 141 York Street, Cheetham Hill Road, Manchester (now 141 Cheetham Hill Road)
1852	9 St Luke's Terrace, Cheetham Hill Road (now 385 Cheetham Hill Road)
1854	Seedley Grove, off Tanner's Lane, Pendleton
1855	16 Islington Square, Salford
1864	1 Gore Street, Greenheys, Chorlton on Medlock
1865	May, to Canada on *SS Moravian*; New Market, Tennessee
1866	Noah's Ark, outside Knoxville, Tennessee
1868	Vagabondia Castle, Knoxville
1872	To New York
1872–3	Fifteen months in England, mostly in Manchester
1873	19th September: Frances married Dr Swan Burnett at New Market, Tennessee
1874	20th September: Lionel born at Temperance Hill, Knoxville
1875	To Europe in the spring: 3 Rue Pauquet, Paris
1876	5 April: Vivian born in Paris. Visit to Manchester; returned to New Market, Tennessee
1877	1104 F Street, Washington, D.C.; M Street, Washington; 813 13th Street, Washington
1879	1215 I Street, Washington; February, first visited Boston; June, Newport; 28th August to Canada
1880	April, Canada; New England on way home; June, Nook Farm, Hartford, Connecticut
1881	Summer in Long Island (New York)
1882–4	Summers at Lynn, Massachusetts Bay; to Boston in the autumn of 1884
1885	Returned to Washington; Boston again in the summer
1886	Moved to 1734 K Street, Washington. In Boston again
1887	May, to England: 23 Weymouth Street, London; August at Southwold and Elm Farm, Wangford, Suffolk; Paris; Florence

1888   Back to London; house in Regents Park West; Joss Farm, St Peter's, Thanet, Kent; to Boston, New York, and back to Washington

1889   1770 Massachusetts Avenue, Washington; to England: 44 Lexham Gardens, London; Manchester; bungalow at Bellagio, Surrey, for summer; back to London; French Riviera; Rome

1890   5th April, sailed from Rome to US: Atlantic City and Philadelphia; Göbersdorf; Marienbad; Paris; London

1891   Cannes; San Remo; London; Southport

1892   London; 1770 Massachusetts Avenue, Washington; Swampscott, near Lynn

1893   May, to England: The Glade, Hampton Court; 63 Portland Place, London W.1.; 9th December, sailed to US; Washington

1894   May, to England: Portland Place; back to US.

1895   January, returned to England: Portland Place; summer at Broomfields, near Frensham

1896   Portland Place; back to U.S. in the autumn

1897   1770 Massachusetts Avenue, Washington; New York

1898   January, returned to England: Manchester; Portland Place; Maytham Hall, Rolvenden, Kent

1899   Maytham; October, returned to Washington

1900   February to Genoa; Maytham for summer; 48 Charles Street, London for winter

1901   To Maytham in the spring; autumn to Holland and Belgium; returned to US.

1902   Fishkill-on-Hudson; East Hampton

1903   New York; East Hampton

1904   New York; North Carolina; to Italy; June, returned to Maytham; 21st December, sailed for New York

1905   Returned to Maytham for the summer; 16th November, sailed for US; 25th, Atlantic crossing

1906   New York; Washington; 12th May, sailed back to England; Maytham; Montreux

1907   February, back to Maytham; 21 March, returned to US: Sands Point, Long Island

1908   Frankfurt; Tavistock; New York

1909   New York, Plandome, Long Island

1910   Spring, back to England again: London; the Dolomites and Austria; returned to US: Plandome

1911   March, to Bermuda; Plandome; cruise; Bermuda; Plandome

1912   Bermuda; summer at Plandome; New York

1913   Bermuda; Trieste; Austria (Vienna)

1914   Salzburg; Rothenburg; Paris; May, back in New York (33rd and last crossing of the Atlantic); Bermuda; Plandome

1915   Plandome; New Windsor on Hudson

1916   Bermuda; New York; Plandome

1917   Plandome; New Windsor on Hudson; New York

1918   Plandome; Nova Scotia visit; Plandome
1919   Bermuda; Plandome
1920   Plandome
1921–4 New York; Plandome

Died 29th October 1924.

Bibliography

I have attempted to include every first publication of a book by Frances Hodgson Burnett both in America and England.★ I have not attempted to list the numerous stories and articles which appeared only in magazines. Magazine publication of the books is normally a year earlier.

Title	New York, unless otherwise stated	London
That Lass o' Lowries	Scribner, 1877	Warne, 1877
Surly Tim and other Stories	Scribner, 1877	Ward Lock, 1877
	Robertsons (Toronto), 1877	
Theo	Peterson (Philadelphia), 1877	Ward Lock, 1877
	Scribner, 1879	Warne, 1877
Dolly	Porter & Coates (Philadelphia), 1877	Routledge, 1877
retitled as		
Vagabondia	Scribner, 1883	
	Osgood (Boston), 1884	
Pretty Polly Pemberton	Peterson (Philadelphia), 1877	Routledge, 1878
Earlier Stories (First Series) "Lindsay's Luck," etc.	Scribner, 1878	Routledge, 1879
Kathleen	Peterson (Philadelphia), 1878	Routledge, 1878
Earlier Stories (Second Series) ("Kathleen Mavourneen" and "Pretty Polly Pemberton")	Scribner, 1878	Chatto, 1879
Miss Crespigny	Peterson (Philadelphia), 1878	Routledge, 1878
	Scribner, 1879	

★ Where there are a number of early editions, I have included them.

A Quiet Life and *The Tide* on the Moaning Bar	Peterson (Philadelphia), 1878	Routledge, 1879
Our Neighbour Opposite		Routledge, 1878
Jarl's Daughter and other stories and other novelettes (adding "Miss Vernon's Choice")	Peterson (Philadelphia), 1879	
Natalie and other stories	Peterson (Philadelphia), 1882	Warne, 1879
Haworth's	Scribner, 1879	Macmillan, 1879
Louisiana	Scribner, 1880	Macmillan, 1880 (With *That Lass o' Lowrie's*)
A Fair Barbarian	Osgood (Boston), 1881	Warne, 1881
Through One Administration	Osgood (Boston), 1883	Warne, 1883
Little Lord Fauntleroy	Scribner, 1886	Warne, 1886
A Woman's Will or Miss Defarge	Lippincott, 1888 (in J. Habberton's *Brueton's Bayou*)	Warne, 1887
Sara Crewe	Scribner, 1888	Fisher Unwin, 1887
Editha's Burglar	Jordan Marsh (Boston), 1888	
Sara Crewe and Editha's Burglar (in one volume)		Warne, 1888
The Fortunes of Philippa Fairfax		Warne, 1888
The Pretty Sister of José	Scribner, 1889	Spencer Blackett, 1889
Little Saint Elizabeth and other stories	Scribner, 1890	Spencer Blackett, 1889
Children I Have Known (English title)		J.R. Osgood, McIlvaine & Co, 1892
Giovanni and the Other (US)	Scribner, 1892	Warne?
The Drury Lane Boys' Club	Moon Press (Washington), 1892	
The One I Knew the Best of All	Scribner, 1893	Warne, 1893
The Captain's Youngest (England)		Warne, 1894
Piccino and Other Child Stories (US)	Scribner, 1894	
The Two Little Pilgrims' Progress	Scribner, 1895	Warne, 1895
A Lady of Quality	Scribner, 1896	Warne, 1896
His Grace of Osmonde	Scribner, 1897	Warne, 1897
In Connection with the De Willoughby Claim	Scribner, 1899	Warne, 1899
The Making of a Marchioness	Stokes, 1901	Smith, Elder & Co, 1901
The Methods of Lady Walderhurst	Stokes, 1901	Smith, Elder & Co, 1902
In the Closed Room	McClure, 1905	Hodder, 1904
A Little Princess	Scribner, 1905	Warne, 1905
The Dawn of a Tomorrow	Scribner, 1906	Warne, 1907
The Troubles of Queen Silver-Bell	Century, 1906	Warne, 1907
Racketty Packetty House	Century, 1906	Warne, 1907

Bibliography

The Cozy Lion	Century, 1907	Tom Stacey, 1972
The Spring Cleaning	Century, 1908	Tom Stacey, 1973
The Shuttle	Stokes, 1907	Heinemann, 1907
The Good Wolf	Moffat, 1908	
Barty Crusoe and His Man Saturday	Moffat, 1909	
The Land of the Blue Flower	Moffat, 1909	Putnam, 1912
The Secret Garden	Stokes, 1911	Heinemann, 1911
My Robin	Stokes, 1912	Putnam, 1913
T. Tembarom	Stokes, 1913	Hodder & Stoughton, 1913
The Lost Prince	Century, 1915	Hodder & Stoughton, 1915
The White People	Harper, 1917	Heinemann, 1920
Little Hunchback Zia	Stokes, 1916	Heinemann, 1916
The Head of the House of Coombe	Stokes, 1922	Heinemann, 1922
Robin	Stokes, 1922	Heinemann, 1922
In the Garden	Medici Society, 1925	

Plays

I have not included dramatizations of Mrs Burnett's books by other writers. The dates are the first nights of production in London and New York. They were often toured earlier, and sometimes single copyright performances were also given earlier.

1. *That Lass o' Lowrie's*
   F.H.B. and Julian Magnus
   Booth Theater, Broadway, New York   28th November 1878
2. *Esmeralda*
   F.H.B. and William Gillette
   Madison Square Theater, New York   26th October 1881
   as *Young Folk's Ways*
   St James' Theatre, London   29th October 1883
3. *The Real Little Lord Fauntleroy*
   Terry's Theatre, London   14th May 1888
   Broadway Theater, New York   11th December 1888
4. *Phyllis* (from *the Fortunes of Philippa Fairfax*)
   Globe Theatre, London   1st July 1889
5. *Nixie* (from *Editha's Burglar*)
   F.H.B. and Stephen Townesend
   Terry's Theatre, London   7th April 1890
6. *The Showman's Daughter*
   F.H.B. and Stephen Townesend
   Royalty Theatre, London   6th January 1892
7. *The First Gentleman of Europe*
   F.H.B. with Constance Fletcher
   Lyceum Theater, New York   25th January 1897

8. *A Lady of Quality*
    F.H.B. with Stephen Townesend
    Wallack's Theater, New York   1st November 1897
    Comedy Theatre, London   8th March 1899
9. *A Little Princess*
    (Originally *A Little Unfairy Princess*)
    Shaftesbury Theatre, London   20th December 1902
    Criterion Theater, New York   1 January 1903
10. *The Pretty Sister of José*
    Duke of York's Theatre, London   16th November 1903
    Empire Theater, New York   10th November 1903
11. *That Man and I* (from *The De Willoughby Claim*)
    Savoy Theatre, London   25th January 1904
12. *Dawn of a Tomorrow*
    Lyceum Theater, New York   28th January 1909
    Garrick Theatre, London   13th May 1910
13. *Racketty Packetty House*
    Children's Theater, New York   23rd December 1912

Mrs Burnett also apparently made plays from *The Making of a Marchioness* (called Glenpeffer), *T. Tembarom* and *The Shuttle*, and another play called *Judy O'Hara*—but I can find no record of productions of these.

Main Published Sources

The One I Knew the Best of All	Frances Hodgson Burnett, Scribner (New York, 1893)
My Sister	Edith Jordan, *Good Housekeeping* (US, 1925)
The Romantick Lady	Vivian Burnett, Scribner (New York, 1927)
As I Knew Them	Ella Hepworth Dixon, Hutchinson (London, 1930)
Mrs Ewing, Mrs Molesworth, Mrs Hodgson Burnett	Marghanita Laski, Arthur Barker (London, 1950)
Worlds Away	Pamela Maude, John Baker (London, 1964)
Happily Ever After	Constance Buel Burnett, Vanguard Press (New York, 1969)

Index